Margaret Laurence – Al Purdy.

A Friendship in Letters

Margaret Laurence – Al Purdy:
A Friendship in Letters

Selected Correspondence

Edited and with an introduction by
John Lennox

SEP 8 1994

For Mia, Anna, and Jeffers
"... cats and roses ..."

CANADIAN CATALOGUING IN PUBLICATION DATA

Laurence, Margaret, 1926-1987
Margaret Laurence, Al Purdy: a friendship in letters

Includes bibliographical references and index.

ISBN 0-7710-5255-3 (bound)
ISBN 0-7710-5256-1 (pbk.)

1. Laurence, Margaret, 1926-1987 – Correspondence. 2. Purdy, Al, 1918-
– Correspondence. 3. Novelists, Canadian (English) – 20th century –
Correspondence.* 4. Poets, Canadian (English) – 20th century – Correspondence.*
I. Purdy, Al, 1918- . II. Lennox, John, 1945- . III. Title.

PS8523.A77Z546 1993 C811'.54 C93-093104-1
PR9199.3.L37Z546 1993

The poem "For Margaret" and lines from "Lawrence to Laurence"
are from *The Woman on the Shore* (McClelland & Stewart, 1990).

Typesetting by M&S, Toronto
The support of the Government of Ontario through the Ministry
of Culture and Communications is acknowledged.
Printed and bound in Canada on acid-free paper.

The publishers acknowledge the support of the Canada Council
and the Ontario Arts Council for their publishing program.

McClelland & Stewart Inc.
The Canadian Publishers
481 University Avenue
Toronto, Ontario
M5G 2E9

Ameliasburgh
Oct. 69

MEMORANDUM

Margaret Laurence to Al Purdy

I may now and later ask all sorts of things -- reassurance,
sustenance, etc, and also give them if needed. But I will only
ever ask one favour. This is it: do not sell my letters *or even give away*
until I am dead. Eh? After that, fm fine, okay , great.

(I am assuming you will
survive longer than I do,
which seems a fairly
reasonable assumption.)

— Personally, I think the
collection of letters would
be damned interesting, &
I can even see it as
a book. But I don't want
to see it. That is for
later.

(Keep this. It can
be the Intro.)
ML

Acknowledgements

This volume is the result of generous co-operation. First and foremost, I am indebted to three people: Al Purdy for permission to publish his letters to Margaret Laurence and to quote from two of his poems in *The Woman on the Shore* (1990) – "Lawrence to Laurence" and "For Margaret" – and Jocelyn and David Laurence for permission to publish their mother's letters to Al Purdy. Without their interest and goodwill, this project would never have been realized.

Ellen Hoffmann, University Librarian, and Barbara Craig, University Archivist, both of York University, provided invaluable space and help. Phyllis Platnick and Grace Heggie of York's Special Collections allowed me to make good use of equipment and expertise. Thanks also to Chantal Dussault, Stephen Moses, Hirem Kurtarici, Catherine Morlock, and Dennis Skinner of Special Collections, and Mary Hudecki of Interlibrary Loans.

Outside York, I would like to acknowledge the co-operation of Anne MacDermaid, former University Archivist, Queen's University, who with her colleagues made my examination of the Purdy Collection such a pleasure. I am also grateful to the archives of the University of Toronto.

For their assistance at different stages, I express my thanks to Michèle Lacombe of Trent University, Brandon Conron and Edward Phelps of the University of Western Ontario, Donez Xiques of the City University of New York, Mary Adachi, Ronald Weyman, Ruth Panofsky, and also John Handford of Macmillan Publishers in England.

York's Faculty of Arts awarded me a leave fellowship for

1991/92 that enabled me to work full-time on this project. York's Document Processing Unit under the able supervision of Patricia Cates and the never-failing patience of Patricia Humenyk gave consistent and careful attention to the preparation of the type-script.

McClelland & Stewart's commitment to this project reflects their long support of the work of Margaret Laurence and Al Purdy as of so many other Canadian writers. Douglas Gibson initially indicated strong interest in the manuscript, Ellen Seligman gave valuable advice and wholehearted editorial support in each of the succeeding stages, and Peter Buck's sharp eye caught questions and inconsistencies that I hope have been clarified. That McClelland & Stewart brought this collection forward for publication in a period of severe financial constraint is cause for gratitude and admiration.

And finally, to Clara Thomas, who encouraged me to undertake this project and who initially paved the way: Give without remembering, take without forgetting.

Contents

Introduction

By the end of 1966 Margaret Laurence had been living in England for four years. She had separated from her husband in 1962 and had left Vancouver for London with their two small children after sending ahead by surface mail the only manuscript copy of her second novel, *The Stone Angel* (1964). Laurence intended to work full-time on her writing and felt that she could best do this in England, where she anticipated becoming part of a stimulating literary community centred in and around London. As she records in *Dance on the Earth* (1989), she found no such group of writers and her early years in England were difficult and lonely. By 1964, however, she was established at Elm Cottage near High Wycombe in Buckinghamshire. There she immersed herself in writing the other works of her Manawaka cycle and had no time for anything else, except her children and the time she took to write letters.

Those with whom Margaret Laurence kept in touch during the Elmcot years were, by and large, Canadians, some living in Canada and others resident abroad. Apart from her immediate family and Adele Wiseman, her early correspondents included Ethel Wilson, Jane Rule, Marjory Whitelaw, and Malcolm Ross. Of those whom Laurence came to know in England, she was closest to Alan Maclean, her publisher at Macmillan, and Lovat Dickson, a director of the same firm, both of whom did a great deal to support and encourage her during this time. By December 1966, she was established as a writer whose African books were highly regarded and whose Canadian books – at this point *The Stone Angel* and *A Jest of God* (1966), for which she was to receive the Governor-General's Award the following spring – had brought her especially wide popularity and critical favour at home. Both novels had earned respectable notices abroad, and movie rights to *A Jest of God* had been bought for what would be the highly acclaimed film *Rachel, Rachel,* starring Joanne Woodward and directed by Paul Newman. For Canadian readers, these novels – especially *The Stone Angel* – had struck a particularly evocative and powerful chord.

A number of factors – four years' absence, the success of *The Stone Angel,* the publication of *A Jest of God,* plus the good offices of Robert Weaver, editor of *The Tamarack Review* and producer of the CBC literary program "Anthology" – played a substantial part in Margaret Laurence's decision to make a brief return visit to Canada in the summer and early fall of 1966. *A Jest of God* had been published in early July in the United Kingdom by Macmillan and later the same month by McClelland and Stewart in Canada. Laurence's Canadian publisher, Jack McClelland, never backward in encouraging the sales of his books, saw her presence in the country as an opportunity to introduce Margaret Laurence the author to her Canadian public. The promotional tour was exhausting, but in the high summer before Canada's centennial year, it marked Laurence's emergence at home as a literary and cultural celebrity.

Someone who had hoped to meet her in Canada that summer, and whom she herself had wanted very much to meet, was Al Purdy, another McClelland and Stewart writer, who had just earned the Governor-General's Award for his collection of poems *The Cariboo Horses* (1965). In fact, as Laurence was to tell him, it was the poetry of *The Cariboo Horses* which had initially sparked her interest in returning to Canada for a visit. Eight years older than Laurence, Purdy had also come to recent celebrity and, like her, he was both gratified and overwhelmed by the sudden attention it brought. At first glance, they seemed to be very different from each other. He had little formal education; she was a university graduate. Apart from a brief trip to Europe in the fall of 1955, Purdy had lived all his life in Canada, while Laurence had spent a total of eleven years in Africa in the 1950s and in England in the 1960s. He had worked as a cab driver and mattress-factory worker, while she had experienced, though uneasily and unwillingly, the perquisites attached to being a white woman in colonial Africa. He lived in conservative, rural, eastern Ontario, where he had spent most of his life; she was an expatriate who had chosen a far more cosmopolitan environment.

Beneath these ostensible differences, however, were origins, interests, and allegiances that were to draw Purdy and Laurence together. They were members of the same generation and came from small Scots-Irish Canadian towns. Both had been raised in the inter-war years and had experienced directly the effects of the Great Depression of the 1930s and lived through the Second World War. This gave them a common cultural vocabulary. Both shared a concern for social issues – Laurence had covered the labour beat for the co-operatively owned *Winnipeg Citizen* and Purdy had been involved in the formation of a labour union – and each was fiercely democratic and without social pretension. Outspoken and anxious by nature, both were intensely political, but these qualities were leavened by a healthy sense of humour. As time went on and their reputations grew, they were prepared to take on, for public and private reasons, complementary roles as cultural icons, though neither was easy with this aspect of their fame.

Purdy and Laurence had experienced the consolidation of their sense of a writing vocation in the late 1950s. By the 1960s they had acquired an important measure of confidence in their own success and knew that their work must claim first place. They made appropriate arrangements to this end and were prepared to undertake commissions from various magazines and periodicals. Coincidentally, the sixties were to create and reflect in Canadians a renewed and intense cultural nationalism for which, in retrospect, the country and its creative community had been preparing since the late 1940s and all through the 1950s. The Massey Commission had examined Canadian culture and had made recommendations that Isaac and Dorothy Killam and the Canada Council were to put into effect with dramatic results in the 1960s and 1970s. In the early fifties, Contact Press in Toronto and the literary magazine *CIV/n* in Montreal anticipated cultural change and growth, as did the establishment of *The Tamarack Review.* CBC Radio was instrumental in this process in its long-standing tradition of presenting original Canadian plays, some of which were written by Purdy, and in programs like "Anthology" which allowed new Canadian writers to read from their work. In July 1955, a meeting of writers, editors, publishers, and critics was held at Queen's University to discuss Canadian writing and publishing. Two years later McClelland and Stewart began issuing inexpensive paperback reprints in its New Canadian Library series. *Canadian Literature,* the first quarterly journal devoted exclusively to the discussion of Canadian writing, appeared in 1959. The climate for general and academic readership of Canadian literature had not been as good since the 1920s. Most significantly, Canadian universities, hitherto regarded as élite bastions of higher learning, were on the verge of tremendous expansion and, ironically, of a concomitant dissemination and popularization of Canadian culture that was to be without precedent in the history of the country. As they did so, existing and new post-secondary institutions created year after year a large and sustaining audience for Canadian writers, artists, and historians.

Laurence's fiction and Purdy's poetry were characterized, in part, by an idiom and by a sense of place and continuity that this growing audience recognized and appreciated. These were writers who wrote about ordinary people and everyday life and who, in the process, powerfully described Canada's historical and cultural geography. As their fiction and poetry became more technically and thematically ambitious, they never forgot their fundamental responsibility to matters of language and form. Their idiom represented a common starting point from which they and their readers could move into new and uncharted territory by means of a vocabulary whose accents and rhythms remained familiar, even if the syntax and patterning became more ambitious.

In the late 1960s, Purdy and Laurence were becoming public personalities and were beginning to experience the adulterating effects of that role on their privacy and creative energy. They were, therefore, glad of the chance to escape to their refuges of relative tranquillity – for Laurence, Elm Cottage and, for Purdy, his A-frame in Ameliasburgh – where they could be alone and write. In December 1966 the first letter from Ameliasburgh was sent to Elm Cottage, where it was waiting for Margaret Laurence when she returned from Egypt in mid-January. She had gone there with her children on a one-month assignment commissioned by *Holiday* magazine. She read the letter with delight. Purdy's humour, lack of pretension, and bluff, direct voice were instantly familiar and appealing. The letter, dated 10 December 1966, began with Purdy's correction to his typed misspelling of Laurence's surname and the printed comment "AINT THAT AWFUL?" He lamented their missed meeting:

> Bob Weaver said I was going to meet you when I came back from Newfoundland this fall. However, you were in Manitoba at the time. Perhaps later.

He informed her that he was "just another admirer, and you have those ad nauseam I suppose." He had bought her books for her to sign, and concluded: "Incidentally, I hope you bawled out someone at McStew for the paper they used in Jest of God."

Laurence wrote a lengthy reply which she began by telling Purdy that

Owing to one of those ironies of life, you were the person I most wanted to meet when I was in Canada this summer and the only person in the whole country (almost) whom I didn't meet. Actually, it was owing to a line from a poem in THE CARIBOO HORSES that I went back to Canada at all last summer. It wasn't exactly one rural winter – more one rural spring, when I sat beside my wet-beech-log fire, surrounded by nothing but beautiful trees, reading your poem and thinking at that moment with both amusement and rage that I also hated beautiful trees. The next day I walked into the CBC office in London and said "I'm homesick, and I'm going home", and my friend Ken Black there said "Okay, you can – let's see what we can do", and from that beginning sprung Bob Weaver's miraculous work in getting a Canada Council grant for me, including a travel grant which allowed me to go to Canada for the summer (16 January 1967).

Laurence went on to announce her aversion to Toronto with its traffic and big-city pretensions, talked about her family, and then got down to what mattered to her most – her work as she prepared to "get started on another novel." She declared her reluctance to complain about the production of *A Jest of God* – "I dearly love Jack McClelland, although we fight quite often" – and described her interest in other writers and writing. During the next seven years, while she finished *Long Drums and Cannons* (1968) and *A Bird in the House* (1970) and wrote *The Fire-Dwellers* (1969), *Jason's Quest* (1970), and *The Diviners* (1974), and while Purdy edited the collection of essays published in *The New Romans* (1968), and wrote the poems that were to appear in *Wild Grape Wine* (1968), *Love in a Burning Building* (1970), *The Quest for Ouzo* (1971), *Hiroshima Poems* (1972), *Sex & Death* (1973), and *In Search of Owen Roblin* (1974), they wrote freely and frequently to each other.

After the initial exchange in December 1966/January 1967, they communicated by letter two or three times a month. This set a pattern that (apart from Laurence's visits to Canada on vacation or on an extended basis as writer-in-residence and Purdy's travels abroad) was to last until the end of 1974, shortly after Margaret Laurence settled permanently in Lakefield, Ontario. There were, in addition, visits between them in England and Canada with the result that the families came to be very fond each other. Once Laurence returned to Canada and distance was no longer a factor, written communication gradually dwindled although they remained loyal friends. They wrote each other sporadically until 1981 and in subsequent years communicated occasionally by telephone except for one or two very brief notes, the last of which was sent by Purdy shortly before Margaret Laurence's death.

Purdy was the first male writer that Laurence came to know well and the perspective he offered – at once Canadian, masculine, and writerly – was one she admired. In a voice that she recognized as authentically Canadian, Purdy spoke trenchantly and often poetically from another perspective about what was most important to her: language and the work that flowed from it. Language, in fact, was the cornerstone of their friendship. Margaret Laurence had wanted to meet Purdy because she admired his poetry and had responded totally to his idiom. His voice reverberated with the rhythms, accents, and diction that she had rediscovered to her great joy in writing *The Stone Angel*. As a novelist talking to a poet, Laurence relished the candour that a lack of vested interest ensured. In June 1967 she met Purdy for the first time in Ottawa where she had gone to receive the Governor-General's Award for *A Jest of God*. She wrote him after her return to England:

I'm always slightly uncertain about meeting someone with whom I get along well in letters, because some people are different in print, but you talk just the way I thought you would (6 June 1967).

The Laurence-Purdy letters resonate with the energy and directness that idiomatic talk embodies, and they took pride and pleasure in being able to communicate frankly with each other. The idiom of their published writing, however, carried the rhythms and allusive power of poetry. It was this use of language to which Laurence had first responded so strongly. In fact, her first letter to Purdy began with a postscript characteristically placed at the beginning of the letter: "have seen your Eskimo poems in Parallel and Tamarack, and think they are – what? Difficult to say without sounding phoney. I like them. The people come across. And so do you" (16 January 1967). In response, Purdy sent a letter which contained a draft version of his poem "Interruption," which was later published in *Wild Grape Wine*. Laurence commented:

> Thanks for your letter, and even more, thanks for copying out the poem about the house at Roblin Lake. I liked all of it, but what hit me most were the last three lines. How damnably difficult to remember, ourselves, to avoid the traps. The mice are certainly one's brethren in this respect – so who isn't terrified? This poem was like a kind of gift, and you are lucky in that way, in being able to do that. Writers of prose can never reciprocate. (Imagine sending anybody a copy of the first chapter of a novel, and if you did, it wouldn't mean a thing in isolation anyway) (19 February 1967).

From the beginning of their correspondence, they talked always and passionately about writers and writing. Laurence's first letter talked about Purdy's poems and their effect on her and, in his reply, Purdy included the draft of an uncompleted poem. This tended to be the pattern of their letters – Margaret Laurence talking about her or Purdy's or others' writing, and Purdy, who was far more reticent about describing the process of writing, including poems in or with his letters, composing poems in his letters, or writing poetic letters. From Ottawa, he wrote:

> Have also three bushels of wild grapes to clean, a legacy from Roblin Lake, which are bubbling in the tiny kitchen like a spillage of whispers. Squirrels walking upside down on screens of windows; yellow, red and green leaves outside deciding what to do when the wind comes. Days getting so short they seem no more than the click of a camera shutter; a tall tall crane fumbles heavy weights out the side window like a gigantic mantis. Crazy ordinary (13 October 1967).

Laurence replied: "Your last paragraph in your letter seemed like a poem to me, the description of Ottawa and the wild grapes and the cranes ... 'crazy ordinary'.[...] Wish I could write description like that, so selective, so apparently light in touch, so much unspoken appearing under the surface" (23 October 1967). Letter-writing was also incorporated into Purdy's creative process as he wrote and revised poems in his letters. After quoting six lines from a poem he was composing, Purdy added, "So I just come up with another line writing this" (10 May 1971) and told Laurence what it was and where to insert it. Purdy was very aware of the way in which his letters could serve as a kind of workshop for his material: "I hope you don't mind my working on this while I'm writing you, because obviously that's what I'm doing" (5 January 1969).

Part of the process of writing poetry for Purdy was travel and his letters often bore postmarks from far-flung locations: Greece, Mexico, Japan, South Africa. Laurence had done most of her travelling in her twenties and thirties, and came to loathe it in later life. Purdy, however, had only really begun to travel in his forties and did so for aesthetic reasons. In his second letter to Laurence, he told her that

in order to write I have to go out and look for things I want
to write about, i.e. put myself in a physical position where
I'm enough involved in strangeness and the strands of an
existence outside my own norm (never finish this sentence)
so that I both want to and have things to write about. (what
a tangled sentence) (2 February 1967).

Laurence replied:

I don't know about your comment that you have to put
yourself in a physical position where you're enough
involved in strangeness so that you have things to write
about. I can accept this as valid and necessary, for you. For
myself, the external strangeness seems to happen almost
continuously without my planning it (like going to Somalia
last spring for a week, fare ludicrously and insanely paid for
by Somali government – how bizarre), but the internal
strangeness which relates to writing seems to be there with
very little reference to immediate external happenings (19
February 1967).

Change of scene became something that Purdy saw as essential
to his work. Perhaps with the success of *North of Summer* (1967) in
mind, he described himself as "somebody contemplating all
sortsa trips in order to write poems. But I stress that where I go is
of interest for itself, itself blends with me and the poems, I'm now
such a goddam litperson that all these things are inextricable" (27
August 1970). If anything revealed the intense self-consciousness
of Purdy, it was his travel correspondence. His comments to
Margaret Laurence anticipated what he was to write George
Woodcock a year later from Hiroshima:

I think life for me is wrapped up in poems, which is the way
I discover what I think and feel. All the genuine emotions
and feelings etc other people have felt have also been
wrapped up in poems for me. Incredible selfconsciousness

I guess, probably common to most writers or all. Also a beforehand thing. I make up my mind previously (sometimes) what will provide poems, and then aim directly for them. Not always, but fairly often. In any CC fellowship, tho, you have to do this.

Probably anything I ever thought was important got into a poem sooner or later. And I *discovered* what was important thru poems.[1]

As well as directing Purdy to new sights and sensations, these journeys were equally marked by an intense introspection which prompted him to examine his own creative impulses. From Johannesburg he wrote to Laurence, "Odd thing: I am well aware that, with an act of will, I can write poems. Here or anywhere I've exercised this will sometimes. And yet, much of what I wrote was written as I breathe, as I talk or consider something pleasurable i.e. involuntary" (16 December 1972). He visited Cape Kennedy two months later to see the rocket museum or "graveyard," as he called it, since he had "read a book in Africa that made me think a poem possible re the graveyard" (11 February 1973). Curiously, his letters depict him as a diffident rather than enthusiastic traveller, as aware of the interior as of the exterior life.

Where Purdy might occasionally harness the energies of letter-writing or travelling directly to the process of making poems, Margaret Laurence would write about what she was doing. Her letters are a chronicle of the stages, challenges, doubts, false starts, and satisfactions of her fiction. As she began corresponding with Purdy, she was finishing *Long Drums and Cannons,* her study of Nigerian dramatists and novelists, and in the throes of returning to the writing of *The Fire-Dwellers.* She said that "the only thing I really care about is to try to write about three more novels" (19 February 1967). The composition of *The Fire-Dwellers* – as later of *The Diviners* – was a recurrent topic in her letters. Laurence wrestled with my difficulties with this new novel – how to get across the multiplicity of everything? Not by thinking about it consciously, that's for sure. And snaring the subconscious becomes *not* more easy as the time passes. The attempt to deal with the shifting and ambiguous nature of reality seems to me to be the only important thing that's happened in the novel in the past decade (6 June 1967).

Her subsequent letters trace the fascinating vicissitudes of writing *The Fire-Dwellers*: the 300 pages of an earlier draft that she burned in June 1967; her undertaking of the fifth attempt to write it; the process of "paring down to the bone, of shedding gimmicks, even of shedding many explanations" (23 October 1967). When Laurence described her procrastinating techniques, Purdy replied by outlining his own when he was writing plays for the CBC: "before I'd settle down at the typewriter I'd do all sorts of silly things, like making coffee, washing dishes (I was alone most of the time), just walking back and forth back and forth thinking about the damn thing. Does all this have a familiar ring?" (26 November 1967).

It was about *The Diviners,* however, that Margaret Laurence wrote most extensively to Purdy. That part of their correspondence traces the long and difficult gestation of the novel and the intensity of the three-year period of its composition. As early as the fall of 1968, she talked about travelling to northern Manitoba and driving from Churchill to York Factory, "the trek the earliest Selkirk settlers walked, when their ship landed at the wrong place. Don't know how many miles – about 150? – but they walked it in early spring, men, women and kids, plus bagpipes – that story has some meaning for me, but am not sure yet what it is" (31 October 1968). Throughout the summer and fall of 1970, Laurence worried unremittingly over her next novel: "I don't want to think of that goddam novel. Dunno how to tackle it. I realize more and more that realism bores me to hell, now. No way

I can do it in straight narration. Can't think of any other way. Stalemate. Words fail" (5 August 1970). She described "the symptoms of pre-novel neurosis" (22 September 1970) on her return to Elm Cottage after having been writer-in-residence at Massey College for the 1969/70 academic year. She then observed:

> It is so rejuvenating at the moment simply to be a totally private person (not "a real live author") and to read lots of books written by others and look at lots of idiotic TV and pick out curtain materials and harvest apples from ye olde orchard, and so on. Maybe I am simply building up my strength? (22 September 1970).

Purdy's response was humorous but trenchant. For him as for Laurence, the personal and the professional could not be compartmentalized; they had too integrated a sense of their lives and their writing for that: "Work is work and not work, and it wouldn't be lovely not to do it. You're talkin like a woman, not a writer at the moment. Curtain material! Shame on you" (29 September 1970). She was grateful: "Surprisingly, or maybe not surprisingly, I need from time to time to have a friend saying, in effect, for god's sake quit messing around and get on with it. You are, of course, quite right – I will have to think of a way to write it" (26 October 1970).

After a number of false starts, the novel began to take shape in the spring of 1971, and Laurence worked on it at Elmcot and at her newly acquired shack on the Otonabee River near Peterborough until the late summer of 1973. She wrote Purdy:

> I am into the third section and that is all that matters. Spent two damn-nearly-sleepless nights while portions of this opening part of S. III were composing themselves in full technicolour in my head. Too tired to get up and write it down; unable to shut the TV inside off for the night. Terrible. Got up and scrawled down key words, and in

morning would look at them and think "what did I mean by *jerusalem*?" (7 September 1971).

When the final revisions to the novel had been completed, Laurence wrote to Purdy about what she considered to be the differences in rhythm between the novelist and the poet:

> I'm a novelist and I have just finished a book and don't want even to think about my own work for at least another year. Whereas a poet's writing doesn't move in the same kind of cycle. With you, or anyway this is my impression, the possibilities of a new poem coming along are always there, and you really want to keep open to them (27 September 1973).

Purdy replied, "You have it exactly right re the poet, or so I think. One wants to 'keep open to them' etc. So you must have the novelist right too" (4 October 1973). His agreement was typical of the affinity between them and their ability to speak plainly and sincerely to each other.

Laurence was an intuitive and skilled reader of Purdy's poetry. She reread *Wild Grape Wine* and wrote in 1969 of her reaction in a way that suggested that she found in his poetry resonances that were already playing in her imagination:

> I was struck once more with the way you have quite often of delivering an absolutely stunning last few lines, which connect everything – the poem to itself and to the reader, and then go on to reach out like the ripples when you skip a stone in a lake (6 June 1969).

Among the lines she quoted was

> "They had their being once/and left a place to stand on" … it seems to me you've said damn near everything in those lines that I was trying to say in the short stories. They *did* leave a place to stand on, and we are standing on it.[…] These are lines which take up residence in the mind, and

remain there, the kind of lines to say to oneself in moments
of pain, crisis, disaster or earthquake.

And, she might have added, of composition.

While not as extensive, Purdy's comments on Laurence's writing were consistently perceptive. Purdy wrote that he thought
The Fire-Dwellers was "like breaking into someone else's life – a
phrase I kinda like as you might guess. I can't remember when –
how long ago – since I've read a book I thought as good.[…] I disagree all to hell with the idea that your idiom-jargon-slang is 20
years outdated" (13 February 1969). Eight years later, describing
The Diviners, he commented:

> I have all sorts of feelings about the book, one of them
> being one you perhaps don't prize as much as I do: the fact
> that you seldom or never write a line that isn't, of itself,
> interesting.[…] There are things I did think about the
> book, as I remember: that the earlier years in it over-
> matched the other sections in some degree. But the best
> part of it was what I talked about in the first para. of this
> letter, the homogeneity of time and what happens, how
> incidents float in time (18 February 1977).

Then, as if to answer Laurence's reiterated statement that *The
Diviners* was likely her last novel, he continued, "I do think it's
one of the three top novels written in/of/about this country. And
when one develops the ability to do this, I think one should go
farther. Always farther, exploring, developing etc."

As writers, they shared common experiences and could com-
miserate with each other about them. Both worked as writ-
ers-in-residence and found it exhausting and short on rewarding
returns for the energy they expended. Their gratitude for a steady
income, however, never faltered. They wrote articles on commission for *Maclean's,* the *Vancouver Sun, Weekend Magazine,* and
Purdy agreed for a time to write a critical monograph on Earle

Birney until he realized that it was not the job for him. Throughout, they wrote each other letters of support and advice. They
discussed other writers, Laurence recommending African writers
to Purdy, and Purdy describing his assembling of an anthology of
young poets, *Storm Warning,* and his friendships with Milton
Acorn and Angus Mowat. They agreed that Margaret Atwood's
Survival was a *tour de force,* Laurence confessed her passion for
Joyce Cary's novels, and Purdy, a confirmed bibliophile,
described his most recent finds.

The person they shared in common was their Canadian publisher, Jack McClelland. Laurence had been published by
McClelland and Stewart since 1960, Purdy since 1965. The firm
had been publishing Canadian books since 1906 and by 1960 was
the premier publisher of Canadian writing. McClelland, the son
of the founder, had brought many important and widely read
authors into M& S. In addition to Laurence and Purdy, he was the
publisher of Gabrielle Roy, Farley Mowat, Pierre Berton, Margaret Atwood, Mordecai Richler, and Irving Layton. A dedicated, tireless, and colourful personality, Jack McClelland filled
his role with an obsessive sense of mission and North American
entrepreneurial ingenuity. He believed in his writers and was prepared to take financial risks on behalf of selling their books, and
the near-bankruptcy of the firm in 1971 preoccupied Laurence
and Purdy at the time. In return, McClelland expected them to
work with the firm and, more and more as time went on, to
undertake arduous promotional tours. Only a few – among them
Gabrielle Roy and later Margaret Laurence – were prepared and
able to refuse.

Al Purdy's relationship with McClelland was ambivalent,
although Purdy recognized the extent to which he depended
upon "McStew," especially when efforts to have Random House
publish his *Selected Poems* in the United States fell through. One
particularly difficult episode involved a proposed collaboration,

arranged by McClelland, between Purdy and Harold Town on *Love in a Burning Building.* When McClelland and Town had a change of heart, Purdy, who disliked Town intensely, made dismantling the project as difficult as possible. It was inevitable that these men, temperamental, strong-minded, and belonging to the same generation, should experience a clash of wills. Purdy, however, remained with McClelland and Stewart who published his most recent collection, *The Woman on the Shore* (1990).

Although she had her difficult moments with McClelland, Margaret Laurence was less willing and motivated than Purdy to rock the boat. She had high admiration and affection for McClelland, was impressed by his professional skill and promotional ingenuity (especially the water-divining contest held at the Ontario Science Centre in honour of her last novel), and recognized his personal charisma in the world of Canadian publishing. She appreciated his friendship, valued him highly as a reader, and was especially grateful for McClelland's professional modesty in acknowledging her unique and fruitful working relationship with Judith Jones, her editor at Knopf.

As an early and vocal cultural nationalist, Purdy's convictions struck a responsive chord in Laurence who, at the beginning of their correspondence, was feeling more and more displaced as an expatriate. She was the first person he approached about a contribution to *The New Romans,* an anthology he was preparing about Canadians' views of the United States. Laurence tentatively agreed and eventually sent "Open Letter to the Mother of Joe Bass," which had been prompted by the American race riots of the summer of 1967. Partially projecting from his own experience, Purdy suggested that England was the wrong place for her and that she should sell her house and move back to Canada. He added, "In Africa I would think you lived emotionally off the people around you, but are not doin it now" (8 July 1967). Laurence replied, "The truth is, Al, I don't know where the hell

I belong – nowhere, I guess" (26 July 1967) and by the end of
August she was saying, "What has been bugging me, under the
surface, for months now, is that I really do not belong in this
country, Al" (31 August 1967). She vacillated between staying in
England and moving back to Canada. It was natural, given her
immersion in the writing of the Manawaka cycle, that she should
feel a more intense connection to her country than ever before.
She decided, however, that the continuity of her children's education and the opportunity her relative isolation in England gave
her would provide the essential psychological and creative advantage that she needed to write.

For all that, Laurence was not as isolated as Purdy imagined.
Her letters to him record visits from many Canadian writers,
among them Margaret Atwood, Dave Godfrey, Gary Geddes, and
Percy Janes. She had congenial meetings with Mordecai Richler
and Jack Ludwig. In addition, there was a continuous stream of
family and friends who came to visit. She was no less a nationalist
for being in England, denouncing the sale of Ryerson to the
American publishing firm of McGraw-Hill, holding her breath
over the future of McClelland and Stewart, and agonizing about
the FLQ crisis. After she arrived home, she became very active in
the establishment of the Writers' Union of Canada, discussed at
length the future of the country in the event of the possible separation of Quebec from Canada, and coped with the attempt in
the Peterborough school district to ban *The Diviners* from high
school curricula. Much of what she felt about these issues she
expressed most fully to Purdy.

Their own correspondence became a subject of discussion
between them. At the end of 1967, Laurence had asked, "probably unjustified curiosity, but why do you put Margaret Laurence
at the top of your letters to me? Do you make carbons and stash
them all away? I hope to Christ nobody keeps my letters to them
– they are not for keeping" (11 December 1967). Purdy's reply
was blunt:

I do make carbons of all my letters, because sometimes I
say things I want to look up later that seem good to me on
imperfect reflection, also because I may want to peddle
them to a univ. later. I also keep all letters to me, not business letters or notes, but those that are about writing etc.
Shall I send yours back to you? Wouldn't be any trouble at
all – ? (31 December 1967).

Laurence answered quickly and apologetically, telling Purdy to
keep her letters and confessing that she herself kept friends' letters
about writing "because I like to look back from time to time and
read about other writers' problems and comments on work,
especially if I am feeling low myself" (5 January 1968). Purdy saw
letters as a literary form and commented to Laurence that "even
in [your] letters the prose-ability comes thru like a palimpsest of
the mind" (13 January 1969). Laurence herself admitted, "Strikes
me now that this correspondence might possibly make interesting
reading someday when we are dead, for what the letters say about
writing and what goes on there" (16 January 1969). In October
1969 she spent Thanksgiving weekend with the Purdys and
wrote a memorandum to Al that, following her injunction, serves
as an introduction to this edition of their letters.

To writers as obsessively committed to their work as Laurence
and Purdy, "saving laughter"[2] was an important release and
sometimes a source of mischief. From Purdy's first letter and his
comment on his mistyping of Laurence's name, humour was an
abiding feature of their letters to each other. Discussing the masks
that the writer wears, Laurence told Purdy that when she first met
him, he looked like a cowboy. She went on to describe how she
could turn herself into the "good middleclass housewife-type …
possibly because this is what I partly am. Can hear myself taking
the part, and think – *Christ, it can't be!*" (23 October 1967). Purdy
responded, "Me – a cowboy? Christ, any horse I got near would
crap on me sure. Milk wagon horses used to give me that sneering

lip-lifted equine look, and I was so pleased when they started using trucks" (30 October 1967). Purdy had a gift for humorous anecdote: his account of going with his wife Eurithe to Cape Kennedy; the tall-tale descriptions of the tidal wave in his kitchen and of being trapped in a toilet factory during a torrential rainstorm in the Yucatan. Laurence also had a lively sense of anecdotal humour. Her account of her meeting with Miron Grindea, the editor of the *Adam International Review*, and of her sprint across a lawn in a "long greenblue silk robe and a long black cape lined with scarlet silk […] looking like a combination of an Indian witch and Batwoman" (14 November 1973), are two hilarious examples. Both had the Scots-Irish love of the slightly contorted anecdote and of ironic self-deprecation. In the early months of their correspondence, Laurence gave Purdy a droll image that was to remain vividly in his mind. In late August 1967, she wrote of her longing to return to Canada. Explaining that most of her friends were Canadian and that the best part of her income came from Canada and the United States, she projected an image of herself in ten years' time "surrounded by cats and roses – and nothing else, and the prospect is a little less than pleasing" (31 August 1967). Purdy commented, "Perish the goddam cats and roses. What a title! Makes me wriggle to think of it" (16 September 1967). They kept returning to this image throughout their correspondence. It became a kind of talismanic shorthand for lurking self-pity, a code word for the writer's need for community. In his poem "Lawrence to Laurence," published after her death, Purdy wrote:

> And remember a remark by Margaret Laurence
> "I expect to grow old raising
> cats and roses –" (but she didn't) [3]

Throughout their friendship Purdy and Laurence felt a connection with one another as writers and as individuals.

Sometimes they shared work, as when Purdy collaborated in the adaptation of one of the stories from *Bird in the House* for CBC radio. Each felt that the other was a kind of creative listener, and both had a profound sense of the importance of history. They experienced at the same time a sense that their work was becoming harder, Laurence declaring that *The Diviners* was her last novel and Purdy writing: "You talk about The Diviners being your last novel, and I think lately I haven't been able to break thru to another stage another thought I might flatter myself is original, either in saying or meaning" (3 June 1974). Later, he talked about "writing a few poems now and then, but not in the outpouring I seem to have lost forever" (26 September 1974).

They both experienced at the same time sustained hostile reviews. Laurence wrote that she wished "people wouldn't think that I am in a state of despair, or am bowing out of life. Gee. It's not that way at all, Al.[...] If another novel is given, I'll be grateful. If not, I won't be too upset.[...] To me, life depends on doing what you are given to do, and no excuses. And if one door may close, then another opens" (15 February 1977). Purdy's curmudgeonly reply was astringent. He acknowledged the way in which Laurence had become a public personality and the extent to which, by contrast, he insisted on remaining a fiercely private individual, choosing the marginality of the writer to protect his essentially creative interests and energies:

> I doubt that people think you're "in a state of despair" and "bowing out of life." That's a wild exaggeration. And people who keep pestering you to do this and that, well, one learns to dispose of those things in order to do the important things. I am saying: a talent is to be used, even if you let it lie fallow for a time. If you never write another novel, you won't think you're useless in this life, as you say. Of course not, and that's not the goddam point. Because

neither novels nor poems are entirely gifts, only in one sense. The qualities that enabled you to write your novels are still there, and one owes both one's self and other people (18 February 1977).

Purdy spoke with the concern of an old friend and with the passion of a writer. Like Margaret Laurence, Purdy celebrated the importance of continuity for the writer and the writing. This quality – a product of their backgrounds and sensibilities – was a characteristic of Purdy's writing to which Laurence returned again and again. Speaking of the revised edition of *Poems for all the Annettes,* Laurence described how the collection conveyed

> the sense of oneself and everything being so ephemeral and momentary, contrasted with the equally strong feeling that the aspects of life are interconnected and continuing.[...] You can convey an almost eerie sense of hearing the voices of the dead and the unborn, and I like this very much (4 September 1968).

She returned to this theme early in 1969 as she identified the stirrings of a new novel:

> Interesting, your fascination with the ancestral voices – it bugs me, quite a lot, too, and yet in some way mine at this point are all connected with the old celtic bit, although in other ways with the caveman, too, I guess. I don't know what the hell I'll write next as a novel, if it ever comes, but something seems to be going on and I hope someday it'll crystallize (10 January 1969).

In his reply Purdy sent a draft copy of his poem "The Game Before the Egg" and Laurence described enthusiastically how that poem had vividly captured the sense "of being both unique and in another way connected right from the inside with every amoeba that ever was, every creature with gills, every ancestor who made gods in his own shape, every human unborn" (16 January 1969). A year and a half later she wrote to congratulate Purdy on "The Horseman of Agawa":

> It gets across that quality which is in all your best poems, I think – ie the sense of the present being part of the past and also of the future; the sense of everything being connected, somehow, so that the ancestors are everybody's ancestors, and we ourselves are ancestors-in-the-making, or something like that (5 August 1970).

Four years later Laurence wrote about how Purdy expressed in his poetry what she had tried to do in *The Diviners*:

> The sense that the past is always the present is always the future, and that the future, altho in one way totally unknown, in another way *is* kind of known to us.[...] One thing I have always loved in your poetry is the recurring themes of the connectedness of life – which is why, in yr poems, deeply out of Canada, you can make reference to the Greeks (ancient, i.e.) and the old Egyptians, etc etc etc, with perfect ease and naturalness, because it fits and we are not isolated nor ever have been, if only we can see it that way. I guess in The Diviners a lot of the same ancestral feeling comes across (I hope), and the sense that in some ways, after a certain time, *the ancestors* are everyone's ancestors – mine, in some ways, are not only the Scots but also the Métis; I was born in a land which they had inhabited, shaped and invested with their ghosts.[...] what comes across more than anything, I mean the emotion or whatever, under the words and under what you are saying, is a kind of sombre and yet enormously strong affirmation of life and continuity – the kind of thing that you could not possibly have written 20 years ago because you didn't know it yet, not in that way (12 June 1974).

This sense of continuity was what allowed each to hope for the other. Laurence added: "you say you feel you haven't been able to break through to another stage, etc etc. Maybe you have done it somehow without realizing it." In his turn, Purdy wrote in the hope that there would be other novels after *The Diviners*. For Laurence, the image of connectedness was articulated in the last two lines of "Roblin Mills (circa 1842)": "but they had their being once/and left a place to stand on." Purdy's poetry served as a kind of creative confirmation for Laurence of one of the basic preoccupations in her work: the web, both mythic and human, that makes possible an imaginative vision of human community.

The culmination of the most intense period of their correspondence coincided with the publication in 1974 of *The Diviners* and *In Search of Owen Roblin,* a long poem incorporating previously published and new poems. Both works trace personal and cultural journeys into the past and the history in which Laurence, Purdy, and their work were rooted. As such, they were journeys home, characterized by the elegiac counterpoise of lament and affirmation. For Laurence, the journey home was also literal. In the final months of writing *The Diviners* she wrote of "Project Canada, re: moving back in spring" (30 December 1972). Six months later she announced that she had decided to settle in Lakefield. Purdy himself felt an unusual urgency about the poem which was to commemorate the ancestral past of his own Prince Edward County. Laurence had written to him the previous February about the completion of *The Diviners*. His reply to that letter indicates that he may well have had in mind Laurence's protracted wrestling with her novel as he thought about *In Search of Owen Roblin*. He told her that he saw himself "perhaps like a novelist in this instance, I wanta get everything about me into this, obviously ego eh? If I inhabit those goddam early settlers then they are me and I am them. I'd like to get a farmer in there who's a failure, can't keep up with more successful ones, dies trying and knows his own failure. How in hell do I do that?" (11 February 1973).

Margaret Laurence sold Elm Cottage and sent *The Diviners* to her publishers in April 1973. In July she returned to Canada for good. After that, demands were made on her that she had not experienced in England and she felt an increasing responsibility to take on many of them. It was inevitable that she and Purdy should go more and more their separate ways, although they kept in touch by occasional letters and by telephone. Their friendship had been marked by candour, respect, and affection. Although as writers they were ultimately alone with their separate selves and their work, they had been delighted to discover common ground. Laurence had found in Purdy a voice she recognized and an ear that was prepared to listen. In Laurence, Purdy found a perceptive, articulate, and supportive audience. Their letters created a dialogue that continues to speak vigorously today about what is and always has been central to any writer – the language that words speak.

FOR MARGARET[4]
We argued about things
whether you should seek experience
or just let it happen to you
(me the former and she the latter)
and the merits of St. Paul
as against his attitude to women
(she admired him despite chauvinism)
But what pitifully few things
we remember about another person:
me sitting at her typewriter
at Elm Cottage in England
and translating her short story
"A Bird in the House" into a radio play

directly from the book manuscript
in just two or three days
(produced by J. Frank Willis
on CBC his last production)
and being so proud of my expertise
Then going away to hunt books
while my wife recuperated
from an operation
Returning to find the play finished
Margaret had taken about three hours
to turn my rough draft
into a playable acting version
fingers like fireflies on the typewriter
and grinning at me delightedly
while my "expertise" went down the drain
And the huge cans of English ale she bought
Jocelyn called "Al-size-ale"
and the people coming over one night
to sing the songs in *The Diviners*
(for which I gave faint praise)
And the books she admired –
Joyce Cary's *The Horse's Mouth*
Alec Guinness as Gulley Jimson a Valkyrie
riding the Thames on a garbage barge
– how Graham Greene knew so much
that she both loved and cussed him
for anticipating her before she got there
and marked up my copy of his essays
These are the lost minutiae
of a person's life
things real enough to be trivia
and trivial enough to have some permanence
because they recur and recur – with small
differences of course – in all our lives

and the poignance finally strikes home
that poignance is ordinary
Anyway how strange to be writing about her
as if she were not here
but somewhere else on earth
– or not on earth
given her religious convictions
Just in case it does happen
I'd like to be there when she meets St. Paul
and watch his expression change
from smugness to slight apprehension
while she considers him as a minor character
in a future celestial non–fiction novel
And this silly irrelevance of mine
is a refusal to think of her dead
(only parenthetically DEAD)
remembering how alive
she lit up the rooms she occupied
like flowers do sometimes and the sun always
in a way visible only to friends
and she had nothing else

---

1. Purdy to Woodcock, 24 May 1971. In *The Purdy-Woodcock Letters: Selected Correspondence 1964-1984,* ed. George Galt. Toronto: ECW Press, 1988.

2. Clara Thomas, "Saving Laughter." *Canadian Woman Studies/les cahiers de la femme,* "Margaret Laurence: A Celebration," 8, 3 (Fall 1987), 46-48.

3. Al Purdy, "Lawrence to Laurence." *The Woman on the Shore.* Toronto: McClelland & Stewart, 1990.

4. Al Purdy. From *The Woman on the Shore.*

A Note on the Text

From December 1966 to December 1986, Al Purdy and Margaret Laurence exchanged approximately 300 letters, the largest number of which were sent in the seven-year period between 1967 and 1974. The selection in this volume reflects the characteristic energy, wit, and candour of their friendship and speaks eloquently to what preoccupied them most – writing and its work.

In preparing this volume I have kept editorial intervention to a minimum. For example, idiosyncratic spellings (e.g., Purdy's spelling of "pome," "writ," "wanta," "hafta," etc.) have been retained, as have spellings of proper names, with correct spellings of the latter appearing in a footnote. There are rare cases where, in the originals, a word or punctuation has apparently been omitted, and these have been left as is. Supplementary information, when required for clarity, appears in square brackets.

The format for addresses and dates has been standardized, although the variable spelling of Ameliasburg/h and the designation of Elm Cottage or Elmcot follow the instance of each letter. Since Purdy often wrote on letterhead that he collected on his travels, letterhead addresses have been included only in the case where letters were written at that location. Purdy's usual typing of Laurence's name above his opening salutation has been omitted. To prevent any confusion in the reading of the letters in this volume, all postscripts appear at the end of the letter rather than at the beginning where lack of space sometimes occasioned the writers to put them. Margins have been spaced and ruled for addresses, salutations, and signatures.

Almost all of the letters in this selection were originally

typewritten. Any handwritten additions and/or annotations made to a letter are, where the context requires, identified as such in the footnotes. In keeping with typographical convention, words or phrases which were underlined in the originals are set in italics. In cases where poems were appended to letters, only those not previously published at the time have been included here. In all but a few specific instances, poems are identified in the footnotes by book publications. Detailed information on periodical publication is available in the *Annotated Bibliography of Canada's Major Authors* and elsewhere. Footnotes have been prepared for a broad readership. They contain information current to the date of the letter and, where literary works are mentioned, publishers are indicated only when the context requires.

Letters are reproduced in their entirety except in rare instances where material is no longer pertinent or has been omitted at the request of Al Purdy or Margaret Laurence's children. Such deletions have been indicated by ellipses in square brackets.

John Lennox
York University
February 1993

Letters

॰

Al Purdy
R.R. 1
Ameliasburg, Ontario
10 December 1966

Margaret Laurence
(wherever)
Dear Margaret Laurence,[1]

Bob Weaver[2] said I was going to meet you when I came back from Newfoundland this fall. However, you were in Manitoba at the time. Perhaps later.[3]

I am just another admirer, and you have those ad nauseam I suppose. Went so far as to buy your books tho, and that's goin pretty far for me – I generally try to wangle used or review copies or some damn thing like that. Must admit tho, I intended to get you to sign them if I ever caught up with you personally. Incidentally, I hope you bawled out someone at McStew for the paper they used in Jest of God.

All best wishes,
Al Purdy

---

1. Purdy typed this as "Lurence" and corrected the misspelling by adding the missing "a" in ballpoint, followed by the hand-printed comment "AINT THAT AWFUL?"

2. Robert Weaver (b. 1921). Editor, anthologist, and radio producer, he was one of the founders of *The Tamarack Review* (1956-82) and launched and produced the CBC radio program "Anthology" (1953-85), which featured the work of new and established Canadian writers.

3. Laurence had returned to Canada between late July and mid-October for a visit and promotional tour for *A Jest of God,* which had been published in July.

§

Elm Cottage, Beacon Hill
Penn, Bucks., England
16 January 1967

Dear Al Purdy:

I was really glad to get your letter. Owing to one of those ironies of life, you were the person I most wanted to meet when I was in Canada this summer and the only person in the whole country (almost) whom I didn't meet. Actually, it was owing to a line from a poem in THE CARIBOO HORSES that I went back to Canada at all last summer.[1] It wasn't exactly one rural winter – more one rural spring, when I sat beside my wet-beech-log fire, surrounded by nothing but beautiful trees, reading your poem and thinking at that moment with both amusement and rage that I also hated beautiful trees. The next day I walked into the CBC office in London and said "I'm homesick, and I'm going home", and my friend Ken Black there said "Okay, you can – let's see what we can do", and from that beginning sprung Bob Weaver's miraculous work in getting a Canada Council grant for me, including a travel grant which allowed me to go to Canada for the summer. Naturally, as soon as I hit Toronto I discovered that I didn't hate beautiful trees at all – what I hated was Avenue Road and that everlasting traffic which makes sleep impossible unless you are half stoned or preferably more so. It was good to see people like Bob, but otherwise I couldn't wait to get back here to my kids and this house which must have the frailest plumbing in the world (the tank on the toilet says charmingly but with vast inaccuracy, Pontifex's No-Sound). I guess I like this place because it doesn't claim perfection – it just staggers along somehow, with damp walls and other blemishes but it has elegance and warmth (spiritual; the physical warmth you have to work for constantly). I find it reassuring. Those beautifully appointed houses in Toronto give me the creeps. So I'm stuck here, and at the moment I have to buy this house, because it has to be sold, and either I buy it or I

4

move out, and I can't bear to move out. Thus it was that I have spent the last month in Egypt, on an assignment (this sounds professional – but I've never done this sort of thing before) for *Holiday* magazine.[2] I am hoping to raise some money thereby. I took my two kids along (daughter 14; son 11) and we had a terrific month, so it wasn't wasted even if the magazine doesn't buy the articles. As it turned out, the Egyptians are very fond and sentimental re: kids, although they were a little uncertain about my nubile daughter (marriageable age in the U.A.R.), but in general the presence of the kids paved my way considerably. I think they also believed that no one travelling with 2 kids could possibly be a spy. What I really want to do is to get these articles written and get started on another novel. A lot of life seems to be the process of clearing the decks, or maybe it only seems so to me because I only started earning my own living when I was 36 and that is probably leaving it a little late.

I didn't bawl out Mc & S for the paper (and, I may say, printing, binding etc) of *A Jest of God*, because I think they wanted to bring out their fall list of novels in some kind of uniform form and anyway what's the use. Also I dearly love Jack McClelland,[3] although we fight quite often.

You were in England about a year ago, I think, re: the Commonwealth Arts Festival[4] (what a fiasco), and I had wanted to go to the evening which ludicrously combined Canadian poetry and W. Indian poetry, but unfortunately had to go to see a Yoruba opera that night. A friend of mine at Macmillan's told me about driving you and some other Canadian poets home that night, and thinking "My God, if we crash, Canadian poetry is finished".

If you can ever get to England some time, please phone and perhaps we can meet. Phone – Penn 2103.

Best wishes.
Margaret Laurence

p.s. have seen your Eskimo poems in Parallel and Tamarack,[5] and think they are – what? Difficult to say without sounding phoney. I like them. The people come across. And so do you.

---

1. The lines "surrounded by nothing/but beautiful trees/& I hate beautiful trees" are taken from Purdy's poem "One Rural Winter" in the collection *The Cariboo Horses* (1965) which had won the Governor-General's Award for poetry.

2. The articles that resulted from this assignment, "Good Morning to the Grandson of King Ramesses the Second" and "Captain Pilot Shawkat and Kipling's Ghost" were not published in *Holiday*, but appeared later in Laurence's collection of essays, *Heart of a Stranger* (1976).

3. John G. (Jack) McClelland (b. 1922) had been president of McClelland and Stewart Publishers since 1961.

4. The Commonwealth Arts Festival took place 16 September–2 October 1965. The Cardiff conference of Commonwealth poets was part of the Festival.

5. A bi-monthly journal of opinion and the arts, *Parallel* published in its second number (May-June 1966) three of Purdy's Arctic poems: "Canso," "Looking at Swinton's Book of Eskimo Sculpture," and "What Can't Be Said." In its Spring 1966 issue, *The Tamarack Review* had published as "Arctic Poems" the following: a prelude poem, "Dead Seal," "At the Movies," "Metrics," "The North West Passage," "The County of the Young," and "When I Sat Down to Play the Piano." This selection was preceded by Earle Birney's poem "In Purdy's Ameliasburg."

§

3 Anglesey Blvd, Apt. 1

Islington [Ontario]

2 February [1967]

Dear Margaret,

Hadn't realized you were already flitted back to England. Bob Weaver had said by letter that we were all to have lunch together –

Just as well you didn't get to the Commonwealth Arts thing at the Royal Court – Was a shambles. And the thing at Cardiff was far worse. Bunch of American expatriate beats there, only a few, but they brought to my mind all the American articulateness of their State Department and public relations people, as poets, tho bad ones. The Africans, who didn't know English too well, couldn't keep talking pace with them. As you see, I am extremely anti-American, a Canadian trait said to be predominant.

Yeah, the ambivalent bit about "the beautiful trees". Of course maybe it's the soggy sentimental associations and heritage that one dislikes. Many poets have raved over nature, and the tendency still exists. But if you're marooned among the damn things by lack of money you don't appreciate nature quite so much. One always (I think) wants to reserve the power to say, "to hell with this place" – always a matter of money.

Your Egypt trip sounds good, and the idea of using kids as a front –! And I would love to go thru the touristy places, pyramids etc. Which I did last time in London, with John Colombo.[1] Birney[2] was busy keeping social engagements.

Your house sounds attractive etc. – tho from my point of view, in order to write I have to go out and look for things I want to write about, i.e. put myself in a physical position where I'm enough involved in strangeness and the strands of an existence outside my own norm (never finish this sentence) so that I both want to and have things to write about. (what a tangled sentence) Anyhow, maybe you're the sort of person who can hibernate in a cottage and write like hell at the same time, I suppose about past

7

experiences filtering into now. I do that too, but generally feel like litmus paper about to change colour. (Violent purple?) Incidentally, have just written a piece about the house at Roblin Lake, which I'd like to copy, but it will take all the space. Will anyway.

INTERRUPTION[3]
When the new house was built
callers came:
black squirrels on the roof every morning
between sleep and wakefulness,
and a voice says "Hello dead man".
Chipmunks look in the windows
and you look out,
but neither moves
for their lifetime and half yours.
Orioles, robins and red winged blackbirds
are crayons that colour the air;
something sad and old
cries down in the swamp.
Moonlight in the living room,
a row of mice single file
route marching in the silver shade
until they touch one of my thoughts
and jump back frightened,
but I don't wake up.
Pike in the lake pass and re-pass the windows
with clouds in their mouth.
For 20 minutes every night
the sun slaps a red paint brush
over dinner dishes and leftovers
but we keep washing it off.
Birds can't take a short cut home
they have to go round the new house;
and cedars grow pale green candles

8

to light their way thru the dark.
Already the house is old:
a drowned chipmunk in the rain barrel this morning,
dead robins in the roof overhang,
and the mice are terrified –
We have set traps,
and must always remember
to avoid them ourselves.

Anyhow, I see there is extra space. Re. Jack McClelland, I feel under the skin we don't like each other much. More feeling than anything. Incidentally, the same paper was used on Layton's new book,[4] and Irving is steaming a bit. Thankfully my own new book (May) is a sort of art book, with both Arctic poems and A.Y. Jackson repros,[5] so they can't very well use anything but good paper.

I hope you can finish articles and necessary money-making and get back to novels, your strong point – I suppose I'm doing an equivalent of articles in CBC work, couple of plays, hour long program of poetry and prose, also reading scripts to pay the rent.

In the event I get my fellowship this spring,[6] I will be in England on the way to Greece, and we shall have a drink or meal or whatever.

Best,
Al Purdy

---

1. John Robert Colombo (b. 1936) editor, anthologist, translator, poet. His first book of "found" poetry, *The Mackenzie Poems,* had been published in 1966.

2. Earle Birney (b. 1904), well-known Canadian poet and creative writing teacher.

3. The finished version of this poem was published in the collection *Wild Grape Wine* (1968).

4. Irving Layton's (b. 1912) most recent collection of poetry, *Periods of the Moon* (1967), had also been published by McClelland and Stewart.

5. *North of Summer. Poems from Baffin Island* (1967) with illustrations by A.Y. Jackson (1882-1974), one of the Group of Seven.

6. Purdy had applied for a Guggenheim Fellowship.

§

Elm Cottage
19 February 1967

Dear Al:

I have the feeling that you may have moved from Islington (wherever that is)[1] to somewhere else by the time this letter arrives, but probably it will catch you up sometime. Thanks for your letter, and even more, thanks for copying out the poem about the house at Roblin Lake. I liked all of it, but what hit me most were the last three lines. How damnably difficult to remember, ourselves, to avoid the traps. The mice are certainly one's brethren in this respect – so who isn't terrified? This poem was like a kind of gift, and you are lucky in that way, in being able to do that. Writers of prose can never reciprocate. (Imagine sending anybody a copy of the first chapter of a novel, and if you did, it wouldn't mean a thing in isolation anyway).

I can imagine what the poetry sessions at Cardiff must have been like – the African poets do, in fact, know English extremely well, I think, but are operating on a different wave-length to the Americans (beat-type, anyway). There is a kind of American intellectual talk that is so slick that although it may be directed against the establishment, it still seems like advertising. I wonder what African poets were there. Christopher Okigbo[2] of Nigeria seems like one of the best, to me, but I'm pretty uninformed about contemporary poetry. Have you seen Okigbo's HEAVENSGATE? If not, and you'd like to, I could send you a copy. I'm still attempting to finish a book about contemporary Nigerian prose (novels and plays),[3] and why I ever wrote it I can't think, as I am certainly not a literary critic, and the North-American scientific-academic school of literary criticism scares the hell out of me (they are all so bright, one feels gloomily). Anyway, I want to get this out of the way, because I got hooked on the whole subject sufficiently to make it impossible to proceed until this particular thing is done. The only thing I really care about is to try to write about three more novels, and writing a novel is what I am supposed to be doing at the moment, with the Canada Council's financial help, and I am not doing it. I worry greatly over what they will think if (God forbid) they discover this unfortunate fact. Will I be cut off with a shilling, etc? If the novel is really there, it will be written; if it isn't, it won't – it is as simple as that. But it isn't always possible to do things to schedule. It would be great not to have to worry about money.

I don't know about your comment that you have to put yourself in a physical position where you're enough involved in strangeness so that you have things to write about. I can accept this as valid and necessary, for you. For myself, the external strangeness seems to happen almost continuously without my planning it (like going to Somalia last spring for a week, fare ludicrously and insanely paid for by Somali government – how bizarre),[4] but the internal strangeness which relates to writing seems to be there with very little reference to immediate external happenings. I just feel that with great luck there may be three more novels which I may be able to write if I can survive that long, and after that it may well be finished unless a miracle happens which is unlikely and I do not relish much the thought of trying in a minor way to imitate Sarah Berndhardt and playing Juliet with a wooden leg.[5] Say what you have to say and then shut up, or so it seems to me. As to what happens after that, I don't think it really bears thinking about, not yet. We step carefully around the traps we've set.

I don't mean this to be a gloomy letter. You know, one of my very beloved aunts wrote to me about A Jest of God, and said "Dear, I'm terribly sorry, but I'm afraid I didn't like it very much, because I wouldn't want people to start getting the wrong impression of you and think you were gloomy and sexy." I was very touched by this comment, and refrained from writing back and saying "Brace yourself – I'm both." When I was in Canada last summer, some guy in the CBC in Toronto said "Why is your writing so obsessed with death – why is it so downbeat?" And in Vancouver, another CBC type asked me, "Why is your writing so overly optimistic?" Can you win?

If you get a fellowship this spring, try and look me up on your way to Greece. I envy you even the possibility of going to Greece, as it is a country I really love, not so much for the ancient monuments as for the way it is now. Also, if you happen to like Retzina, it's bottled like Coke and much cheaper.

Good luck –
Margaret Laurence

---

1. Islington is a suburb in Toronto's west end.

2. Christopher Okigbo (1932-67), a major in the Nigerian army, was killed later the same year in the Biafran War. *Heavensgate* (1962) was his first collection of poetry.

3. *Long Drums and Cannons: Nigerian Dramatists and Novelists 1952-1966* was published in London by Macmillan (1968) and in New York by Praeger (1969).

4. Laurence had gone to Somalia for its annual Independence Day celebrations on 1 July 1966.

5. Sarah Bernhardt (1844-1923), the famous French actress, continued to perform after the amputation of one of her legs.

❦

Ameliasburg

[16 March 1967]

Dear Margaret,

No, I'm still at Islington, but by the time any other possible letters could reach me I'll be back at the above. Have just returned from Edmonton and Wpg. and readings and yak-yak there. Those parties! – and I can't help drinking some of that free liquor, end up feeling I'm wasting time. Don't like reading poems much anyway, seems kinda phony to stand up there and exhibit your sensitivity. If the stuff was any good they oughta read it anyway.

I don't think CC will cut you off with a shilling, in fact I think you'll do very well in the near future. Call it a hunch.

The bit about saying what you have to say and then shutting up is true, of course – except by the time you get all those novels written another will be biting inside you trying to get out. Of course if you run out of bright new ideas, that's different; but I can't imagine your going dry for really long periods. Some do, of course, and it's a nasty thought, and it's why I want to drink deep as long as I can.

I'd love to read the Okigbo book if you think it's really good, and will send it back after. Have you heard much of Sylvia Plath?[1] I knew about her some time ago, but first time I really looked at her was in an American mag that featured her, and the woman is rather marvellous. Earle Birney knew her and Ted Hughes in London before she committed suicide. Rather formal structural poet, but such insights – wow! I expect you know all about her, – If you're in London and see her books and have any spare energy to get them for me I'd love it. However, it's a bother to do such things and I know you have writing to do –

Just heard from a Can. friend of mine in London on some academic fellowship, Tom Marshall,[2] young, shy (rather) Queen's prof., doing writing on poems of D.H. Lawrence. He's involved in Poet's Workshop etc. Reason I mention him is – Canadians

13

sometimes flock together in London, and you might run into him –

Your comments re other people's comments on your novels very pertinent to me. I get somewhat the same. Some publisher (I really forget his name) years ago said my stuff was nothing but sex and death. That's fine with me, of course. Newspaper interviewer named Sinclair for Free Press in Wpg. kept saying my stuff seemed like prose to him and why did I take this pose etc. I said I was glad he knew how to distinguish prose from poetry since I didn't and the pose might even have a man behind it and did his? What the hell, I'm more concerned with those readers I respect, such as Weaver, Milton Wilson[3] and Birney – Every now and then one gets this gratuitous criticism under circumstances that don't call for it, like some stranger picking a quarrel with you. Reason I say this is: expect you meet the same remarks, judging from your aunt and CBC quotes.

Guggenheim turned me down (the bastards!) so I won't be in Europe this year – but I'm not really so sad about it, for it'll give me time to work out in more detail what I want to do in Greece and what archaeological books to read etc. I'll try CC in the fall, and hope like hell. In the meantime I'll be stuck at Ameliasburg I suppose, with a few weeks in Ottawa to visit parliament and see if it's as silly close up as it looks at a distance. I guess I am a little sad about Greece, but hell I'll get there. Am sure I'd write some poems there, also Sumer and Ur, which names are mnemonics for poems – Once started to write a play about Gilgamesh, got to an hour and then got onto something else and never finished – Ah well – But to look for maenads among the Athens waitresses!

Best,
Al

1. Sylvia Plath (1932–63), American poet and wife of the British poet Ted Hughes (b. 1930).

2. Tom Marshall (b. 1938), Canadian critic and poet.

3. Milton Wilson (b. 1923), critic and professor of English at the University of Toronto. He edited two collections of Canadian poetry, *Poetry of Mid-Century 1940-1960* (1964) and *Poets Between the Wars* (1967).

Elm Cottage

7 April 1967

Dear Al:

Of course it is no trouble to get the Sylvia Plath books. I merely wrote to my tame booksellers, Dillon's University Bookshop, who can get anything and everything, any time, and a few days ago they kicked through with *The Colossus, Ariel,* and her one novel, *The Bell Jar.* I wanted to read them before I sent them, and now have, and will post them tomorrow. I found *The Colossus* less interesting than the other two, although her real true terrible themes are adumbrated there – she hadn't yet faced them completely openly, I would guess. *Ariel* I found so painful that I could hardly read it, and one evening drank a lot too much wine in trying to read it without having it affect me too much. It is, simply, terrifying. The awful thing is that her father – the Nazi-Super-Authority figure, may really not have been that at all, and she knew it and knew all the nuances of her need of him, her hatred of him. What I was reminded of, strangely enough, when reading both *Ariel* and *The Bell Jar,* was Amos Tutuola,[1] a Nigerian writer who also has walked in the pit of hell, but who, in contrast, was never consciously setting down the horrors. Sylvia Plath seems to have been about a hundred percent conscious the whole way. The novel is a good novel, as such, but one feels that it is almost entirely autobiographical – what is amazing is the retention of humour, perhaps as a defense, but no – not really as a defense, because she can see the ludicrous aspect of her dilemma in situations where defenses cease to have any meaning (like, when getting shock treatment in a mental hospital). The suicide theme goes through everything, though, doesn't it? Even from the time of *The Colossus.* And it continues and builds up through the novel and finally is faced and looked at absolutely straight in *Ariel.* What is truly grim is that someone who could see so much and who could and did love, could also want so much to die. This is what bugs me about her. I remember reading, at the time when she died, about the circumstances (British newspapers are very specific about these things). She had 2 kids, remember, and before she put her head in the gas oven, she left breakfast all prepared for her kids. Knowing, I suppose, all the unanswerable ironies involved – so, your kids find their breakfast ready and their mother dead. And of course, the other part of the thing, which I can't entirely dismiss (even though it probably makes me appear hard-hearted) – the element of self-drama and self-pity. She leaves breakfast as a kind of gesture towards duty, and what her kids want is not breakfast. I sometimes feel this iron-in-the-soul in myself, knowing that it is mistaken in some ways and yet unable to pre-vent it. I feel guilty about this same feeling towards someone like Gerard Manley Hopkins, when he says "Thou art indeed just, Lord, if I contend/ with Thee, But Sir, so what I plead is just/ Why do sinners' ways prosper and why must/ Disappointment all I endeavor end?"[2] (Sorry for the hashed-about quotation – I did it imperfectly from memory, then looked it up).[3] But you think, really, who are all these sinners? Who are all of *them,* who are less sincere, less perceptive, less everything than I? I haven't seen many of them about. It seems to me that the true horror is to see that there is no enemy. That the enemy also feels pain; is real; hurts when kicked in the teeth; doesn't know what to do, either. This is almost not to be borne. When I think of somebody like Sylvia Plath, I only have one basic reaction – she *knew* all this, and a hell of a lot more; if only she could have decided to *survive,* despite everything. But there it is.

On to lighter topics. I would guess from the comments in your letter that you either have a kind of second-sight or else you were talking to Bob Weaver. I mean, when you say you have a hunch that the C.C. will do well by me in the near future, etc. I was pretty astounded to hear about the Gov-General's award, [4] and I guess you must have felt slightly odd about it when you got it, too. Actually, at this point in history, I think the money means most of all to me. This is not because I am so mercenary, but because I need the dough right now, as I am buying this house and suffering terrible anxiety re: mortgage payments etc.

I guess I will be in Ottawa whenever the ceremony is to be held. They don't seem to know when, yet. I can't leave my kids on their own for more than a week, so I think I will just stay in Ottawa 1 or 2 days and then go to Montreal for a few days to be with my friend Adele Wiseman. [5] How far is Ameliasburg from Montreal? Hundreds of miles, probably. Anyway, it's a thought.

I'm sorry Guggenheim turned you down, but you'll get to Greece, no doubt, and will probably find (lucky devil) maenads among the Athens waitresses. I paced the goddamn beaches of Crete, but did I find Zorba? [6] Like hell. Never mind – I didn't really expect to. And if I had, I probably would have dropped dead. "Who're you?" "I'm Zorba, woman, my lady." "Sorry, I promised my kids I'd be back by 9:30 p.m." "Oh?" Etc.

Good wishes.
Margaret

ps. I'm also sending you Christopher Okigbo's poems, *Heavensgate.* I don't know if they are good poems or not, because I don't know enough about poetry. I'm still working on this awful book on Nigerian literature, and I am really fed up with it.

1. Amos Tutuola (b. 1920), Nigerian novelist, whose first book, *The Palm-Wine Drinkard and his Dead Palm-Wine Tapster* (1952), was published by Faber and Faber to international acclaim.

2. The first verse of Hopkins' (1844-89) untitled poem:

> Thou art indeed just, Lord, if I contend
>
> With thee; but, sir, so what I plead is just.
>
> Why do sinners' ways prosper? and why must
>
> Disappointment all I endeavour end?

3. Laurence had corrected by hand the inaccuracies of her transcription of the verse.

4. For *A Jest of God*.

5. Adele Wiseman (1928-92), whose first novel, *The Sacrifice,* was published in 1956, had been a close friend of Laurence since the late 1940s.

6. Nikos Kazantzakis' novel *Zorba the Greek* (1952) was a celebration of its free-spirited hero. It was adapted for the screen under the same title and released in 1964.

Ameliasburg

20 April [1967]

Dear Margaret,

Thanks much for the Plath books (didn't know she'd written a novel and curious about it), and let me know how much please.

Re. Tutuola, I picked up a couple of his in England in Faber softcover, started to read the Palm Wine Drunkard but never got far, started to do something else probably. (Incidentally, William Golding is another of my enthusiasms, I have all his books)

Yeah, the bit about "who is less sincere than I – and who are the sinners?" – Some less perceptive, yes, for you don't expect a guy working in a factory etc to be appreciative of the same things you are, and the guys I knew could hardly think of anything but new cars, women and getting drunk. Of course money too. They spend their lives that way. But doubt if their lives are as much mixed up as my own.

Could be Plath decided not to survive because she saw what you say she saw, and perhaps also because she didn't satisfy herself in her own writing and her own life. Of course it sounds puerile when you put it down on paper, and I can't get around that. I think I used to feel and believe that a corner would be turned in my own life and I'd find the answer to things, the key, a flare would light in my head and my life would change – Rather silly, for it never happens. I guess some, maybe Bertrand Russell, pick some "cause" and fulfil their life that way. Anyhow, it's the sort of thing you can sometimes talk personally about if the other person can talk on a discussion level. Yet, I'm a kinda combative conversationalist sometimes. Met a guy yesterday, should say I talked to him for the umpteenth time, and it always ends the same way. He goes on advancing his rigid fact-theories, I pay little attention to them and think they're mostly silly, and he does the same thing re. what I say. Most frustrating. Enemies are never wholly enemies or friends friends –

Ottawa is 180 miles from here, Mtl. 250. I shall try to get to Ottawa when you're there, likely drive. Will try to catch your eye when you curtsy to Mitchener. [1]

I knew about your award beforehand, but was supposed to keep my mouth shut. However, I couldn't resist intimating you'd get it.

I hope you're writing like hell, because I'm not. Haven't written a good poem since that one I sent you (no connection) and dammit that irritates me tho I can't do a thing about it. I get the Beaver mag (HBC) yesterday with a poem of mine and the A.Y. Jackson repros that are to be used in my own book. I think they're terrible, and Jackson is a study in retarded development. I sure stuck my neck out re. those paintings. Always do that tho, pull some enormous blunder – enormous to me anyway – then cuss my own stupidity. So Jackson will sell a few books of poems, but his paintings look like geriatric vomit done from habit. One step above "Autumn Woods" if you ever saw that abortion on suburban walls.

I think I've worked myself into too depressed a mood to write a letter. Be sure and let me know when you'll be in Ottawa and Mtl., and will see you then.

Best,
Al

---

1. Roland Michener (1900-91), Governor-General of Canada from 1967-74.

§

Elm Cottage
27 April 1967

Dear Al:

No, I'm not writing like hell. I'm sorry to hear you're not, because I feel lousy that I'm not. In any event, what I seem mostly to be doing at the moment is writing bits of a novel but only in my head,[1] and I have the feeling that when I start actually picking up the pen, it will all have vanished. Maybe not. I'm still clearing the decks, though, because I have a one-track mind and cannot seem to concentrate on more than one thing at a time. I used to laugh when I read in books of social anthropology that African chiefs educated at Oxford suffered from "role conflict" – I thought, so what's new? I've been suffering from role conflict for years. I don't try to write when my kids are home, as then I can't do anything in either direction – I'm no use either to them or to the writing. But I must say things are easier in that way now, as the kids are away at school from 8 a.m. until 5 p.m. (The English school system isn't cruelly long in its hours – it just takes them the

20

extra time to get to and from the place where they go to school.) I have had to work on this Nigerian literature book these past 3 weeks, and at last it is finished, for better or worse. I had to re-write parts of it, and do the last chapter all over again, because when I first wrote it, I was getting pretty tired of the subject and so did a horrible job on the last chapter. Macmillan is going to publish it, but God knows if it is worth publishing. I showed Bob Weaver one chapter last summer and he thought it was terrible. I tell myself he isn't interested in African literature. At this point, I don't really care, because it isn't of prime importance to me, but I've invested a year of my life in it and I can't do anything except finish it off as well as I can. I will never try anything like this again.

The Plath books came to £2.18.6, or roughly $9, but I'm not desperate for the money, and as it is complicated to send money here, you might prefer to send me a book sometime, if you see something particularly interesting. I don't mind one way or another. I'm sorry about her novel, because I bought it for you in hardcover, and only discovered later that it was out in paperback and could have got it much cheaper.

Got a cable from Ottawa last week saying ceremony will be June 2nd, and "letter following." However, it hasn't followed yet. What I want to know is do they pay me for expenses for fares before or after? Before would be nicer. I have just finished paying my solicitor for legal fees re: the purchase of my house, so I am feeling a little cagey about money, or at least about putting out large sums.

I don't think I ever felt that there would be some sudden rev-elation, or that everything would change, but I think I used to feel that one day I would achieve a kind of calm and would at last possess wisdom and would stop being afraid. As you say, it doesn't happen, and after a while you see that you've got the only self you're ever going to have, for life. I suppose if you real-ize that, and it really isn't bearable to you, then you do what Sylvia Plath did. I don't think I hate my own failings quite as much as I used to. This could be progress, or just acceptance, which is also okay, I guess.

Sorry to hear about the A. Y. Jackson reproductions. I am illiterate where art is concerned. Do you mean to say that he is still alive?[2] Or are these pictures which were done a long time ago? It's grim to have pictures which you don't like in what is your book not his. Is it too late to create havoc with the publishers? It's very hard, though, I know, to do anything about these things, once the wheels have been set into motion. My only experience of this was with the English dust-jacket of The Stone Angel (which is minor, in comparison to illustrations in a book) – it was the most drab and repulsive dust-jacket I had ever seen, but it was already printed by the time they showed it to me.

Hope you are in a less depressed state now. Don't worry about the poems – they will come when they're ready to. I am great at telling other people this kind of thing – less good at telling it to myself.

All the best.
Margaret

_____

1. Laurence had returned to the writing of *The Fire-Dwellers*.
2. He was still living.

Elm Cottage
2 May 1967

Dear Al:

Got a letter yesterday from Canada Council, with all information re: ceremony, which will be June 2nd, in Ottawa. They say they will be pleased to pay my hotel bill for night of June 2 in Ottawa, so I think I will only stay that one night, as do not want to pay hotel bill for anything further. I spent yesterday afternoon on the phone, talking to Air Canada and BOAC, and was surprised to find that thousands of people from England are going to Expo and flights are all booked up. Couldn't get a flight for June 1 or 2, so have got a booking to Montreal for May 26. Will be in Montreal with Adele Wiseman (Apt 21, 1217 Drummond St, Montreal – phone 861-2261) from May 26 to June 2, when I will go to Ottawa. Back to Montreal June 3 and home, same day. But I do have most of June 3 in Ottawa, as plane does not leave until 8 p.m. So if you can get to Ottawa, maybe we can have some time to talk. I will be staying (C. Council tells me) at Beacons Arms Hotel, Ottawa.

All this seems a bit daft. Last night finished manuscript of Nigerian book, finally and absolutely, and now am in the usual state of physical illness which I always manage somehow to create every time I complete a manuscript – symptoms very acute, streaming cold, swollen glands, ghastly sore throat, all mental, how idiotic.

All best,
Margaret

p.s. I see in newspaper that one need no longer curtsy to Gov-Gen. Thank God. Have never curtsied in my life and would without doubt have fallen flat on my face.

Ameliasburg
8 May 1967

Dear Margaret,

Books received, and ten bucks enclosed, since you'll be able to use it right after you get off the plane. And much thanks for sending them, also the Okigbo book. Just not available over here at all.

I enclose an "Invite to Authors" sheet[1] which, when you read, will see what it's all about. I'm a little uncertain sending out this sheet, because I'm not sure if this is the right way to do it. i.e. I subscribe to most of what the sheet says, but a little worried it's too blatant and may scare off those I'd like to see contribute. Just finished getting the mimeo work done, so you're the first prospective contributor to get one. Anyhow, I hope you can scare up a thousand words about the U.S. (more or less) on whatever angle you feel like writing about. Mel Hurtig[2] mentioned your name particularly, and I feel the same way.

Congrats on finishing your book, tho you sound as if you need sympathy more than anything. Migawd, never been thru such a physical struggle and illness to complete a manuscript. (Incidentally, if by chance you'd like any of my early crap I can dig up most of it and mail it along?) My first book was twelve years ago (apart from a privately printed one when I was R.C.A.F.)[3] and I got a helluva kick outa that, sheer egotistic enjoyment, but all the others have landed with a dull plop as if I didn't give a damn. Of course I do. In your case I should recommend a bottle of scotch, or whatever is handy, and a real good drunk-celebration.

I am not sure whether Jackson is alive or not, technically he is, but these jesus paintings make me think he passed to his last reward about 1920. French impressionists, you have much to answer for!

Well, I hope Bob Weaver is not right about the Nigerian book, but even if he should be I expect the cure is to write another book you think is good to remove the bad taste. And isn't that easy for me to say. Every now and then somebody says or wants me to do a book of criticism, and I think to hell with that. It's enough to do reviews, and there are several people who can do criticism better than I can. Incidentally, I have now got that Ryerson antho the Italian guy did to review, with a story of yours in it, "To Set our House in Order"[4] – And copying a short story I wrote myself more than a year ago, a horrific thing with nasty sex and murder and voyeurism etc. Nearly ten thousand words, and a helluva job to do the final version. I have a passage in it about three thousand words, a story within a story someone else tells: so I neatly begin all paragraphs with quotes, and then I come to dialogue inside the quotes and don't know what the hell to do. Gonna send it to Weaver, and maybe it's so bad it won't matter what the punctuation is like. I can never really tell myself, tho I think I can with poems sometimes.

I'm ashamed of this typewriter ribbon, and it irritates me to get a letter so dim I can't read it like this. I'm trading in this typewriter tho, so damn if I'll change the ribbon.

I mean to say, and should have before, why not come down here and stay at the cottage at Ameliasburg (tho I suppose you've got it all arranged with Adele Wiseman). My wife is a primary school teacher, but is only doing supply teaching this year, and we have lots of room. Lots of birds bees and water here. Then we'd drive you to Ottawa and pour you onto plane a la Dylan.[5] As it is we'll drive to Ottawa and see you there. But I'm sure you might enjoy a lake and country more. On other hand you mightn't, since you presumably live in those surroundings in Eng. I will write C.C. in Ottawa just in case I need a formal invite.

Sorry about the curtsy being dropped, I would have enjoyed watching you essay that one. I wasn't sure if I was supposed to bow to Vanier[6] or not, so I shook hands instead.

Okay, see you in Ottawa.

Best,

Al

---

1. Purdy had decided to edit an anthology of Canadian reflections on the United States. *The New Romans: Candid Canadian Opinions of the U.S.* (1968) was published in Canada by Hurtig and in the United States by St. Martin's Press.

2. Mel Hurtig (b. 1932), publisher of *The New Romans,* was also at this time a well-known bookseller and nationalist.

3. Purdy had published *Pressed on Sand* in 1955. His first collection, *The Enchanted Echo,* had appeared in 1944.

4. "Turning New Leaves." Review of *Modern Canadian Stories,* ed. Giose Rimanelli and Roberto Ruberto. *The Canadian Forum,* October 1967, 163-64.

5. The Welsh poet Dylan Thomas (1914-53).

6. Georges Vanier (1888-1967), Governor-General of Canada (1959-67).

Elm Cottage

16 May 1967

Dear Al:

I realized after I'd posted a letter to you yesterday that I had not even mentioned the matter of the projected book on America. This wasn't from lack of interest in the book, but because I tend to become slightly disoriented when I have house guests, as I don't seem to have any time to myself, and can only think properly when I'm alone (sometimes not even then), so letters suffer. Re: the book – I would very much like to contribute, and wouldn't want payment. I can't promise that I shall be able to write anything, however, as I'm trying to get going on a novel now, and am also trying to uncomplicate my life by removing as many external pressures as possible in the form of promises to do things. Anyway, I'll try, because I really do have pretty strong feelings on the subject. The trouble is that one's feelings and opinions range over a fair amount of territory, and how to write something brief and inclusive enough, without generalizing in a way that misrepresents everything? Would like to discuss this further.

I met Mel Hurtig only once, in Edmonton, but liked him enormously.

All the best,

Margaret

❧

Elm Cottage
6 June 1967

Dear Al:

It was good to have a chance to know you a little.[1] I'm always slightly uncertain about meeting someone with whom I get along well in letters, because some people are different in print, but you talk just the way I thought you would. You know, I enjoyed that week in Canada more than the whole 2½ months last summer. No pressure, I suppose. The touring politician act is definitely not for me. I hadn't known there would be so many people I knew, in Ottawa, such as Henry Kriesel[2] and Kildare Dobbs,[3] etc. I was struck once again, as I was last summer, with how many people there are in Canada that I like, and this sets up the old quandry about whether to return or to stay here. I wish I didn't have such a split mind about Canada. However, having just acquired a house, I can't see myself leaving it for a few years. Must try to wangle a trip back in a year or so, but won't ever be able to ask the C. Council for any more loot, as they have given me a lot of money this past year.

Well, back to the beautiful trees. Strangely enough, I'm always glad to go away and equally glad to come home. (How is that for a cliché?) The place is very much like a jungle at the moment, and I am thinking of ways to con other people into mowing my lawn. I've got tenants (I rent several rooms in my house), a young married couple, and the guy likes to get exercise outdoors and so frequently asks in a polite and almost apologetic way if he can cut my lawn. I generously agree.

Talking of clichés as we were the other day made me think later about the business of autographing one's books. If it's for a friend, I always want to put down some brilliant line but unfortunately can never think of one, so end up putting "Best wishes" or something. Better not to put anything, really, but I can't do that, either, as it seems impersonal. What you said about writers being monsters bothered me because it seems likely that you are right, in many ways. My kids hate it when I'm writing, as I'm often rather absent in every way that matters, and then the little brutes tell me I'm neglecting them, thus loading me with guilt which they don't mean to do at all. It strikes me, however, that I've known people who will look you straight in the eye and maintain that they always do their best and never harbour a mean thought towards anyone – the kind of person who is utterly convinced of his own virtues, and in a way this is worse, isn't it? Or am I just saying that if you *know* you're a monster in some ways, this puts you in a position of moral superiority over the oafs who don't know their monstrousness? You change your perspective by a fraction of an inch, and everything looks different. This was partly what I was trying to get at, when I was telling you my difficulties with this new novel – how to get across the multiplicity of everything? Not by thinking about it consciously, that's for sure. And snaring the subconscious becomes *not* more easy as the time passes. The attempt to deal with the shifting and ambiguous nature of reality seems to me to be the only important thing that's happened in the novel in the past decade. Which isn't to say that no one tried before. They did, but more novelists are compelled in this way now. Who can say any more what really happened?

When I got home, I found waiting for me the most fantastic letter I've ever received. I don't know whether I told you or not, but some time ago my agent in N. York[4] very cleverly sold a film option on A Jest of God. This was great, as it meant quite a lot of money, about $3000. I never expected things would go any further, as many are called but few are chosen. But this letter was from some guy in California who is writing a film script on the novel.[5] This isn't to say that a film will be made, naturally, but only that things have proceeded one step more. Anyway, after almost overly enthusiastic comments on my novel (I tend to become suspicious about this "you're absolutely great, baby" line), he went on to ask questions about the sources of hymns, assuming that I had done masses of investigation and knew about such things as Thomas of Celano's *Dies Irae* (what in hell can that be?) Actually, I'd taken all the hymns from the Book of Common Prayer, picking those that were especially gruesome. He then went on to point out the many levels and symbols of the novel, and here is one prize line … "Rachel is built of so much else, so many darting mysteries – as hard to catch as the bluebottle flies you mention, whose eggs, I discover, (as I plunge through yet another reference – this one, "*Undertaking Science*") are the ones those maggots come from that flourish best in the ears of unembalmed corpses." Al, really, I ask you. Does this guy really believe that I read books on how to be an undertaker, before I wrote the novel? The bit about the flies and the ears of corpses is certainly rather interesting, in a repulsive sort of way, but if he thinks I put in that kind of symbolic reference, he's dead wrong. In a way, this is what makes me suspicious of critics – a person can seize on almost anything and over-interpret it, which is just as bad as under-interpreting it. Well, poor buggers, they will never achieve the right balance, will they? This script writer also asked if there were an "intact Manawaka" where the film might be done. I didn't give him the name of my home town of Neepawa, Manitoba. I just couldn't. Can you imagine the furor? I don't suppose it will all come to anything, but it would be nice if they'd renew the option.

All the best,
Margaret

p.s. I put the cigar box on my desk, for luck.

---

1. Laurence and Purdy had met in Ottawa on 2 June 1967, the day that Laurence received the Governor-General's Award.

2. Henry Kreisel (1922-91) was the well-known author of *The Rich Man* (1948) and *The Betrayal* (1964).

3. Kildare Dobbs (b. 1923) was one of the founding editors of *The Tamarack*

Review and was managing editor of *Saturday Night* from 1965-67. In 1968 he became a literary columnist for the *Toronto Star* and then the paper's book editor.

4. John Allerton Sill Cushman (1927-84) of John Cushman Associates, Inc.

5. Stewart Stern (b. 1922), whose credits included *Rebel Without a Cause* (1955) and *The Ugly American* (1963).

§

Ameliasburg

14 June [1967]

Dear Margaret:

Congrats on the film option, especially the money. It will seem strange if the novel is ever filmed – I have strong doubts that a film script written by someone else could ever satisfy the author of the novel it derives from. But what the hell, money – to do things and go places you want to – So I hope they carry it one step farther yet, might even import you as tech. consultant.

Re. money, B.B.C. is taking a poem of mine for a program called "Canadian Mosaic" and one Jack Beale tells me that they grab nearly half the six pound fee for Br. taxes on someone outside the country. I said send the money to you, if they will. Can get another book later from you if I see one I want and if not – doesn't matter. Don't like giving so much money to a gov't, any damn gov't.

Re. reality, I suppose one can give one's own version of reality, or else portray how shifting and ambiguous it is – but I rather doubt one can show actual reality itself, but only an illusion of it. It has so many aspects that if you attempt to show them all you'd bore the reader to death. I think of a poem of mine I've had occasion to type a few times lately. Way off reality too.

ABOUT BEING A MEMBER OF OUR ARMED FORCES [1]
Remember the early days of the phony war
when men were zombies and women were CWACs
and they used wooden rifles on the firing range?
Well I was the sort of soldier you couldn't trust
with a wooden rifle
and when they gave me a wooden bayonet
life was fraught with peril for my brave comrades
including the sergeant-instructor
I wasn't exactly a soldier tho
                    only a humble airman
who kept getting demoted
                    and demoted
                    and demoted
to the point where I finally saluted civilians
And when they trustingly gave me a Sten gun
Vancouver should have trembled in its sleep
for after I fired a whole clip of bullets
at some wild ducks under Burrard Bridge
(on guard duty at midnight)
they didn't fly away for five minutes
trying to decide if there was any danger
Not that the war was funny
I took it and myself quite seriously
the way a squirrel in a treadmill does
too close to tears for tragedy
too far from the banana peel for laughter
and I didn't blame anyone for being there
that wars happened wasn't anybody's fault then
now I think it is

Not very close to reality there, or even seriousness.

Anyway, I am now sick to death of this anthology I am trying
to edit. I've written something more than fifty letters, had

seven/eight acceptances, and the end seems nowhere in sight. I have visions of spending the next year asking people to write articles or poems, and begin to doubt that I shall ever do anything else. However, my steel will and iron endurance will undoubtedly carry me through to deserved triumph and critical recognition. Ahem.

Talking about reading books re. undertaking, I once wrote a story that involved an undertaker.[2] I visited the local undertaker's union in Belleville, and thought it gruesomely fascinating. For instance, found there is a time right after death when the corpse's temperature rises and rises, as if the body didn't want to die and was in some way going on living after death. I've written only three/four stories, at least those I thought any good, and they've all concerned the most gruesome thing, at least most of them have – necrophilia and thou shalt not suffer a witch – Whereas in poems I try to stick to concrete incidents, even use real names if I can get away with it –

Well, must get back to work on this damn antho, which reminds me, don't forget your own hoped-for contrib.

Best,

Al

---

1. Published in *Wild Grape Wine*.

2. "The Undertaker" was published in *The Canadian Forum,* October 1963, 156-59.

§

Dear Al:

Hope you are feeling less depressed by now about the anthology, and that your steel will and iron endurance has produced a few more acceptances. I know what you mean about feeling that you'll be working on the book for the next year – I had that feeling about the Nigerian literature book I did, and used to visualize myself still plodding away at it when old and decrepit. I haven't begun to think, really, about what kind of article to try to write for you, and have the feeling that when I do, it may not turn out to be anything which you will want to print. I don't mean that it will be too far-out – I think it won't be far-out enough. When it is a question of personal opinions, I'm not sure I know how to make it sound interesting enough, and not too cliché-filled. However, I'll try. When is the deadline? Or what you hopefully think of as the deadline.

I didn't think the poem you included in your letter was way off reality. Not what literally happened, of course, but what was felt to happen, so more real, in a way. I kind of like the mental picture of you saluting civilians.

I agree about not giving any more money than absolutely necessary to any government. I hope the BBC will agree to send the money for your poem to me, but it will surprise me if they do. If they do, however, and you can't think of a book you want, I could send you a cheque in dollars for the equivalent amount, as I have a few dollars in a Toronto bank account and recently discovered that I had $30 more than I thought, as it is a savings account and I had forgotten about the interest. Very seldom do I find I've got more money than I thought.

The guy who is writing the film script for A Jest of God keeps writing the strangest epistles to me. In the last one, he said "One wants only to snatch up a camera and *shoot!*" It isn't that he is actually a nut, but he just speaks an idiom very different from mine. He said in the same letter, "God, but that last speech of Rachel's is beautiful!" One wants to say – yeh, well, maybe, but let's face it – it's not *that* beautiful. I guess I should be glad he is enthusiastic. Except that I feel I don't really know if he's enthusiastic or not.

I'm still at the stage of grappling unsuccessfully with this new novel. I know all the problems and none of the solutions. It is absolutely shapeless and doesn't seem to have a natural form. I've written pages and pages of sheer nonsense. I feel like hell about it, in one way, and yet in another way I *know* the thing is there, if only I can manage to stumble onto the way to do it. I really ought to be feeling depressed, but in some odd fashion I feel quite the reverse, and yet I'm not doing any work worth anything right now. I guess I must believe that one of these days inspiration will strike me, like the spirit of God between the eyes – wham. Which, as I know from past experience, is not at all likely to happen, at least not until I'm well into the novel. My mind creaks like rusty machinery at the beginning. Damn it, I *ought* to feel lousy about this wreck of a novel, and I don't, and so I reproach myself for being frivolous – how is that for presbyterianism? The possibilities for convoluted thinking are endless, so I will give it up and go and weed my garden this afternoon, by which I mean making one or two feeble stabs at a weed, and then deciding that the weeds really look quite attractive after all.

I was glancing through McC & S catalogue the other day to see if I wanted any of the books therein, and I noticed that publication date for North Of Summer was June 24. Hope it got out on time, and that the old firm made a few graceful gestures in your direction, such as a party.

Later: This letter got interrupted because of the sudden arrival of some American friends – a couple with 3 kids. They arrived in England today, and I've been trying to find a house for them to rent for a month, but without success. I told them they could stay here if no house available. Wasn't expecting them quite so soon or suddenly, however. Anyway, they've decided to go to Canterbury today, and will try in that area for a house. They're old friends, so I wouldn't mind having them here, although it would be rather like a circus, I guess, with 5 kids, 3 adults and 2 cats. I have it all planned out – if they stay here, I'll carry on with this so-called novel in the mornings and they will get the meals. Sounds like a good arrangement to me.

When is your next foray into some other part of the country or the world? I think you mentioned that you were thinking of going north this summer. Is that still on?

I feel ill every time I think of my Egypt articles, which I'm sure Holiday won't be able to use now.[1] In the first place, they're wildly out of date, especially the one on the Suez canal, and in the second place, who wants to read an article in America now which is favourably inclined towards Egypt? Anyway, thank God I wasn't in Port Said with my kids when all this happened.

Write when you've got time. Hope the work is going well, I mean the real work not the anthology.

All the best,
Margaret

---

1. The "Six-Day War" pitting Israel against Egypt, Jordan, and Syria had taken place 5-10 June 1967 and had resulted in a decisive victory for Israel.

§

Elm Cottage
29 June [1967]

Dear Al–

I think I am a firebug. I have just burned all the hundreds of pages which I wrote on this novel 3 years ago and which I had been trying recently to sort through and save some of the (as I thought) better bits. All gone. I have to start all over again or not at all. Sometimes I think it will be not at all. It is like looking at the face of someone you love through prison bars (not that I've ever done that) and seeing it but not being able to touch. Do you think it is possible to crack up without knowing it? I jest not. If I can't write this one, I can't write. I'm sorry – I tend to impose myself upon my friends at times like this. It will pass. Probably.

Best,
Margaret

ps. I am giving a talk on Canadian Literature to some Can. students and possibly others, at Oxford, tomorrow. Jesus.

§

8 July [1967]

Dear Margaret,

The way you seem to be feelin a long quiet drunk with a friend, someone you can talk to, would be a good idea. Universal panacea, they say, but at least it does bust your life into before and after. However, it must be fun burnin all that money you coulda had for the typescript. Anyway, I recommend a drunk, tho I ain't qualified to prescribe – that or twenty four hours fucking.

My book[1] is on the way to you surface mail. I suppose it takes weeks.

I sometimes, rarely, feel the same way you describe, tho maybe I am too lazy to take desperate measures. In one way I have an idea that, pleasant as it may be, that England is wrong for you as a writer. Nice pleasant cocoon alright, but what very close relations do you really have with people over there? And really, do you care very much either way? Burning one's bridges by selling one's cottage is just as violent a measure as burning immortal prose, besides you retain the cash deriving from figurative flames, and can use it to move around. In Africa I would think you lived emotionally off the people around you, but are not doin it now. Of course I'm givin you pretty simple answers to problems and it ain't that simple I know. But in a way it's a good thing that you have such violent reactions (to the English desert I'd say), and can realize something is damn wrong.

Yeah, the goddam antho is hovering over me all the time. To say the least, I don't like it. Why the hell did I get into it? Dunno, tho I thot it a good idea at the time. Still is, but wish someone else would do it. Deadline is, say, end of Oct. Lotsa time.

BBC says they won't send the money to you taxfree the bastards. I'll take em into small debts court or something?

Still, there must be something purifying about burning a novel. Can't imagine doing it to poems. I now staple all the handwritten work sheets and then staple a typewritten version to them, so that it must look like twentieth century dead sea scrolls. I can imagine some poor bastard trying to figure out what I'm like from reading them – so many contradictions nobody could do it. Especially me. So anyway, I cheer your pyromaniac self, while my scotch blood boils sympathetically for all that money up in the clouds mingling with Strontium 90.

Now hafta get back to antho, goddam it. One real sizzler, poem, makes U.S. sound like a decadent Assyria over-running the Children of Israel.[2] I hope you get paid at Oxford, which gives me a vision of a lot of old men running around in black night gowns.

Best,

Al

---

1. *North of Summer.*

2. Perhaps Eric Nicol's (b. 1919) "Dat ol' man river," which appeared in *The New Romans,* although many of the poems in the anthology could be described as "sizzlers."

❦

Elm Cottage
26 July 1967

Dear Al:

Thanks for your heartening letter. The panic and crisis is now over, and I feel slightly mortified at having fired off communications to friends informing them I was off my rocker. Premature diagnosis – survival is still a possibility, it appears. As I suspected, I did the right thing in burning the old pages from previous versions of this novel – any of the bits which weren't too terrible have remained firmly in my memory and are coming in of their own accord. But until I got rid of all the garbage, I seemed to be tied to the past efforts, as it were. So although I may have been burning $$$, it had to be done. I have such split feelings about the sale of manuscripts, in any event – I won't refuse the cash, needless to say, whenever it may be offered, but I do believe the whole thing is lunatic in the extreme. The finished work is what matters, and all these scribbled marginal bits are not valuable at all, ever, to anyone, anywhere, in my opinion. Thank heavens many would disagree with me.

Have reached Chapter 2, and am feeling better. Not calm, and not certain that the whole thing is really worth doing, but just slightly better. I don't have any doubt about the characters – they're there, all right, if I can only get through to them. This is the point at which it is an act of faith as well as an act of will. Also, I think the trouble has largely been that for the past year I have been whipping around the world – Crete, Somalia, Canada, New York, and Egypt, and now find it hard to settle down and work. However, when the self-dramatization is over, one has to face the bleak and horrible fact that the only way to write a novel is to commit yourself to about a year of doing damn little else. Sometimes I really hate the thought, but the truth is that it would be worse not to do the novel than to do it, so the basic situation is not a very complicated one – the choices have already been made. I wish there were some way of producing a novel or a short story quickly and at no personal cost. The cost is always more than I'm prepared to pay. But not more than I can pay, so no cause for self-pity.

Can't leave England, or not now, anyway. As usual, with nearly everything, I'm divided horribly on this subject. In some ways would like to return to Canada – have moments when I feel I want to be there, and ought to be there, etc etc. Why am I living my life as an exile, I ask myself, etc etc. Then I come back to the thought that in some ways I seem to be committed to a lifelong concern about Africa and African writing, as well as Canadian, and this place is halfway between Africa and Canada, and from here I can go either way, from time to time, and many people whom I want to see do visit here both from N. America and from Africa, so in some ways it's a good vantage point. Also, I really love this broken-down old wreck of a house, which obviously represents more than a dwelling-place to me. I know I will need to return to Canada some day, just in terms of work, but when I think of living on a 33-foot lot in, say, Toronto, my heart sinks. Through a fluke of circumstance in getting this particular house in the way I did, I've got nearly an acre, and jungle-like as it is, I like it. Where in Canada, on the money I earn, could I afford to have that much space around me, except maybe northern Manitoba? There are, actually, quite a few people I care about, in this country. But there are perhaps even more in Canada. There are some I care about in Africa, too. I worry like anything at the moment about the Ibo writers in Nigeria, especially Achebe[1] – one bullet and the best novelist in Africa could go. The truth is, Al, I don't know where the hell I belong – nowhere, I guess. But for now, this place at least feels like my own home, in an individual sense, no wider affiliations necessary.

Hope the anthology is going well. Have thought about an article, but the more I think about it, the less simple it seems. And now Detroit – well. On the other hand, two American friends have been staying here for the past week – a couple, with 3 kids, and all the things I feel about the race situation and Vietnam are what they feel, too. Not easy to be an American these days. Got a letter from Mel Hurtig re: the book, and wrote back saying I'd do an article if possible.

Why do you think England is a desert? It isn't. Could argue this at length with you.

I'm not surprised that the BBC won't send the money to me tax-free. But I agree it's damn silly. Could you by any chance do me a great favour? Could you get me a copy of the last Chatelaine, which contains a story of mine? The mag. hasn't sent me the 2 copies I'm supposed to get, and I now find I have not got a decent copy of that story, which I may want sometime. It's called Horses Of The Night.[2] If you are embarrassed about buying Chatelaine, which would be understandable, please don't worry. Have also asked Adele.

By the way, thanks for advice re: how to recover from inner crisis upon beginning a novel. The long quiet drunk with friends proved possible. Twenty four hours fucking, alas, is slightly more difficult to arrange.

All the best.

Margaret

ps. thanks for sending book – look forward to seeing it.

---

1. Chinua Achebe (b. 1930), whose most recent novel was *A Man of the People* (1966).

2. "Horses of the Night" appeared in *Chatelaine,* July 1967, 46, 70-77.

§

[Laurence to Purdy] [1]

– this letter got interrupted, and only now resumed. What you wrote for me inside the book ... "for M.L., the best writer not in Canada", started up in me the old symptoms which might almost be called the "exile syndrome" – intense desire to return to home and native land; determination to do so instantly; questioning of how this would be possible without all kinds of undesirable disruptions in life and work; further looking around present situation and observation of the many things one values and loves here; result: stalemate, bewilderment, confusion; resolution: can't live in state of confusion, so will shelve the problem for the moment. There are so many things to be said on both sides (ie whether to live here or there), and I find myself almost totally unable to make up my mind. Also, there are so many difficulties involved in moving, and in moving my kids, although I've now decided I'd really like my daughter to go to the University of Toronto in 2 years' time. For the time being, I think I'll try to write a book instead of worrying about anything else. I guess I have reached the point where if I'm in Canada I'm homesick for England, and if I'm in England I'm homesick for Canada. Doesn't seem to be any permanent solution to this.

I've decided to go to Canada next summer, though. Think I'll be able to afford it, as apparently A JEST OF GOD is being filmed and so I shall get quite a lot of money. The big trouble is that the income tax dept will take a hell of a lot of it. I'm trying to have the payment spread over 2 years, which will help some, although I'll still have to shell out a lot more than I feel I ought to. I suppose the only way to look at it is that I never expected a film to be made and I never anticipated this money, and I didn't do any work for it, so whatever I'll be able to keep cannot help but be a gain. The

41

mistake is in thinking of this kind of money as real money – in a sense, it seems to me to be rather like play-money in the game of Monopoly – we talk in terms of thousands, but the actual meaning is rather less. But it will enable me to get back to Canada for the summer next year, I hope. If I can finish this novel, first. I've sworn not to go anywhere or do anything (or almost) until I've got this novel finished. It's coming along slowly, but I'm no longer despondent about it. It is there, if I can find it. Have 2 chapters – a horrible chaos, but that's not so important at the moment. The big trouble right now is that my kids are home on holidays, and it has now reached the point where I find it almost impossible to concentrate, as life seems to be one long round of shopping and preparing enormous meals and washing dishes and stopping fights. However, they go back to school in another 2 weeks, so I hope to get back to schedule then. In the meantime, in sheer frustration I've quit work on the novel the past week and have been writing a children's story instead, really a fantasy for my own amusement – probably no kid would want to read it.[2]

Saw Jack Ludwig[3] and his wife in London a week or so ago. They are here for a year. Hadn't met him before, although naturally we have many friends in common. He is certainly full of vitality and charm. Actually, I hadn't expected to like him because so many people have told me how charming he is, and this tends to make me a little wary, but I did like him. The BBC phoned me yesterday to ask if I would appear with Mordecai Richler[4] etc on a panel discussion on "Canadian Culture". I said no, but referred them to Jack, who (I think) would not only do that sort of thing well but would probably enjoy it. I don't actually collapse or become paralysed under these circumstances, but TV is such an ordeal that I don't see why I should do it. Also, "Canadian culture" as a subject is not one of my favorites, as nearly everything that is said about it seems to be almost 100% garbage.

Have about a million letters to write, so must go. Hope the

anthology is progressing. Again, thanks very very much for NORTH OF SUMMER.

All the best,
Margaret

---

1. The first part of this letter is missing.

2. *Jason's Quest* (1970).

3. Jack Ludwig (b. 1922), Canadian writer and author of the comic novel *Confusions* (1963). He was a professor of English at the State University of New York at Stony Brook.

4. Mordecai Richler (b. 1931) was living in London at this time.

Ameliasburg
22 August 1967

Dear Margaret:

First congrats on the movie sale, and this should give you money to do what you like and live where you like. The tyranny of money lifted, or I suppose so and hope it's into large enough figures to do that.

Second, I've been looking at Chatelaine's on the newstands, and can only find Aug. and Sept. and your story in neither. As well, I seem to know no one who subscribes to the mag. So I'm writing the publishers and asking for that copy.

Thank you for your reaction to the book. It's probably as good a description, and flattering to me, as I've seen.[1] Even if poetry isn't your specialty you could still review the stuff. I had the idea when I went north, that no book I'd read had given me the feeling of what it was like to be there, the colour, smells etc., just the reality. The authors would describe, but they didn't make you feel the place. All travel writers, just about tho. The way you put words down on the page I envy, and doubt very many novelists can do it so well. I'm often stopped in attempting to describe feelings and have to do it by eliminating the false ones to get at the real ones, those that strike me as right and true. But in a letter your prose still looks good, as if you said exactly or very nearly what you were getting at – Different sort of mind from mine, I suppose – Damned if I know the difference between a poet and novelist anyway, this ability with words is certainly superior to mine.

"Kabloona"[2] is by De Poncins, which I have but haven't read. And yeah, the pictures are not exactly crap, but they seem very old-fashioned to me. But a lot of older people and art addicts may buy the book because of them. I shouldn't complain – Coupla reviews, three – two quite favourable, and one favourable with reservations. The writer picked out the poem INNUIT and said I didn't see the old man at all but "merely some vague person of my own" and how distasteful that was. In a way he's right, since I didn't treat the old man as other than a focal point for my "race-soul" idea, especially since I didn't know the old man. But I don't think the idea of a "race- soul" is vague, altho it might be hard to express in concrete terms, since who the hell has a touchable soul anyway. But Eskimo sculpture, and I suppose African sculpture, is much more representative and typical of those cultures than white sculpture is of white culture, especially since the physical medium of soapstone and ivory is more limited than material available to white sculptors. Anyway, re. the book, I like indulgently to think that I did something re. the north that hadn't been done (other than by Robert Service who is so different from me), treat the north as a real place with real, tho different people. This is pretty egotistic on my part, but what the hell. When all the reviews are in I'll find out what the consensus is. My idea is that the big weakness of the book is that it didn't treat the lousy dirty side sufficiently. But much of the time up there I was in a state of mild euphoria at just being there. The Eskimos at Frobisher Bay, for instance, are in a helluva bad situation, belonging to neither world, white or Eskimo, drinking and the occasional murder. But I didn't see any of the murders and drinking, I did see what I wrote about. And reviewers are bound to ask for things I didn't see. Anyway, glad you enjoyed it.

I don't think that's bad, wanting to be other than where you are, so long as it isn't a continual psychic state. Personally, I get sick of most places if I'm there long enough. I go on these jesus reading tours and drink too much and eat too much and come back perfectly content for a while, then get restless again. But I guess we're all peripatetic travellers over the earth — no, not all, but many of us. That bit you mention about "values and loves here" — one doesn't lose them by going away (or am I being trite and obvious) doesn't one set them in another perspective, perhaps a clearer one? One realizes the value of things gone after they're gone — And I keep thinking I'm speaking crap, and I guess I am. Obvious things.

Yeah, Ludwig's charm — it's undeniable, tho when I met him I had the idea he didn't really see me at all (just as the reviewer thought of me and the Eskimo carver), but likely didn't think of a purdy race-soul. Very confident and sure, so much so that he seemed not to than the obvious cordial gestures, and was more curious about you/me than anything else, and quite a mild curiosity. He also strikes me as the professional academic and speech-giver, at gatherings of students and profs, rather than the pro. novelist. I am envious of his ability to talk on his feet, which I have not got, and yet feel this quality detracts in some way I don't know. It over-balances him into being more a public personality than anything else.

Why don't you get a job as script writer for your own film? That would pay all expenses, give you a trip somewhere in the U.S. and time for Canada too. If you get enough money you can hire a girl to do the dishes etc. and you can write. Does that sorta thing work?

If you are in London and feeling good-natured can you get me some more books? Don't repeat don't, go looking for them if you aren't in book stores anyway. But if you are, and the Hakluyt Society's books are there gettem to send me Vol. CXIII The Troublesome Voyage of Cap. Edward Fenton, ed. Taylor, and Vols CXIV-CXV The Prester John of the Indies, ed. Beckingham and Huntingford. No idea how much money. I hae a passion for authentic sea stuff, partly because of the archaic language and Coleridge, I suspect. For chrissake don't go to any trouble – but can't resist taking advantage of a willing woman????? I paid ten bucks for one of the Hakluyts in a Mtl. book store, which is six bucks over-price. I resent that slightly.

Personal – I am goddam sick of poems and poetry, ALL poems and poetry, even my own. Tho did write one I like, which I copy on reverse, first one I liked of my own in mos. Anthos are awful. Nevermore quoth Poe. Least not till I'm dead broke. Off to Expo as an observer next month, where Pound and Neruda and lesser lights hold forth.[3] I shall get their books autographed to ride my hobby horse still farther. Possibility of short term grant to live three mos in Ottawa and look at the House of Commons, CC of course.[4] Another crazy idea for poems. Culture is for non-writers. Wouldn't mind talkin of books and poems, particular ones, but not god save us culture. See I'm ended. See poem reverse.

Best,
[unsigned]

JOE BARR[5]
In a grey town of seven-week days
during an eternal childhood
where I was so miserable sometimes
at being me that I roamed lonely
over the reeking town garbage dump
unable to talk to anyone
locked in my own body

46

captive of the motionless sun
in an eternal childhood

Old Joe went there too
happy as a young dog
pushing the garbage with his stick
grinning like a split orange
telling himself stories all day
the doors of his prison opening
into rooms he couldn't remember
places he couldn't stay
the river providing a green sidewalk
that bore his mind's feet lightly
his days like scraps of colour
and the night birds always teaching
him songs that because of his stutter
he never learned to sing

I could have learned from Joe myself
but I never did
not even when gangs of children
followed him down the street
chanting "aw–aw–aw" in mockery
children have for idiots
In a town that looked like a hole
torn in blue clouds
where I made–believed myself
into a moonlit grasshopper
and leaped the shadowed boundaries
that bore my mind's feet lightly
forty years ago
in the grey town of memory
the garbage dump is a prison
where people stand like stones
the birds are stuffed and mounted

47

a motionless sun still hangs there
where Joe is a scrap of crimson
when the sun at last goes down

---

1. A reference to the missing part of the previous letter.

2. Gontran de Poncins wrote *Kabloona* (1941) in collaboration with Lewis Galantière. With illustrations by de Poncins, the book describes the fifteen months he spent with the Eskimos in the high Arctic in 1936-39. It was published in New York by Reynal and Hitchcock.

3. Ezra Pound (1873-1972) and Pablo Neruda (1904-73) took part in one of the many arts festivals held at "Expo '67," the universal and international exhibition held in Montreal from 28 April to 27 October 1967. Expo was the centerpiece of Canada's centenary.

4. Purdy was awarded a Canada Council Arts Award and Short Term Grant for 1967-68.

5. This version of the poem was later published in *Wild Grape Wine*.

§

Elm Cottage
31 August 1967

Dear Al–

Thanks for your letter, which was a help in ways probably unknown to you. I've been tied up in knots for some time, as no doubt you have gathered, by the question of Canada or not-Canada. Where your comments have been a help is that you've been careful not to give advice, thank God, but have suggested in some fashion that one is not necessarily trapped – ie that the traps are mostly inner not outer.

What has been bugging me, under the surface, for months now, is that I really do not belong in this country, Al. Once, when I first arrived here, I made a joke with an English friend that some of my best friends were Canadian. Now I have to face the fact that indeed in this country *all* (or nearly all) of my best friends are Canadians. One or two English people are friends from away back, but not many. The people I see most often, and who phone me, and whom I phone, are all Goddamn it Canadians. I look at my income, and what I see is that nearly all my dough comes from either America or Canada. If I had to live on what I made in England, I would have starved long ago. […] I also visualize myself, in ten years time, here, by myself, surrounded by cats and roses – and nothing else, and the prospect is a little less than pleasing. I've tried over three or so years to become a little less isolated here, and have not succeeded. Of course, this is partly because I always want things on my own terms – I want to be able to make contact with members of my tribe while at the same time preserving privacy, and this is a bit tricky. But in many many ways, including the writing, I must go back, and finally I have admitted it, and this is maybe a step in the right direction. I have to write this novel first, and so will try to do so within the next year, ie before next summer, and then will go back and look (I hope) shrewdly around for some place to live – my problem being that I can't bear to live in a city but have to be within reach of one. What I really want is some broken-down old shack on a lake within easy reach of Toronto – a fantasy? I am talented at making a dwelling-place out of a broken-down shack, so perhaps will have luck in finding the right sort of place. I have enormous faith that I'll find what I'm looking for, and have always done so, actually. However, we'll see. Cannot do anything until next summer, and the physical difficulties of selling this place and pulling up roots are nearly overwhelming – I guess this is what has held me back, until now. One has taken so long to establish oneself here, and accumulate all the garbage that is necessary, furniture and refrigerator etc, and when I contemplate disposing of it all, plus sorting out mortgage and income tax etc, I feel weak. I do not contemplate doing anything until next summer, anyway, so all I really have to do now is write a book – very simple?

I had lunch yesterday with a very strange character … Miron Grindea, who is the editor of ADAM International Review. He is doing a Canadian Edition for this year,[1] and about 3 weeks ago phoned me to say that he was an old friend of Geo. Woodcock,[2] and had only found out from George that I was living in England. In a strongly middle-Eur accent he said "I have been vaiting like a bridegroom to meet you …" and at that precise moment, the operator cut us off and the phone went blank. I thought, My God, he will think I'm offended and have hung up on him – so I swiftly looked in the London directory and luckily found his number. As it happened, he is not the sort of person who would ever think anyone was offended – he's a real eccentric, absolutely assured of his own abilities, and I found myself giving him an excerpt from the novel I'm now attempting to write.[3] When I went to his place for lunch, it turned out to be three lettuce leaves and half a glass of cider in the kitchen, and I talked all the time to a Polish girl who is either a cousin or an au-pair, I'm not sure which, while Grindea kept flashing in and out and saying "Excuse me one minute – I must just type out this one page – has to go to the printers today". He handed me a sheaf of stuff from the Canadian volume, and among the litter was a letter from Alden Nowlan saying here is a poem of Alfred Purdy's etc, but the poem itself wasn't there. I asked him (Grindea) and he said he was including one of your poems,[4] so there it is. I do not suppose any-one will get paid anything. When I left, he (in old-world style) kissed me on both cheeks and also kissed my hand, and as we were at that moment standing on the Cromwell Road, this drew a few curious glances, as Mr. Grindea is about 70 and about 5 feet tall, and I was trying not to look embarrassed. Anyway, I enclose the page proofs of the excerpt from my so-called novel – I always envy you, that you can give friends poems, in letters, and I can't do that, so here is something.

I wonder from the poem you enclosed, about your town. Where exactly did you grow up? The town sounds so much like mine – maybe they all are much the same. And I remember, too, a town idiot, who led a kind of doomed and charmed life. And a garbage dump – mine came out, actually, in The Stone Angel, in one episode. It was something from my own childhood ... seeing a whole lot of dumped eggs, some of which had horrifyingly hatched in the sunshine, on the dump, and the chicks, cramped and mutilated there, and someone braver than I, killing them.

Re: Ludwig – you are right about his public personality. As a matter of fact, he would have done more as a writer, in my opinion, if he had not been so occupied by his public image. Even in his first novel, *Confusions,* he protects himself very much. This is really what I meant when I said you were willing to make yourself vulnerable – he isn't, and the work suffers because of it, or so I see it. What did you mean, he was more curious about you/me than anything else? When I met him, he mentioned you and asked me what I thought about you. In my unsuspecting country way, I told him I thought you were great and that I loved you – sorry if I have unwittingly damaged your reputation! I thought he was talking about writing.

Re: books – no trouble; I have written to a bookshop in London, asking them to send the books you mentioned to me. I took the precaution of asking them to let me know if they cost a fortune, as I thought you might want to consider. If I can get them, will send them to you, and you can (if that's okay) deposit the equivalent money in $$ in my Toronto bank account.

All best,
Margaret

ps. if a woman is willing, that is not taking advantage, surely? i speak of books. p.s. 2. in Can. issue of Adam – Richler, Levine, ML, Birney, you, Nowlan, M. Avison, M. Atwood, a number of poets I don't know,[5] and (apparently) lots of French Can. (he didn't show me the French ones).[6] p.s. 3. thanks re: Chatelaine.

PS. Herewith also a few pages which might be considered for your anthology.[8] If you think they are crap, do not hesitate to say so. My feelings will not be hurt. Don't know if it is at all the sort of thing you could use in the book, but I think it's about all I can do right now. I'm not sure that it isn't nonsense.

---

1. Miron Grindea (b. 1909) had been an editor of the *Adam International Review* since 1941. The special Canadian issue (volume 32, nos. 313-15) contained a broad selection of Canadian writers and writing.

2. George Woodcock (b. 1912), writer, biographer, critic, and poet, was the founding editor of the Vancouver quarterly journal *Canadian Literature,* which first appeared in 1959.

3. The four-page draft excerpt from the first chapter of *The Fire-Dwellers* was published in the *Adam* issue as "'Everything is all right' (a short story)."

4. "Return from Kikastan." The issue also contained a poem and a short story by Nowlan.

5. Among the other poets, some of whom Laurence did know, were F.R. Scott, Irving Layton, Leonard Cohen, R.G. Everson, Dorothy Livesay, Miriam Waddington, John Glassco, Michael Ondaatje, A.J.M. Smith, and Ralph Gustafson. There were also articles by Hugh MacLennan and George Woodcock.

6. Francophone writers included poets Rina Lasnier, Gaston Miron, Jean-Guy Pilon, Anne Hébert, Gatien Lapointe, Paul-Marie Lapointe.

7. "Open Letter to the Mother of Joe Bass."

Ameliasburg

16 September [1967]

[Salutation missing]

Hey, you comin back to Canada! I shall burn a candle for your arrival at the H-bomb factory. Or re-invent the heliograph to signal Aldebaran. Always wanted to signal Aldebaran anyway.

I have got your mag, Chatelaine sent Chatelaine, shall roll it up up tightly to cut down air resistance and throw vigorously east.

Have just got back from Expo World Po., Toronto tapings and script judgings, reading at Queen's, and just writ 19 (nineteen) letters tonight, this being the 20th and longest and last. I'm dizzy! You figured that out anyway, of course.

You describe a complicated mental and physical situation in your letter. Migawd, "cats and roses"! Of course, there is the perhaps point, if you get back here all your best friends might be English. I doubt that tho. There is also this: you can go to any damn place in Canada and write about it if you're able to. I doubt like hell if you can do that in England. Course I could be terribly wrong. But I, me, self, do feel this way. I could only write about England from my Can. point of view. Okay, I'll try again. I mean, suppose you take a shack near Toronto, and if things are right there you'll write about it. As a comparison, HAVE you already done this in dear old Bucks? Sure you'll find a shack. Tell Jack McClelland you want one of his smaller outbuildings (say seven rooms) moved to the beach past Scarborough on LakeOnt. Perish the goddam cats and roses. What a title! Makes me wriggle to think of it.

Yeah, moving is terrible. I'm just doing it by the way, Goin to Ottawa on a short term CC grant. After Oct. 1, plan to attend House of Commons and make a fool of myself writing about the other fools. Address: 173 Waverly, Apt. 1.

If you can drive and pick up a car then a city is easy to reach. At least some are. Toronto especially. Of course you'll perhaps get tired of that too, but so what – there are more good places to go. I'm being glib here, for maybe you're not the same as me in that. But if I could write like you I'd wander to all the Can. places and write a book about em. George Woodcock did about B.C.,[1] but you bein you I expect you'd want a thick gooey theme to hold it together.

Your experience with this Adam ed. is odd, but you can think back on it and grin whenever you want. It's not everyone who can do that. A twist of thought and you grin three thousand miles away.

Your bit about the chicks is scarifying. I would write a poem if it'd been me. Birney claims his are exorcism. Mine are not to me – I dunno, what they are. Could I do the poem anyway? I wonder? It makes your insides knot up to think of those chicks. I don't remember that in The Stone Angel, which I read quite a long time ago. I should tho, if you described it there like in your letter. I'll look back over the novel for that garbage dump.

Oh, Ludwig meant what did you think of me personally – Isn't that strange. We all do it, ask people what they think of other people. I think of people whom I'm sure had several different sets of thoughts which they could think simultaneously. Some people can talk about one thing, think another, and have still another in their mind, and maybe some of these thoughts merge around the edges and we're liable to get sunset all over thoughts of our friends.

It never occurred to me about Ludwig protecting himself in his novel. Of course he isn't straightforward in his story, which as I recall seemed to slide one way and another. No, you couldn't put your finger on the author till the end, when he came out with his "life philosophy" or something. I thought it a failure, but an interesting one, good in spots. I don't remember what I meant by that sentence you quote. I sometimes forget the beginning of a paragraph at the end of it.

How would I do a poem about those chicks? Goddamit …

Okay, if you can get books will send money to acc't you let me know about – And thanks. Books are comin outa my ears and nostrils. They tickle too. House is fulla them, on the floor, all tables, shelves, open, shut, half-read, never read, never will be read, blue orange scarlet beautiful beautiful.

Re. Adam, have no idea who's in it – the Can issue bit seems to

54

be into a lot of mags (of course other countries too), but I always think I could do a much better job than the eds, since there have been some pretty awful Can issues. For instance, I don't think much of Levine as a poet,[2] he strikes me as a prose writer, whatever his merit is in that. But what I mean is: editors select friends or contributors for all sorts of reasons. Dunno how come Nowlan would be sending a poem of mine to Adam anyway, since Fred Cogswell[3] asked me for some –

The reading at Queen's was pretty good, Layton and I, about 500 people there, mostly freshmen, some sitting in the aisles. Very seldom get an audience that large or as enthusiastic. I went to the hotel in Kingston, met Layton downstairs and arranged to meet him shortly after washing up. So I went to my room, but it turned out to be Layton's room, and my key surprisingly unlocked his door. I hadn't looked at the number on my key. Anyway, I looked around and saw all Layton's poems ready for him to read that evening, and I said gleefully I'll never never get a chance like this again. So I put all Layton's poems and briefcase under the bed, went out and locked the door and went to the right room. Layton and my wife and I went to dinner and came back. Then I went to Layton's room to get him for the reading. He looked at me grey as a faded maple leaf and said "Al, I left my briefcase at that restaurant and it has all my poems!" I couldn't keep my face straight and told him he hadn't left it at the restaurant and confessed. But I could see a whole train of happenings, Layton and I back at the restaurant asking about his briefcase, the worried arrangers of the reading, myself perfectly innocent but struggling inside. Must stop I see. Thanks for book. Chatelaine on the way to you.

Best,

Al

PS. I haven't read your prose piece, but I am like Thomas, a "prophet who has no doubt" Thanks

1. *Ravens and Prophets: An Account of Journeys in British Columbia, Alberta and Southern Alaska* (1952).

2. Norman Levine (b. 1923), Canadian writer, best known for his short fiction.

3. Fred Cogswell (b. 1917) was a member of the English Department, University of New Brunswick, and an advisory editor for *The Fiddlehead* literary magazine. He had been of considerable help to Grindea in putting together the Canadian issue of the *Adam International Review.*

Elm Cottage

11 October 1967

Dear Al–

Every letter I write recently seems to be a note written in haste. Don't know why I'm so busy – I'm not, really, it's just that I've got down to this novel again and when I finish doing a day's work on it I feel beat. Wanted to write, though, and thank you for sending me the copy of Chatelaine – much appreciated. (Did I thank you already? I think I'm losing my mind – can't remember anything these days). Also, to thank you for sending the money for the books to my Toronto bank account – the bank informed me.

Am resolutely attempting to put all personal dilemmas from mind, otherwise won't have any mind left. Have finished doing the somewhat peculiar kids' book which I started when the summer holidays were going full blast and the house was too full of guests and kids for any concentration to be possible. I always vowed I would never write a kids' book, much less an animal fantasy. This one is an animal fantasy. It sort of sneaked up on me, and seemed to present itself all in one piece, so I wrote it down. Don't know whether it will be publishable, as it doesn't seem to be for any specific age group. Did I tell you one grim detail? The hero is a mole, and at the time I was writing it, I was having so much trouble with moles on my lawn that I finally had to call in a molecatcher, so now I feel like a murderer.

The novel seems to be moving at last – it keeps changing all the time, partly owing to the inner necessities of the thing, partly to the fact that I had originally included, in my idea of it, a hell of a lot of nonsense which doesn't belong and one only finds these things out slowly. Also, one trouble has been that I've felt the old narrative methods won't any longer work – too slow and not immediate enough. Have been trying to figure out some other way of doing it. Needless to say, have not come up with anything stunningly new, but at least I'm trying to have a slightly different focus – and this does seem to suit it better, as it is apparently a little more willing to be written than it was before. Have had to begin almost all over again. This is my fifth attempt, so if this doesn't work, I'm through with it. Thought I had discovered a sensational new narrative method the other evening – there was only one thing wrong with it; in practice, it proved to be unreadable. Thought of it in terms of the inner and outer going on simultaneously, side by side on the page – fine if you had a two-foot wide page and a reader with four eyes.

How long will you be in Ottawa? Hope you're having fun. And also that the anthology is pretty well off your neck by now.

All the best.
Margaret

173 Waverley, Apt. 3
Ottawa
13 October 1967

Dear Margaret,

Have just copied your Joe Bass piece, incorporating corrections, and think soberly, logically and particularly, also, emotionally, that it is a very fine – article? More like a short story perhaps.
It will stand out, in my opinion, as fair-minded, personal and
individual among other prose, some of which will likely be dull.
Yours isn't that. Despite its short story aspect, it's an entirely utili-
tarian piece (which is queer to say about it) that does what I think
you want it to do, and particularly what you want it to do. I have
no doubts about its merit whatever, and you shouldn't have. Incidentally, I also have doubts, perhaps especially in reviews where I
say something that might be interpreted as nasty, instead of the
well-meaning rabelaisian good humor which is my simple characteristic. Or hadn't you noticed.

Yeah, I know Barry Broadfoot,[1] not his wife.

Include a clipping re M. Laurence's riches and movie sales.[2]
There were others, but they dealt more with the glamorous
Newman than the novel and movie.[3] I like him as an actor, but
not sure this liking doesn't consist as much of his physical charm as
anything.

Re. the spoken word, I hope I express myself better that way
too, and it's the only way I can correct previous mistakes also on
paper, and sometimes personal impression etc.

About the kids and their father, I am almost disbarred from
comment entirely. No outsider really can say about those things.
On the other hand, in your own case, you have to judge the situation damn accurately, gauging all the emotional penalties
involved like an irrigation engineer. There being times to take
chances for the sake of the end and times not to.

For myself, I am settled into a shabby little furnished apt. in

Ottawa with wife and visiting House of Commons and it seems a circus of which I can make no sense. I will have to make sudden darts into the confusion, seize something and retreat to examine it. No other way, since I'm no political reporter. Some aspect etc that appeals to something in me. Took the grand tour of parliament buildings yesterday with the parliamentary librarian who knows everything. Was introduced to McEachen (Alan)[4] and couldn't remember his new job or even his face and stood in confusion wondering who I was introed to. They are all so smooth and polite and used to meeting people. I don't suppose I betray confusion exactly, but gather some cliches that have echoed around the stone corridors for years and use them again to whoever I meet. Found they are still doing sculpture in the building, covered with canvas, and work after midnight. This appeals, the idea of sculptors coming back at night after the talk and their chisels making marks on stone as words do not really on silence. Gonna try and meet the sculptors and watch them one night. Woman named Eleanor Milne[5] is in charge, tho I dunno what in charge means here.

Have also three bushels of wild grapes to clean, a legacy from Roblin Lake, which are bubbling in the tiny kitchen like a spillage of whispers. Squirrels walking upside down on screens of windows; yellow, red and green leaves outside deciding what to do when the wind comes. Days getting so short they seem no more than the click of a camera shutter; a tall tall crane fumbles heavy weights out the side window like a gigantic mantis. Crazy ordinary.

Must stop and get outside. Been drinking coffee and seeing the dull day with distaste at the idea of going outside –

Best,
Al

1. At this time Barry Broadfoot (b. 1926) was a journalist with the *Vancouver Sun*. The Laurence letter to which Purdy is replying is missing.

2. These items are missing from the Purdy correspondence in the Margaret Laurence papers.

3. Paul Newman (b. 1925) was producer and director of *Rachel, Rachel* (1968), the film adaptation of *A Jest of God*. It was his first film as a director and featured his wife, Joanne Woodward (b. 1930), as Rachel Cameron. It earned Academy Award nominations for best actress, best director, and best screenplay.

4. Allan J. MacEachen (b. 1921) was at this time Liberal Member of Parliament for Inverness-Richmond and had just been named Government House Leader.

5. Eleanor Rose Milne (b. 1925), Official Sculptor, Canada, since 1961.

Elm Cottage

23 October 1967

Dear Al–

Thanks for your letter of the 13th. I am very glad indeed to hear that you think my article is okay. To have it called "personal and individual" is what pleases me most, as this is always (to me) in some way the crucial point. Interesting that you think it is more like a short story – I can see what you mean. I guess that is because it deals with a few people rather than in generalities. I always remember a line I read once (in a Josephine Tey who-dun-it novel, of all unlikely places), which said, in effect, "A thousand people drowning in a flood – that's news; one child drowning in a pond – that's tragedy."[1] It oughtn't to be that way, because the thousand are all individuals with names, too, but it *is* that way until the thousand are all explained, one by one. Did I tell you about going to a conference of W. Indian writers at the Univ of Kent recently?[2] God knows why they asked me – they wanted a few outside observers, I think. It was quite interesting, but one odd aspect of it was the American negro writer who was there. I sat beside him (unfortunately) in the bus, and in my naive way, and also not realizing he was an American, began to talk, as is my wont. I've never met anyone who radiated hate as he did. In icy waves it came from him. So after a bit, I thought, oh well this guy doesn't want to talk, and alas whatever I say will be wrong, so I shut up. The first evening many W. Indians read their own poetry and prose, and some of it was marvellous, and then the Amer got up and read a long long poem about Harlem – God, Al, all the emotions expressed are so bloody understandable, but it was a hell of a bad poem, at least in my opinion, as it was full of lines like "There is terror in Harlem tonight" ... all in very generalized terms; all abstract; not one real actual individual human face among the words. It contrasted very much with a poem of one of the W. Indians, which described one Harlem streetwalker, just one, and it all came across. The Amer's poem reminded me of the old days in Winnipeg when I once worked for a Communist weekly, The Westerner[3] (that was my second job after college – seems strange now; when I began I didn't even know enough to know it was a Party paper – thought it was left-wing vaguely; why they hired me I cannot think; I did book reviews and reporting – and did I learn a lot in that year!) My big break with the editor (whom I still feel enormous affection towards) was when I reviewed some novel or other and said "this novel stinks", and he said, you can't say it stinks, it's on the right side, and I said I thought otherwise. Anyway, us liberals (ha!) are agin' generalizations, and this is probably why we are so ineffectual.

Yes, I had noticed your care in reviews, not to slide the knife between anyone's ribs, while at the same time putting down your own assessment of the work. Your well-meaning rabelaisian goodhumour which is your "simple characteristic" ... yeh. It's a mask which is more appealing than most masks. It wouldn't seem to me, though, that many of your characteristics were very simple, except as you deliberately make them so, perhaps both for yourself and for the purpose of encountering others. When I first saw you, looming suddenly up in the Country Club, Ottawa, my instant reaction was "My God, he looks like a cowboy", closely followed by "... but he *isn't,* however much he sometimes might like to be." Could be wrong; don't know. I guess that myself I sometimes have to let on that things are simpler for me than they in fact are – if you're living simultaneously in a couple of different worlds, why burden the people in one with those in another, especially (for me, anyway, writing fiction) as the people in one of the areas aren't externally real to others until much later on – and by the time they exist for some others, I am no longer living with them. Or do I make any sense at all?

Understand to some extent your feeling about the people in Ottawa who are smooth and polite and used to meeting people. I am not used to meeting people, either, but I think I take a different way out from yours – although maybe similar in some ways. I use the cliches all right, but seem to have some (unwanted) knack of turning myself temporarily and chameleon-like into good middleclass housewife-type ... possibly because this is what I partly am. Can hear myself talking the part, and think – *Christ, it can't be!* But when I do it, everyone for miles around is convinced. Most people are always more convinced when one is telling lies than when one is attempting not to tell them, I find. I also have much more fear of rocking the boat than you have, and this is a quality I dislike in myself, but think I'm probably too old to change.

Re: returning to Canada – have, in my usual open-mouthed way, told about three or four close friends about my dilemma, and I find that with all of them (as with your letters) I am much less alone than I sometimes suppose myself to be. Adele, and also a friend now at Dalhousie,[4] have both been working away in an underground sense, to try to wangle a writer-in-residence job for me somewhere. My God, I don't deserve it, but I certainly am grateful. So I've been bashing off letters, and trying to see how we might work it for myself and kids to go for 1 year and then reconsider at the end of that time. One has also the unpleasant feeling that the major decision has been made, and that one is only going to go through the usual process of gradually making the arguments stronger and stronger, finding more and more logical evidence why it is essential for myself and kids to move back, and suffering sufficient guilt and pain so that in the end one feels justified in taking the selfish decision which one had in some submerged way made some time ago. I wish I did not see this about myself, as I think it is a very sneaky and unpleasant characteristic but these past 5 years have shattered my self-image, and I am not quite so astonished any more by my own basic unscrupulousness. Once I believed I was a person who meant well – amazing, eh? Now I see that I love my kids, care about my friends, value and break my heart over my husband, and perhaps most of all, am aware that I'm 41 and not liable to live forever and am therefore (disbelieving in violence) just as prone to spiritual violence as anyone else. If you see it, though, you feel you have to guard against your own potential for the destruction of others. But I think in the end I will act selfishly. If the other way were clear, it might be possible, but I've known enough martyrs to know that their actions are just as suspect as my own.

The novel, in the meantime, proceeds in some odd fashion. I do not think at this point that I will ever be willing to submit it to any publisher. Don't laugh – I'm not joking. It is a question of trying to transform the ordinary, and I've never yet tried to transform anything quite *this* ordinary, so it may not be possible with the means at my disposal. So many things have got chucked out in the process – the whole thing is a matter of paring down to the bone, of shedding gimmicks, even of shedding many explanations. It is a mess at the moment, but I am trying not to look back or not yet. If it proves to be unpublishable, it will still have been worth doing. There isn't any possible doubt about that, and that is the only thing there isn't any doubt about. The only time I feel okay these days is when I'm actually writing, but days often go by when I don't or can't, and then I bend all efforts towards not thinking about it, and am reading a really astonishing amount of Science Fiction, and also looking at the most moronic programs possible on TV.

Your last paragraph in your letter seemed like a poem to me, the description of Ottawa and the wild grapes and the cranes ... "crazy ordinary". Did you keep a copy? If not, please tell me and I will return the paragraph to you. Wish I could write description like that, so selective, so apparently light in touch, so much unspoken appearing under the surface.

This has turned out longer than I intended. Now have to do domestic tasks and then try to start Chapter 4 – am evading it, and know I am. My feeling about the central character is, "Baby, I'm afraid I won't be able to do well by you". I had that feeling when I finished A Jest of God ... I thought I wanted to apologize to Rachel. And then my little Rachel took off and went to Holly-wood – but I don't suppose either she or I were too deceived by that, only somewhat surprised, but not in essence altered, still our uncertain selves. I suppose one always has basically the same prayer – God, just let me do this one novel, and I'll never again ask for anything of you. One hopes He smiles tolerantly, and says – yeh, I've heard that one before.

Best,
Margaret

ps. this letter probably makes it sound as though I'm brooding about methods in fiction all the time – not so. The other life goes on, in the usual trivial-chaotic-sustaining manner. Kids now home for one week's mid-term holidays – we wisecrack and battle in the normal ways, each of us being one another's chain but also anchor; the cat has to be taken to the Vet to be neutered – she has hysterics in the taxi and I almost do, too; we buy a new extension ladder which proves to weigh about ten tons, and put it up in our orchard in order to pick the apples; we go to David's school for Parents' Evening and I talk in genteel fashion to teachers; and so on.

---

1. Josephine Tey, the pseudonym of Elizabeth Mackintosh (1897- 1952), published romantic novels, crime fiction, and plays.

2. The first Conference on Caribbean Arts was held at the University of Kent in Canterbury, England, 15-17 September 1967. It included writers, painters, sculptors, and actors from the West Indies and elsewhere.

3. *The Westerner,* under the editorship of Mitch Sago, was published between 21 July 1946 and 11 September 1948.

4. At the instigation of Donald Cameron, a Killam Post-Doctoral Fellow at Dalhousie University, Laurence was asked by Dalhousie's Department of English to apply for a position as writer-in-residence for a year. Laurence applied, then cancelled her application because she decided it was best to stay in England and write.

30 October 1967

Dear Margaret:

I shall sheer off entirely from any comment on your personal problems, which are so much yours that I shouldn't say anything anyway.

Your kids book sounds wonderful, or rather I dunno – except I suppose the mole talks (don't all moles talk) and I hope there's some nice moley dialogue. You mean there are molecatchers in England? The place must be honeycombed and infested with the things. Is there a price on their heads like wolves? Can you put salt on their tale, or do you just tip your hat politely as Dr. Doolittle would have in my long ago childhood?

Sometimes the novelist must feel like that old woman on Old Dutch Cleanser before they changed the label, the one whose face you don't see, whose housecleaning never ends.[1] But the sitting down at the typewriter, is my idea of the worst part of it. Because it has to be only once and a while that you feel carried away and brilliantly original etc. Thanks christ I never intend to write a novel. I used to yearn for a novel like a childless woman, but now I regurgitate prose in small chunks and don't care – Poems are enough, just so I write what I think is good. (Why don't you call your child's book "The Hero is a Mole"?)

The antho seems like it will never be off my neck. And now Copp Clark writes to say they want me to do a book on birney (only 100-125 pages) and offer five hundred bucks down. My greed is gonna get me into a lotta work. Haven't accepted, but might. George Bowering[2] is doing a book about me, so it's gettin kinda incestuous.

You mention the hate in this American negro – what an awful thing. I never ran into it like that, haven't had enough to do with negroes, tho I think Austin Clarke[3] in Toronto feels like that, but in him it seems more like a personal oddity. Such a waste of time to hate, as if you had nothing else to do. So many better things. I mean – take part in these civil rights things because you believe in them, not because of hate. Of course, how can a white man put himself in their shoes? The poor bastards have had to endure so much over the years, like Jews too. But most Jews are not virulent in their dislike of Gentiles, and I have the impression many negroes are.

Me – a cowboy? Christ, any horse I got near would crap on me sure. Milk wagon horses used to give me that sneering lip-lifted equine look, and I was so pleased when they started using trucks.

The bit about poems (the Laurence wisdom I mean) strikes me as true. Kid poets tend to philosophize and generalize, use great wild rainbow adjectives and pile them on horribly. Many never learn to be specific, and even if they do they may never learn to round a poem off, make it progress and move and circle around to its beginnings. But after you realize abstractly how a poem should be written you're liable to be haunted by the fear that you won't or can't write any more. Like you with a novel. It's as if knowing how a poem or novel should be written in your own mind sort of invalidates your previous methods. I see myself repeating myself in so many things I feel like a continual stutter.

Re. simplicity tho, you couldn't carry on social intercourse very much if you paid attention to all the nuances you feel and hear. I've sometimes felt another person's brain ticking over on thoughts other than they were talking about, and I think people are stupid if they don't realize other people are liable to realize this about them. Of course one is always liable to see this quality in others to some degree but one can also feel it very strongly, masked only slightly by manners.

Well, I am drinking beer while writing this letter, and wondering what effect it has on what I write. Migawd, just thinking about writing a book about someone else appals me.

Best,
Al

---

1. The old woman on the label was depicted holding an identical can of Dutch Cleanser with an old woman on its label who, in her turn, was holding a can of Dutch Cleanser in an endlessly repeating pattern.

2. George Bowering (b. 1935), poet and fiction writer, had recently published a novel, *Mirror on the Floor* (1967). His *Al Purdy* appeared in 1970.

3. Austin Clarke (b. 1932) had just published *The Meeting Point* (1967), a novel about West Indian immigrants in Toronto.

❧

Elm Cottage
8 November 1967

Dear Al:

Thanks for sane and sensible letter. I think that very likely all my personal dilemmas (whether or not to return to Canada; etc etc etc) could be expressed in one short sharp phrase – attempt to evade novel. It now occurs to me that this is a recurring pattern, and that with the previous 2 novels I also went through a terrible period of intense upheaval, mournful letters to long-suffering friends, floor pacing, determination to alter entire structure of life, and one damn thing and another. When the smoke cleared, having upset nearly everyone I knew, I settled down and wrote a novel (or in the case of The Stone Angel, re-wrote it). One would think that a person ought to have more insight into themselves at this point, and to recognize the symptoms, but no. Will undoubtedly return to Canada one of these days, but can't at the moment for obvious reasons, and really – at this point, to consider taking a writer-in-residence job would probably have been insane. I won't be finished this novel by next summer. If it's done in 2 years I will be lucky. It is only in the past week that I have been able to face that awful fact. What bugs me about it is that I apparently find it essential to write this goddamn novel, having tried 4 times before, and being unable to drop it, and yet I cannot delude myself that it is anything more than 1 novel out of the thousands. With luck and the grace of God, it may work reasonably well. I can't yet tell. I only know that if it doesn't work, it won't be mediocre – it'll be downright bad. It's a chance I have to take, and every time I think of it (say, 1500 times a day) I feel sick at my stomach. (Nobody can suffer like I can, when I really put my mind to it!) The old narrative forms won't work any longer, so I've spent ages in trying to figure out how it can be done – not that my forms of writing this are very new; they're only new to me, that's all. The subject seems so unlikely as to be the choice of a

68

nitwit. Well. But it's there, so it's got to be written. I have never felt such cowardice and terror at sitting down at the typewriter. Damn it, if only I could write it as it really *is* – as it exists, somewhere. If only I could write in three dimensions and technicolour, or something. I don't mean for flamboyant effect – only to get across the feeling … this is how it was, for these particular people. You are right about the ways one thinks about form – at first, one doesn't think about it at all, and then later on, you do – you can't help it, and then you wonder if you know too much about the mechanics and are in danger of forgetting the life and breath of the thing. Of course, in all honesty, I am scared, too, at this point, of writing a really dreadful novel. Which is daft, but there it is. I hope I would *know* it was dreadful, before letting a publisher see it. You know, some very young writers whom I seem to keep meeting (they're all Canadians, by the way) are always saying to me how great it must be to have published a certain number of books, and to have been given this and that, and how reassuring it must be – little do they know that it is the exact opposite. I had far less fear about my first novel than I do with this one – I didn't know then how difficult it is, and how many things can go wrong. Anyway, am on Chapter 5, and am determined to write 1 chapter per week until the first draft is finished. After that, the re-writing, which will be interminable. Not that I care how long it takes, really, if only it comes across even partially. Strange that you should say you used to yearn for a novel – I guess everyone wants something that they aren't given to do; I have always felt I would like to write a novel that was like a poem … absolutely no verbiage, everything pared down to the bone, every word reverberating in the mind. I tried to do it with A Jest of God, but I didn't succeed. Maybe in a novel it isn't possible. This one is completely different – it won't fit into any known pattern, and I've been fighting this for a long time, but am trying to quit fighting and let it do whatever it wants, however disorganized etc.

Can't recall what I said in my previous letter(s) which could possibly be misconstrued as "the Laurence wisdom" ... probably I was drinking wine when I wrote whatever it was, and undoubtedly wouldn't have seemed like wisdom to you unless you'd been drinking beer. Good idea for achieving a reputation for deep thought – request all one's friends to have three stiff drinks before reading one's letters?

I think it would be splendid if you'd write a book on Birney. Can see it would be a hell of a lot of work, but can't think of anyone who could do it better. You would be fair to him – you wouldn't damn him for not being 20 years old, nor would you salaam thrice. I read the review (can't remember where) which you wrote on his collected poems,[1] and thought it managed to be both personal and impersonal, ie affectionate and yet dispassionate. Glad that Geo. Bowering is doing a book on you – he's a good poet and is going to be a good novelist as well, I think. I thought Mirror On The Floor came across very well – maybe the taperecorder bit was slightly gimmicky, but the selection of material was damn good.

Best,

Margaret

ps. Macmillans didn't think my kids' book would do – they said they were amused (they were probably letting me down easy) but the story was too much connected with current fashion in swinging London and by the time it was published, all might have changed. I think they are right. Don't know why in hell I ever wrote it – guess it was another evasion of novel. One's methods of self-deception are endless.

---

1. She may be referring to Purdy's review of Birney's *Near False Creek Mouth* in *Fiddlehead*, 65 (Summer 1965), 75-76, in which Purdy felt compelled to look at "*all* the poems" that Birney had written.

§

173 Waverley, Apt. 3

Ottawa

26 November [1967]

Dear Margaret:

Reading your letter again about writing this novel, have decided I never want to write one, not unless I have everything in my head and the thing absolutely demands to get out. I am slightly familiar with this idea of evasion, since I used to write plays for C.B.C., or perhaps should say I tried to, since I had about fifteen accepted and produced of the more than hundred written. I used to try to get to work every day on the play I was writing, after having presumably got the plot complete in my head (tho it never was complete), and before I'd settle down at the typewriter I'd do all sorts of silly things, like making coffee, washing dishes (I was alone most of the time), just walking back and forth back and forth thinking about the damn thing. Does all this have a familiar ring? I would get the mail first, I'd do any damn thing before getting to work, and when I did get to work I'd work all sorts of odd times, some days for only a few minutes, others for hours and hours. I had the idea then, and I probably still have it, that I ought to feel absolutely mentally alert and bright, that I ought to have had a good long sleep the night before, and that this sharp edge obtained would only last a short time. Therefore I had the readymade excuse to stop whenever my head so much as nodded. And I believed I had some sort of God-given right to go off on tangents whenever I felt like it, to write poems etc etc. It's a wonder I ever got any work done.

If you're right about assessing your own difficulties, they are much more complicated than mine. You believe most of your difficulties unconnected apparently with writing, are actually and really connected with writing. You'll be having your husband and cottage and kids in the next novel (not that I suppose they aren't in

71

the previous ones somehow as well as yourself) and the whole structure of your life. The trouble is that one sees thru one's own self-deceptions in these matters, but just being cleverer than one's non-clever self doesn't enable one to surmount it. There must be yet another self that observes, cynically or otherwise, that sees the two selves struggling with each other and the physical world of writing and non-writing. We don't know about the third self, and the proposition that "it" is there at all must be arrived at like astronomers predicting new stars and comets and such on the basis of the way the solar system acts (that's the first two selves), and some hunk of rock behind Jupiter is causing a hitch in its orbit. Therefore, I wonder if I still do want to write a novel, just because I say I don't? The bastard me is watching the first two me's, and I don't like being manipulated by another me because I don't like outside interference even tho it is by me, if you follow this which I'm beginning not to –

I seem to be doing a lot of different things here, and if I could split up the work among my different selves I'd be willing to pay myself union wages. Writing reviews and coupla short pieces about poetry for local paper, anthology, readings at Carleton, talking to creative writing class and denying the necessity of being a prophet (they all want you to be that, and it irritates me) reviews for lit mags. Bob Weaver asked me to do about a dozen poets for a coming ish, [1] and I couldn't refuse Weaver very much, and ambiguously not sure if I wouldn't want to anyway. Also writing poems. Meant to include a short one here if I can find room. The hell with the Birney book, their "advance" is not really an advance, and the money comes only when the book is done and accepted. Besides, I'd like to get Birney's love-life and everything else in such a book and he and they wouldn't like that – Wow! Always, or rather used to, tell Birney if he died before me I was gonna grind him up and marinate him for an aphrodisiac. I like the guy, but could never figure out his apparent attraction to women. He uses his poet-self of course ...

IS THIS THE MAN?[2]

When I see the cabinet ministers rising
un-Venuslike from the sewage
of words and one particular old
buffalo assumes by accident a pose
of statesman delivering cost estimates
like a police lieutenant I say to myself
"Is this the man?"
Or the member left over after redistribution
rises during the question period
to say we stand on guard and how
patriotism swells the bosom and the member
rises for royal commission to investigate same
again Mr. Speaker I question myself
"Is this the man?"
No doubt the Minister of Trade and Commerce
and the Minister of External Aff. & Transport
and the Minister of Economic Integration with the U.S.
are all honest and some bilingual
but the cost in time and money
comes high to find the man I'm looking for
and none here seems remotely capable
of running the affairs of my small
village of Ameliasburg
when the reeve retires next month

These goddam air mail letters[3]
are a fiendish business, since
you either have too much or too
little space and can't feel comfortable
knowing the sentence is gonna end with
a whimper and all the meaningful and
delightful things you mighta said can't
be goddam said because a word

from a poem (in this case) projects
like a phallic whatever into your
thoughts – Which gets silly,
   but the blank space below irritat
es me, but it irritates me more to
say silly things to fill it. Of cou
rse another air mail letter right now,
   but that's cheating, must be
        concise etc. I was never con-
        cise, always shapeless,
   formless and blundering off
outside the edges of whatever it was.

Best,

Al

---

1. Purdy's review appeared in *The Tamarack Review,* No. 49 (Spring 1968), 81-96. Entitled "Aiming Low," it commented on new collections of poems by George Jonas, D.G. Jones, Roy Kiyooka, A.J.M. Smith, Dennis Lee, Raymond Souster, P.K. Page, Lionel Kearns, Dorothy Livesay, George Woodcock, and Alden Nowlan. Also included in the review was *The Making of Modern Poetry in Canada,* edited by Louis Dudek and Michael Gnarowski.

2. This version of the poem was published in *Wild Grape Wine.*

3. Purdy's poem occupied the left half of the last page of the aerogramme. His concluding message was written in the only remaining space on that page and is here transcribed as the prose poem that the space apparently helped to create.

§

Dear Al–

Thanks for your letter. Your description of yourself in the throes of writing a play certainly does sound familiar – damn you. When it's all put down like that, the evasions sound awful. I go to any lengths to avoid beginning a novel, and when I have begun, I go to any lengths to stall the beginning of each new chapter. The tension between opposite feelings is what I find difficult – I want more than anything to write the damn thing, but I find it so hard to write that I want desperately not to do it. In the end, what happens is that I can't stand the tension, so have to write it in order to free myself, temporarily. I guess it ought to be a pleasure to write, and in some way it is – but it is so damn painful as well. I keep wishing there were some way I could wave my magic wand and the novel would spring into instant being, with everything in it that ought to be in it, the characters being themselves, speaking in their own recognizable voices, without my having to write it. But many a good novel has been written only in the mind, and this is really an unwillingness to make oneself vulnerable, to risk writing it. It isn't going to turn out as I would like it, but if I don't write it, it won't exist at all, not even in a flawed and imperfect state. So each goddamn scene has to be lived through, from the inside, and as I get older I find this process of going inside the thing harder and harder to bear. I know what's there, but I bloody well don't want to look at it. Isn't any other way, though. It has to be looked at. I write with the accompaniment of bizarre physical symptoms – I write a scene and I really feel as though I'm going to throw up any moment. All this is self-dramatization, too, to some extent. It would all be worthwhile if one could know that the final product was going to be good, but for this there isn't any insurance. This is what bugs me all the time. To turn yourself into a kind of non-human monster unable to make more than a cursory contact with your external life, for a period of time, might be okay if you were going to produce a really good novel. But I know that at best this novel will be a competent middleclass one, nothing more, one out of the thousands published that year. At worst, it will be a flop, and won't see the light of day and I will have betrayed my characters. The trouble is that I know very precisely what I want to do – no, that's not the way to express it – I know what is *there,* with the characters, what they are and exactly how they could come across, if I could do it as it should be done. But I can't. I can't ever catch verbally all that they *are.* My sense of apology isn't directed towards the publishers or readers (whoever they may be) but towards the characters. I keep thinking – okay, I know you; we've lived together a long time; and I don't think I can really do well by you. There is the book which exists only in the mind, and this isn't the one which gets written – the actual one never gets enough across. What bothers me almost unbearably about this novel is that it could be a terrific novel, if it had been given to someone with a hell of a lot more talent, perseverance, perception, intelligence, faith and truthfulness. I hate to see a thing not being done as well as it deserves, but this is what happens all the time with me. Don't mistake me – this isn't false modesty or any crap like that. There are some things which I know I can do; others, I know I can't. Anyway, I have reached the point where I know this novel will get finished, however ghastly it may turn out. Have finished chapter 6 and am going to get ch 7 done before Xmas or die in the attempt. Then only 3 more chapters. I don't dare look back at what I've written, or like Lot's wife I will be turned into a pillar of salt. But really, to overcome fear I guess one has to consider what the worst would be – and in my case, right now, the worst would be for this novel to turn out to be pure garbage. And when I think of it like that, I think – yes, that would be pretty grim, but it wouldn't kill me. The thing-in-itself is *not* garbage – that is the trouble; I know it's there; what I don't know is

76

whether I'm striking through to it. In fact, I know I'm not – it's only a kind of dim approximation.

Your activities sound enormously varied and interesting – hope you are getting paid well for them. Do you mean you aren't going to do the Birney book? I can see the difficulties – the love-life couldn't really be included at this point. I agree re: him and women – I don't know him all that well, but have a terrific admiration and affection for him, but can't see why his woman-appeal should be – maybe I am just impervious to father-figures at this point, don't know. I guess it is right that he uses his poet-self – which, in a way, is okay, because it really only works with those who can settle for that role – I Was Stephen Spender's Mistress – or like that. If you know what I mean. So he isn't conning them.

Thanks for poem. I agree with your mistrust of politicians – more and more, one feels that it is all such a bloody mess that maybe the best thing is to concentrate on one's village. Re: poems – I feel, as usual, how lucky you are to be able to send a poem in a letter to a friend. I wish I could do something like that. (Want 50 pages of a godawful novel, anyone?)

Best,
Margaret

ps. MERRY CHRISTMAS AND HAPPY NEW YEAR

p.s.2. probably unjustified curiosity, but why do you put Margaret Laurence at the top of your letters to me? Do you make carbons and stash them all away? I hope to Christ nobody keeps my letters to them – they are not for keeping.

ps.3. have you ever thought of a book of your plays?

§

134 Front St.
Trenton, Ontario
31 December 1967

Yep, Margaret Laurence
Dear Margaret:

I do make carbons of all my letters, because sometimes I say things I want to look up later that seem good to me on imperfect recollection, also because I may want to peddle them to a univ. later. I also keep all letters to me, not business letters or notes, but those that are about writing etc. Shall I send yours back to you? Wouldn't be any trouble at all – ?

Plays, yes, thought of it several times, but not really sure I think they're good enough. I am sure, on looking back, that I had several unusual ideas (if they weren't just silly) like a race down the fallopian tube among the sperm cells, all of which were given human personalities and trained like olympic sprinters – ending with a presumed future murderer born to a queen. I enjoyed writing that one, feeling ingenious and inventive as hell, more like an athletic coach than a writer – But as a book, might make a few bucks with the best of them, but unless I need money in the future which seems quite possible, to hell with it.

Moved to Trenton from Ottawa, with me bearing great loads of belongings down stairs, packing car, driving 175 miles, unpacking car and being useless for about two days after – Age and fat have overtaken me all at once. Two weeks before leaving Eurithe fainted on the downtown streets of Ottawa. She had felt faint and asked me to find a restaurant where she could sit down. I was about 150 feet away and looked back to see her start to fall. Ran like hell to get back before she hit the pavement, but didn't make it, and she hit her head on the concrete with a sickening impact. Raced to hospital in a taxi with tires screaming and horn blaring, at which place I sat about four hours before I found out what was wrong. She had had over-fulsome menstrual flow, and this had weakened her until she was anaemic, which led to the fainting. Okay now, but has to eat liver and drink juices and things like that.

From a time angle we are supposed to be near the end of the U.S. antho bit, but there are about 15 promised pieces that aren't in, and I have to write, phone, beg, plead etc. to try and get them. Also doing one of those omnibus reviews of books for Bob Weaver in Tamarack. I couldn't refuse to do this for Weaver, and maybe I wouldn'ta refused anyway, tho it's a bad time, what with everything else. Copp Clarke say they'll cough up an advance in cash, which makes the Birney book on again. And I hafta figure out a method for that which won't result in just another dry textbook. Also Ron Grantham at the Ottawa Citizen gave a coupla review books,[1] nice expensive books that'll keep their value and one can run one's hand over the expensive cloth bindings as if they were human skin. Can't resist reviewing when I can get good books. One is about wooden building construction in 19th century Ontario, log construction mostly with many photos. Amazing the variety of those bldgs.

Anyway, I'm now sitting in a room full of books overlooking the snowcovered Trent River in the dreary little town of Trenton, wishing to jesus that antho were over and done. Trenton amounts to the dingy reality of my misspent youth. The house here amounts to the shell of a huge snail that I can't seem to get rid of, marine creatures, some of them, can leave their shells but must scuttle back at signs of danger, and so do I it seems. Goddam umbilical cord to the past.

Neurosis no doubt, and there are many happy wholesome loving people living in the miserable place, rearing cooing happy babies that will grow up to be mongoloids and cretins as a result of environment. I will dust the place with DDT at a later date.

I am, of course, writing a poem on rushing my wife to the

hospital and all that[2] – saying to myself purdy you are a jesus priest continually confessing yourself, also you are the ultimate god who judges literary excellence and personal moral excellence, the last of course coming second to the first. I remember Lionel Kearns at U.B.C.[3] telling me he wanted to be "a good guy" more than he wanted to write fine poems. Don't know what his definition of good guy is, but I've seen enough people who were judged good guys that I don't want to be that, not in the sense they seem to mean anyway. It gets down to something narrower than that with me I suppose. Always feel, or generally, a reaction to publicly labeled nice guys, and want to call them nice guys which seems to me the ultimate insult. Niceness being to me a quality that must be defined by its absence rather than its presence.

Must stop and write my long series of letters to delinquent contributors dunning them for their public thoughts.

Best,
Al

———————

1. Review of Elizabeth Collard's *Nineteenth-Century Pottery and Porcelain in Canada. The Ottawa Citizen,* 13 January 1968, 23. The second review, of John Rempel's *Building with Wood and Other Aspects of Nineteenth-Century Building in Ontario* (1967), has not been traced.

2. "Alive or Not," included in *Sundance at Dusk* (1976).

3. Lionel Kearns (b. 1937), poet and a member of the English Department of Simon Fraser University.

TO: AL W. PURDY
REF: ML/Elmcot/1/68

Elm Cottage
5 January 1968

Dear Al:

Please don't feel you have to reply promptly to this letter – I'm only answering with unaccustomed swiftness because I feel kind of like a louse about the comment I made to you in my last letter about letters. It was only after I had posted my letter that I realized the remark sounded churlish, although I didn't mean it to. No, don't return my letters – I am not concerned about them, and if you can ever flog them to a university, more power to you – have a drink for me. Actually, I keep friends' letters when they're about writing, too, because I like to look back from time to time and read about other writers' problems and comments on work, especially if I am feeling low myself. I suppose when I last wrote to you I was probably in a phase of thinking what a lot of drivel I was writing, in novel, etc, but it was only a phase. That is the only trouble with letters – you write some remark like that, and next day you feel differently. I think, also, that I tend to fight the current tendency of many people (especially academics) to be more interested in a writer's methods and personal life than in the writing itself, so I don't really like to believe that any university would want my letters – I want to shout in fury, "Read my goddamn books and never mind the scribblings on the margins of old manuscripts". On the other hand, I don't refuse the money offered for scripts.

What a hell of an experience for you and your wife, the accident in Ottawa. In my slight experience of emergencies like that, the hospital always seems to take eternity to do anything – although it is actually probably only a matter of minutes, but time takes on a different quality entirely. Also, when it is someone you love, you feel an overpowering sense of rage and panic and help-lessness – a kind of protest against fate, I guess, or at least that is how I felt when my daughter had convulsions when she was a month old. Anyway, I'm glad your wife is okay now. I seem to get the impression from your letter that it was this happening in Ottawa which led to your going to Trenton, or are you there for work? Not that it's any of my goddamn business. I can see very well why you periodically question yourself re: writing poems on personal events – but how can you help doing so? I don't think it has anything to do with being or not being a good guy or even a good man. You don't really have any choice in the matter. I don't write directly out of personal experience, but all the same I often wonder how much of myself I'm revealing in novels and stories – in fact, I'm revealing the whole thing, but I always fondly hope that this isn't obvious to everyone. And in a peculiar way, the characters are definitely not me, while at the same time express-ing aspects of myself. Did you read Brian Moore's AN ANSWER FROM LIMBO? The main character is a novelist, and at the end, at the death of his mother (whom he has treated horribly) he finds himself already transposing the event into fictional terms – he hates himself for it, but knows he can't do otherwise.

I like the outline of the play with the sperm cells racing to see who'll win – the murderer born to a queen could be Oedipus.

I haven't worked since before Christmas, as I went mad and invited all sorts of friends here on various days and for a week never got a meal for less than nine people. I now have about a mil-lion letters to do, and then am going to Spain with my husband for 2 weeks. After the end of January, I hope to God I can get back to work, as every day I'm away from the novel it seems a worse mess to me. Actually, I'm not too discouraged about it – I can finish the first draft in a month, and then begin to make some kind of pattern out of the chaos. I keep making notes about things I've left out or done wrongly, and will soon have more notes than manuscript. All I want to do in 1968 is finish 3 books. I feel heartened when I think that they are all at least more than halfway done.

You sound tremendously busy. Will you send me a copy of the anthol. when it is out? I don't mean for free – with that number of contributors, I think you should charge them. Very glad you're going to do the Birney book – don't think you need to worry about its being dull – he's not a dull subject and you're not a dull writer. I've just received proofs of Sinclair Ross's book of stories, coming out in the New Can. Library, for which I wrote an intro-duction.[1] I take some credit for the appearance of the book, as Bob Weaver and I twisted J. McClelland's arm about it – it's long overdue, as Ross's stories have been in many anthologies but never in a collection. I think they are doing THE STONE ANGEL in N.C.L. this year also.

I know what you mean about good bindings on books – when I got Knopf's editions of 3 of my books,[2] I sat with them most of a day, stroking the binding which was unbelievably beautiful and wishing that English publishers could afford to put out books like that.

All the best for the new year.
Margaret
(i.e. MARGARET LAURENCE)

1. *The Lamp at Noon and Other Stories* (1968).

2. Knopf had published *New Wind in a Dry Land* (the American title of *The Prophet's Camel Bell*), *The Tomorrow-Tamer*, and *The Stone Angel* all on the same day, 15 June 1964.

Elmcot
10 March [1968]

Dear Al–

Novel completed. HURRAH!

Jubilation reaction

But is it any good or not?

Apprehension reaction

All I have to do is put in the parts that have been missed out; cut out all the garbage that should never have been put in; type out 300 pages in triplicate; submit to publisher; pace floor telling myself I don't give a damn even if it is the worst novel ever written in English.

Survival is the main thing.

Best,
Margaret

§

134 Front St.
Trenton, Ontario
18 March 1968

Dear Margaret,

Hooray for you! Jubilation reaction oughta prevail. Apprehension one having to do with your own feelings about whether it is a masterpiece or not oughta be clear enough too. Undoubtedly it is a masterpiece. To hell with the critics etc. (there is perhaps an implication of wondering what the critics will think in the apprehension reaction) It has to be your judgement – and now peel, cut, prune, deface, destroy, maim, cripple (no, no!) and generally bugger around with it.

But congratulations!

I type this on the Contents page of THE NEW ROMANS, which we've decided on for title. Thought you might be interested in who's in the book. 3-4 are omitted.[1] Pub. Sept. Now all I hafta do is the Birney book. I got a Canada Council, by the way, and will be in Europe some time this summer or fall. Hope to see you then.

Best,
Al
Purdy[2]

---

1. Three writers listed on Purdy's contents page who did not appear in the published book were Fred Cogswell, Patrick Scott, and Joe Rosenblatt. Missing from Purdy's list of contributors was Larry Zolf whose article – "Boil Me No Melting Pots, Dream Me No Dreams" – appeared in *The New Romans*.

2. The "Al" is handwritten and the "Purdy" typed below it.

§

Elm Cottage
6 June 1968

Dear Al–

Goodness knows if this will ever reach you, as I am not sure where you are at the moment, so will probably send it to wrong address.

It seems to me that the lights are going out everywhere. Have just heard a few hours ago about Robert Kennedy,[1] and have been strangely compelled to write letters to quite a few friends and relations – the motivation being, I suppose, *Are you still there?* What has struck me is the difference in feeling now from the time when John Kennedy was killed five years ago – I was in Calcutta at the time, and there was a terrible sense of shock and almost disbelief, plus the feeling (looking at the Calcutta beggars) that someone of good intent and considerable influence was now gone. But now – it isn't a surprise, and this is the appalling thing. It is becoming a commonplace. Robert, whatever his political opportunism may have been, was at least headed in the right direction, and at least stood for some of the necessary things. And one heard it and thought – Yes, there goes another of the leaders who were basically on the side of life. And there is no sense of astonishment – only the feeling that this was to be expected. The New Romans indeed. What to do except mourn?

I received today Mel Hurtig's bookmarks, the publicity thing for The New Romans, and think it looks good. Am anxious to see the book, and have the feeling that when it is published it will actually be more relevant than it was when it was first conceived, which seldom happens to books. More usually the reverse.

On the personal front, the news is heartening. I go a bit berserk when I finish a novel and can hardly bear to have anyone look at it, and pace the floor until I find out what their reaction is, for better or worse. I can bear to know a book is awful but can't bear not to know, at this point, how other individuals have responded.

86

Macmillan's knows my neurosis and they are terribly kind on this score, letting me know as soon as possible – within a week, actually, which is pretty good going. It seems that they have had, to date, 2 very favourable reports from their readers, and Alan Maclean,[2] a Macmillan director and a man whose judgement I trust very much, has read the novel also and thinks it is better than A Jest of God. So this is an enormous relief to me, to know that the characters do actually speak to someone apart from myself. Some minor things may have to be done to manuscript, but in general Alan and his readers feel the form is right, so praise God for that, as I spent quite literally years figuring the bloody thing out. Haven't sent J.G. McC.[3] his copy yet, as I wanted first to get some opinion on it, but now feel slightly more steady in this respect. I guess I care about this one like hell, and so was pretty frightened that the people wouldn't speak to anyone except myself. But it seems they do. I thought, actually, that everything was against me. Instead of writing a novel about a negro homosexual heroin-addicted dwarf, I had written a novel about a white anglosaxon protestant middleaged mum – ye gods. It remains to be seen whether Knopf and McC& S like it, but at least it has come across to somebody. It is called THE FIRE-DWELL-ERS. That's all of us, or so it seems to me.

All the best,
Margaret

---

1. Robert F. Kennedy (1925-1968) had been assassinated at the Ambassador Hotel in Los Angeles on 6 June 1968 after winning the California presidential primary.

2. Alan Duart Maclean (b. 1924) was a director of Macmillan and editor of many numbers of *Winter's Tales*, Macmillan's annual anthology. Laurence published short stories in the anthologies of 1960, 1962, 1963, and 1965. She had rented and subsequently bought Elm Cottage from Maclean.

3. Jack McClelland.

§

Ameliasburgh

13 June 1968

Dear Margaret,

Yah, I know, what a world! Poem of mine in Star Weekly comes out today which I hope to include in this letter.[1] Last section is best. For much of the earlier part I am maybe too damn clever.

One's friends and loves drop away on all sides, public and private. One feels like a comma in an ancient manuscript. Do I touch, feel, think, see as a human being is said to? Or do I just kill? Do I kill something good and delicate in other people, knowing and unknowing?

I'm afraid The New Romans is out of date already. The situation is far worse there, and the polite mealy-mouthed bastards like Pacey and Edinborough[2] who contributed (we wanted fairness and balance) will probably not even now see that the place is a madhouse. I wish it were more relevant, but events seem to me to have passed the book.

I think of a poem of Millay's (Edna St. Vincent) about her friends dying around her, something about the good and the beautiful dropping away – can't quote it but you may know it.[3]

That's a *good* title of yours. It's fine that people you respect like it. I expect to myself, but I will be a little frightened to read it because of your feelings about it. But one (the author of a book I mean) fairly often has those feelings about novels and poems and stuff don't they? Tho lately I say to hell with it, and when some sonuvabitch like Barry Callaghan[4] dislikes my stuff I say it's for personal reasons, as I'm sure it is. You have a big (I said it) international rep, and there are always a few who wanta knock down a person like that, like you. You've met em, I've seen a few myself. Okay, fuck em all. One does one's best, and the good honest critics and friends can judge. They're the ones. The only ones. Call em the Kennedys of one's personal life if you like. The real people, and I descend into cliches.

I have a book of earlier poems out in about two weeks and will zip a copy to you.[5]

I have a thought that the Kennedys too turn into conformists when they assume an office like the Presidency, that the pressures of people around them change them. But they do have some of the necessary good qualities and perhaps retain some of them even later. I think Robert had many, perhaps only slightly changed by his drive for power. I heard him a few times on tv and he was personally very appealing. You had to believe him and goddam wanted to, it was necessary to believe him for your own well- being.

I liked Richler's COCKSURE and wrote him a congratulatory note and he replied saying the Penguin people were gonna do me, Cohen[6] and Layton, and he strongly suggested calling it THE GOY IN THE MIDDLE. Richler's wit makes me think of the minotaur in his maze waiting to devour the stupid. I love that title, but they won't use it.

Strange about men like Kennedy, that their physical presence is so attractive – and of course we say it's what they are as well which makes their physical presence what it is. I heard him on tv, sunday I guess, and he said to a big crowd: "Will you give me your votes?" They roared yes. Then he said "Give me your hands" and they roared and raised their hands. That "Give me your hands" is magic.

Did people feel this way when the Duke of Wellington died, and Churchill, and Alexander the Great and Caesar and all those others? It is a personal love one has for Kennedy, and if one knew him would it verge on the sexual? I suppose for a woman it would.

Christ must stop. Yah, I'm still here. Are you?

Best,

Al

1. "Lament for Robert Kennedy."

2. Desmond Pacey (1917-75) was a well-known critic of Canadian literature and a member of the Department of English, University of New
Brunswick. He had contributed an article to *The New Romans,* as had Arnold
Edinborough (b. 1922), who was the publisher of *Saturday Night* from 1963 to
1970.

3. Perhaps "Dirge Without Music" by Millay (1892- 1950), particularly
the final stanza:

> Down, down, down into the darkness of the grave
>
> Gently they go, the beautiful, the tender, the kind;
>
> Quietly they go, the intelligent, the witty, the brave.
>
> I know. But I do not approve. And I am not resigned.

4. Barry Callaghan (b. 1937) was literary editor of the Toronto *Telegram*
from 1966 to 1971.

5. *Poems for All the Annettes* (rev. ed. 1968) was first published in 1962.

6. Leonard Cohen (b. 1934), Canadian writer and poet, who was best
known at this time for his controversial novel *Beautiful Losers* (1966).

Elm Cottage

4 September 1968

Dear Al–

Thanks for your letter and for sending me the book of poems –
odd about the latter, and maybe you wouldn't agree with me, but
I like the later poems better than the earlier. What I like best about
a great many of them, though, is the terrific way you have of conveying what seems to me a basic dichotomy (and yet maybe it isn't
a dichotomy at all) – ie. the sense of oneself and everything being
so ephemeral and momentary, contrasted with the equally strong
feeling that the aspects of life are interconnected and continuing.
I specially liked SONS AND LOVERS and ENCOUNTER in
these ways. You can convey an almost eerie sense of hearing the

voices of the dead and the unborn, and I like this very much. I'm very glad to see the collection, as it was about time someone brought it out. Is Dave Godfrey still running Ananse[1] Press?

Also many thanks for sending me the two novels from McC& S – I accept gratefully and gracefully, and hope I can find a book or two sometime in which you'll be interested, and send it along.

I expect you'll have gone on the tour by the time this letter arrives. Hope all goes well. The advance sales sound pretty good, although I know they are returnable but let's hope none are returned.

I like the concept of a mermaid with athlete's fin.[2] Not sure if it applies in my case or not, but it sounds impressive as hell! You're right about the title of my novel – it does refer to those who live under stress and danger continually, but not in the sense of what many people would consider to be stress and danger; in this case, merely middleclass city dwellers in (as it happens) Vancouver but really in almost any city.

I think I'm almost as much involved in England as I am in Canada, but really never quite so much. I still feel tremendously split in mind over this question of where to live. I can see all the drawbacks for me personally in Canada – I can't stand to live permanently in a city, but as I don't and won't drive a car, how could I live in a small town near a lake – I'd be utterly isolated. And many other difficulties, some practical and some inner. And also I do care a hell of a lot about this house here, and sometimes wish I could transplant it to Canada – you know, like the Texas millionaires used to do with Scottish castles, etc. But despite all this recognition of the drawbacks of moving back to Canada, I still keep wanting to do so. Not all the time, but it sneaks up on me, leaving me feeling intensely depressed and kind of displaced. Maybe I just haven't yet accepted that you can't go home again. (On the other hand, is it so certain that one can't? Not in the sense of home as you once knew it, but in another sense). I guess if

I didn't have to consider anything or anyone else, I'd probably move back. Sometimes I wish I were quite alone, with nobody else to consider, but I know people who are and they haven't found it such a hot life. It all seems too complicated to think about, so I brood over everything from time to time and analyse it all in my mind and usually end up right where I began, so then I say the hell with it and start writing instead. I guess you are right about following our ancestors' patterns – one never thinks it is going to happen to oneself, only to other and less determined/perceptive/etc people such as one's parents, and when you begin to see the archetypal mould growing around your own life and fitting you into it, it comes as an astonishment – who, me? Yeh, me. So you try to break out of the pattern, and this involves floundering around and battling like crazy, and in the end you find you really have moved somewhat – maybe ¼ inch, like. I remember in my first novel having the idea and viewpoint about the characters that people *could* change within one generation, although only in a limited way. I guess then that I thought (without realizing it) that this was true of everyone except me, and that if I really put my mind to it, I could transform myself. Well, now I am older. All the damn cliches.

It's a good thing you made a poem from your thoughts about that campaign film of Robert Kennedy's. The choice between the two possibilities of the mass reaction seems to me to be frightening because in the end the two reactions amount to the same thing – it's a thing that Wole Soyinka[3] brings out in several of his plays, I think, the intimate relationship between saviour and scapegoat. Should I send you some of Soyinka's plays? He is still in prison, if not dead. Current rumours here suggest that he was killed by the Federal side, but the Federal govt refuses to confirm or deny. He is, or was, the best writer writing in English in Africa, I think.

All the best,
Margaret

ps. why is it Ameliasburg in the poems and Ameliasburg*h* on the address? (I can see you trying to avoid being sued by an irate town council)

---

1. "Ananse" is the British spelling of "Anansi."

2. In an earlier letter to Purdy, Laurence had said that writing *The Fire-Dwellers* made her feel that she was leading a double life with six children (her two and Stacey's four) and two husbands. In his reply Purdy compared this state of mind to "a mermaid with athlete's fin."

3. Wole Soyinka (b. 1934), Nigerian playwright, poet, novelist, and political activist, who was imprisoned from 1967-69 for his efforts on behalf of Biafra's secession from Nigeria.

Elmcot
18 September [1968]

Dear Al–

A brief note to congratulate you on THE NEW ROMANS, which I've just finished reading. I think the book is *good*. Varied, interesting, balanced. Can't help feeling it would be of interest to some Americans, at least, and hope it can be distributed there. I think George Woodcock's article[1] is the best in the book – he has such a strong grasp of history, and such a fair and reasonable mind, in my view. He doesn't emote; he writes it all in low key, but it is so damn effective. Also liked the most of all: Margaret Atwood's poem (she is really good, that girl);[2] your own poem on Che Guevara[3] (which has the same integrity that all your writing seems to have); Robin Mathews' poem;[4] Dave Godfrey's story[5] (which I'd read before; Dave is going to be the best Can prose writer, at least of fiction, in a long time, I think). Also much liked

93

Naim Kattan's article,[6] and Minifie's.[7] Also Mordecai Richler[8] and Larry Zolf[9] (had never previously read anything of Zolf's but think he is clearly very talented). In short, I liked the book. Which is not to say I liked it all – naturally. But what I did think admirable was your choice of a true variety of opinion. I hope it sells forty million copies.

All the best,
Margaret

1. "Various Americas."

2. Margaret Atwood (b. 1939) had contributed "Backdrop Addresses Cowboy."

3. "The Anti-American."

4. "Centennial Song" was the poem by Robin Mathews (b. 1931), who had just returned from two years in England and France to take up the post of Assistant Professor at Carleton University in Ottawa.

5. Dave Godfrey (b. 1938), co-founder with Dennis Lee of the House of Anansi Press in 1966, had submitted "The Generation of Hunters." In 1967, with James Bacque and Roy MacSkimming, he established New Press.

6. Naim Kattan (b. 1928), Head of the Writing and Publishing Section of the Canada Council, had written "Besieged, Neglected, Violated, and Ignored."

7. The journalist James M. Minifie (1900-74) was the author of "Eagle's Feather."

8. Richler had submitted "The North American Pattern."

9. Larry Zolf (b. 1934) was a journalist and producer with the CBC.

§

Ameliasburgh

8 October 1968

Dear Margaret:

Just back from tour in aid of "Romans" and magawd what a lot of chatter I came out with. Joining the Trappists next week. Some sixty interviews.

No, Godfrey is in Europe somewhere on a CC, Dennis Lee[1] is at the Anansi helm, if it has one. Sure, I agree the later poems are better, tho I felt when this book was projected it would bring all the earlier stuff in one place and also give me a chance and a wish to revise. I always get the desire to revise when I have to copy.

Last I heard on "Romans" the sale was over 32,000, which seems pretty good, tho I hope for better. Am supposed to go to N.Y. and Chicago for more yak-yak, so I can't join the Trappists yet. Besides, I have to go to Europe.

Yeah, I can see the car bit when living in country (Canada) would be unpleasant. It takes 90% of you when you drive a car at least, and leaves the remainder of the time you have a bit jangled. That's extreme but it's at least partly true for me. But there's no way out where I'm living.

When you talk about people changing within one generation I wonder how much you have and how much I have. On the surface I've changed a good deal from my own parents who couldn't be more unlike me, or vice- versa. If my parents had really known me they would have thought me some kind of monster. Of course they didn't, and I didn't know them. I suppose you feel much the same, tho it would be difficult for me to consider your parents more hidebound and cast in a mold than mine. You obviously did break out, not just in the matter of place, but in the mode of thought etc. I did too, long ago. Don't think such cliches as "happiness" should be considered either, for I have the feeling most people have about the same degree of contentment unless they are radically mentally different from their fellows, or else a little nuts. Out of a year there's so much sun and so much rain, and kinda think it's nearly similar with people. Of course it's simplistic, can never be verified, not unless we strap on electrodes in the marriage bed. Of course there's sickness of all sorts, but I think one lives with a physical sickness, and in the end as day by day floats by the person parallels in himself a healthy person. Mental sickness is another thing of course. I probably have flaws in all this????

Yes, often thought of that bit about transforming onself. Can one really? My discontent provoked or induced me to break thru into a different sort of personal thinking and writing, or at least I say that's the reason I changed. Does that come from genetic inheritance? I think yes, but it's a combination of many inheritances, therefore not directly parents. Besides they were so conventional in all I know of them that something had to give – or take. Shall we pray for our children?

Yeah, I wouldn't mind seeing Soyinka's plays, tho there's no time. I leave too soon. I met him for a handshake when in England in '65. Saw his truckdriver's play[2] at some rural London theatre. I take it he is/was Biafran.

There is a U.S. ed. of Romans you know? That's why I'm going to U.S., where I shall undoubtedly succumb to the Dylan Thomas disease, at least I would if I had his attractive personality. I'm much too abrasive (or so I'm told) to succumb to anything but hangnail.

Of the contributions you mention, I except myself, but like the others you mention except Mathews' poems and Kattan's article. The latter a bit naive and the former too one-sided, a thing you were not. "I too am North American" – but you can't prove it by your place of residence hey? (I couldn't resist that dig.)

It was pointed out to me by Douglas Fisher[3] in Ottawa that Zolf and Richler are both professional Jews. I didn't like the term at the time, thinking of racial connotations, but I guess it's true. They both use their race as an intimate part of their writing's fabric. I don't do that really, nor do you, (and some would say we are unfortunate in our racial origins, tho I don't for I don't think race that important), believe it's much more subtle and less deliberate on the part of either of us. Of course being a pro Jew is legitimate, but after a while it begins to wear. I've heard so damn many Jewish plays with a smaltzy mama and pop saying oy oy I'm sick of em. Turn em off right away. Shows I'm anti – Still, I really can't say the way Zolf and Richler did their thing is wrong, it's just that so many Jews do that I get tired. That was their boyhood, they talked from a point of view, and so do I even if it isn't so obviously racial. Really, one gets so damn sick of race, difference difference, difference, No, that's wrong, I mean difference in a way that submerges common feelings we all have, like being human is submerged to the degree that we're some particular race. That's better. Okay, I guess it's gonna go on tho.

Best,

Al

P.S. Leave at the end of this month for Europe. Hope to see you some time next year.

----

1. Dennis Lee (b. 1939) was the author of two books of poetry, *Kingdom of Absence* (1967) and *Civil Elegies* (1968). A cultural nationalist, he was co-founder with Dave Godfrey of the House of Anansi Press.

2. *The Road* (1965).

3. Douglas Fisher (b. 1919), former member of Parliament (1957–65), was at this time a syndicated columnist for the Toronto *Telegram* and a member of the Parliamentary Press Gallery.

Elm Cottage
21 October 1968

Dear Al–

Hope this reaches you before you take off for Europe. I meant to reply right away when I got your letter, but life has been unbelievably hectic these past couple of weeks. There are quite a few things I want to say, of a practical nature, so this will be a très practical letter.

First – it now seems almost definite (well, hell, it *is* definite as long as I don't die first) that I shall be going to Toronto as writer in residence next September, [1] and will be in Toronto from beginning of Sept to mid-May. I am delighted at the prospect, although have not yet got all my domestic arrangements arranged. Saw Dave Godfrey when he was in London about a week ago, and we discussed possibilities of some Canadian writer (he's going to suggest several) and wife taking over house and being able to work here for that time, rent and food free, in return for making my kids' dinner at night and generally looking after the place. This seems to me to be a better idea than asking my mother-in-law (who is a dear, but not used to English houses in winter and probably less flexible than a young couple who might not faint at the sight of my coal boiler). Anyway, I hope I can fix it all – in fact, I'm *going* to fix it, or die in the attempt. What this leads me to is this – I have a flat in the house which is now occupied by a young married couple who will be moving out soon, as they now have their own house. I don't plan to re-rent the place, as I want to keep it for whoever comes in when I'm away – my husband will be here most weekends, and if a Canadian writer and his wife were here, it would be nice for them to have their own livingroom etc in case rapport is not supreme. So for the next year – or rather, from about the beginning of December until next July, we will have one large livingroom and one large double bedroom with sink and one kitchenette empty, so if you and your wife want to come and park here for a time, remember that you're welcome, eh?

Thanks so much for sending Brian Moore's novel and Jack Ludwig's.[2] Haven't read either one yet, but am very glad to have them.

Please don't join the Trappists yet. Not that I can believe this is much of a danger, with you. (Al Purdy Quits Talking – can you see the headlines?) I know how you feel, tho, about these publicity tours – they are murder. Have only done it once, the summer A JEST OF GOD was published, and at the end of the time I tottered into McClelland's office and said "I'm a physical wreck", at which he laughed cynically, and said "Well, you'll know enough not to do it again, Margaret" and he was certainly right. But I'm glad THE NEW ROMANS is doing so well, and also very glad about the Amer edition. I think you need to get away now, though.

I was going to send you a copy of my book on Nigerian literature, which comes out this month, but will wait and give you a copy. You don't need to read it – it will be the least read book published this year, I think. Never mind – it's got a lovely dust-jacket.

So much for your crack about me being a non-resident North American!! Yeh, I know. But at this point I've decided I have to stop brooding about it all the time, because then one only feels caught in some kind of trap – I want to go back and live in Canada; my kids are at school here and I don't want to move them; I love Elm Cottage more than anyone should love any place; my husband is established here and working in Surbiton and although our relationship is far from ideal, it is by no means nothing. So I sometimes feel caught and fall into the self-pity trap, which is bloody useless. I've got some things to do this year, and I pray I can get them done, and after that, I guess one plays it by ear. I'm not really ready to make any kind of major leap again, as I did in 1962 when I came here, but I'm not any longer trying to accept the fact that nothing can change – it will, and when the right time comes, I guess I'll know. You're right about change – one does change, but within limits. The thought of one's parents is sometimes too painful to bear (I think of my husband's parents, too, so this gives me two sets of that generation, which is really awful). *Shall we pray for our children?* That's what you said. I guess it is about all we *can* do for them. But they're pretty strong and determined to survive, too, just as we were, so maybe all we can do is to accept the fact that they have to speak a language which we will never be able to hear in its entirety. Where did I start out, and where have I ended up in this letter which was meant to be only practical? Hell. Well, I guess you won't mind.

I saw RACHEL, RACHEL, which was the film of the book, as they say, and thought they had done a splendid job. Al, it was the weirdest experience of my life. I saw my characters and my town (I don't own them, but you know what I mean) *there,* and Joanne Woodward *being* Rachel – it isn't given to many writers to have this kind of truthful portrayal, in another medium, so I'm grateful. Met Woodward last week when she was in London – she is a very intelligent lady.

Let me know your address when you get to wherever you're going.

> Best,
> Margaret

---

1. Laurence was at Massey College, University of Toronto, from September 1969 to May 1970.

2. Ludwig's comic novel *Above ground* (1968) and *I Am Mary Dunne* (1968) by Brian Moore (b. 1921).

❦

Dear Margaret,

Well, congratulations, which I seem to be saying to you continually these days. I mean re the U. of T. thing, which allows you to re-enter Canada as a famous expatriate. Hey, I was on a television interview program in N.Y. in which William Shatner[1] the actor also took part. Leaving with him on the elevator, I said something to the effect that since he's gonna live the rest of his life in the U.S. (he expects to) won't he in effect be a U.S. citizen? But he said no, tho I'm not so sure he won't – Amusing bit on that program, the interviewer asked me if I thought the U.S. of all countries was most permanently on a war economy. I said yes. Then he asked Shatner who said no, and the latter said I was a good poet but not much of an economist. So I said that while William Shatner was a very good actor etc – Not so funny when I repeat it, but at the time I was pleased with myself simply for not being at a loss for words which I generally am on these damn gabfests.

The movie, yes, must've been peculiar for you. I suppose one's thoughts are shadows in the head, but to see the shadows emerge from the brain, someone else's brain, to be still shadows but coloured ones, out of one's own and someone else's head –

Thanks much for the invite to your cottage – now if I just knew where Penn Bucks and Beacon Hill were. But I will stop an average Londoner in a pub and say "Where does Margaret Laurence live?" If he says "Who's she?" I will say "Why, the woman in the movie, 'Rachel, Rachel'."

I really think the U. of T. thing is the best thing that could happen to you – then your decision to live in England will be decidedly confirmed (I think it might be) because it calls for a different sort of thinking to come back permanently (add cliches) – Yes, I do think the outcome will be that you say to yourself nodding wisely, I did the right thing. But it will give you a chance to say that. I don't expect any writer is any longer an integral part of his culture/country the way a postman is, say. Our milieus become excessively literary, and we both love it and hate it. But I hope when you're back here that you'll be able to get away from that scene sometimes, I mean hit the trains, the prairies, the woods etc etc. I guess nothing we do, or any writer does, can escape being considered as grist for the mill rather than for itself –

By the way, you can have New York if you want it, which I doubt. About three programs, yes, three, one cancelled because the book was "scurrilous anti-Americanism" and another stopped after about two minutes because I "had no constructive things to say" which left me chortling all the way down 5th Ave. on the bus gazing up the great empty canyons feel life really had something. There's more to that story which I hope to relate verbally. The three programs that did go on were okay I guess, tho the Trappists are less remote than previously. There is a projected purdy selected poems in the wind with Random House, tho as to how far it goes[2] – …?

Life is still chaos even now we get back (Eurithe came along to N.Y.), and seem so many little things to do before we get away. Trouble is they get in the way of poems, I have three in longhand and don't know what they're like so long since I wrote them – Well, see you sometime in the spring or before then I guess, not sure exactly,

Best,
Al

---

1. William Shatner (b. 1931) began his acting career in Canada and left the country in the mid-1950s for Broadway and American films.

2. *Selected Poems* (1972) was published by McClelland and Stewart. There was no Random House edition.

§

Dear Al–

Brief note, in case it catches you before you leave, as your letter seemed to imply you weren't instantly on the point of takeoff.

Hurrah for you in New York interviews – those things are murder, anyway, not that I've ever done any in N.Y. Thought N.Y. was terrifying when I was there 2 yrs ago, and was so depressed by no trees around anywhere and all the huge buildings that I thought were about to descend and crush me. And yet some of the people I know there – my agent, and people at Knopf, seem to me some of the wisest and least frenetic people I know.

Don't ask in Eng pub re: me – blank stares all around, even if you asked in offices of literary publications. Well, it's better that way, really. The novels are only novels among the millions published here every year, and I work best in that atmosphere. Not that I'm falsely modest – I take great pleasure, as a matter of fact, in the way that for the moment my books are read in Canada. But I think you have to live as a human being, not a writer, and this is what I can do here. Still have awful dichotomy of mind, and don't know how I'll feel about Canada after being in Toronto next year. I love the damn country, that's the trouble – I mean the country, not the cities, and I love quite a number of people there. Of course I love quite a few people here, too, now, and I love the country here, as well – so total split mind.

Have just discovered in one blinding flash of the obvious that I may have 2 more novels there, not just one. Well, well. Maybe I'll go on writing into my old age after all.

What I hope to do when in Canada, at some point, is go to northern Manitoba. This may be a fantasy, but not if I'm determined to do it, I guess. Want to get up to Churchill somehow and then drive if possible from Churchill to York Factory, the trek the earliest Selkirk settlers walked, when their ship landed at the wrong place. Don't know how many miles – about 150? – but they walked it in early spring, men women and kids, plus bagpipes – that story has some meaning for me, but am not sure yet what it is.

Please drop a line from wherever you are in Europe – Greece? If Greece, how I envy you. When you can get to England, write or phone (Penn 2103) and let us know when you want to come out – will give instructions about travel at that time. Very simple to get out here. One takes a train from Marylebone station, smallest station in London, only 4 platforms so that even I can't get lost.

Best,

Margaret

P.S. Wonderful news about the Random House collection! Congrats.[1]

---

1. This was added on the back of the airmail letter.

c/o Canadian Embassy

31 Vass. Sophias Ave.

Athens

2 December 1968

Dear Margaret,

Greeting – Seems like quite a while since I wrote, but life is extremely disorganized here – How are you? Damp and cold in England's famed muggy climate? Here I hasten to mention, things are even worse. The damn rain rains all the damn time every damn minute. Sun? That's for Greeks, I guess, not foreigners. Anyway, Eurithe and myself wound over Europe from

Luxembourg in a "couchette" most of the way, thru Germany, Austria, Yugoslavia and finally Greece. With a Greek porter who must have either liked us or decided there was something to gain from good treatment (he asked me to write a letter saying how well I was treated by him to Wagons Lits Cook in Athens, which I did) for he guarded our privacy like God, in a six person couchette we were the only passengers all the way from Munich to Athens, a helluva long way. Before Munich we were in an ordinary compartment which had eight people, including two Greek women so pregnant it was like a herd of elephants inside a ping-pong ball.

But finally Athens. Around ten days now. Have climbed the Acropolis like good little tourists, listening to other marvelling tourists (Gee whiz, Myron, you just don't know what to say, you're just speechless), went to the national museum where the Mycenaean masks are (wrote a poem)[1] (also poem about the acropolis), wandered the Kerameikos graveyard (where Pericles is buried),[2] but to hell with Lykobettos hill, which is too much for my leg muscles – I was gonna copy a poem, but keep changing it as I read it over

THE SHOUT[3]
Walking among chattering dodging jostling
Greek pedestrians in the street of the shoemakers
whose middle-of-the-road progress
is a human dogfight with motor traffic
– thinking of Pericles in Kerameikos graveyard
with the Eridanos River oozing along the Sacred Way
with human millions under the ground and being
the ground itself as if there was some puzzle
among the dead as if their non-existence
is a clause in some ancient contract baked into
a clay tablet of which I am a codicil
The kid came from nowhere

behind me shouting loud in my ear leaving
me slightly startled his red sweater
a flash of light bound for that other
Eridanus which is a sky
constellation known to astronomers
and the gods whom I am ignorant of
Not Munch's shout of personal terror
on the bridge of nowhere nor
derisive mockery of foreigners in Attica but
something to say thank you for and
I do say thank you you little bastard
and notice I'm walking in cold shadow
on the sunless side of the road jump
back to the middle among reckless Greeks chuckling

Our friends the McDonalds here in Athens, had dinner with
them last night, drinking Dutch beer and feeling it today – We
shall leave for Crete in the next few days, looking for a little sun in
this sunless country. Temperature isn't that cold, but it seems cold
anyway.

Best,

Al

---

1. "The Death Mask," included in *A Handful of Earth* (1977).
2. "Kerameikos Cemetery," included in *Sundance at Dusk* (1976).
3. A revised version of this poem appeared in *A Handful of Earth*.

[Athens]

3 December 1968

Dear Margaret,

Saw "Rachel, Rachel" last night, and felt like writing you a
note afterwards – I think you mentioned that the picture is a

triumph for Joanne Woodward (and I think for Paul Newman by the same token) – And I think the old stream-of-consciousness techniques have seldom been put to better use, nor one person more thoroughly explored.

Nothing much happens yet a great deal happens, and this suggests the large areas that many novels and films neglect, or perhaps suggests a misplaced emphasis on such things as violence etc., the on-the-surface more dramatic things that produce the sudden flush or swift paling, and floods of words. Whereas Rachel was an inward movie – or does all this seem elementary to you? It might well seem that way to you, since you've thought of it in connection with the film more than I – As I remember, your "Stone Angel" was similar re the inward stuff –

Anyway, it was an excellent film, and I can recall few unfaithfulnesses to the novel. In one way, you might say it's a novel and film of repeated anti-climax, lesbianism being incipient only, pregnancy that turned out to be a cyst; the religious affair was pretty horrifying. I thought Rachel was gonna get up and run frantically away from it all – And the continuous rapt smiling expression of Calla – There was something wrong with the sound in the theatre we went to, or else Woodward threw away some of her lines – and I had difficulty making out some things – At the end I had the impression that Rachel has acquired strength from the abortive abortion incident and others, and now is as much in control of her life as she can be.

We are getting ready to leave for Crete in the next few days, hoping it will be warmer there, and being assured it is to some degree.

Best,
Al

§

Dear Al–

This won't reach you before you take off for Crete, but maybe you will pick it up somewhere along the line. Thanks for your 2 letters. I was glad you liked RACHEL, RACHEL, and was fascinated by the thought that you and your wife were seeing it in Greece. Seems odd, somehow, as though the messages get sent out and are picked up by the most unlikely radio receivers. Not that RACHEL, RACHEL was really my message, but I did feel it related to the book quite a lot, and personally thought they had done a very good job on it. The oddest things to me, apart from seeing Rachel in some kind of flesh, were the signs in the town – MANAWAKA THEATRE, etc, and then the graveyard, much later on, with the Cameron's stone, black granite, and I felt very peculiar, because the town name Manawaka came first to my mind about 20 years ago, when I made my first abortive attempt to write a novel (it was never finished) – and that town, mine, I guess, has been known in my mind by that name ever since – how odd to see it in letters, like that, externally. The cemetery likewise – the people who did the film knew or sensed the way the thing should be, and that goddamn stone could have been my family's burial stone in the town I came from – it, too, is black granite, and looks just the same. The last time I visited Neepawa, I went (crazily, as I knew) to the cemetery, and looked at my family's stone – my father and my mother being skeletons somewhere there, quite meaninglessly, for if they exist at all (and they do – all the ancestors do) it is not in crumbling calcium bone but in my head. In short, I was moved by the film – thought they did as well as anyone could possibly have done, and was also surprised by the themes which when I saw the film I recognized as recurrent in my writing. Like Barry Callaghan once said to me in an interview, "Why are you so obsessed with death? Why are your characters so neurotic and gloomy?" and one tried to say they were *not* more neurotic than anyone else, but of course the red-blooded young man could not buy that one.

Dave Godfrey has been here for the past week – returned to France last Friday. It was lovely to have him here, and to talk a lot with him. He will be the best prose writer in Canada, within 10 years, and will almost certainly extend far beyond Canada. It nearly frightens me when I talk to him, because in some ways he knows his own value but in other ways he can't quite yet believe it and also maybe feels he has a lot of time in which to work. God forgive me, I keep batting at him to ignore all else, within financial reason, and do the books he has to do, because maybe he will have 10 or 15 years but he won't have forever, and the most important thing is to get the books written. He is so bloody talented he scares me. He knows a lot more than I do, of course, about organizing one's life – finances, for example, he is really good about. But he is only beginning to see that he isn't going to live forever and he damn well better get his work done while he can. Of course nobody can be protected – and Dave doesn't need protecting; he can do it all himself. And he will. I guess I care about him in something the way one might care about one's children, although the guy is nearly 30 – it is just that he has really got it, and one would like to ensure that he has good writing conditions and not too many money worries for the next decade, so the essential things can be accomplished. But he knows all this, basically, and like anyone else who has to get the writing done, he is pretty canny about providing somehow the means.

How I envy you in Greece. Thanks for poem. It reminded me so much of once when Jack and I went on what was called the FIVE DAY ULTRA CLASSICAL TOUR, namely bus ride around famous places. At Mycenae, I did not want to listen to the guide reeling off the facts about how the step-graves were discovered, etc, so I left the party and walked to the top of the hill, where – at least mythically – Agamemnon, King of Men, fell by his wife's hand. Lots of primitive stones – the whole place was the fort of a barbarian king. And when I reached the place, on top of the hill, where Agamemnon fell (either in his bath, stabbed by Clytemnestra, or in the banqueting hall, according to various interpretations), suddenly a small high-pitched voice said in American to me, "Hi." And there was this kid, both less and more real than Agamemnon. What could you say? I said "Hi." Agamemnon was the ancestors, in a sense the romanticized ancestors. The kid was now, here, real, and possibly mine. One couldn't cast off either one.

Crete – well, I hope you've loved it. I did. Was very very uncertain about Sir Arthur Evans work at Knossos[1] – his reconstruction seemed only an educated guess, but maybe better to have some physical reconstruction rather than the broken columns one sees at Delphi etc etc. When you see in the Heraklion museum just what *was* left of the murals of Knossos (one or two tiny fragments) you see that the reconstruction was a kind of fantasy.

Best to you both. Visit here when you can.

Margaret

---

1. Sir Arthur Evans (1851-1941), British archaeologist, best known for his excavations and studies of the ancient Minoan civilization of Crete.

Athens
5 January 1969

Dear Margaret,

Thanks much for the mag,[1] was a nice-good thought – I had read all but R.S. Thomas[2] among these poets, but he made up for the rest. Despite his rigidity of form (which I find a barrier sometimes), he has some very effective ways of saying things. The things themselves? I dunno – Long acquaintance with Hughes, Gunn and Larkin[3] have made them seem very tame to me, tho that's not the word – they describe excellently things I don't find very important, which is likely my own fault. In the poem by Thomas called "Iago Prytherich" which ends with the guy in the fields: "Marring the simple geometry/Of the square fields with its gaunt question./My poems were made in his gaunt shadow/Falling coldly across the page/"[4] this strikes me as very well-expressed, but I am a bit repelled at the idea of writing in anyone's shadow, and perhaps this is my own ego speaking. Not that I don't admire others etc. and I know Thomas means a bit more than just being influenced – But he writes well, very well.

We are still stuck here in Athens, as if it were a rut. I've written some fifteen poems which, in some sense, leaves me conscience-free re Canada Council. But I feel guilty about the Birney book which I dislike doing, and probably will try to wriggle out of – I'm just not a lit-man in the sense of writing critical books, reviews is the best I can do.

Noting your comment on skeletons and ancestors, that they do exist in your head I state the obvious agreement – they also exist as unknowing and unknown influences: tho when I see my kid use me as an excuse for his actions I am enraged. He's right, but not that much right. Your reply to Callaghan your characters not more neurotic than anyone else, I think that this is true except for the many near-vegetables in the world, and I insist there are these.

Had a letter from Dave Godfrey asking wife and I for Christmas which was "nice" of him, but letter arrived too late. In any case I feel sodden and anchored in Greece thru my own inertia right now. Incidentally, I agree about his ability, and that he knows it too – but in some obscure sense this knowing is almost a handicap. For instance, I sometimes alternate between exultation at what I think I am and have done, then depression at what I can't do, which is defined by itself and its coming into being. I don't know if Godfrey feels any of this, and wouldn't ask him, since I believe his own ego gets in the way and he might sense some insult or slight, in fact probably does somehow anyway. As I know some of his thoughts that are quite wordless, he also knows some of mine – And this hangup I somehow do not have with you. I have seen so many people, promising people, fall flat in the mud, that I do not believe in promise only, or at least not as equating with accomplishment. The latter is far too chancy; also I do not or am not either quite sure that the attitude that knows it can do a thing tho the thing is not yet done – I'm not sure if that's good either.

Bob Weaver has written me asking me to do a poem-for-voices re Canada now, and despite the deadline of July 1, I'd rather try this than do other duty things. Except, I don't like the damn thing being so explicit as to now. Here's my capsule plot. New ruins (imaginary) are discovered in Anatolia, plus clay tablets which are translated by a prof with a brief intro to the p.f.v. This ancient country of ruins was next door to say the Hittites or other larger ancient country. Its settlement was two (by) waves of barbarians, and it had neolithic inhabitants who are subjugated by the two later races. "It is a cramped little state with no foreign policy" and is dominated by Hittite neighbours, who use its timber and horses etc and protect it from other warlike neighbours for that reason. Of course these ruins have their parallel in Canada, with the U.S.A. as dominating neighbour. After the prof's intro, setting the stage, the whole p.f.v. is taken from the newly translated clay tablets. The scribe who wrote and baked them is perhaps fled, but he mourns in non-lachrymose degree his lost country which some great catastrophe had overtaken, "and I only am left to tell thee –" This is the reverse of the science-fiction plot that has some star travellers finding ruins on earth which has been done to death, and by the same token, has this been done to death? Also, what is the great catastrophe that overtakes Canada

and the ancient one? And here I have to look straight at Canada
and decide what fate will overtake it.

THE POPE'S 1968 ENCYCLICAL[5]
"No pills
              no raunchy rubbery pleasure rubbing
against rough duty in the luke-warm
vulva robbing the rich seed-bed of sons
Rather stumble betimes from cold coition
cursing haggardly the name of Onan
wiping dry musk thy member remembers
and swear to the dank meat-eyed bone-faced
creature fronting the boudoir mirror
cunt was never wholly thy motive also
swear to the blood-god donating false dawn
who must be truthfully answered master
fucking and love were not different matters" – However
a rose is a rose is a rose

I thank thee lord that to mine eyes
leaf-shine and springtime were complete accidents
and pike some cold January in Roblin Lake
romantically mistaking a drowned rubber boot
for female may give it their best try
they have seasons tickets and my blessing
I thank thee that nothing was laid on previously
and breasts like unto the roe feeding among lilies
may hunger greatly despite thy maidenform brassiere
I loved equally the sun's yellow menstrual blood
& irregardless the cold menopausal thrust of winter
In short and to wit and with due modesty
I don't wish to be taken credit for
I don't wish to be earmarked on an assembly line
I insist on entire anonymity
I reject all odds of being anyone else but me

I am my own my entire my sole responsibility

And when in the course of time and the fullness
of my years I go down eventually
into the valley of the shadow of death
I expect to make my own travel arrangements

(Wanted to copy above while there was room, in case you might
chuckle)
(It will still take some working, since the bit about love and fucking at end of first verse not quite what I wanted –)

Anyway: play, I mean poem for voices, plot. I use the Ventris
translation[6] as a basis for my prof's, and the nostalgic scribe bears
the body of the play. i.e. we are listening to the past and also
present and future. Is this just silly? I hope you don't mind my
working on this while I'm writing you, because obviously that's
what I'm doing. (I am drinking Triple Sec to help hinder my
mental non-processes) I am looking for a catastrophe just as
Cafafy in "Waiting for the Barbarians"[7] – But I also and self-
consciously want something workmanly poignant, craftsmanly
meaningfully movingfully goddam real. i.e. not all craft. That's
the frame, but what can be placed inside it? There are all sorts of
obvious things: the scribe has a dream of armed Hittite horsemen
crossing the borders. The neolithic inhabitants (golden age
Indians) rebelling as their number swell thru improved techniques of birth. But those are very obvious, and will probably be
included anyway. Such a play could fall flat so easily and likely
will. But I believe the reversal of the usual star travellers in future
discovering ruins of past is a good idea. It's far-off from what
Weaver wants tho. I can think of hitch-hikers on camels as paral-
leling riding freight trains, which I did as a kid. But that sort of
nostalgia fucks up the straightforward parallels I want to get
across.

I'd better leave it. The poems I've written are mostly about
Canada, as your novels in England are – hey? (tho not your african

short stories) Objectivity elsewhere? Shove that in thy maiden-form brassiere.

Anyway, feel my physical energy is running all downhill, and should write that play whether Weaver wants it on that theme and treatment or not. But poignant love love love has gotta be in there like a dirty shirt which is real real real. (I have stood upon a hill/And trembled like a man in love/A man in love I was and I/Could not speak and could not move (W.J. Turner))[8] Anyhow, 'twill take time.

Another short piece:

ST. PAUL to the CORINTHIANS[9]
We decided some time back that
we were stuck with each other more
or less when I said "You bitch" it no
longer meant she was exactly
that but conversely it ain't
no valentine dear when she says
"You bastard" it means I may
be one but she forgives me
which is rather harder to bear
And I want the people to know
                    Corinth

Dunno how long intend to stay here, since if I prophesy always wrong. Some cold sleepless dawn stumble downstairs with bagg[ag]e to hulk morosely on a boat or train – But Turkey appeals somewhat, since I may find those Canadian ruins some-where in ancient Anatolia.

                    Best,
                    Al

THE POPE'S 1968 ENCYCLICAL
"No pills
        no raunchy rubbery pleasure rubbing

against rough duty in the luke-warm
vulva robbing the rich seed-bed of issue
Instead stumble betimes from cold coition
cursing haggardly the name of Onan
wipe off the dry musk thy member remembers
and swear to the dank meat-eyed bone-faced
creature fronting the boudoir mirror
cunt was never wholly thy motive also
swear to the blood-god donating tumescence
who must be truthfully answer[ed] master
fucking was not mine only intention but love
divine love certainly that kind
or another must definitely be included" – However
a rose is a rose is a rose

I thank thee lord that to mine eyes
leaf-shine and springtime were a complete accident
irrespective of the Julian calendar
and pike some cold January in Roblin Lake
romantically mistaking a drowned rubber boot
for female may give it their best try
they have seasons tickets and my blessing
I thank thee that nothing was laid on previously
and breasts like unto the young roe feeding among lilies
may hunger greatly despite the maidenform brassiere
I loved equally the sun's yellow menstrual blood
& irregardless the cold menopausal thrust of winter
In short and to wit and with due modesty
I don't wish to be anticipated
I refuse to be earmarked on any assembly line
I insist on entire anonymity in fact
I reject all odds but me in the unprofane lottery
I am my own my entire my sole responsibility

And when in the course of time and the fullness
of my years I go down eventually
into the valley of the shadow of whatever-it-is
I expect to make my own travel arrangements

Margaret,

Revised this on accounta copying it for the letter to you – So
(tell me true) is "whatever-it-is" better or worse than "death"?
Typewriter acting up.

Best

Al

---

1. The identity of the magazine is unknown.

2. Ronald Stuart Thomas (b. 1913), Anglo-Welsh poet.

3. Thom Gunn (b. 1929) and Philip Larkin (b. 1922), British poets.

4. The poem, "Iago Prytherch" (Purdy had misspelled the title), was published in *Poetry for Supper* (1958) and its second last line is "my poems were made in its long shadow."

5. A later version of the two drafts of the poem included in this letter was published in *The Quest for Ouzo* (1971).

6. Michael Ventris (1932-56) had published with John Chadwick *Documents in Mycenaean Greek: Three Hundred Selected Tablets from Knossos, Pylos, and Mycenae with Commentary and Vocabulary* (1956).

7. This is a poem by Constantine Cavafy (1863-1933), the Greek poet.

8. Walter James Turner (1889-1946), poet and novelist. Purdy quotes a stanza from his poem "Epithalamium":

> I have stared upon a dawn
> And trembled like a man in love
> A man in love I was, and I
> Could not speak and could not move.

9. A revised version of this poem was published in the collection *Love in a Burning Building* (1970).

〜

Elm Cottage
10 January 1969

Dear Al–

Thank Gawd for your letter! It arrived like a rain in a dry season, and I do mean dry, as I shall explain presently. So if this turns out to be about 10 airletters long, it is only that I feel a decided need to communicate with someone who knows what I am talking about. First, re: your letter. I didn't actually read the poems in the little book I sent you – saw it in a bookshop and thought it would be a good Christmas card; was in too busy a state even to read it, but thought the poets might be of interest to you. Should've realized you would have read most of the poems.

Re: your comment on Dave Godfrey – odd, really, that you should say it concerned you that he knows his ability, because when he stayed here for that week, in December, I felt exactly the same thing – in fact, I deliberately refrained from talking about his ability, when I was talking with him re: his novel which he's working on, and about his future work. I only urged him not to take on too many other jobs, ie teaching and publishing, all at once, because it is important for him to have time to write, and he is young enough to think he'll have forever, but he won't – he'll probably have about 15 years, and those will be the most important for him, and if he doesn't get the books which are in him done in those years, he'll likely not get them done. But I kept thinking – don't tell this guy he is good; it's a danger to him. In some weird way, I know precisely what you mean by a sense of uncertainty being some kind of help, because I feel as you do, when I want to begin something, that it's there to be done, but whether it'll get itself done even halfway right is something unknown to me, something that is a gamble each time, luck or the gods or what? I can't sit down and think "Now I am going to write a novel" – I feel convinced that the characters exist in some other dimension, and I pray like hell to make direct contact with

118

them, and not to try to manipulate them, and to let the thing happen by itself, and all that kind of thing. But certain is not what I feel. In a way, everything is like starting from scratch. Maybe Dave feels that, too – I don't know. But I like him enormously, and can talk in some areas with him extremely well, and yet there is a feeling I get when I'm with him – I feel he is much younger than I am, and yet he is also a lot smarter and knows more, and this makes me feel uncomfortable, because it's true and also not true, if you know what I mean. I guess I feel he really is enormously talented, but I wish he either felt or expressed a little more doubt or – maybe not doubt, just homage to some non-existent protector god? Do I know what I'm talking about? Do you? Also, he doesn't seem to have to grapple with many personal faults, and maybe I find this hard to take in some ways, which is idiotic of me, as undoubtedly he does have to grapple with same, just like I do. I guess I feel a little in awe and yet resentful of people who don't smoke, who never drink too much, never have to go on diets, who aren't in any way beat-up.

Re: your play, or poem-for-voices – I can see it is taking shape, and probably it is working away like yeast in some subconscious wine-vat of your mind, and I'm glad you told me about it. I think the reverse of the usual SF theme could be terrific, and I think the whole thing really depends on how it works itself out – ie. I think you'll sweat blood trying to figure it all out, and in the end, with a hell of a lot of possibilities churning around, you'll find that the right combination of concepts, words, ancestral voices etc, comes out – or of course doesn't come out; that's the gamble. Anyway, I think it sounds fascinating, and maybe when you write it, you'll discover the ending – I hope it doesn't appal you too much. Interesting, your fascination with the ancestral voices – it bugs me, quite a lot, too, and yet in some way mine at this point are all connected with the old celtic bit, although in other ways with the caveman, too, I guess. I don't know what the hell I'll write next as a novel, if it ever comes, but something seems to be going on and

I hope someday it'll crystallize. I sure as hell don't want to write an historical novel, God forbid. Something in the area of legend, or half-legend, or legend even seen distortedly through contemporary eyes – who knows? It's peculiar, this feeling that something is there, but so far mostly invisible, and you can't catch it by trying to pounce on it, but just wait for awhile and think about it sort of casually, as though pretending not to think of it, like the Chinese giving their sons girls' names so the gods wouldn't be tempted to take them away.

Re: your poem, thanks for copying it twice – the revised version is better, there is no doubt about it. I like it; agree with it – what more can I say? Except to say that I don't, personally, much like either "whatever-it-is" or "death" for the next-to-last line, and wonder if perhaps in some way either word is necessary? It's none of my goddamn business, but you did ask for an opinion, and I throw this out to you for free but very hesitantly – could it just be "the valley of the shadow" or "the valley of the shadow of"? Probably not. Anyway, there it is for what it's worth.

I loved ST. PAUL TO THE CORINTHIANS, although actually its meaning to me was more personal than biblical or impersonal or whatever-the-hell, which maybe was what you meant and maybe wasn't and it doesn't matter except I understand one meaning of it which is as close to me as my own neck-vein, (like the Muslims say of Allah, and I've always liked that expression). See my forthcoming novel for yet another version of this fascinating and eternal theme. Ho ho.

Well, re: all my many problems – they are less than sometimes, but the situation is bloody well chaos at the moment, although controlled chaos, if you see what I mean.

In a word – HERE I AM WITH FIVE CATS, 25 GOD-DAMN FUSCHIA PLANTS AND NO BOOZE. (Could one make an Eliot-like poem of that sentence?)

Wait. I can explain. A Canadian friend of mine (nearly all my friends are Canadians; odd, eh?) is moving house and like a fool I said I'd look after her three cats for a time, and also her fuschia plants. Now I have her 3 cats and 2 of my own, and they all hate each other and act like miniature tigers and I am beginning to hate all of them. Thank God my tenants moved just before Christmas, so I have their large livingroom and have stashed the guest cats in there, where they eye me with suspicion and malice when I go in to feed them. They won't go outside, as they are experiencing some kind of trauma, so they lurk in there, thinking sinister thoughts. They are like three versions of Bast, the Egyptian goddess of (war? death? something), and in a way it is all kind of like a musical comedy. I don't actually mind them, but it is just sort of peculiar. The fuschias are quiet, and need watering only once a week – they are supposed to grow better if you talk to them, but I don't – I snarl, so goodness knows what colour they will be when they bloom. Black, probably. The booze – I decided I had to quit. [...] However, will probably not remain a teetotaller all my life; but at least will try to go through this regime for awhile, in the interests of survival and so on.

Like a damn fool I agreed to give a lecture on TRIBALISM IN NIGERIAN CONTEMPORARY LITERATURE, both at Univ of Leeds and at Univ of London, Institute of Commonwealth Studies, and have been working like hell on it, and it is still a mess and I do not even get paid for it. I know how you feel about the Birney book – I really am no good at this sort of lecture, article, lit. crit, etc – I just do not LIKE doing it. Next year, in Toronto, as writer-in-res, I hope I can get away with only about 2 lectures, and the rest just chatting and seminars and reading kids' unpublished fiction, etc. Otherwise, it will be hell. Why does one agree to do these things? Weakmindedness, and the desire to please, or sometimes to make money, I guess.

Good news, though – Macmillan has accepted my re-written version of the kids' book I wrote, and they even like it! Hurrah. I still have to do some work on it, if ever I can forget about African novels – never want to see an African novel again, ever. The kids' book was the one where the hero was a mole.

By the way, have discovered non-alcoholic wine, like grape juice, really, of different kinds, some dry white and not bad at all, and I drink bottles of the stuff. In a way it is rather pleasant to drink without any effects, although not always. When I think of the retsina in Greece – my God, how I envy you! Not just the wine, tho, because I love the country. Hope it warms up soon there and you experience an upsurge of energy, etc.

Re: cats – Al, I truthfully never thought I would end up keeping a cathouse!

All the best,
Margaret

[P.S. deleted]

§

Athens
13 January 1969

Dear Margaret,

It is to laugh – years ago in high school at the age of 13 I admired a poem of Carm's, which may be why I'm writing now. "Arnoldus Villanova/six hundred years ago/said peonies have magic/and I believe it so."[1]

[. . .]

I have writ the best poem yet, and will copy it later, so probably shouldn't have said I think it good. Incidentally, by the time I got your letter I had already made the change you suggested – odd, eh? I'm so pleased with this one that some of the burden of duty-guilt is lifted from my shoulders for not writing more and better stuff. Feel no guilt at all for not doing more on the Birney book, I mean not the same kind of burden at all –

Had a letter from Dave inviting me to live in his house in France while he is away for a month and "I felt for him a transport of cordiality" which is Dickinson isn't it?[2] But had to refuse graciously as is my nature, since I would've just had to come back to Greece later anyway, to go and do the things and places I want to visit. But very good of him to think of it –

There is something about writers, novelists, poets and most of them – that want you to see them as if they had already done and written their good fine books: probably it's part of human nature in any line of whatever – Except maybe athletics, which so definitely goes by compared times and knockouts and such. I suppose we do, most of us, admire people for their capabilities and potentialities as much or more than anything – but it seems somehow wrong. I don't believe – if there's any relation – in the genius who has been passed over indefinitely. Obviously one doesn't hear of them. I mean you gotta lay it on the line, take your chances with what you write, and let the chips fall etc. And with some the esoteric schools and cults like Black Mountain and others – they have the excuse that the public isn't ready yet for them, and can point to people like James Joyce for proof of their own pudding – i.e. experimenters don't get the recognition they deserve right away (tho sometimes they do, for many think there's virtue in experimentation as such rather than what is said) – I'm getting off the subject tho, which is meant to be Dave. Sure, I agree all the way down the line about him – but have the odd feeling that so many (Celtic feeling, which I am one third?) break a leg or something before they write the novels everyone tells them they can and deserve to write – "Break a leg" isn't what I mean – the mere telling them (as you say) acts against their doing it, almost like talking out a good novel or poem – I guess I'm saying much the same thing you did –

Your bit about cats and fuschias is great, makes me see the hammy novelist peering behind a letter. (By the way, I lost twenty pieces of mail in the post my paw-in-law sent along in a large envelope, the which disgusts me) – The bit about you seeing your people in another dimension is hard for me to grasp, since I discover things in writing, rarely have them worked out – but that too is what you're saying, that you discover what already exists. That somehow seems to take some credit away from you, which I don't like. At least, nobody but YOU could discover them. It would take a better man than Freud (and certainly me) to figure that out. I've said sometimes that: the mind leaps very rarely in the act of creation, does more than it's really capable of – which is my own way of explaining me to me, always assuming my leaps are higher than a typewriter shift lever. But I try to reconcile another dimension with my own so-called leaps. It can be reconciled, but I don't like the assumption that things already exist – Neither one is really any explanation, as I think you'll agree. I suppose some part of the stuff I do is mere reaction: I look at something that's bad and say it wasn't like that at all, and reaction leads one into opposite excesses. (like my "crudity" maybe)

Re the Celtic stuff, I like it sometimes in Yeats, but it too causes reaction in me. It's much like, at least related [to], the visions some people have told me they have – one beat writer told me that in particular – I don't know whether to be envious or not, since I've never had a vision in my life, and perhaps take perverse pride in not having them. Always know where I am and what I'm doing and take responsibility etc., which is equally revolting. I have the feeling I'm being very dull in this letter, whereas yours are beautiful –

The neck-vein meaning in St. Paul is probably the right one – Your description of cats and fuschias gives me an inferiority complex apart from enjoyment, since I can't go and do likewise – On the other hand, you snarling at fuschias is too much for me, and I'm forced back into poems screaming protest that you're takin advantage – Christ, it's a good thing my ego is solidly seated in rubber – Even in letters the prose-ability comes thru like a palimpsest of the mind.

It seems your booze problem and my own are also similar. As you know, booze is cheap here, esp. brandy which I love – and have had a head enough to take it easy. Now drink one or two beer a day. I like triple sec like a glutton and liable to drink half a bottle, jesus!

Have you thought that Dave saying "nobody drinks any more" was a kinda thoughtless thing for him to say? If so, why didn't he think of it? But then, I shove my foot in my mouth so many times I should talk. Well, drugs have never appealed to me thank Bacchus! Mention makes triple sec necessary, alcohol and vitamins wow. Please note effect if any succeeding –

Your lecture title sounds awful – there, I have foot & mouth disease. So why not save all lectures for possible use at U. of T. and I will listen to you and laugh? Poet has a big advantage there, he can just read his bloody stuff – comment if he feels like – Course you run outa material much sooner. Wow, Tribalism in – You must save that one for U. of T. – go great with C. Bissell,[3] who is not really a bad guy since he was perceptive enough to write a good review of New Romans on accounta M. Laurence was included. (triple sec?)

Hurray for your monster book, I mean children's – ! African novels? I got Tutola's "Palm Wine Drunkard" and "Life in the Bush of Ghosts" four years ago and never read em – are they good? As the author of "Tribalism"[4] – you should be able to tell me – I would like [to] take "Stone Angel" – By the way, I've read only three books of yours, the two last novels and a book of African short stories which the library kindly loaned me – Can one pick up the first eds of the others in London so one (me) can get em signed by author? It's a lotta fun doing that, since then I feel half collector, half financial entrepreneur, and half lover – Which is three triple sec halves – works fast, eh?

Non-alcoholic wine is revolting, don't do it, will ruin your intolerance. Can't stand retzina, which I find is pure idealization on your part. The brandy, however, might be made the source material for an address on "Periclean Alcoholism Among the Early Mycenaeans" ?? In fact, I'm beginning to hate Mycenaeans. In fact, shit on the Dendra curiass.[5] (reaction, ah reaction!) I suppose really I hate the Canada Council which forced me to improvise reasons for going to Greece, yet I applaud the Canada Council, so how do I explain that?

Vitamins are being got the best of by alcohol, and I see I will have to copy poem later, even tho I would much rather send the damn poem by telepathicommunication or something – BUT, MUST SEND POEM. REPEAT, must, s e d .y ... god dam poem –

(don't drink nonalcoholic triple sec with deja vu)

> Best,
> [unsigned]

THE GAME BEFORE THE EGG[6]
Childhood – when toads and frogs rain down the sky,
which is summertime, of course ...
In winter water pours from gardenhose
to ice in town backyards,
coal-shovels clear a battlefield for boys,
and mothers watch anxiously from rear windows:
King Arthur's court, with Eaton's catalogue
for breastplate, a hockey stick for lance –

The later legend has a big league scout
sitting in smoky small-town rinks,
watching the local flash, signing him
to a contract guaranteeing fame & riches –
Begin before the beginning,
shortly after birth, even before school,
with ice luckily thick or drowning thin:
the kids swarm like mustard seed,
and never practise always play –

126

And sometimes on hard-crusted river snow
I've seen the game escape its limits,
and leap the width and breadth of things,
become a mad chase going nowhere out
past dangerous places where the current
nibbles cheese holes – out to the wide wide bay:
where iceboats leave their track to race with birds,
and fishing shanties are small castles beyond the town,
and slow clouds lift their bodies like giant goalies –

Miles out in the far country
of Quinte the child stands
– senses he is being watched,
glances down below his feet
which seem supported
by nothing above black glass,
and shadows with eyes,
green shapes look back:
"Gills for lungs, good sir?"
Motionless as a waterfall,
he stands outside time,
and the deep-buried self
becomes aware of what looks
like a small hockey player
reflected on ice watching him:
– or else a boy with raw cold nose
– or else a complete stranger,
standing inside the big blue barn:
and yet this four-foot carbon
copy is not exactly himself either –
An order from somewhere makes one arm
lift up, holding the stick high;
the pinched face smiles grimly;
the body above mirror ice is instructed

to bend in order that the owner's eyes
may permit a glimpse of the owner
himself, clothed in flesh but aloof
from flesh remaining invisible: Politely
the boy's mouth opens his lips slowly
carefully form the words: "Thank you —"
After which a whoof
of expelled breath shrieks
a sudden "YEE-OUUW" at the sky,
and black ice with a mile-wide spasm
over somewhere beyond the world's horizon cracks —
He skates wildly back to town,
With long swooping twenty-foot strides,
batting an old tin can ahead of him —
A cold moon hangs above the town clock tower
that strikes hard iron of sky;
the elderly pumpmaker in his shop
crowded with pine smell decides to eat;
the blacksmith in his glowing cave
drops the hot shoe and a red foreleg falls —
On either side the river lie
long fields of houses tucked in snow:
the boy dashes excitedly to one
of them aching with news
of an event real or imagined, bursts
the door open: "Mom, you —" and forgets.
The weather turns colder, the house
shudders and rocks, frost creeps
along white windows: and under
its patchwork quilt time moves
in a drift of birds a dream of horses,
and sticky buds breaking out of snow,
premeditations of flowers and lifting tides,
the sleep of men —

Even the shadow shapes inside their black prison
stay where they are, surviving the night,
and have been known occasionally to sleep –

Margaret:
   I've revised the end in copying this, and now the title does not
apply. Maybe I've screwed it up, but suddenly more and more of
my own childhood got into it – also Tennyson's Shalott: "On
either side the river lie/long streets of houses tucked in snow" – I
was thinking of the blessing and curse of awareness with its monsters under the ice of being human. It has got farther and farther
from hockey, into something wider and larger, at least I hope it
has – The pumpmaker and the blacksmith are two dream-realities
of my own childhood, and I consider modern kids deprived that
they don't have them. If you're curious about the original, it
goes on after the above line: "batting an old tin can ahead of
him" ———:

      the self inside himself forgotten,
      tho not quite ever forgotten again,
      as the ice cracks & cracks & cracks –

      The legend hardens to permanence,
      and whether it's worth it is beside the point:
      tho few ever reach those fabulous arenas
      where money grins green and freckles fade –
      The game is not hockey but an earlier game,
      one that precedes hockey as egg does chicken:
      and the closed ego splits itself,
      amoebas separate,
      the mother painfully gives birth,
      red-faced and yowling the child lies there;
      beside him in the crib a hockey stick:
      as time passes he seizes it
      and skates slowly away from her –

Of course it's a larger thing now, I do believe that. All sorts of implications, tho I wonder over the validity of the Tennyson paraphrase. But it makes the curse or blessing of awareness stronger –

Best,
Al

---

1. The opening quatrain of "Peony" by Bliss Carman (1861-1929), a Canadian romantic poet.

2. From poem 986 by Emily Dickinson (1830-86) in *The Complete Poems of Emily Dickinson* (ed. Thomas H. Johnson, 1970): "I feel for them a transport/Of cordiality –"

3. Claude Bissell (b. 1916), member of the Department of English, University of Toronto, and President of the University of Toronto (1958-71), was a critic and teacher of Canadian literature. His review appeared in *The Globe Magazine,* 7 September 1968, 15.

4. A reference to her lecture at the University of Leeds and at the Institute of Commonwealth Studies, University of London.

5. A reference to a piece of Mycenaean body-armour associated with the ancient Peloponnesian city of Dendra. Ventris's study has a chapter devoted to metals and military equipment.

6. This poem was published in revised form as "The Time of Your Life" in *Sex & Death* (1973).

§

Elm Cottage
16 January 1969

Dear Al–

If this letter gets lost in the post, like the ones sent to you from Canada in large envelope, I will be pretty annoyed at the postal systems of the world.

Got your letter this morning, and am bashing off reply now for reasons which will become obvious in the course of this letter.

First. I think THE GAME BEFORE THE EGG is one of the best poems you've ever written. For me, anyway, you really do capture it – the moment of awareness, of self-awareness, the astonishing sense (only dimly comprehended maybe or only ever seen in flashes but ever afterwards always there somewhere) of being both unique and in another way connected right from the inside with every amoeba that ever was, every creature with gills, every ancestor who made gods in his own shape, every human unborn. The sense of time – the awareness of time past and future because the present is over the instant you say it; the awareness of change and growing and nothing remaining the same yet always the same; the enormity of time; the knowledge both of one's own existence and of one's own death. For me, this is what the poem says. The fantastic thing is that you can catch all this in such a few lines. Maybe this is what a good poem can do, and nothing else can do. In prose it takes me 264 pages (both THE STONE ANGEL and THE FIRE-DWELLERS are exactly 264 pp.) to make a stab at it, and then it becomes too diffuse. Al, I think this is a hell of a good poem and I hope you continue to be happy with it, because you damn well should be. The revised ending is about 2000% better than the original, because with the revised version you do get exactly that sense of both the continuation of life and the presence not only of death but of an awareness of death, just as the shadow shapes the child sees in or under the black ice become the shapes which will always now inhabit his own skull and only sometimes sleep. God, it's terrific. It really is a fantastically good poem.

Other details about it – I think the line with echoes of Tennyson is good, because it *does* have echoes – for those of our generation, anyway, and the slightly outdated flavour of the Tennysonian line brings back the small towns of childhood and the poems studied then in schools, and connects with those towns in a way that is right. The hockey game which escapes its limits – that is exactly the right framework in which to set the poem. The whole thing, on the level of the child's experience, in terms of outer event and places, carries for me a lot of connotations – the prairie town where I grew up, where the boys learned hockey as soon as they could walk, nearly, and the river where the kids skated before a rink was built, and where some drowned, and the blacksmith, all that. I don't see how you can capture all that background in so few words, but you have done it.

I think the last lines of the poem … "in a drift of birds a dream of horses …" on to the end, are wonderful.

After this, to send you anything of my writing seems like an invitation for you to say you like it, and this would embarrass both of us unless we are quite clear that this isn't my intention, which it isn't, as I am damn sure you know, so don't know why I even mention it. If you say anything at all about the novel, it will be straight and I trust you for that.

You know I've always envied you, being able to send poems in letters? Well, I bet this is the first time you have ever received a novel in a letter! I have been wondering whether to send it to you or not, and yesterday decided to do so, then got your letter this morning and when I read the poem I decided to send the novel[1] because it relates in some ways or maybe conveys some of the things I feel about aspects of life.

This is an uncorrected proof copy – Macmillan sent me an extra copy of the page proofs when they sent a copy to be corrected, and so this is it. I also got a couple of copies of the dustjacket, which I like very much, as it seems to sum up the novel in the way I hope the title does.

[. . .]

I guess the booze problem *is* similar. I don't intend to stay off for the rest of my life, but will try to stay off for about 3 months anyway, just to get used to not drinking. The non-alcoholic wine is really not so bad – it is one way of drinking while writing letters to friends and not getting drunk! I get all involved and carried away by the desire to communicate and then my hand reaches for the glass, and I guess if I can substitute grape juice for the real vine it will be a good thing. Don't think I can live forever without wine. I have the same affection for retzina as you do for brandy – I can't stand Greek brandy, but I love the wine.

Incidentally, after I wrote last I nearly wrote a post-script in another letter, as I felt I had been kind of unfair to Dave – I was damn grateful to him, because it was through him that I found a young Can writer and his wife who will take over Elm Cottage and be company for my kids while I'm in Toronto. He also advised me on investing some money, and put me in touch with his broker in Toronto. He is one hell of a nice guy. I think the reservations one feels are due mainly to the fact that he is a member of the cool generation, and I am not. My natural impulse is not to play anything cool. When I do, it is only consciously imposed, not spontaneous.

You're right – the title of my goddamn talk sounds awful. Have finished it now and don't want to think about it. Yes, THE PALMWINE DRINKARD and MY LIFE IN THE BUSH OF GHOSTS are good, fantastic, weird, and I like them.

Don't know whether or not I want you to read my first two books, a novel set in W. Africa (THIS SIDE JORDAN) and a book on Somaliland (THE PROPHET'S CAMEL BELL). I don't much like them now. The first is very amateurish, which is not strange, seeing as it was written by an amateur, and the second is not true enough, being non-fiction. Both now probably out of print.

Remember once when you told me you saved friends' letters so you could make a fortune out of them someday, and I wrote back saying you damn well didn't need to keep mine, etc? I later changed my mind, and said go ahead and keep them, of course. Well, I guess I was kind of sneaky about it at the time, because I had kept your letters, along with letters from some few other writer friends, because they were so damn interesting. Strikes me now that this correspondence might possibly make interesting reading someday when we are dead, for what the letters say about writing and what goes on there.

I'm finishing the kids' book and although it isn't what anyone would call serious work, it gives me some kind of great amusement to be doing it. I hope they get good illustrations.

Enough for now. Have a triple sec for me.

All the best,
Margaret

ps. Know what you mean about the possibility of a potentially good writer breaking a leg before the novels and poems get written. Do you ever get scared you'll die before the poem you're writing gets finished? I always do, when I'm writing a novel, and I've heard of other writers who feel the same way. It's daft, but there it is.

Re: what I said about feeling my characters existed in some other dimension – I only meant that they seem that real to me, although in fact I know where they exist, and of COURSE they couldn't be recorded by anyone else! No visions for me, either, and no mystique about writing. Although sometimes when it is going well, one has a kind of sense of "possession", like I guess the West African masked dancers feel when they perform better than they really can. Something like that. It just happens sometimes, for no apparent reason. I think that feeling is okay, provided one takes a hard critical look afterwards at what has been written – I don't go along with the inspirational bit and not changing a word, etc. One *is* responsible for it, and it's *not* all okay the way it comes out first. As witness the revised ending of your poem. I guess I'm saying much the same as you did. I wish you could have seen the original manuscript for my novel – I couldn't get anyone else to type it, it was so scribbled over. Could hardly read the bloody thing myself.

P.S. 2 My novel will be published in April in Eng, I think, and in May in USA & Canada

P.S. 3 Odd that you'd made that change in the other poem. I'm glad you had.

---

1. *The Fire-Dwellers.*

[Ameliasburg]

20 May 1969

Dear Margaret,

Greeting and all that. Arrived home dog dead to catch the damnedest cold, the which I am treating with scotch and bromo quinine and sullen anger.

We pulled quite a boner at Can. Customs by declaring only two bottles of scotch, which was all we had with us, me forgetting entirely about the two Harris tweed jackets that had preceded us by mail. I threw away the customs declaration on the bus returning to Belleville, and then found $20. duty payable on the jackets at Belleville, and nearly as much later when a couple of pairs of slacks arrive by mail from Burton's, London. Have writ to Ottawa pleading ignorance of which I have a great deal, also stupidity which overcomes me as well. Dunno how it will come out. Point of mentioning all this is wondering if the jackets go back, whether you will have enough on your own customs allowance to get them in for me. However, rather than do that I will probably pay to the accompaniment of breaking teeth.

I dug up a copy of an earlier book of mine for you which I send separately, along with a Cariboo Horses for Dave Bellingham. [1] Incidentally, McStew's sales records arrive for past six mos and find Wild Grape Wine sold nearly 1000 copies in that period,

135

which I think is damn good. Trouble is the $500. advance fucked me up and they don't owe me anything on that book, but also sold 4-500 copies of the two earlier books, and I end up with $400.

I see I'm talking about nothing but MONEY! Terrible. Shit. Fact is I'm scared to type the poems I wrote in Crete, Rhodes and Turkey – or am I too sick and lazy? Two extremely good reviews of my stuff in CanFor[2] and the Queens Univ. mag Quarry.[3] One rather sentimental, but I love being slobbered over in print now that age removes my basest sexual instincts. I mean, but real Sentimental! I quote the end of the CanFor one: "One note more. If Purdy speaks, as the depth of feeling indicates he must, for himself as well as the young man whose death he mourns in 'Death of a Young Poet', if he truly feels, if only sometimes, that 'only the written extensions of myself are alive' and 'I move … touching no live thing', then I must make personal response. It is not so, Al Purdy. I am alive and touched and moved by you (ed. note: Gee whizz!) not by any cold 'written extensions,' but by the fulness of yourself that lives in your poetry. You will be loved a long time, alternatives or not, because you give."

I alternate between narcissistic enjoyment of this, and dislike of the sentimentality. Naturally the reviewer is a woman, and will now write and ask for a photostat of her birth certificate. Probably born 1879. Actually, that scares me, makes me sound like the third law of thermodynamics. Let us pray?

Anyway, this goddam cold is getting me, and I have to read at Albert College[4] tomorrow, a prospect that frightens me, since I wish they'd just mail me the $150. plus some more bromo quinine. Those are my late doins, what are yours?

Best,
Al

1. Dave Billington (1939-87) was a Canadian journalist working in London for the Reuters news agency. After his return to Canada in 1969 or 1970, he worked as entertainment editor for the Toronto *Telegram* (1969-71) and the Montreal *Gazette* (1971-76).

2. Mary Keyes, Review of *Wild Grape Wine. The Canadian Forum,* April 1969, 17-18.

3. Doug Fetherling, "Al Purdy's Recent Poetry." *Quarry,* 18, 2 (Winter 1969), 42-3.

4. Founded in 1857 and affiliated with the United Church of Canada, Albert College is located in Belleville, Ontario, and is Canada's oldest co-educational, residential private school.

§

Elm Cottage

24 May [1969]

Dear Al—

Thanks for your letter. I think our letters crossed. I'm sending an airletter which arrived for you – it has been so scribbled over that I thought I better not forward it on its own. Also sending a clipping re: Geo Jonas, which appeared in the Guardian last week.[1] I wonder what publishers he tried? And with what result? Have you heard anything about possibility of your collected poems, or have you yet approached J.G.McC about it?

Re: your jackets – I don't think there would be any problem about my taking them in, as I won't be taking anything else under customs allowance, but I'm not sure how I fit into Can customs allowance, having been resident in Eng for all these years. Anyway, I'm quite willing to try, if you like. There might be a problem re: weight on luggage, but probably not, as the kids get full baggage allowance.

Thanks for sending the book of yours. Also, it is nice of you to send WGW for Dave Billington. By the way, a book or books arrived for you from Ryerson – do you think it could be Milton Acorn's book?[2] Shall I open it, or do you want me to forward it back to you? (Forward it back – that sounds Irish)

I like what the lady reviewer has to say about you. It is a little fulsome, and I can understand your suspicion about sentimentality. However, everything she says is true – probably more true than she suspects, actually, as it applies to you in life as well as in poetry. (Guaranteed unsolicited comment, for which I expect no cash payment, although perhaps wrong of your friends to add to your already gigantic ego??)

Hope your cold is better by now. The treatment sounds good – scotch won't help the cold but it certainly makes you feel less grim. I'm in better shape than I was, having now figured out why J's news affected me so oddly.[3] It took me a long time when I first came to Eng to build up a self-image of a person who was a professional writer, not a housewife, and who could (wonder of wonders) actually cope with things like getting a mortgage and earning a living etc. Then when we decided to try again, I had to try all over again to return to self-image of housewife, while actually the outer and inner were in considerable conflict (probably not a bad thing at the time, as I was writing the F-D). Then, last week, another psychic change necessary. Back to self-image of professional writer etc etc. Actually, that being, as they say, the Real Me. Which I always knew. All the other bit was suppression suppression all the way, which worked not too well, as you undoubtedly know. I see now that I have to stick with this present concept of myself, as it is simply folly to try to pretend to be something you're not, even if you don't have to do so with your close friends (I would have cracked up during those 2 yrs if I hadn't had any close friends). So whether or not he decides to go through with it, as far as I am concerned, I will have to go through with it now. This decision fills me with panic and alarm, but it is 100% necessary, as I guess I have long known although

not admitted. Well, in short, I feel better now that I think I understand what was and is happening inside.

INSTANT ANALYSIS
CONSULT GYPSY ROSE MARGARET
MIND-EXPANDING AND HEAD-SHRINKING

Also, of course, one does feel slight terror at thought of
advancing age etc and me without a penny of insurance and no
intention of getting any. And can I keep on writing and earning
money? Well, one has to have some faith. As you say, rightly, you
can't run scared all the time. Did you ever see that film, years ago,
on the Dreyfus case?[4] Paul Muni took the part of Zola, I think.
When after years in prison on Devil's Island, Dreyfus was finally
released, they opened the cell door and he walked out into the
sunlight, blinked, and – walked back into his cell. The horror of
that moment I still remember. But one just has to put on one's
sunglasses and go out. I know all this very well, and in about a
fortnight I will have assimilated it. At the moment I sometimes
quite suddenly start shaking. But it will pass. I dramatize myself so
damn much that any moment of crisis can be turned into a real
panic.

Well, let us end on a cheery note. Joke from last week's Rowan
& Martin's Laugh In[5] – SEE GEORGE WALLACE IN
RACIAL, RACIAL.[6] I liked that.

Am trying to begin thinking about possible talks and lectures.
What a sweat. I suppose if I talk beguilingly about myself at least
no one can accuse me of getting my facts wrong.

I hope the reviewer wasn't born in 1879. Re: Let Us Pray – I
did an interview with Marjory a few days ago,[7] and somehow
found myself telling her (this for the CBC!) that I was a religious
atheist and writing was my way of praying. God knows what they
will make of that in Halifax!

All the best,
Margaret

ps. please tell Eurithe I haven't yet got around to taking her tights back to Marks & Spencers but will try to do so this coming week. Also, my best regards to her and I hope she's feeling better and better, while still not attempting to lick her weight in wildcats (hey, no, I didn't mean you, Al, honestly!) [8]

---

1. "Matured in English" by Terry Coleman. *Manchester Guardian,* 19 May 1969, 8. George Jonas (b. 1935) was a Hungarian-born writer who had made his name in Canada as a poet, playwright, and librettist.

2. Milton Acorn (1923-86) had just published *I've Tasted My Blood: Poems 1956 to 1968,* selected and introduced by Purdy.

3. Jack Laurence had asked for a divorce.

4. *The Life of Emile Zola* (1937) starred Paul Muni as Zola and Joseph Schildkraut as Dreyfus.

5. A popular American television comedy review hosted by Dan Rowan and Dick Martin.

6. George Wallace (b. 1919) had been governor of Alabama (1963-66) and had sought to prevent black students from enrolling in public schools and at the University of Alabama.

7. Marjory Whitelaw, co-author with Derek Patmore of *Canada* (1967), was employed by the Public Affairs Department of the CBC in Halifax.

8. Eurithe and Al Purdy had spent the month of March at Elm Cottage while she recovered from surgery.

Ameliasburgh

31 May 1969.

Dear Margaret,

Yeah, letters must've crossed. Re Selected, McClelland said yes. Suppose I hafta write Random House now and see if they wanta – Glad to see the Jonas clipping, more bio than review tho.

Re jackets, thanks much, but wrote Ottawa and getting them without duty, plus the liquor I did declare. Which – dammit! – is nearly finished. What did I say about teetotaling?

Have another review that really alarms me. This by Pacey, who has condemned my stuff for centuries now.[1] That he should suddenly like it means I must be finished, the poem I writ this morning has to be shit. I can hear the nasal intoning of "Dearly beloved, we are gathered here to celebrate John Philip Grove and Al Purdy who was not the least of these in life –" I mean Frederick Philip Grove, which mistake illustrates what I mean.[2] Life indeed has its turn-arounds not to mention its upsidedowns.

Re the books from Ryerson, there ought to be two. Please take the best one for yourself, then could you mail the other to: Dr. Earle Birney, 2030 Barclay, Apt. 406, Vancouver 5 – book rate naturally. It could be mailed to me here, but what's the point if it's going elsewhere anyway.

Hey, did you get Greene's essays?[3] If not, buy one for me, read it to yourself then mail it to me. Let me know cost – which is $8.50 here and hurts. This way looks after both of us, and two birds make better pot-pie than one. Besides, after reading another review I can't resist Greene.

Milton Acorn came down here for a – groan – several day visit. I would have you know that Acorn is not like other acorns, he does not lie still on the forest floor and shut his big yap. He talks. He wakes at 6 a.m. and stalks thru the house reciting poems, all of which sound like the King James version. Luckily Eurithe went north to clean mouse shit from farm, Acorn and my own child went with her, and I am happily free and alone a short time. But my watch stopped, and I phoned to find out the time to find out as well that Eurithe is on her way back down south with a sick diabetic aunt who refuses to take insulin, apparently visiting woodsy witch doctors instead. So I'm fucked up again. Acorn is the only person I can think of off-hand who won't let me work. Or sleep. Or even sit in silence. He just got sixteen hundred dollars from

CC and is happily basking in liquor and contented ego, expecting me to celebrate both. I expect pity by return mail.

Just writ pome called ASTRONOT,[4] which I feel will set back space exploration to Jules Verne,[5] if not stop it forever.

Read poems at Albert College – very peculiar biz. Once went to Albert myself way back in Thirties. Figured when I got the invite: old grad returns (I didn't grad – I ran away in the night) to accept honor due etc. Funny thing – I wasn't there because the Eng. Dept. wanted me but because the graduating class did. Very religious school, Albert, god in every classroom and chapel 99 times a day. Hear from the one teacher that arranged it to suit grad. class that I am a stench in the nostrils of religious men which I feel kinda flattering. Anyway, I read, same as always, and hear the headmaster sneaked in and departed quick. No real nasty words in my poems, least not many, but I don't sound cultured I suppose. Anyway, drank beer in this teacher's apt. later after all students under 21 screened out – Peculiar, eh? Also $150. and it makes me wonder how the students dug it up.

You and your talks and lectures. Me, I gotta teach two weeks, believe me baby, no more. Never still not once again more no sir.

No outsider could comment really on this break-up of yours, tho outsiders always do. All one can say if he wants it to go ahead and ditto you, which is heartless nothing. Must admit from you that it sounds like it's gone too far for any mending, the ass being out of the marriage, which I like and is hereby copyrighted. Phone Belleville, 962-7809

Rather amazingly the Canada Council sent me a copy of Ray Souster's manuscript, asking me if I think it worth publishing and deserves a subsidy. I'm surprised that Souster can't find a publisher and the CC thinks his book needs any opinion.

Have somehow come up with a headache, undoubtedly from the sediment in the last bottle of scotch. I didn't even get the Racial-Rachel bit till after re-reading your letter, so I think you're a bit prejudiced in favour of understanding. The Laurence books are all lined up on my shelves in one spot. Impressive. Did I say St. Martin's Press sent me a de luxe leather bound ed with marbled end papers of "New Romans"? Surprising, but I suppose they must do that for all the books they publish. But if the pub. binds such a minor book as "Romans" they oughta come up with some good copies, really well-done, of yours.

Must stop, coffee and codeine I guess.

Best,

Al

1. Review of *Wild Grape Wine. The Fiddlehead,* No. 79 (March-April 1969), 106-07.

2. Pacey had published *Frederick Philip Grove* in 1945.

3. *Collected Essays* (1969) by Graham Greene (1904- 91).

4. Published in *Love in a Burning Building.*

5. Jules Verne (1828-1905), the popular French writer who was the first novelist of modern science fiction.

Elm Cottage
6 June [1969]

Dear Al–

INVOICE – herewith one cartload of pity, by return mail (or nearly), as per your request. Charges already paid.

Acorn sounds like a great guy, but not, perhaps, at 6 a.m. Actually, I can't think of anyone I know who would sound even passable at that hour. I know what you mean about need for silence and aloneness – you must need that quite a lot at the moment, with thoughts of ancient monuments floating around and the picture of yourself – an Ontario farmer's son in a far country thinking of your fathers. (I re-read a lot of the poems in WGW

143

the other day, as I had not really read them in sufficient undistract-edness before. More of this later). How did the poems you wrote in Greece and Turkey turn out? You don't mention them. Are they typed yet? Also, what about the freight train sequence – do you think you'll retrace that trip one of these days? Yeh, what with one thing and another, I can see that you really could do without friends, visitors, lectures and so on for awhile.

I think it is a very good thing that it was the students at Albert College who wanted you. The hell with the faculty. Hope it may happen with me like that at Toronto from time to time – when I think of a year of maybe talking to no one but faculty and their wives, I could almost shoot myself in advance in case it happens like that.

Haven't got the Greene essays yet, but will order them this week. We can share the cost. Will also send Acorn's book to Earle. Thanks very much for my copy – haven't read it yet, although I read your Intro last night (I did not feel I could open the parcel until I heard from you). Also, this morning the book for Dave Billington arrived, and THE BLUR IN BETWEEN[1] – many thanks. Will write reactions later, as haven't yet read it.

How long is ASTRONOT? Would like to see it. I know sweet nothing about the techniques of poetry, so a lot of the structure and the finer points escape me. Nonetheless, in looking again at WILD GRAPE WINE, I was struck once more with the way you have quite often of delivering an absolutely stunning last few lines, which connect everything – the poem to itself and to the reader, and then go on to reach out like the ripples when you skip a stone in a lake. "Bring out your dead and come yourself/ I am not at home/ I am not at home"[2] … it is the truly deceptive simplicity and terrifying ambiguity of these lines that really hits. Another – "They had their being once/and left a place to stand on"[3] … it seems to me you've said damn near everything in those lines that I was trying to say in the short stories. They *did* leave a place to stand on, and we are standing on it. Also "All I have is

144

wine and laughter/and the spring came on forever/the spring comes on forever/Yes I do."[4] These are lines which take up residence in the mind, and remain there, the kind of lines to say to oneself in moments of pain, crisis, disaster or earthquake.

I am personally going through pain, crisis, disaster and earthquake, and am surrounded on all sides by hellish problems, but luckily, most of these at the moment are focussed on the short stories.[5] Al, I'm really in trouble about them. Judith Jones, my ed at Knopf, wants me to make a more "unified" book of them – in other words, to "de-story" them and make a continuous and chronological narrative. You know the stories well, so you will appreciate what this would mean – buggering around with at least 3 of them, taking bits from here and putting them there, in short making a christly mess of the whole thing. Then, if I did do it, I would lay myself wide open to the charge of having tried to do a kind of mock-up of a novel. I just CAN'T do it. But when I think this will probably mean Knopf won't publish the book, I feel sick. The English publishers agree with my viewpoint, but it is not in Eng that I make any money or get interested reviews, it is in N.Amer. McClelland will likely publish anyway, or so I hope. But I feel upset as hell about it all, and really do not know what to do. Or yes, I *do* know what to do, but I dread the long battle which will ensue. Anyway, I can't do a hatchet job on my own characters. I can see Judith's point of view, and I can even visualize the kind of book she wants. But it would be like plastic surgery – the end product might be prettier but it would not be so true. This was just what I could have done without, at this point, when I am trying to get ready to go to Canada.

Great news about the Selected. I certainly hope Random House agrees.

Re: my personal situation – have recovered from slight panic and process of self-image-changing, and now feel encouraged about whole thing. It *had* gone too far for mending, which I have known for years. Anyway, I am determined not to try to settle the course of the next 20 years in five minutes – I'll see when I've lived in Toronto for a few months how I'd feel about moving over there. It might be better to wait until David is finished school, but no doubt all these things will work out. I must try to cultivate patience, of which I have none, (except where writing is concerned, where I have quite a lot of patience – odd).

Good reviews of THE FIRE-DWELLERS in Atlantic Monthly[6] and New Yorker,[7] so thank God for small mercies. Don't worry – you're not finished even if Pacey (horrors) likes you now. If I can withstand the awfulness of having something published in the Ladies Home Journal,[8] surely you can withstand Pacey!

All the best,
Margaret

---

1. *The Blur in Between: Poems 1960-61*. Toronto: Emblem Books, 1962.

2. "Further Deponent Saith Not."

3. "Roblin Mills (circa 1842)."

4. "Dark Landscape (Oct., Roblin Lake)."

5. Collected and published as *A Bird in the House* (1970).

6. Edwards Weeks, *Atlantic Monthly,* June 1969, 112-13.

7. A brief review appeared in *The New Yorker,* 31 May 1969, 115-16.

8. "To Set Our House in Order." *Ladies Home Journal,* March 1964, 80-82.

Ameliasburgh
14 June 1969

Dear Margaret,

Re *Blur,* don't bother reading it, since it's just a curiosity as an earlier book, of interest for the drawings – the poems were accepted for pub. in 1960, but not actually printed until 1963 – I had changed my mind about doing it at all by that time, since

Annettes had come out and was a great deal better: so I sent a registered letter to Jay Macpherson[1] and also the printer saying they had not permission to publish. Immediately I was involved in nearly panicky letters etc. back and forth, and thought what the hell I can't screw up their plans, so went ahead.

I completely agree with you re the short stories. I'm not you, obviously, but me I wouldn't change it, not unless I was broke. But of course it's your baby as you know well.

Just had a card that one, Gordon Elliott,[2] is sending a record you asked him to send me. Well, thanks, but my guilt over having so many of your early books is compounded – tho I suppose not really. I did like that record very much, the cowboy songs one, and of course I lost the number of it, and was beginning to forget altogether. Most things just pass in and out of the mind like pissing beer. Lest you should doubt it tho, I did love that record and appreciate it. Shall I now send back that gaelic bible which I know you treasured? Thanks.

We have now got a room fixed upstairs here (one climbs a very dangerous ladder, first signing a release form) with you in mind principally. As the house sways back and forth in the wind you will be rocked to sleep to dream of sexual retzina.

Pot pourri: good about your reviews, must make you feel you might just be a fair writer – I say that because I have all sorts of self-doubts when I read bad reviews of myself. Read at Classic book store in Toronto two days ago with Acorn, on behalf of his book and mine,[3] crowd of about 200, so we had to go outside and read at the entrance to some apts at the back, and the super called the police, who attended the remainder of the reading listening hard for the word fuck, and of course our pictures in the Telegram without Barry Callaghan's personal okay. I haven't written Random House yet, because I don't want to until I have a manuscript ready, and I have a strong hunch that the guy I met there, Jason Epstein, will have left Random House by then. Which calls for immediate work (if I'm right) on the selected, but I don't feel like it. Besides, there's a young poet in Trenton whose father is a printer and he wants to do a de luxe ed of fifty copies of my stuff, with drawings by a Trenton artist. [4] A Trenton artist seems in itself a most dubious fact given the nature of that town of my up-downing, nevertheless said artist consumed beer one night which has to be proof of something if not existence.

I probably told you Maclean's phoned about a poem about the astronauts? And I probably told you *Astronot* was too long. So I wrote another which I didn't like. Then another which I rather do. I wanta copy this last. The title is from Yeats, and the poem is certainly not what Maclean's wants.

NINE BEAN-ROWS WILL I PLANT THERE? [5]
No woman has ever lost her man
to another woman here
or had him just go
because he didn't want to stay any longer
No woman has spent the night rocking in pain
knowing that even in her grave and after
she will not see him again
The grief of a child's death has not touched
this place
or the dumb grandeur of mourning for the lost
     And the inconsolable [6]
walkers in the storm
cursing at the locked gates of fact
refuse to be satisfied with fiction
board a leaky ship for the past
not to be seen again among us
except as our knowledge that pain and death
have their own glory that lifts them
sometimes over our limitations
of being dust to dust
but more than human

After the landing
on that torn landscape of the mind
and the first steps are taken
let a handful of moon-dust run thru my hand
and escape back to itself
for those others
the ghosts of grief and loss
walking beyond the Sea of Serenity

George Bowering & wife, Doug Jones[7] & wife, spent the night here last night. We drank, a bottle of rye, half a gallon of wine and a dozen beer – today – OW! I really can't drink any more, too fuckin old. Acorn just phoned from Toronto – seems he was upstairs somewhere at the time we left scene of reading – That is one helluva bad way to read a poem as above, on a blurry typewriter and the poem broken in half! With transposed letters in a word too. The Yeats title is maybe not so hot – Anyway I write Earle and said I wasn't doin the book on him. He said fine and meant it.

Best,

Al

---

1. Jay Macpherson (b. 1931), poet, teacher, and publisher. Emblem Books was her own small press. Her collection *The Boatman* (1957) had won a Governor-General's Award for poetry.

2. Gordon Elliott (b. 1920) was a Canadian critic, Professor of English at Simon Fraser University, and editor of *Klondike Cattle Drive: The Journal of Norman Lee* (1960).

3. *I've Tasted My Blood*.

4. *The Quest for Ouzo*, in a limited edition of 69 numbered copies, was illustrated with lino-cuts carved by Tony Lassing, and printed, silk-screened, and bound by M. Kerrigan Almey of Trenton.

5. Published with minor revisions as "Nine Bean-Rows on the Moon" in *Maclean's*, August 1969, and in *The Quest for Ouzo*.

6. This had been misspelled by Purdy who had corrected his mistake by typing at the end of this line "'inconsolable' dammit."

7. D.G. Jones (b. 1929), whose most recent collection of poetry was *Phrases from Orpheus* (1967).

Elm Cottage
20 June 1969

Dear Al–

I did read BLUR, naturally. I was interested to hear that the poems had been written quite awhile before the book was published, because most of them read to me like much earlier work and I was puzzled by the publication date, as it looked later than I thought it would be. I liked best Kispiox Indian Village, partly for what it would express to anyone and partly because I was there, too, and felt like an intruder (some of that came out somewhere in THE FIRE-DWELLERS), and ... the best poem in the book, for me ... the last one, Decree Nisi ... which I think is good, and especially the last part ... who hasn't been afraid in that way (maybe lots haven't ... yeh, I guess so), and the last line ... "I think it will be colder." I think it undoubtedly will.

Was surprised to find so many of Acorn's poems so tenderly personal ... I like them the best. I loved "I will Arise And Go Now ..." (another poem taking title from that one of Yeats) [1] ... but the last verse is great; the whole thing is. Was interested in what he said about you in one poem, not able to trust your own delicate poems in case they were better than you were ... something like that ... can't find the right page. I don't know. In a way I see what he means, and in another way I would have said that the fact you may have always known your poems were better than you were was one thing [that] kept you going. Could be wrong. I don't mean I think you're a swine (au contraire, as we say in

Quebec) or that *you* think you are … only that of course your best poems are better than you could have written them, only you did write them, so how peculiar … something like that. Guess I'm looking at it the way I feel about my own writing, too.

Maclean's won't like NINE BEAN ROWS, but I think it is like some forms of good SF … a reminder of what is inside the space-suit. Last line hits.

I am damn tired. I won my fight with Knopf, and the Amer ed, who is a great lady, really, has written to say she can understand my viewpoint about being totally unable to alter the basic nature of the stories and that I should go ahead and do whatever revisions I feel I can, and the hell with the others. So … whew! Massive relief. But it was a bad fortnight, and I tend to over-react to these crises. I decided after I wrote you last that I would rather not see the book published in Amer than chop it all to hell. But thank God it hasn't come to that. She says it won't get such a "wide audience", but I don't care. Have airmailed her the manuscript, all revisions done, so pray it is off my shoulders at last. Now only have to do final revisions on the kids' book before I leave. Will likely be doing them as I step on plane.

My young writer-in-res, Ian Cameron and his wife Sandy are now here, and are very likeable and we seem to get on fine. My kids are slightly withdrawn at the moment, but may loosen up. Have talked non-stop to the Camerons for 4 days now, trying to establish contact, not forced, we all wanted to, but tonite I am drinking red wine and writing in the livingroom alone to friends. All this company after awhile drives me into compulsory solitude.

Delighted to know you have spare room fixed up but how in hell do you expect me to climb dangerous ladder? I get vertigo even on a stepladder. Couldn't I just take a sleeping bag out into the back yard when I come to visit you? Will crawl under the back step along with the squirrels and skunks.

Have sent you Graham Greene's essays. Pay half if you like, but maybe you shouldn't, as in a fit of enthusiasm I scribbled comments on margins of some pages so have ruined book. Also have sent Malamud's THE FIXER and John Cheever's BULLET PARK, the former mine which at last was returned by the person who borrowed it, but I've read it so don't bother returning it unless I change my mind about wanting it back. The Cheever was sent free to me by Knopf … they actually by mistake sent me 2 free copies, so I pass on one. It's a very very good novel indeed. Nothing explained, nothing wasted. He trusts his readers. A hell of a good writer.

My young couple are terribly nice but so intellectual it tires my middleaged brain. Two nights, yes, three, yes, even four, yes, but tonight, goddamn it, I am going to look at the British Comedy Film. In sheer self-defense. I can talk for just so long about modes of communication and the audio-visual bit and so on, which is really very interesting and relevant to me, but then I get so my brain feels like a squeezed-out sponge. These kids nowadays are so *bright,* so well-educated, and of course so relatively clueless about some of the dilemmas to which the human frame and spirit is prone, at least I think so altho maybe not. – Glad it is okay re: Earle and not doing book.

Yrs in relative exhaustion,
Margaret

these new airletters are hell. like a roll of toilet paper.

------

1. "The Lake Isle of Innisfree" by William Butler Yeats (1865-1939).

§

Massey College
University of Toronto
25 September 1969

Dear Al–

Letters crossed. Got yrs this morn at office, and many thanks. You *did* say comforting things re: my low state of mind, when I was at yr place; they didn't have to be said *as such* – the message came across. Especially in the kidding, I guess. Strange. But in other ways too – like the folk music, etc. And some poems, intentionally or not.

My Toronto address is: 9 Westgrove Crescent, Tor 305; phone 489-6577. Office phone is 928-8684. Incidentally, for yr information, Westgrove Crescent is between Avenue Rd and Bathurst, along Glengrove. I sound like I knew Toronto – I know how to get to and from office; to bank; to hairdresser; to Eaton's; to doctor. I order groceries and have even (clever!) discovered a means of ordering booze. Have been on the wagon for the past 3 days, taking my anti-booze pills again, as I was overcome with thought – I MUST CHANGE MY LIFE. However, it will not last. It never does. I'm reasonably okay when not too depressed, but the crises come and go. There seems some chance of getting going at one or two interesting things here – re: contact with young writers – so that cheers me. Have also made a firm decision – will turn down any more invites to speak. Have accepted invitations from about 6 various organizations, mostly Univ Women's Clubs, hither and yon, and also Dalhousie, because I want to see something of the country, but enough is enough. Accepted an invite this morn from Mrs. W.L. Morton in Peterborough – the historian's wife.[1] Ho ho – the one time I ever met W.L. Morton was (incredibly) when I was 16 and he was about 19 … he was a Gladstone, Man., boy, home from univ for Xmas hols with a pal who had a girl friend in Neepawa, Man., who happened to be my best friend. Bill Morton was assigned to drive car and I was dragged

153

along as company for him, while the other pair necked untroubledly in back seat. I was petrified of Morton – he seemed a million miles away, and so bored with a 16 year old Neepawa girl he could hardly stay awake to drive car. What a laugh. I will remind him. That is really why I accepted invite to talk in Peterborough. Am going to talk on my Prairie Background. Hope you find this small irony as appealing as I do.

I don't think you should worry unduly (maybe you aren't – hope not) re: the poems in the Trenton book which you aren't crazy about. There are some good poems in the collection, and others which don't have as much reach as you would like them to have. So what? You know why. It wasn't an especially easy time to be writing poems, and anyway, as you say, when you feel it is incumbent upon you (even if it really isn't) because of the C.C., the poems tend to go away, I would have thought. But it seems to me we ought not to worry that all our work is not of the same (high) standard … for God's sake, whose is? Not even Shakespeare's. I feel that way about THE PROPHET'S CAMEL BELL, and about the Nigerian book – there are some okay things in them, but they're not true enough, not penetrating enough, or at least they don't speak as much of my own truth as I have sometimes been able to speak in novels. But I think this is a fact of life, and damn well better than not writing at all if it makes you miserable at that particular time not to be writing. The Nigerian book was a life saver for me – saved me from despair and booze, probably. So it's got a few decent parts, and that's all, but that's okay, I think. This doesn't mean a drop in standards – it only means that you don't operate at the same pitch or tempo or whatever it is, all the time.

But the poems in LOVE IN A BURNING BUILDING are mostly damn good, and the 2 new ones you showed me communicated a hell of a lot. You *should* be very happy with them. Also, the poem in CANLIT[2] is one of yr best, as I said when you sent it to me some time ago.

Lines overheard on the subway this morn … "Myrtle was so incensed that they hadn't paid their rent that she went out to the garage and the lady had this piece of marble there, like, that she was gonna use for a coffee table top, and Myrtle got a sledge hammer and busted it up and threw it all over the lawn." Honestly … I *did* hear just that! Life's small gifts.

Best,
Margaret

ps. is Thanksgiving the weekend of Oct 11? Will you be there, or is there a family gathering in Belleville?

---

1. William Lewis Morton (1908-80) was Trent's Vanier Professor of History and the author of, among others, *Manitoba: A History* (1957; rev. 1967) and *The Kingdom of Canada* (1963). His wife was the former Margaret Orde. Laurence was obviously mistaken about his age.

2. "The Time of Your Life" appeared in *Canadian Literature,* No. 41 (Summer 1969), 62-65.

[Ameliasburg]
28 September 1969

Dear Margaret,

Your letters remind me of me, even if that sounds a bit silly. If I ever have to appear on television, write a bio piece, or this poem for Weaver, etc – I worry a little about it. And time, and death and all that crap. Not worry in any overwhelming sense, I don't suppose, but things do weigh on me. Scheduled things, I mean. Probably I drink about the same amount as you, and every now and then I say, must cut down! Think what a disordered life I am leading, without aim or direction except my own. But then I wouldn't change that last, and neither would you. Still, you once said you saw yourself an old lady among your cats and roses: I would have neither, in all probability, likely Eurithe tho, who is omnipresent and nearly omniscient and ubiquitous. I hope, by the way, that you were able to go to the farm when she phoned, as she told me she was going to ask you to do when she phoned me from there. As she probably told you also, we're leasing the place to Doug Fetherling,[1] and there won't be quite the same chance later. Fetherling is, I've decided, a politician in every sense, and I mean a literary politician. You've undoubtedly seen them before, and perhaps Douglas Hill[2] is one in England. I find Fetherling likeable; but he dances a slow dance of attendance on those people (probably me too) whom he thinks can do him good. These are unpleasant thoughts, but they've been much on my mind since he was here. However, that can be talked about later –

Jack and his entourage came down very late (about 11.30 p.m.) Tuesday night. Town[3] also, and his entourage, which was masculine. Jack's was feminine, his editor, hired sight unseen he said, but quite good-looking by accident. We argued most of the night, even talked a little. He and Town do not want to do "Burning Bldg." with Town drawings, because the poems are not romantic enough, Town describes them as "hard." While admitting I am not a romantic in the ordinary sense of the word I feel I am romantic in another and advanced this point of view – to no avail. Jack said he'd do the book, and I felt he felt he was doing me a favour – as an ordinary book, and I was correspondingly grateful. He has an antho of "significant" poets planned, which he wants me to edit and Town to illustrate with twenty portraits.[4] I said this was a sop and felt it was dreamlike, which Eurithe said Jack didn't like; but then we were just a mite drunk. Town, by the way, is one of the most egotistic people I've ever seen; the least mention of any other artist causes Town to put him down, declare his work to be inferior. I think Town's intelligence, at least from his appearance, eyes and alertness and so on, is repellently sharp. But he seems very inhuman, cold if you like, by reason of this lack of

156

sympathy and appreciation for anyone but himself. This would be a usual reaction of mine to someone like that, I guess, even tho it seems an over-simplification. Perhaps here I think of two lines ending a poem by Phyllis Webb, the two best lines by far in the poem:

> What are we whole or beautiful or good for
> but to be absolutely broken?[5]

Incidentally, if she had a few more lines like that she'd be a great poet. Anyway, people like Town with this absolutely crystalline pure ego seem inhuman, as if they'll never be "absolutely broken." The net result of the visit was (probably) that Jack and I are both confirmed in our opinions of the other and detente remains repugnant.

Then Fetherling Thurs, and Gary Geddes[6] today. He said he hoped he'd meet you this year, and I said he probably would. In case I haven't mentioned him, he did that Oxford antho, Twentieth Century Poetry and Poetics, a sort of a school book. He also edits one of the modern writer's series, the Copp Clark one. Very bright too, and more human. We had a long involved argument about the mythologizing of people in the U.S. and Canada, which latter place, R. Fulford[7] holds, does not mythologize, I say that's a good thing, and Geddes rebuts by saying I do it myself in poems. Not quite impasse tho. I generally remember some little thing people say previously that contradicts what they say now, and confront Geddes with this (admittedly a very irritating little habit of mine), but he passes this off after a moment of hesitation. But I am so amused by my own cleverness that I think Geddes shares the amusement, at least good humour. He brought the beer, six bottles, so we drank it before he left for Toronto on 401. In some ways, it's interesting to take the opposite side of an argument, just for the sake of seeing what happens: or, seeing you're wrong and refuted, still uphold the discredited theme to see where it leads.

Yeah, I'm dissatisfied with the poems, and your words of comfort don't help. They're just not good enough, even if I know why. Nothing very basic happened to me (internally) in Greece etc. And I'm some kind of echo chamber or reflector. I guess you are too. On the other hand, I can't remember whether I felt very strongly about some of the poems I now consider "not bad" or "pretty good", and therefore mistrust my own ability too. I dislike this goddam poem thing Weaver wants too. Hell, I wanta take a year to write a poem like that, twenty minute piece for voices, I mean. Oh, I can probably do it, but I can do much better with a moon-poem or a Kennedy poem on very short notice. Shit, that is! The way I feel, I mean. Guess this requires another page.

Too lazy for another page.[8] Or tired, or something – It is 3:15 a.m. A cricket stammers in the kitchen. I stammer here.

Love

Al

Come down, eh? Before we leave, at least once? Need the sanity of your insanity –

What would a graphologist say?
I mistrust a place called Westgrove Crescent!
Essentially hostile to humans!

---

1. Doug Fetherling (b. 1947), editor and poet, was working at House of Anansi Press. He was later included in *Storm Warning: The New Canadian Poets* (1971), edited by Purdy.

2. Douglas Arthur Hill (b. 1935), a Canadian free-lance writer who had moved to Britain in 1959. He was an editor, poet, anthologist of books of science-fiction, and author, among others, of *The Opening of the Canadian West* (London: Heinemann, 1967).

3. Harold Town (1924-90), painter and sculptor.

4. The collaboration never took place.

5. From "Breaking," by Phyllis Webb (b. 1927), in her collection *The Sea Is Also a Garden* (1962).

6. Gary Geddes (b. 1940), anthologist and poet, was editor of Copp Clark's "Studies in Canadian Literature" series.

7. Robert Fulford (b. 1932) was at this time editor of *Saturday Night* magazine.

8. This sentence to the end of the letter was handwritten.

Ameliasburgh
October 1969

MEMORANDUM
Margaret Laurence to Al Purdy
I may now and later ask all sorts of things – reassurance,* sustenance, etc, and also give them if needed. But I will only *ever* ask one favour. This is it: do not sell or even give away my letters until I am dead. Eh? After that, fine, okay, great. (I am assuming you will survive longer than I do, which seems a fairly reasonable assumption.)
– Personally, I think the collection of letters would be damned interesting, & I can even see it as a book. But I don't want to see it. That is for later.

(Keep this. It can be
the Intro.)
ML

* Jesus, even Beaver Pond, maybe!

§

Dear Al—

Dr. M. Laurence, indeed – I swear I am going to get even with you by putting something even more flamboyant on the address of this letter! Thanks much for invite to go out and drive back with you and E, and see dinosaur footprints. Would love to, naturally, but fear it isn't in the cards. Have to go to Montreal week after next, and then early in March to Maritimes, and don't want U of T to feel I'm never here. How come you'll be here Mar 13? Will it be a flying visit? I get back from Maritimes on Mar 12, so please phone if you're here. Also, if you want to stay here, please do, altho if you haven't got yr car, it might be an inconvenient place to be. However, you know the door is always open. (Metaphorically speaking. Actually, it's got about 6 locks, as the people who own the house are even more neurotic than I, if that is possible).

I'd like to stay the summer and move out to my shack and get it fixed up,[1] but dunno what situation will be re: my kids. Jocelyn wants to hitch-hike in Greece with Paul, her boyfriend, so she'll probably do that. But Dave might like to come over for summer. It all depends, too, on whether Ian and Sandy Cameron are willing to stay on in Elmcot for a few more months. As far as I can see, neither has done fuck-all in terms of work this year, but that is their problem, not mine. They've looked after the house and got the meals and they get on okay with my kids. The only complaints I get are rather practical ones – Sandy tends not to do the washing until no one has any clean clothes, and Joc says "Mum, if you can write books which are good enough to get published, and do the laundry on time, I can't see why Sandy can't" ... oh joy ... one sentence of appreciation from one's young, AT LAST! However, Sandy is about 1000% better cook than I am. Think both Ian and Sandy, especially Ian, really lack a kind of intensive driving force, which is what compels us to go on and finish a poem or a novel, eh? Like, one cannot *not* finish it, however unwilling, tired, beat-up or hungover one may be. He wanted to finish his M.A. thesis, and hasn't, and wanted to write a novel, and has not written more than 1 very short story, but he has done a few good songs. People really mostly do what they want to do the most, would you agree? Like, if you don't get the poems written or the novel written, it is because maybe it wasn't there to be written. It isn't really a question of discipline – did you ever have to force yourself to write something that really was there to be written? I would bet my life you did not. Nor did I. No credit to us for writing – it's an addiction. Some credit, however, for doing the other attached things, like re-writing the thing and shipping off the manuscript to what one guesses may be the right place, etc etc. A kind of practical cunning which every writer has to develop, I think. One young writer (the only really promising prose writer who's come into my office so far) is developing this quality in ways that give me pleasure to behold. Already, he's trying to figure out how he can get two (very good) stories published and also get some publisher to consider taking his thesis on John Updike. He's got the right blend of the real need to write plus the recognition that a certain amount of unscrupulous gamesmanship is necessary. And it bloody *is,* as you know only too well. Remember years ago, when strictly amateur, I had my first novel accepted provisionally by Jack McClelland, on the chance that we could find either an Eng or Amer publisher. It had gone, then, to Macmillan's of London, and I decided that this was the right time to submit to Macmillan's a long African short story for Winter's Tales,[2] so they might (hopefully) connect the two. And in fact this was precisely what happened.

What in hell do you mean, you handle the job inadequately?[3] Listen, if you did prepared lectures, all full of academic bullshit, you would be handling the job inadequately. If you simply go and get the kids talking, and talk right back, you will be great. I'm convinced that this seminar method is much more valuable than formal lectures, and I think that you probably feel much as I do about the situation – I am no bloody good at formal lectures (altho I have to give about 6 more, damn it) but in a to-and-fro situation I am just fine. We talk in a kind of down-to-earth way; no one is up there preaching; and it's an encounter, not a dry and bloodless variety of academic prozeletizing(sp?). I have done both ways, so I feel very strongly. Okay, some people can lecture, but I am not one of them and I suspect you are not, either. But we *can* talk, and it isn't really ever off the top of our heads, because we're talking about things we've been discussing innerly for years. Also, the kids can surprise you with bizarre questions which make you take another look at your own work or someone else's work, and that's a good thing, I think. So don't worry about the lecture bit. Just go and talk *with* them, not *at* them, and all will be well.

[. . .]

Did I tell you? I got an advance copy of A BIRD IN THE HOUSE from Knopf. Paper is lovely, print is lovely, everything is just gorgeous – but jesus, what a dustjacket. It is a nice sky-blue, but the bloody bird on it looks like a crippled seagull. It was supposed to be, as you may remember, a sparrow. The English dustjacket is beautiful – white background, black lettering, and two hands half-folded and a sparrow flying up out of the hands. It could hardly be better. But the Amer (and of course the Canadian, as J.G.McC is buying pages etc) is unbelievably awful. Okay, so we had land gulls in the prairies, but when did one ever get caught in a house? However, no point getting worked up about it. Will send you a copy when the rest of the advance copies come in. I'd really prefer you to have the Eng edition, so will try to get them to send a few to me here.

[. . .]

You know, Al, I find the kids who come to my office awfully easy to cope with, in relation to the older people who ain't made it and who won't. The kids are mostly (in my view) very unpromising; I am tactful with the really unpromising ones, but who knows ... they may develop. With the really promising ones, I'm hard as nails and tear their work apart, because they can take it, and whatever I say, they're going to be okay anyway. But these goddamn people who are paranoid at the age of 45 and who think the world hasn't treated them right – how to cope? I can't. You can't really say – look, the reason you have not had universal recognition is that you actually do not write very well. So you have to think up other things to say, I guess. However, one good thing – I have met about 2 really good prose writers this year, and 1 good poet (or so I think). The poet (I've met dozens, Al, but this is the first guy who seemed to communicate something to me) ... is a kid who was a dropout from York last year, and who is going to Scarborough this year and who reads enormously widely but does not feel that courses in 18th century literature are very relevant to his situation. You might be amused about his poems. Some of them are very personal, very mythical, very historical, in somewhat the same way as yours, some of yours. I said to him "I like this poem VINTAGE YEARS very much, and I like the way you've treated the theme of your grandparents, but isn't it a little derivative? Like, Al Purdy?" He fixes me with a serious stare, and says "I guess it's my fault, but I really haven't read much contemporary poetry; haven't read Al Purdy." I was very glad he hadn't, you know? He will, now, because I discussed with him the whole question of the forming of our mythology, and quoted to him some of yr poems, especially Roblin Mills ... "They had their being once/ And left a place to stand on ..." When I quoted that line, he clued in directly. This was what he had been trying to do, with his own background, in his own unique way. He actually didn't know that anyone else had been trying to do it. I pointed out in my subtle fashion that I'd been trying to do the same thing

163

with THE STONE ANGEL. What he is worried about is how to earn enough money to pay the rent and have 1 meal a day. I gave him the line which I reserve (I may say) only for the really talented dropouts – and maybe it could be the title of a book which either you or I write, as advice for young writers – "Al Purdy worked 12 yrs in a mattress factory." Hope you don't mind my using yr experience … it is more dramatic and in a real way more meaningful than saying "M. Laurence worked 15 yrs as a suburban housewife", because in a sense I didn't; in Africa, had (undeserved) servants etc.

Fear not for the lectures, eh? Just get them talking, and talk back, and all will be well.

Write soon.

Love,
Margaret

ps. was stoned when I phoned, so undoubtedly talked nonsense. please excuse. have gone off the booze … let us hope willpower lasts for a while.

further p.s. got my phone bill this morning, for last month, and I had phoned everyone I knew, nearly, across Canada, when I arrived back from England – have now decided that I've dialled my last long-distance call!

It is this damn direct dialling which is my undoing – I can't believe it's anything but a local call, until the bill comes in. Ah well, what would life be without the occasional folly? (It would be less poverty-prone, that's what it would be)

ps. had lunch this week with Will Ready,[4] of McMaster Univ, who is the guy who is buying up everyone's manuscripts. He has got for McMaster the letters of Bertrand Russell, and also manuscripts of Samuel Beckett … what a coup. It occurs to me now (and okay – I know I've fought it, so make fun of me) that our correspondence might be interesting, in time to come. I ain't got copies … have you? I got yr letters, that's all.

---

1. Laurence's "shack" was the cottage she had bought on the Otonabee River near Lakefield, Ontario, in the Fall of 1969.

2. "The Perfume Sea" was published in Macmillan's annual anthology *Winter's Tales 6* (1960), as was "The Rain Child" in *Winter's Tales 8* (1962). Both were later included in *The Tomorrow-Tamer* (1963). The series, edited by Alan Maclean, also published "The Sound of the Singing" in #9 (1963) and "The Mask of the Bear" in #11 (1965).

3. Purdy was Visiting Associate Professor of English at Simon Fraser University, January-April 1970.

4. William Ready (1914-81) was McMaster's University Librarian from 1966 to 1979.

English Dept., Simon Fraser U.
Burnaby 2
1 February [1970]
mail to that address

Dear Margaret,

Since just talked with you, felt like writing a note. Don't worry so much about the goddam letters. Will give you a contract of non-sale, will make a deal not to sell, you can sue, besides I have enough goddam letters, just won't sell – but in case I do I'll split the money.

Okay the lectures get me down. The kids in class know fuckall about CanLit, or just about any lit, with some notable exceptions. This being the case I feel I should try to *make* them know something about poetry by *liking* the stuff. Which is the way I aim what I say. I don't mean shove it down their throats. I do mean reading a helluva lot of it, also talking about the particular poets, disagreeing with excerpts of criticism I read to them (almost always) (disagree, I mean) – But it still gets me down. There are some students in class who, from their comments, want great elaborate theories built up, to explain not only CanPo but all. Well ————? I mean, I can't. This makes me feel goddam inadequate.

However – however – the money! You know I got a thousand bucks (less tax) for a month's non-work? I mean, show me the ditch where you can do that, even if you write a poem about ditch-digging. Must admit I'd rather do that, write the poem that is. But the stuff I'm writing seems crap. Have to go to the metrical analyst's for an overhaul. This bit about Annette[1] also bugs me. I'm goddamed if I'll give her a pass for a crappy paper, or honors which she says she has to have – if she does nothing as I expect. Eurithe seems to think I'm a cold-hearted bastard about it, which bothers me. Because sometimes I show signs of being that to myself, and how can a cold-hearted bastard write good poems? I ask you – Therefore, because of the lit gain involved, I must not be a cold-hearted bastard. Right? So pass the bitch. To hell with that, I won't, not unless she writes a good paper. But it bothers me. Am I wrong? Anyway, sometimes I think all the poems I would consider good are already written, which is a nasty thought. Then I will have to bone up on Parmenides, Rilke, Coleridge's Bigraphia Literaria (which someone left in my office) etc.[2] And that's hell. I wanta find out things for myself, as I said in the last letter.

Re poems, I once thought of getting/having Eurithe get a job teaching on an Indian reservation and me being an invisible entity nearby drifting etc. That's what I am too. Three/four years back when I thought of that, and still think it's a good idea.

Don't you feel this lit guilt yourself? – writer-in-rez and all that? Or is it the washed-up writer talking? Anyhow, this fucking place is dull, television at night, *walks,* (dunno how Eurithe stands it, and she hates me for not goin to Mexico) – I think there's a pressure on me I put there myself, to write better, to always write better. Right now, I can't. And don't like it.

So what else is new? Birney I sympathize with, for he is a friend, tho I can't talk to him the way I do in letters to you, or in person. I do agree that he's a phony lothario, whether he realizes this or not. But in a way, perhaps unexplainable, I do sympathize with his wish to stay young thru others. In another way I do not, for it makes him a phony if he knows it, an idiot if he doesn't. I think a lot of men – at a certain more youthful age than him – have the wish to fuck every beautiful woman in the world. Some women perhaps too, vice-versa. It's not altogether silly, perhaps has to do with one world psychologically, one human world etc. But really, the only important women are those with whom there is some kind of rapport, whether instant or developing. And beyond that again is death.

That brought Lawrence to mind, D.H. Since the more I read him the more I know he's the poet that talks in the language and uses the thoughts I aim towards. Not just death, but that too, since it's always so mixed with life – I mentioned his poems to you before, and do now emphatically again. I wish you'd get his two vol collected from library and read quickly quickly, particularly "Birds, Beasts and Flowers", then return to the poems that seemed good.[3]

I am thinking of all sorts of ways and stratagems to get books and mags I want. You'd be amused. Eurithe says I'm the oddest mixture of ethics and complete disregard for them she's seen – of course her experience is a bit limited. She has been pushed and prodded in the direction my mind takes because of her connection with me, else she couldn't stand me at all. And yet I am quite amoral about some things, material things, a dichotomy she doesn't seem to get. But then why should she? But the dichotomy is not one to me, since I separate all things into compartments –

Yeah, and hark back, all women are not symbolic of one world etc.

Love,

Al

Hey – I put the carbon inbackwards, so you have the only copy. Burn it? Sell it? Zerox it? Use it for toilet paper? One page at least shall escape this mercantile world –

P.S. A student, who is quite possibly trying to curry favor (I can't tell) has sung one of my poems to me over the phone. Sounds like Leonard Cohen, Eurithe says. I am buying a guitar tomorrow.

---

1. Purdy's student and one of the women celebrated in *Poems for All the Annettes* (1962).

2. Parmenides (515-450 B.C.), a Greek philosopher of the pre-Socratic period; Rainer Maria Rilke (1875-1926), a German poet. Samuel Taylor Coleridge (1772-1834), poet, philosopher, and critic, published his *Biographia Literaria* in 1817.

3. D.H. Lawrence (1885-1930), novelist, poet, and essayist. *Birds, Beasts and Flowers,* originally published in 1923, appeared in volume II of *The Collected Poems of D.H. Lawrence* (1928).

Massey College
University of Toronto
5 February [1970]

Dear Al–

Thanks for yrs of Feb. 1. Ye gods, what shall we do re: the carbon put in the wrong way? Shall I return the page to you? Maybe I'll just keep same, and – no, maybe I better send it back to you, as you are well organized re: this, and I ain't. I've got all yr letters (I think) in various files, mostly in Eng and will put all together when I return, but damn it, now you've converted me to yr way of thinking so I'm concerned that this immortal correspondence should survive and future students or gossips or whatever can read them and think "Well, hell, *she* sure was more of a slob than the world knew at the time", or "Imagine Purdy being so business-like, albeit intermittently — we thought he was a *poet*." I don't remember what I said to you on phone re: letters — or anything else, come to that — so ignore what I said. My judgement was at that moment somewhat warped, no doubt.

Sorry to hear the lectures are bugging you. Honestly, I think that if you just get up and read poetry and talk and get the kids talking, it will do a hell of a lot more for them than formal lectures. Naturally, some of them want elaborate theories — that is their heritage in the academic world, and a bloody poor one it is, in my view. The viewpoint of someone like yourself, non-academic but knowing what poetry is all about, will be like a breath of fresh air through the stifling corridors of their minds. Seriously — I am being serious, Al. For heaven's sake do not feel inadequate — I know what you mean, tho, because sometimes when talking to either kids or faculty here, I get bowled over and bewildered by their abstractions, theories, jargon, excessive talk of symbols etc. Then I think — what the hell; I wrote the damn thing they're talking about, and I knew all the various threads involved but it does NOT have to [be] explained in highly abstract terms. There is another way of looking at it. In some ways, I almost feel that every poem or novel should be read the way it is (I think) written — as though it were the first one, ever to be encountered, and yet with the (subconscious) knowledge and accumulation of all the others, like approaching it all anew and yet with some acquired feeling for the nuances, which doesn't necessarily have to be verbalized at all, and certainly doesn't have to be verbalized in highly theoretical and jargon-like terms. (Like, I suppose, making love is best when it happens like that, too — the two are always in some way comparable in my mind).

Yeh, the money. Well, you are building up a reserve which will let you be free for awhile, that's what it's for, after all.

NO YOU ARE NOT WRONG ABOUT ANNETTE … for heaven's sake, man! You know bloody well you are right. You're a cold-hearted bastard if you don't give someone an A unless they write an A paper? That must be the most ridiculous statement I've heard in weeks, as you know only too well. Out with these self-doubts, Purdy! You know perfectly well that you can't do otherwise than mark on what kind of paper anyone turns in. And it is not only academic standards we are talking about, here, is it? It's the fact that there is one thing you don't dare betray – and that's whatever it is that is connected with your own poetry. You don't dare because like all of us you are aware that the poems can't be turned on and off at will, and so this is mysterious. Hell, don't mistake me – I'm superstitious in this area, and maybe you're not, but I know you well enough to know that you feel something the same about this whole thing, what makes us able to go on writing. And that in some ways one would sooner betray one's nearest and dearest, on account of the other is – well, you know. (I never really knew whether I left J originally because of all the many differences of personality, or whether in the end it was because he said he didn't really think I was a novelist, and nothing much happened in THE STONE ANGEL – so I packed my manuscript and took off!)

Yeh, I do feel literary guilt re: w-in-r. When I've got time to think of it, I think – what the hell am I doing here? It's fun in some ways, exhausting in others, but I'm not really doing anything for young writers. Any of the good ones don't need any help, and the others are not possible to help anyway, so I'm really spending the year chatting away to a whole lot of kids, to no particular purpose. Way I try to justify it – I'm not doing them any good except to provide someone for them to talk about writing with, but I am probably doing myself (hopefully) some good by getting away from my writing for a spell, which god knows I needed to.

In 5 minutes have to go out to a woman's residence to have dinner and talk with the girls oh joy oh joy. Would like to go home and have double scotch.

Yr not amoral … you just have basically a one-track mind (apart from the obvious question of women, I mean) … and that is connected with yr work, it is just loyalty or whatever to something difficult to explain. Like, one walks to a different drum or some such thing. Or so I like to think about myself, dunno about you. A justification for being at times unscrupulous? Maybe.

Love,
Margaret

§

[Simon Fraser University]
3 March [1970]

Dear Margaret,

The book is lovely! [1] I didn't like the idea of a seagull when you mentioned it, but doesn't seem to matter in actuality. Forget whether this cloth matches all the other Knoph – how in hell do you spell Knohp Knoph nuff said – books, but the lover of books and other things hopes it does – One sees a four foot shelf of books, all dust covers off, lined up for a receiving line at a book show. No book show, on a personal shelf.

I seem to remember all those stories well, the people in them, tho not perhaps the incidents. I guess that's wrong, for I remember these stories better than any by anyone else. Why is that? Obviously because of the author's genius. But it's true, I can remember those people. They do somehow exist imaginatively for me, and I believe that's gotta mean they're very very fine. For instance, it's years since I read Chekhov, Hemingway, or even Callahan,[2] and can't remember any of those. Strange.

Enuff tho, you're probably away by now. This is just to say the book is great fine splendiferous etc. It's even good.

Love,

Al

---

1. Laurence had sent him a copy of *A Bird in the House.*

2. Morley Callaghan (1903-90), Canadian novelist and short-story writer.

9 Westgrove Crescent

Toronto 305, Ont.

5 March 1970

Dear Al–

Thanks much for letter of Mar 3. I am so glad you think A BIRD IN THE HOUSE is okay. Knopf is spelled *Knopf.* Yeh, the binding matches all my other books except that THE FIRE-DWELLERS was done in a slightly more jazzy way, with bright orange binding (good), and zigzag gold lines on binding, so it is really the only one that doesn't match, and I was sorry. I thought it ought to match, too, just to have a set, but that really is nonsense, I guess. This one, now, reverts to type and MATCHES. Does it matter? It doesn't, really. But one has these small vanities and hang-ups – like, let us have a matching set of books, when we know perfectly well that it is all crazy and we are certainly none of us in the immortality stakes. We'll last about as long as we live, and probably not after that, and so what.

Glad you liked the stories, tho, and that you remembered them. Hell, you remembered them probably on account of you had worked on them, eh? You have not forgotten those terribly long days in Elm Cottage, when you were not able to work on your own work on account of circumstances and had to work on *something* or you'd lose yr mind?

I didn't write in A BIRD IN THE HOUSE what I wanted to write to you or intended to write. Dunno what happened – loss of memory, maybe. Wanted to send the book quickly to you, and did not say what I had intended. I wanted to say thus: (you can glue it into book): [1]

The life here remains the same, hectic. I am getting rather fed up with seeing young writers, to tell you the truth. As I said in last letter, I am getting homesick for my goddamn typewriter. You notice that yr letters to me and my letters to you are getting shorter and shorter? This is because both of us are involved with work we feel responsible for, but don't really now want to do. Or so I think. It has been an okay year for me but I want to go home now, please. I am not thinking of Home as Eng, or Can, just somewhere where I am myself and do not have all these duties which I feel I oughta do, on account of being paid for same, like real and fantastic money (academics do not, you know, know what money *is* – they feel threatened if they do not have yearly salary of 12 thou dollars or much more – how strange).

What I really want to do is tell you everything that has happened, all the whole kooky bit, but cannot, as it is too detailed and I am too tired. Every week is filled with strangeness. The number of really promising (I hate that word) young writers I've met could be counted on less than the fingers of one hand, to tell you the truth. But a very few of them are interesting. The rest? Well.

There are about ninety million things I want to say to you, but cannot on account of being so bloody tired I have to retire now and get 10 hours sleep before the Maritime trip. I sort of get the same impression from yr letters – all that terrible stuff about courses and marking essays. Incidentally, I laughed pretty hard re: the article on you in the SFU paper. I loved it, that you said the reason you went there was money. Terrible thing is – they probably thought you were kidding. Little did they know that they had been told the truth. Why else would anybody do that kind of bloody awful thing, as you were landed with, it seems to me.

How do you really feel, Al? I feel really *tired*. The amount of psychic energy poured out in one week is simply fantastic, and all of it goes to talking with young writers or talking with seminar groups or personal radio or TV interviews, and all of it means really nothing NOTHING. I really want to go home. I wanna go home, wherever that may be. What I am doing now seems to me to be nonsense. Like, the kids who are any good do not NEED any help or encouragement, of COURSE. And those who ain't – what can you do but be tactful?

Have, incidentally, had about 5 dozen letters just recently from some people across Canada who say "will you read my manuscript and give me advice about how to get it published?" And I have to write back and say No. But the fucking letters in this vein have bugged me, I suppose, to some extent, because so many of them are from people who are virtually illiterate. What do you say? It is pretty awful, because here are people who are actually nearly inchoate, but needing to *SAY*. And they can't. Their writing is just perfectly dreadful, but that does not mean that they're the same. I write cold letters, wishing them luck. Jesus. But you can only take on what you can take on, and part of the thing about our tribe is that we are in some deep way unscrupulous, and have to be. But these goddamn illiterate letters still bug me.

[. . .]

With love,
Margaret

---

1. The inscription reads:
   To be put into *A BIRD IN THE HOUSE*
   For Al Purdy –

whose words told me something about what I was doing – "My Grandfather's Country," and "They had their being once, and left a place to stand on". You have to know where you're standing. After that – who knows? We'll see.

Love,

Margaret Laurence

§

Elmcot

5 August [1970]

Dear Al–

The poem is splendid.[1] Thought so when I heard it over the phone but only certain now that I see it and read it. It gets across that quality which is in all your best poems, I think – ie the sense of the present being part of the past and also of the future; the sense of everything being connected, somehow, so that the ancestors are everybody's ancestors, and we ourselves are ancestors-in-the-making, or something like that. Also some kind of sense of reaching out beyond our planet and yet the acute ever-present and also painful feeling of awareness of an individual's humanity.

– Looking back on that paragraph, I see how right you were in the poem, too, about the translation of feelings and responses into words. It's all I can do, too, but one feels sometimes (most times, I guess) that it's goddam inadequate. And faced with any kind of direct thing – like the rock painting and a person's unverbal and deep response to it – one almost wonders if someday the human race won't outgrow words. Maybe we've had to work, as a species, through all these christly knots of verbalism only in order to get back to something we once had and now only have sporadically, or maybe we never did have that direct response in any very

175

subtle way, in, say, the caveman era, but it's possible to have it. I dunno. Words are very baffling. And yet, on the other hand, it's only your words which can communicate to other human beings the whole feeling of your response to the Horseman, and your catching of Eurithe's response (migawd, that part is lovely!) I sort of catch the (you should excuse the expression) purity of her response to the Horseman, to the ancestors, and I have to see it as something complete in itself, somehow very strong and with great integrity, almost impossible to anyone who is even at the time translating it all into words. (You remember the scene from Brian Moore's An Answer From Limbo, where the writer at the funeral of his mother is fictionalizing it all in his mind, already, and sees himself doing it?) I thought, reading the poem, as I've thought before (also with other poets etc), how strange to be Eurithe (please pass on these comments to her – they're for her maybe more than you, or as much) – like being Sarah, with Gulley Jimson in The Horse's Mouth;[2] only a very strong-in-herself woman could be, I would suspect, just because you *do* do most of the talking, but there's another dimension of life where the living is done directly, which is her dimension but also the one you're trying (like all writers) to catch in your impossible net. Jesus. Anyhow, the poem made me think of all these things, which I record in words. We serve an ironic god.

The illustrations were pretty rotten, I thought. Purdy in Mod garb was a little peculiar, and Eurithe as Sprite-Of-The-Forest was a damn sight too pixie-like. General effect, actually, for most readers, would be okay. But what they should've done was to print very plain that pic of you and Eurithe which is on yr living-room wall, plus an exact reproduction of the cave painting, very stark, something like that. Newspapers and mags, however, never do these things right. I speak from gloomy experience of having stories idiotically illustrated for many years.

Odd thing – the day after the poem arrived, two dear friends arrived from Canada;[3] have known them for 20 or more years.

They are from Toronto; he teaches in Library School, U of T. Said they damn near missed plane because John at last minute said "We have to take that page from the Globe & Mail with Al Purdy's poem; Margaret will want to see it". They couldn't find it. Chris (his wife) is pacing floor while John fumbles through old newspapers and finally they leave without it. Both very enthusiastic about poem, in real way. Relieved when they learned I'd seen it. I pass on this little episode with no charge. Thought you'd like to know. John is great admirer of yr work, and is (unknown to you) a v. good PR man on yr behalf.

House is a shambles. I think I'm running a hotel here. I love it, actually. I hate the thought of autumn, when all visitors will have departed and I will have no more excuses to keep me away from work. I don't want to think of that goddam novel. Dunno how to tackle it. I realize more and more that realism bores me to hell, now. No way I can do it in straight narration. Can't think of any other way. Stalemate. Words fail. Maybe I should take up painting or music? No? No. Anyway, thanks for poem.

Love,
Margaret

---

1. Purdy had sent the pages from *The Globe Magazine* of 25 July 1970, which contained an illustrated version of "The Horseman of Agawa."

2. *The Horse's Mouth* (1944) by Joyce Cary (1888-1957) was one of Laurence's favourite novels.

3. John and Christine Marshall.

§

Elmcot

14 August [1970]

Dear Al–

Brief (didn't turn out all that brief) [1] note, in case you thought
from my last letter I'd really gone round the bend at last. Was very
struck by your poem, and only slightly drunk when wrote letter,
but thought later that I should've specified I meant Sarah Monday
when she was Jimson's subject all those yea-many years, not the
latterday Sarah – otherwise Eurithe will hate me for life, if she
doesn't know which Sarah I was referring to. Verbal expression is
often puzzling and misleading, as one has often remarked.

What with a spate of N.Amer visitors, plus trying to get house
in shape (builders and painters trekking through all the time, but
never mind ... God bless them), plus long converse with daughter
who is breaking up with boyfriend and thinks she is falling for a
boy from Belfast (it couldn't, of course, have been Cornwall,
where all they have is oil-polluted beaches, not petrol bombs),
plus digging my rose garden and overestimating my ability and
wrenching my back ... well, what with the normal course of life,
in other words, I am feeling just a shade exhausted. However, it's a
healthy tiredness, not that nerve-frazzling kind I underwent in
Toronto from yakking too much about that which shouldn't be
yakked about in public, namely writing. Feel depressed sometimes when I think this coming novel, if it ever gets written, will
be my last. But there. Maybe I'm fated to end my days running
some kind of lunatic hostel for young Canadian writers who need
a decent meal from time to time. It's the matriarch in me. I would,
of course, administer their Can Council cheques for them, taking
a considerable cut. I kind of fancy myself as a mean-eyed con-
cierge (spelling?). I don't actually feel very humorous about it, as I
think it *is* my last book, altho of course one can't tell. But I'm
damned if I'll do any mock-ups of novels ... and by God, I mean

I *would* be damned. For life, with spears of fire in my bones' marrow.

I have been scared as hell, because I've just received from America, for Knopf royalties on all the books plus paperback eds plus a book club ed, more money than I thought possible for 6 months royalties, namely about $ 12,000. When I got the cheque I deposited it with shaking hands. Feel kind of spooky about it, as tho it will mean disaster or something. Or as tho it will be the last, ever. Also, of course, at other moments, feel astonished and delighted. Trouble is, I think I've got Celtic 2nd sight, and I don't *imagine* what situation will be like re: my writing in 10 years (should I survive, by some miracle) … I *know* what it'll be like, and I don't much like what I know.

Never mind. For the moment, the sun shines, the roses battle against the bindweed, and I'm beginning to feel like a human being again after a year of pretending to be a real live author.

Love,

Margaret

ps. have just got my old Remington reconditioned, and it is like welcoming back an old friend. I never did feel totally at ease with my new typewriter … think I'll keep it in reserve or let my kids use it. Every book that means anything to me now I wrote on this Remington. Hell, no, of course I'm not superstitious! Revelation! Have just realized that I got this typewriter when first in Vancouver in 1957 so in fact have virtually written all books on it, with exception of first (awful) version of first novel, plus final version (unimportant) of last book (the childrens' story one). Heavenly days! How could I have borne to part with it for several years? Answer: because it busted a key when I was typing fair version of THE FIRE DWELLERS and in a rage I went out that instant and bought a new typewriter, which never really got along with me that well. I shall now pour a libation of Tio Pepe over my old buddy and maybe my luck will be in, and I'll find out how to do this christly novel. Yeh, and God will give me grace, and my children will rise up and call me blessed, and at the end of my life I will say like (wait for it!) St.Paul, "I have fought a good fight; I have finished my course; I have kept the faith." Yeh. Or, more likely, the reverse. The goddam novel will never be written; I will get vile liver complaint and be taken to my ancestors screaming blue murder; my kids will ultimately go on Can TV shows to speak of life with a neurotic mother; the last of my books will be remaindered for sixpence on Charing Cross barrows. Vanity, saieth the Preacher. And it really is. Something goes on ... I believe it not personally but in the other way. Sometimes.

ps. when appears Love In A Burning Building? Also, have you heard anything re: grant from Ontario Arts Council or whatever the hell it was?[2]

---

1. This parenthetical remark was added by hand.

2. Laurence had written a letter to the Ontario Arts Council supporting Purdy's request to visit Northern Ontario for several weeks.

Ameliasburgh
19 August 1970

Dear Margaret:

Judging from what you say about poetry – mine and others – it seems to me you oughta be doing a poem-antho. I know you continually disavow knowledge of the stuff, and I suppose you mean knowledge of the more academic and esoteric levels kind, but still you get at the vital parts of it, which is what an anthologist needs. If it weren't a fate worse than death, I'd say go ahead and do it, but take back what I said before. Still, I didn't think much of Richler's selection from me,[1] louse choice.

Hope you've got your OUZO by now and no double enten-dres.

Yeah, the illos were pretty bad, me mod and Eurithe pixie, to be expected I guess. Asked Andy Suknaski,[2] who was a student in my class at SFU, if he wanted to do anything with the poem. This guy does illos on chinese paper and just sent me a three-foot-long book with cardboard covers, all sorts of weird paper made of pla-typus-egg membranes and stuff. I hope he does something, because I really don't think much of the other broadsheets either, the ones that Kerrigan and Tony Lassing did ...

It seems there are a bunch of Can poets over there now, Atwood, Fetherling and several others. Anne McDermid of David Higham Assoc. is trying to get their work pub there, and there are readings in Sept. Wants me to come. But I think this is not a good enough reason if I didn't intend to go for other rea-sons. The English poem scene puts me to sleep anyway, and I had nothing to do with it before, and don't feel like starting. Of course if they could dig me up some money I'd like the trip, but they won't since readings don't pay money there ...

Your mention of hating the thought of all the writers depart-ing and no more excuses sounds a bit like me. My excuse is doing anthos and reviews. I've more or less found what interests me in poems now, like Indian paintings, Indians themselves, the crunch moments in life etc. etc. So I don't wanta write poems about the everyday trivia in the hopes they'll blossom into something larger. This is a wrong attitude on my part, I know, and probably prevents me from finding some new things ...

George Bowering says he's writing a porno novel and finding it very hard work. Is that amusing?

Luv

Al

1. *Canadian Writing Today* (1970), edited by Mordecai Richler, had been published by Penguin Books. It contained Purdy's poems "The North West Passage," "Trees at the Arctic Circle," and "Eskimo Hunter." An excerpt from *A Jest of God* also appeared in the anthology.

2. Andrew Suknaski (b. 1942) had published chapbooks of his own verse.

§

Ameliasburgh

27 August 1970

[No salutation]

Greeting! And the letter to OntArts is fine. If the bastards turn me down this time I'll ——— try again. I have all sorts of plans and projects in my mind, including a visit to Hiroshima. What about that one, eh? There are some places that breed poems, as I was sure of writing the Indian rock painting poem. Hiroshima is the same, and there would be several poems there, a real mother lode. Now go ahead and tell me one shouldn't *look* for poems, they should just catch one unawares. There's a fairly good argument for that sort of thinking, except that the things that enable you to write poems are what interests you, you being what you are; and this is also the point behind fellowships and bursaries. Who knows if I'll ever get there, but I'm thinking of it right now anyway – Anyway, thanks for that letter.

I hope you've received Ouzo by now. If you have a red ink ballpoint, run it lightly over the nose on the old gink on the box. I did it with a felt pen after I sent the book. One copy is sold, incidentally, $ 50. return on a $ 700. investment. Also, *Love in a Burning Building* appeared briefly and disappeared back to bindery on accounta three pages were missing. Maybe Harold Town tore em out. It is a pretty good looking book, with flames progressively devouring the first four-five pages, sand coloured genuine cloth covers (genuine? sure), black paper wrapper with photo of two young lovers embracing dispassionately to the tips of the gal's breasts can show bare on the jacket. No photo of me, which is good taste, since I would leer at the hired models. One poem in the book has a short verse on right hand page, turn over another short verse, then remainder of poem on succeeding left hand page. I never figure what they're gonna do from page proofs correctly. Printers must be ignorant sobs. I suppose it's up to me to scream loudly before the book goes to press, and I do, but only about things in the text, and layout eludes me. Anyway, a copy will be along in due course.

Congrats on those royalties. Loan me ten thou, eh. Of course I know why you're feelin spooky about it – I mean you're writing on the increment of the past, the memory-increment, that is, without much thought of manoeuvering your novelist's equipment (which includes the usual body and emotions) into a spot to gain more increment. i.e., fuck the roses battling the bindweed in Molanium! Why not do some more travelling? Sure, being in Canada a year was travelling, but I'm sure your mind is on the marital problems of the recent past.[1] So why not *look* for material as well as for the grist of your own living self, ... The marital problems are close to the bone, I know, but getting around and doing some living won't stop you from writing about that will it? – it might even give you some perspective. It's a helluva time to talk about it just after you get back there, I know ... I don't really feel that being writer-in-rez for a year and keeping speaking engagements in various places here is travelling except in the strictest sense of moving around. And now you've backed yourself into an Elmcot corner again, just as you get that twelve thou ... My sage and foolish advice is: make sure the house doesn't fall down and I mean repairs, then wander without anything in mind but what interests you as a person – to hell with novels that is ... I suppose these are strange things to say from me, somebody contemplating all sortsa trips in order to write poems. But I stress that where I go is of interest for itself, itself blends with me and the poems, I'm now such a goddam litperson that all these things are inextricable. You say *survive,* survive in Molanium or the world? Now isn't that dirty pool or cricket or baseball? Using your own book agin you, but it's not agin you at all, it's for you. Have been writin poems, first one after Horseman Eurithe says it ain't (isn't in her mouth) as good as the Horseman. Jesus, I say, what'd ya expect; a masterpiece every time I open my mouth. Ya think I'm John Donne or somebody? – This quelled her briefly, until she says, It ain't half as good (isn't) as Agawa. Have been nursing a bosomy viper that's plain!

Jack Jenson[2] (Cole book buyer) down last weekend with pictures taken previously, those little postage stamp things that gota be enlarged. When taken, we were all drinking, and decided to move a huge stone into position on the point, and rolling it thru the shallow water. There is a Can. essay by Peter McArthur (an old crappy up-the-buffs writer) about the debt of mankind to the man who moved the stone from life's common roadway.[3] The guy remained anonymous, but has been identified. They were Jenson and Purdy, swigging beer and posing grandiloquently and a bit drunk. At one point I have Eurithe sitting on one arm and Mary Lu (Jenson's gal) on the other for a camera moment, then sprawled into the water which the camera didn't record. Incidentally, that picture with you, Rosemary Eakins[4] and the big guy, what eager just-discovering-the-word expressions. (Who is the latter-day Sarah? I give up!)

Luv,

Al

---

1. Margaret and Jack Laurence had been divorced in December 1969.

2. Jack Jensen was a book buyer for the Canadian chain, Coles Books.

3. Peter McArthur (1866-1924) was a satirist, rural essayist, and poet, whose most famous poem was "The Stone."

4. Rosemary Eakins was a friend of Margaret Laurence and had been at Oxford completing a thesis.

§

Elmcot

4 September [1970]

Dear Al–

NOW HANG ON THERE, PURDY ... NO SNEAKY ATTACKS ON MY HOUSE, eh? Many thanks for yr 2 letters, second of which I got his morn containing sage advice from ye olde master-traveller. Yeh, it's okay – I know your words of wisdom weren't agin me but for me. And I do mean to survive in the world if possible. I swear it! Also, I agree about travelling, but for me it ain't quite that simple. First, it's not that much fun travelling alone (no, this isn't the poor-me syndrome!). Second, I can't just take off, on account of David is going to school. I *am* going to Canada next summer, God willing, and hope to be able to spend the autumn there as well, if I can find a nice young Canadian couple who would like to keep house here while I'm away. Also, am rapidly trying to get myself into a situation which will allow me to take off when I feel like it, in 3 yrs time when David finishes school. Dunno where he'll be then, whether in Eng or Canada, but whichever it is, I'll be more free to go hither and yon then. I've decided to pay off the mortgage on Elm Cottage (with my ill-gotten gains) so that in 3 yrs time I can rent the place if I want to. I'm at the moment forbidden to do so under the terms of my agreement with the mortgage company. Also, if I can pay it off now, it'll save me a lot of money in the long run, or so it seems to me. Anyway, I feel better about owning land than shares and that kind of stuff which always seems meaningless to me. So – don't worry, I don't plan on spending the rest of my life tending my roses. You're right, tho, in a way – of course I'm nervous about material for future novels. Don't care in a sense, because I think something will turn up. I know what I want to try to do for the next one, and maybe (just maybe) one after that, and that's as far ahead as I need to see. I don't think you're wrong to go looking for material – as you say, the poems and the life can't really be

185

separated. Somehow, tho, the traipsing around the world which I've done in the past 8 yrs hasn't made me want to write about it except in articles. Maybe ultimately. You're damn right that being writer-in-residence isn't either a rest cure or a means of experiencing anything much. On the other hand, I think I learned a lot from all those kids, you know. Dunno yet exactly what I did learn, but sense that it's all there somewhere. I know it has changed my view of what I want to do (or have to do) with this next novel.

Anyhow, old friend, thanks for the timely blast – probably this kinda thing pulls me from my rural reverie or state of dimwitted-ness from time to time. At the moment, don't seem to be inter-ested in writing – keep thinking migawd what a terrible profes-sion. Can't seem to focus my mind. No doubt this lassitude (is that the right word) won't last. I think I got so bloody weary last year that I am just beginning to recover. Excuses, excuses. But I did overspend my psychic energy, and didn't even realize how beat I was until I left Toronto. Am really just beginning to feel human again after that gruelling experience. Also, I guess the whole mar-ital bit took a lot more out of me than I realized at the time. For the first time in about 10 years I don't have to think about that sit-uation, and quite honestly, I *don't* think about it. This is a relief, but at the same time leaves a kind of vacuum, which is ironic I guess. Sometimes I feel like a bloody mass of mangled nerves, as tho after a long battle, but think I'm just not going to force myself too much to get going on writing again … it'll come. Or so I trust. What with the gangs of Canadian visitors, all very welcome I may say, plus the gangs of painters and builders who are this moment tramping in and out with gusts of idiot laughter and whistled snatches of In An English Country Garden and other gems, I have not really had much concentration.

No, I haven't yet received Ouzo, but then, the mails have been so terrible that it isn't really surprising. What a terrible thing re: Love In A Burning Building!! How in heaven's name could three pages be left out? Cover sounds great, but Mc& S certainly need to get a few experienced proof readers.

Re-reading yr letter – God damn it, I haven't backed myself into an Elmcot corner again, blast you! What the hell do you expect me to do? Go off on a short snappy tour of Siam? Poison my kids? Sail a yacht across the Atlantic? Put an ad in The Times … ("wanted: temporary lover; own TV") Don't be ridiculous. Can't remove my kids from England … they're going to have to finish their schooling here. And if I weren't here, where would I be? In my shack on the Otonabee, which is where I'll be next summer. Not exactly the thought centre of the world, maybe, but I have to organize my life so that I can be alone a lot of the time but also so that people can come and see me. And they do. Save your sympathy for someone who needs it. Am I over-reacting? I guess so. Well, you know what I mean.

Would love to see the pics of you and Jenson … they sound perfectly dreadful, but in a kind of appealing way, more or less.

Well, must sign off and go and write a great novel.

Love,
Margaret

ps. Sarah Monday in Joyce Carey's The Horse's Mouth … who else? I always think I'll die like Sarah … getting drunk and falling down stairs.

Elmcot
22 September [1970]

Dear Al–

A brief note to thank you for IN QUEST OF OUZO, which arrived today. It looks great! The new end-papers and the box make a hell of a lot of difference, and the whole thing now looks magnificent. How are sales? I would imagine you will undoubtedly sell the lot, sooner or later. Anyway, many thanks and also for the tender inscription – what the hell do you *mean,* "who prefers England and retsina"?? I don't *prefer* England – I am simply an innocent victim of a totally split personality, that's all, a sufferer from double-vision and dual view and passionately held but conflicting opinions. My two dwellingplaces, in Canada and in Eng, express outwardly the inner conflict. Gawd, nobody knows how I suffer when I really put my mind to it! Actually, there is really no conflict, as I can't decide between the two dwellingplaces, so will have to live some of the time in each, as long as possible. As far as countries are concerned, I'd pick Canada. But this goddamn ⅔ of an acre here is so beautiful and this house is so comfortingly huge – you can walk around in it for days hardly running into even the other members of yr family, and I like that. Also like the fact that I can have lots of visitors and I don't have to move out of my bedroom and sleep on a camp cot when they all descend. Sorry to go on and on about Elmcot. But have decided to pay off the mortgage and also to get the rest of the things done to the old dump which I've wanted to do for years … ie carpeting all the bedrooms, etc. Then I will not touch it for about 10 years unless the roof falls in. But at least it will be in good shape so I can rent it if I want to. Also, if it is mine (and God's), I *can* rent it, which is not permitted under the terms of my mortgage. Well, no more of these domestic details, so fascinating to me and so boring to others.

Dave Godfrey has finished his novel.[1] Last night he sent me a *230* word telegram, informing me of that interesting fact! Wow. It must have cost him the earth. The GPO operator was absolutely stunned – she could hardly read the blamed thing, so full of astonishment was she. She was also flustered by my gusts of laughter as the cable went on and on. I'm terribly glad the novel is done, and hope he can get it taken in USA and Eng soon. New Press is doing it in Canada.

Got a copy of QUARRY[2] today. Thought it was folding. What's the situation?

Got to get down to writing 3 promised articles for Van. Sun.[3] Know what I want to write, but it is difficult to get down to work when house is full of painters and so on. Spend hours totting up finances to see how imminent penury is. Otherwise, just mooch around or work on stone tile floors to improve their appearance. Evasions, evasions. I know it. By now the symptoms of pre-novel neurosis are so familiar that I often think I'm only mocking them up at this point. So I take out the file of scribbled notes, relating to novel, stare [at] pages for some time, and put it all away again. You know, Al, I don't honestly think I am suffering anguished doubts about never writing again – I think I am just being bloody lazy. It's so *difficult* to write a novel; how lovely it would be never to have to work again. Of course I know it wouldn't. But right now I can't remember how it feels to be writing, when it's going well and one's only fear is that death will snatch you away untimely before this jewel is polished, this everest clumb. It is so rejuvenating at the moment simply to be a totally private person (not "a real live author") and to read lots of books written by others and look at lots of idiotic TV and pick out curtain materials and harvest apples from ye olde orchard, and so on. Maybe I am simply building up my strength? Well, like all my brief notes, this one turned out unbrief. Again many many thanks for OUZO. Why don't you hire a guy with a sandwich-board to advertise the book on Bloor Street? Better still, wear the sandwich board yrself?

What news from Ont. Arts Council?

Please give Eurithe my love and tell her next time you come to Elmcot, she won't freeze, as back bedrm will be carpeted. Of course, by that time we will be so splendid, accommodation-wise, that likely we'll be charging 30/- per nite, bed and breakfast.

Incidentally, Eurithe has *ruined* that blue eiderdown in my mind –
every time I see the damn thing, I think "blue marshmallow".

> Love,
> Margaret

---

1. *The New Ancestors* (1970).

2. *Quarry* (est. 1952), a literary quarterly published in Kingston, Ontario.

3. Laurence wrote several articles for the *Vancouver Sun*. The first three that
appeared after this letter was written were: "The Natives Are Restless
Tonight" (26 December 1970), 6; "Down East" (20 March 1971), 6; "Salute of
the Swallows" (22 May 1971), 6.

> Elmcot Poetry & Prose Factory,
> Beacon Hill, Penn, Bucks.,
> Merrie Olde England.
> 28 Sept 70

Dear Mr. Purdy –

We understand that you are one of those rare but beautiful
creatures, a POETRY LOVER. We are therefore enclosing a
little brochure which arrived last week with our copy of The
Spectator, in the expectation that you will be interested in its
implications. A POEM OF THE MONTH![1] Signed! Sealed!
Delivered! Wow! What we want to know, Mr. Purdy, is this – has
anyone thought of this great idea for CANADA? If not, why not?
And why not *you*??? We suggest, out of our considerable business
experience, that you should instantly contact those Canadian
poets whom you esteem most, and sign contracts right away. One
poem per month from one poet means only 12 lousy poems per
year – hell, it's so easy it seems like a summer vacation. With our
country's great culture-buying public in the state of titillation and

admiration which it now is, how can the scheme fail? We suggest that our percentage for suggesting this inevitably magnificent scheme should be 15% on total monthly receipts.

Just visualize – Poem of the Month! The first of the next awful month rolls around, and one is sitting at the breakfast table doing the accounts and chewing one's pencil wondering how to cope with the rising cost of all, the coal strikes here, the post office strikes in Canada, the general bloodiness of the world, when – presto! – the postman gently knocks. He hands over the precious document – Allah, it is the Poem! The Word Made Flesh! The monthly insight into Deep Thought and all that. One is restored to human status immediately; one is, in fact, only a little lower than the angels. One flies on fantastic spiritual wing. "Earle B has writ to me personally! Al Purdy has signed his illegible scrawl on this piece of newsprint containing four lines of four-letter words! M. Atwood has poured into my personal ear two stanzas of death-ful poetry! M. Acorn has metaphorically and in jest clobbered me with his carpenter's adze! Yipee! I am in the KNOW. In the KNOWESPHERE."

Mr. Purdy, I appeal to you. Surely you can see the great possibilities of this great scheme.

> Yours in faith, hope & clarity,[2]
> M. Laurence
> Mehitebel Laurence
> Business Manager,
> Elmcot Enterprises Inc.

---

1. Laurence had attached to her letter an advertisement/membership form for the "Poem-of-the-Month" Club located in London. It promised, "Personally signed original poems by W.H. Auden, Sir John Betjeman, Roy Fuller, Robert Graves, Laurie Lee, and Stephen Spender can be yours."

2. The typed word "charity" had been crossed out and "clarity" handwritten in its place.

§

Ameliasburgh

29 September 1970

Dear Margaret,

Glad you found the book decorative. I hope these jesus Can air mail letters are better to open than English – which I always cut with a knife and lop off the bottom part and then hafta use scotch tape to see what the rest is – Yah, the book, don't look too bad, I think. Ad just appears in current CanFor. Tho sold three copies to friends before that – well, not *close* friends, one might say, which seems to be what it boils down to when you sell fifty buck books ...

My small news: workin like hell as usual: trip to Tor. to plug new book (which you oughta have got: Love in Burning Bldg) (or alternatively: Love is Bilge). Three radio shows and a television thing. Two of which, to my slight surprise, I got paid for. Birney in Tor., lunch with him today before we drove back. McStew paid for two nights hotel rooms at Park Plaza and Westbury. I was fairly bored, whereas in the past I woulda been scared at havin to be an intellectual six hours a day. Bruno Gerussi,[1] Robert Fulford and someone called Deirdre something, to whom the McStew woman passed a note about how I was "gruffly offhand" kinda warnin her about me, since Deirdre had been somewhat chastened by another McStew writer called Ian Adam who wrote something about the invisible poor.[2] Anyway, their furtive motions with the note aroused my curiosity and I got it from where they hid it under my book. Eurithe on the same interview and dismayed me by sayin I was the centre of her existence or like that. Too much for my poor shoulders.

The cable is funny all right, I hope the novel is only partly.

Did I say I phoned Dennis Lee (?) and said: "Dennis, howed you like to go on a trip with me?" "Uh," said Dennis, "where?" "Hiroshima," says me. I enjoyed that one. Only hafta find the money. He has a wife and kids, he says finally three weeks later, also much work at Anansi, but would like to etc. Reason: would like to tackle a big thing in a small way ...

We went to Mtl. a coupla weeks ago, stayed at Ron Everson's,[3] drank so much one night I gurgled as I walked out to the car with Eurithe to go to the U.S. for a book hunt. Part over. Some bargains, like Voyage of the Fox, by McClintock, about 1860, for two bucks. First U.S. ed. of Moodie's Life in the Clearings, writ in Belleville, for five bucks. Lotsa fun. Course I made some bloopers too, and paid too much. Five bucks (less my dealer's discount) for 1st ed of C.F. Hall in Arctic. (Won't mention the mistakes!)

Quarry's still goin.

Work is work and not work, and it wouldn't be lovely not to do it. You're talkin like a woman, not a writer at the moment. Curtain material! Shame on you.

Luv,
Al

---

1. Bruno Gerussi (b. 1928), actor and media personality, was the host of the CBC radio programme "Gerussi!" from 1968-72.

2. Ian Adams, *The Poverty Wall* (1970).

3. Ron Everson (b. 1903) had recently published *Selected Poems: 1920-1970*.

Ameliasburgh
5 October 1970

Dear Margaret,

There's a long review of Bird in the House in CanFor this month by Hilda Kirkwood,[1] and it's pretty good, I think. Be sure and get a copy of this yourself. If you don't or can't let me know, and I'll try to get another copy or have this one zeroxed. Have a sequence of them so don't wanta break it, or would send this.

Re Poetry Lovers, I am immediately instituting a similar organization in Canada for the benefit of Canadians and all human-
kind. Letters have gone out to all known-throughout-the-world
Can. poets, asking if they wish to confer the inestimable benefits
and beauty of their minds on a people trembling with the ecstasy
of unfulfilled expectation, as the lily cup trembles before receiving the fucking bee.

Best,

Al

---

1. The review appeared in *The Canadian Forum,* September 1970, 221-22.

Elmcot

13 October [1970]

Dear Al–

Thanks for both yr letters. Re: what you said in yr first letter,
like, I oughta be ashamed of myself for thinking of curtain material and the like – well, yes, yes, OH HEAVENS YES YOU ARE
RIGHT. Don't I know it. I am, actually, in true fact a great nest
builder from way back, and go through life setting up these
homes in various corners of the globe, and that much is genuine.
But of course in very many ways this recent attack of nest building
is a kind of evasion, as I may have mentioned before. It is coming
to an end now and I am faced with the agonizing prospect of this
novel. Actually, I have been thinking of little else, really, other
than the novel, altho the house has taken much attention ostensi-
bly. But underneath only the novel really occupies my mind, and
I don't feel brave enough to tackle it yet. Trouble is, I know in a
vague way what I want to do and I know almost too many details
about the characters, etc, but I don't yet see *how* to do it. I only

194

know many ways how *not* to do it. Every form and voice I've used before are useless now. This has to be quite different, of course, because it wants to attempt something different. Form, naturally, can't be developed or thought out in the abstract, by itself, but only in connection with the characters and the whole thing, and maybe I'm beginning to see, a little, how it might work. But it is always an uncharted sea, and one would not want it any other way, except that at this stage it is pure hell to try to visualize it and not be able to get through to it in the way one wants to. That the novel is there, somewhere, I have no doubt. What I doubt is whether I can pierce through to it; connect with it; establish a direct line, as it were. That is only one problem. The other main problem is that of proximity to oneself. I think – holy Jesus, how vulnerable I'll be making myself and probably other people, too, altho in fact the characters are not based on myself or anyone I have ever known, but what *is* personal is the viewpoint and some of the dilemmas – and even then, these are by no means limited to myself, as I know very well, so what am I worried about? The irony is that the basic fictional situation has been in my head for some 7 years, and in that time, the life situations of several people (not only myself) have followed a somewhat parallel line. What do you say to anyone who knows you and who thinks you've based it all on actual happenings? "I had that line of events in my head since 1962, long before it happened sort of that way in real life"? Because that's what it amounts to, which seems kind of spooky and also unconvincing, altho true. Another thing – the basic thing itself contains many pitfalls, most of which I can see, alas, and I can visualize how *badly* this kind of thing could be written, which terrifies me. (Like, I'm writing the bad reviews in my head before the damn novel is written, even!) There is, of course, only one answer to the whole situation, and that is to get to the point where I am no longer aware of anyone looking over my shoulder; where I do not give a curse whether it turns out well or badly, but only know I have to go ahead and do it anyway, for my own sake;

and where, finally, I sit down and begin, and try for the time I'm doing the thing to forget about my constant sense of anxiety about the financial future and my depressing sense of personal vulnerability and my equally depressing sense of responsibility in perhaps making other people vulnerable. I don't, at least, fear lawsuits ... my fiction isn't ever that directly related to actual events. What I really lack at the moment is the guts to begin. It will come, I hope. It seems to me I want to try to get quite a few things into this novel, but it mustn't be 900 pages ... it has to be very very concentrated, and also not in the tradition of realism, I mean detailed social realism, which now seems to me totally unviable in fiction (I've felt this for some time and tried to get away from it in my last 2 novels, especially The Fire-Dwellers). In short, I can see only too clearly all the problems and can't yet see what partial and eternally inadequate solutions there may be, but I'm convinced they're there somewhere. If I don't get started soon, I will no doubt end up in a mental hospital. The tension is terrible, and I don't really care about anything else, except my kids. As always, I wish there were an easy way to do it, or even a difficult but guaranteed way. But no dice. I hope to God I don't make about 4 false starts, as I did with the last one.

Re: yr letters – I'd like to have the review from Can Forum, if you can get a copy, but if not, don't worry. M& S should send one, but they have been totally unreliable lately in this area.

Haven't yet received LOVE IN A BURNING BUILDING. Hope it didn't get lost in the postal strike.

What of Hiroshima? Are you going? If not, why don't you and Eurithe come here for Xmas? Yeh, those TV interviews you mention ... one does get, finally, not so agitated about them. I had enough to last me a decade.

Have to write 3 articles for Van. Sun. Wrote one three times and tore it up three times. This is getting boring. I must do them, tho, as I both want to write them and want the money. After that, nothing but this damn novel. A better idea than the Poem of the

Month – an insurance firm dealing only with policies taken out by writers on unwritten books; if the thing flops, the writer collects. No one would collect on purpose.

Love,
Margaret

ps. is Doug Fetherling still in Eng? Have you got his address?

Dear Margaret,

While I'm sure there's room I wanta copy a poem.

F.L.Q. KIDNAPPING[2]
We heard all about the kidnapping
in newspapers and on TV
and talked it over between ourselves quite a lot
"Of course we should accede
to the ransom demand or two men die"
she said to me
and I had to ask her what she meant by accede

The second day of the crime we amused ourselves
by devising a dinner menu for the prisoners
it was roast beef and oranges
we cut out photographs of roast beef and oranges
from a women's magazine and mailed them
to the two wives
marked *Please Forward*
which was something I thought of

"On the other hand
Their wives can take lovers
with perfect freedom from pregnancy if –"
(she said)
"Do you mean they shouldn't be ransomed?"
(I said horrified)
"Why yes – after about nine months"

I have sent the woman I love to Quebec
with enough ransom money for two prisoners
No I guess that isn't exactly right
I went myself with as much money as I could
Either way
because we love freedom
it was necessary that one of us should go

Have you heard about the doins of the FLQ and the kidnap-
pings and War Measures Act in Canada in that cocoon over there?
Anyway, I'd have a more serious poem on the same subject, since
we went to Ottawa and were there at Parliament Hill for the big
weekend. (Yeah, I wanted to write a poem!)

I've written the Canadian Forum to send you a copy of the
Sept. ish with the Kirkwood review.

Tell me, for god's sake, have you gotten either *Quest for Ouzo*
or *Burning Bldg.*?

I'm a bit fucked up re Hiroshima. Must have money, and too
late for senior grant application, hafta take short term of $1,350.
which, since the fare is a thousand bucks return allows a stay of
only a month or so. If I went for that short a period my enthusiasm might die (see, I predict myself always) and not return:
whereas if I was there for a long period enthusiasm wouldn't matter, since it would wax and wane and then wax again. Sound silly?
Don't think it is entirely silly. Trouble is I hafta wait for 18 mos for
a senior to begin if I get it, and I might be dead or have no energy
or enthusiasm whatever. You see? Or do you?

About your own gestating novel, is it possible to write something of it, the middle or the end, in any way you like, then sit back and take a look at what you writ? I was kidding about the curtain material, obviously we hafta think of such things at times … As we both know. Wild suggestion, set it in the 16th or 17th centuries. No, too wild! I guess I'm a big help. The bit about what do you say to anyone who knows you etc., well, you say the same thing as you did re all the other novels, whatever that was. You lie like hell, and say it's pure or impure fiction. Besides, a helluva lotta writers have been thru that one, as you know, and maybe there were a lot of books that didn't get written on that account. To hell with that tho. I want the books written, and you'll have to think of a way. If you don't you'll cuss yourself and that's worser no havin other people cuss you. Isn't it?

Love,
Al

Jesus, all that space! [3]

---

1. Purdy had misdated the letter, writing "August" instead of "October."

2. In a gesture of nationalist defiance, a cell of the radical Front de Libération du Québec kidnapped British Trade Commissioner James Cross from his Montreal home on 5 October 1970. Several days later, a second cell of the F.L.Q. kidnapped and subsequently murdered Pierre Laporte, Quebec Minister of Labour and Immigration. The "October Crisis" prompted the federal government to impose the War Measures Act suspending civil liberties. Cross was ultimately released in December 1970. Purdy's poem, in slightly revised form, was later included in the collection *Sex and Death*.

3. Purdy had completed his letter without using all the space provided on the air mail form.

§

Elm Cottage
26 October [1970]

Dear Al–

Got yr letter of Oct 22 today and hasten to reply – yes, I received OUZO some time ago; thought I had thanked you for it, but maybe I didn't, so many thanks. It looks very good now, and the box is a great addition. You'll sell them all ultimately – but you really need them to be handled by one or two bookshops, don't you? Anyhow, many thanks … and what the hell do you mean by saying both England and retzina will figure in my next novel??? England, maybe … (but in a minor role).

You'll have received my 2 letters re: LOVE IN A BURNING BLDG, I hope, by now. I am certainly glad you stuck to your guns re: the title, as it is a splendid title, in my opinion. H. Town sounds like a nitwit – I don't think I really want to meet him. Okay, a strong ego is necessary, but *that* strong an ego is like having halitosis.

Yeh, we hear about the FLQ and all, here in this backwater. What annoys me is that something like this has to happen before any Can news is printed in the Eng newspapers at all. They are all full of it now, complete with lead editorials nearly every day on Mr. Trudeau's agonizing decision.[1] It is, however, as you suggest in poem, a very delicate question. Like, if you were Pierre Elliott T, which way would you have decided? I *think,* altho I am not sure, that I would have gone along with the FLQ's demands and tried to get the 2 guys back alive, while at the same time I would've been convinced that in many ways this was the wrong decision. Funny thing, Al – it's almost as tho by answering that question "What would you have done?", one reveals with perfect precision one's basic stance. In my case, a liberalism which I have known for 20 years to be ineffectual, but cannot help. I will always choose the individual before the principle; my friends before my country. I detest Nixon and Agnew[2] but would not shoot them, or any member of the industrial-military oligarchy which rules America, even tho I believe the establishment will not yield one inch without force. This is what both the Old Left and the New refer to as the ineffectual fence-sitting bourgeois liberal ... yeh, they're right. But I am not capable of any other course, and any other course would kill me dead as far as the only thing I'm meant to do, ie write. The revolutionary and the reactionary both have to quit thinking of people as having names and identities; if the writer quits thinking of people that way, he or she is finished as a writer. So one's dilemma won't really ever be solved, I think.

Yr notion of staying more than a month or so in Hiroshima makes sense, because I know that you would have to stay long enough to become in some way not a tourist. Not that you would belong, in any sense, but it was the same re: living in Africa; a brief visit to a place seldom tells one very much.[3] Hope you make it.

I've decided that in order to allay my terrible anxiety re: going broke, I may apply next year for a C.C. grant, partly because I want to visit N. Manitoba either next year or the following. For a purpose. Or so I think. Will you pen a tender message to the Council, if I do? (Don't need to reply; I know you will).

Re: yr comments on my embryo novel ... thanks much, and I mean it. Surprisingly, or maybe not surprisingly, I need from time to time to have a friend saying, in effect, for god's sake quit messing around and get on with it. You are, of course, quite right – I will have to think of a way to write it. (Not, I think, by setting it in the 16th or 17th century!) Actually, I think I may have found a way to do it – haven't set pen to page yet, but at least the goddamn voices are chattering away inside the brain, often at night until about 3 a.m., which is slightly tiring but not boring ... if yr going to have insomnia, better you should have something interesting to think about! I'll begin, never fear, and how it will turn out is anybody's guess, but I'm approaching the point where I DO NOT GIVE A DAMN whether anyone else except myself ever sees anything in it; it's got to be written anyway. I wish to christ I had more talent, more intelligence, more everything. But one has to do what you can with what you have. I wish I could write it as it deserves to be written, but that is probably how all novelists feel even if they are *great* novelists like Patrick White. Anyway, was it Goethe who said "Begin, and the mind warms to it"? It's true. By the way, yr also right about the personal bit re: novels … one lies like hell. That kind of lie is totally acceptable.

Love,

Margaret

ps. am trying to get my life in order before beginning novel … how impossible. Have written 30 letters in last week, some which needed replying to since last year in Can. Would like to do 3 more (promised) articles for Van. Sun, for $$$$, but am totally uninterested in doing same.

---

1. Pierre Elliott Trudeau (b. 1919), Prime Minister of Canada (1968-79; 1980-84), had invoked the War Measures Act and refused to meet the F.L.Q. kidnappers' demands.

2. Richard Nixon (b. 1913) and Spiro Agnew (b. 1918), at this time President (1969-74) and Vice-President (1969-73) respectively of the United States. Each was later to resign in disgrace.

3. The Laurences had lived in Somaliland (now Somalia) from 1950-52 and on the Gold Coast (now Ghana) from 1952-57, before their return to Canada.

❦

Dear Margaret,

Really screwed up today. Yesterday (Sat.) it was announced Ryerson Press would sell out to McGraw-Hill Monday. I've worked four mos on antho of young poets, but I will not work for a goddam US company.[1] So I expect ructions when this is made plain to Ryerson – and of course and not least, the newspapers, if necessary. And in something like this, I think publicity is good.

About your novel, I can only guess what it's like to be screwing around the way you are doing before beginning, on accounta my big projects don't take the same form, they're enthusiasms and spurts and have little consecutive endurance necessary. I'd cite the aforementioned antho, but it's not at all the same. I just stick grimly to that, day after day, of course as you do with a novel – but very differently. When I was writing plays, there was more similarity. I'd try to work the things out in my head completely, then found that if I did that sometimes I'd lose the whole thing, lost all inclination etc. The two stools, lies and truth, and how to blend the two so it doesn't matter which is which. Or at least, so that they become the same fictionally, become one truth ... I say you absolutely must write the bloody novel. It'll kill you if you don't and might if you do. But there's no way out, positively not. It's probably a good thing you're stupid, since I revel in my own stupidity at times, which was like (years ago) taking pride in operating machines and also in not being able to repair them. Bull-headed stupidity can be a good thing and it's pleasant we both have it. Deliberate hurting no, but finally and if all else fails even that.

Along these lines, I agree with the Trudeau govt. Dislike risking the kidnapped men etc. – but what kind of human beings are we if we don't resist a rule of force and terror? Maybe if I was the wife or close friend of Cross or Laporte – as in some sense we are all wives and close friends of those two – then I'd disagree with the War Measures Act. If this seems schizophrenia so be it. And maybe I'd even feel the same as I do now if I were wife or friend, and feeling the same then would be that much more agonizing and tough. One has to say no at times – which reminds me I discovered an aphorism I wrote maybe a year or two ago,

> Yes is a personal feeling
> but no is a cause ...

Of course this reverses the meaning of Joyce's yes yes yes in Finnigan ...[2] But I think no is affirmative in what I'm talking about, without any weaseling around with meaning and words. (I wonder if those two lines are good enough to publish? What do you think?)

The 30 letters you wrote last week are entirely escape. So are the Sun articles, even if you did promise them.

Of course I'll write CC letter, any time you like. Say when.

I don't believe one has to shoot Nixon or Agnew, just remove their power, and the power of the U.S. elite – by saying no.

We are getting ready to look at some land, and Eurithe tells me I should get dressed. So I guess I should ... just when I'm getting interested.

Love,

Al

---

1. *Storm Warning: The New Canadian Poets* which Purdy was preparing for Ryerson Press, was published in 1971 by McClelland and Stewart. Purdy urged other writers not to publish with Ryerson.

2. Purdy may be confusing the conclusion to *Ulysses* (1922) by James Joyce (1882-1941) with Joyce's *Finnegans Wake* (1939).

§

Elm Cottage
5 November 1970

Dear Al–

Once again I hasten to reply, this time because I've got a suggestion to make. First, I think yr quite right re: Ryerson. I got a very worked-up letter from Dave Godfrey a short time ago, telling me that this sellout was in the offing and saying how furious it makes him to see Can publishers who apparently do not care if American firms control our textbooks. What about taking the antho to Anansi or New Press? It would give them the opportunity (that is, if they want the opportunity) to break into the textbook field, and would also prove a point and would also mean yr work hadn't been wasted. Incidentally, I got a letter from Bill French[1] of the Globe & Mail today, giving me the same piece of news and saying "all hell is about to break loose over another sell-out to the Americans", so I feel pretty sure he'd welcome any raging statement you cared to make on the subject. Good luck! Wish I were there to do battle. Dave Godfrey, incidentally, said also that he had heard M&S were in the same kind of fix, but personally, what with J.G.McC being some kind of official in that organization (can't recall name) for restoring Canada to the Canadians, I can scarcely believe he'd sell out to Amer.[2] What have you heard? I'm crucially concerned about all this.[3] Sometimes I really wish I were back there. On the other hand, that would be a dandy way *not* to get a novel written, at the moment. I'm hoping at least to be back for next summer. I'm pretty certain I can work okay at the shack.

Thanks again for the shot in the arm re: the novel. Of course I know I have to write it. Whatever the pitfalls (and they are legion). In the end, I am more worried about conveying the thing convincingly and uncornily than I am about the personal vulnerability angle. I think now that there is absolutely no further use in trying to plan the thing … the only thing to do is try to sit down and write it. Yr right of course about the Sun articles being another evasion ... but at last I've got the bloody things done.

Also, Ron Weyman[4] has taken a 2nd year's option on The Fire- Dwellers and thinks maybe he can raise the dough for a film after all. However, whether or not he raises it, the option means a further $6,000 ... actually, after agent's fees and income tax, I'll probably clear about the equivalent of $3,000, but at least that gives me the assurance that I can live for the next 3 yrs while attempting to write novel, so now no financial excuses for sitting around brooding, which is good. My agent phoned last nite from New York to give me the happy news. He (my agent) is really a fine guy ... every time a good piece of news comes in, he phones. Chatted for some time to him, his wife and his young son, and then said to friends who were here "The call was from N.Y." ... astonishment all round. Thank god I wasn't paying for the call!

Gary and Phyllis came out last weekend ... actually, they were supposed to come this weekend, but got the dates wrong; however it was fine and I was delighted to see them. We had about 8 people over the weekend, including another 2 Can writers. Gary has written a very good narrative poem called Letter Of The Master Of Horse,[5] triggered off apparently by his reading about the Horse Latitudes where the Spanish jettisoned horses. I have just written a letter for him to the CC and hope he gets grant. I think he kind of wanted to ask you, but somehow felt shy or hesitant about doing so. He asked me for a ref. *very* hesitantly, but I had been going to offer one anyway.

What is this about looking at land? Are you and Eurithe slowly buying up the province?

Guess I won't need to apply for CC grant next year now, with film money. Won't apply unless I really need to, as I have some kind of personal superstition that my next application, if there is one, should be saved for a really rainy day, which no doubt will eventually arrive.

News here says Can govt believes Cross in USA ... what is

news there? Can news here is absolutely non-existent … papers have virtually dropped the whole story.

I have bought five very large notebooks. I stare at them. They remain empty. (This is a joke, not self-pity). I am getting embarrassed about the whole thing. Actually, tho, when I returned from Can, I reckoned I wouldn't get going until mid-November. If I don't get going by then, I'll poison myself. No, I don't mean it. Sometimes, tho, one looks at the reviews of the millions of novels and wonders why we all bother. (It's okay … I *know* the answer to that one).

Anyway, thanks much for moral support.

Love,

Margaret

------

1. William French (b. 1926), literary editor of the *Globe and Mail* (1960-90).

2. Jack McClelland and Claude Ryan, editor of *Le Devoir,* were co-chairmen of the Committee for An Independent Canada, a citizens' committee founded in September 1970 to promote Canadian cultural and economic independence.

3. Early in 1971, Jack McClelland announced that financial difficulties were forcing him to put McClelland and Stewart up for sale. In the spring of that year the Ontario government provided a $1,000,000 loan to prevent sale of the firm to American interests.

4. Ron Weyman (b. 1915) was a producer/director with the CBC. He wrote and directed *Stacey,* his screenplay based on *The Fire-Dwellers,* which was presented on CBC television in 1977.

5. Geddes' poem was published in 1973 by Oberon Press in their "New Canadian Poets" series.

§

Dear Margaret,

Sorry to have been so slow writing, but here's a list of what I've been doing so you'll understand there are reasons.

Of course, first, finishing the antho of young poets. This has called for literally hundreds of letters from me and to me, and has been more work than any other book I've done. Some of the letters to me have been highly interesting, such as a five-page single space roar of rage from Bryan McCarthy wanting to know why he isn't in the book, alternately pleading with me and berating me and praising me – Kinda revolting, as you might agree. Another from a guy praising himself so much, and indulging in so much self-pity at the same time, that it just about makes one throw up. But it's all part of such a job, I guess. There are good letters too, having generosity towards other poets – Also some twenty re my own action with Ryerson Press – I simply don't answer some of them, just can't and have any time left.

I've written three articles, two for TorStar, of which one has appeared; a third for MacLean's, which hasn't appeared.[1] Peter Newman, Star ed.[2] has offered me a job at $13,000. in the ed. dept of the Star, which regrettably I have to turn down. (I have promises to keep/And miles to go before I sleep) Like I may not have said, I got the money from Ont. Arts Council for the Ont. project. Also applied for money for Hiroshima, which application was also successful. The last being only a short term grant, but since the air fare is $950., the short term amounts to well over two thou.

Also, have just completed a record for C.B.C., 12″, which will be broadcast on CBC sometime this spring before record release.[3] Finished taping for this last night, or Wed. nite, some 30 hours ago. Went thru both sides of record, some 45 minutes, with only about three fluffs, and the producer said that's good, we'll leave it at that. Was supposed to have the studio from 7 p.m. to 10, but finished at 8. I was pleased at first, at this early finish, but then I got uneasy, knowing damn well if the tape had been played back I'd notice weak spots that should be re-done. But shit, it wasn't bad generally, I guess.

Angus Mowat (Farley's pop)[4] was here last Sunday, with his forty year old mistress, he being 73-74, which seems kinda sweet, eh? Also six other people, including Acorn, Jack Jenson and his Mary Lu, Kerrigan and the high school head from Trenton. What a night! I swear Angus doesn't like Farley much, tho he doesn't say this. Little tiny man, cocky as hell like Farley, wears a kilt, won't write any more (has written two novels), I tell him because Farley has given him an inferiority complex. He has a school inspector sort of rooster hectoring manner, which I met head on, twitting him about Farley and his inferiority complex.

Anyway, you get the idea, I HAVE BEEN BUSY. No poems for about two months, and only miss not writing in my wistful moments. I have written, but not poems. Fourteen minutes of narrative for record, for instance, which is not the same thing at all.

Right after I pulled the book outa Ryerson, the phone rang long distance about 5-6 times a day. Some reporters trying to trap me into admissions, the CBC interviewing and all that crap, as if I were a writer in rez at U. of T. Did enjoy it for a while, but jesus it got exhausting. All over now, the nine day's wonder finished, the Ryerson sale gone ahead and completed as expected, everyone talking a good fight but not much action otherwise.

And I find I can't really get along with Acorn anymore at all. Expect it's my own fault too. I've changed, gotten impatient with circumlocutions and sloppy reasoning – or so I say re other people, you will note, not about myself.

Before this page ends, should say we leave for Mexico in 2-3-4 days, however long it takes to get ready. We have no address down there, but will write when there is one. (Come back in Mar. at which time I take off for Hiroshima.)

Hey – Canada Council just sent me a huge long novel by James Houston, about the Eskimos etc.[5] Of its genre, I think it's a masterpiece, if a masterpiece can be limited to genre, or by genre. Do you know of Houston? He's the guy that got the Cape Dorset people carving in soapstone. And he knows his subject. His subtitle is "An Eskimo Saga" and it sure is. CC wants to know if the book should be trans. into Fr., since it has an English publisher. Of course it should be.

Love,

Al

---

1. Probably "Why I Won't Let a U.S. Branch Plant Publish My Poetry." *Maclean's,* January 1971, 14.

2. Peter C. Newman (b. 1929), journalist and author, was editor-in-chief of the *Toronto Star* from 1969 to 1971.

3. Probably *Al Purdy's Ontario,* CBC Learning Systems.

4. Angus McGill Mowat (1892-1977), librarian, author, and Belleville resident, was the father of Farley Mowat (b. 1921), the well-known writer.

5. James Houston (b. 1921), author of *White Dawn: An Eskimo Saga* (1971), had been in charge of development of Inuit Art Co-Operatives in the Canadian Arctic (1948-52) and then was appointed civil administrator of West Baffin Island (1953-62). At this time, he was Associate Director of Design, Steuben Glass, New York.

Elm Cottage

28 December 1970

Dear Al–

Thanks v. much for both yr letters – haven't replied sooner because of the mad onslaught of Christmas. Gary and Phyllis Geddes were out for Christmas, plus another couple of friends, and it was really nice to have them here. I thought it might be only the kids and myself, kind of dull. We had 12 for Christmas dinner, and on Boxing Day had a party, sort of, with about 15 people, so I have spent more hours slaving over a hot stove recently than over a cold typewriter. However, it was worth it, and compared to last Christmas, which was traumatic for me on account of the divorce, this year was like paradise. It was lovely not to have to pretend to be enjoying myself, because I really was enjoying it all.

Lucky you to be in Mexico. I don't mind the winter here, but it snowed on Christmas Eve, and the countryside, altho v. beautiful, is bloody cold and I have to go out with my little kerosene stove for the outdoor john each night or the pipes may freeze.

The only thing which has come of the novel so far is that I now have a tame robin who sits on the rosebush outside my liv. rm window and stares fixedly at me while I brood over the notebook. I've started the damn novel about a dozen times, but each time after about 10 pages I know it isn't going to work this way. There are still so many unsolved problems about how to write it. I change my mind about the approach every other day. It's too complicated and I'm trying to get too much in, I think, and yet I have such a strong sense of its *existing* out there in space somewhere. If only I could pierce through to it. Well, either I will or I won't … it's as simple as that. I think on the whole that last year was not good for me … I did too much analysing of my own writing process, and now I can see too many drawbacks with every method I try. I have to try to forget all that. Also am still scared about its being too much related to my own situation, but again, that doesn't matter and I know it doesn't – just find it hard to have enough guts to do it. I've considered making the main character a sculptor, or an artist, but what in hell do I know about that kind of art? Nothing. Anyway, as a ploy it is so obvious as to be not worth doing, unless one can really get inside an artist's skull, as Joyce Carey did with The Horse's Mouth, or Patrick White with his recent novel The Vivisector. I think that writing was easier in the days when I knew virtually nothing about form or voice or anything … now in some ways I know too much about what I'm trying to do. I think I have reached a period of some kind of real crisis in my work – one hears about this with others, but never believes it will happen to oneself. Like every other kind of crisis in life, I suppose. I have a sort of doublethink about all this … on the one hand, I always believe that disaster is just around the corner; on the other, I don't really actually believe it will happen.

The Can Forum with that review of my stories arrived today … had been posted months ago. Thanks very much indeed. Yeh, it's a good review. Whenever I see a review which sort of does a survey of all my writing, I feel a desperate need to write the next one very very differently from anything I've ever done. One has a kind of dread about repeating oneself. This is one problem with this novel – part takes place in Africa somewhere, but *cannot* be done realistically, partly because I haven't lived there for years and partly for other reasons. ie. I'm not all that interested in writing straight realism any longer. Also, how to condense enough to get a whole lot of years in, without writing a long novel, which I definitely do *not* want to write. Nowadays, a long novel has to be a work of semi-genius for me to be able to read it – it just does not seem a viable form any longer, except in a few rare cases.

I feel lousy about this novel from time to time, but less lousy than I did a month or so ago. I've somehow stopped feeling frenzied about getting down to it. I think it will come if it's meant to. God knows I think about it all the time. I am an impatient person, but maybe it is time I learned patience. What I really have to do is to feel my way into a totally different (for me) kind of writing – I've known this would be necessary for quite some time now; in fact, knew it about this unwritten novel as long ago as 1967 when I had not finished writing The Fire-Dwellers, and even knew what direction I had to go – why, then, do I keep fighting it? Partly, I guess, because I have not yet learned the new language which I feel will be necessary for this thing. Migawd, if only I could wave my magic wand! I have a sense of the novel's totality but can't seem to come to grips with the building materials. They keep eluding me, and the harder I try (sitting down and just *writing*) the worse it becomes. Maybe I should heed the Zen proverb about the best way to hit the target being not to aim at it? Anyway, as they used to say in my family when I was a kid, I'm badly battered but still in the ring.

Peggy Atwood and husband[1] coming out for the weekend Jan 9. I kept trying to phone her (she'd written to me, giving me her phone number) and had a bizarre evening in communication with the telephone operator ... I said the number had been busy for about 2 hours and could they check on it; they did, and this operator came back and said "That number is a phone booth in Earls Court Exhibition"!! So I wrote, finally, and when Peggy replied, she said well yes, their room did feel rather like a phone booth in the Exhibition. This country has the best postal service in the world, but the worst phones of any country except Egypt.

Heavens, you must've been busy before leaving Canada – those anthologies are a fantastic amount of work. Was amused (and saddened) by yr descrip of the letters you had received from various poets.

Charlie the robin is outside my window at the moment, staring reproachfully at me. "Why the hell haven't you got the first chapter written?" he is clearly saying. Ubiquitous is the word for Charlie ... if I'm in the liv. room, he's outside the window; if in the kitchen, he's outside that window. Not hundreds of robins ... they apparently in this country adopt a garden and only 1 pair hangs around. His wife is more shy than he, and she wears a small white feathered apron under her scarlet breastfeathers. Goddamn! Reduced to bird-watching! In my old age and literary inability! Charlie is a people-watcher. We stare at each other, both of us wondering what it would be like to be the other. Robins may suffer from chill in winter, but at least they don't have to get tied up in knots over a novel. Or so I believe … but could be wrong.

Jocelyn's boyfriend from Belfast arrived today for 2 weeks. The meat I'd bought some considerable days ago for meatloaf went bad in the fridge over Xmas, so a low-class meal of Spanish rice – there are moments when I feel inadequacy creeping over me like a shroud. The hell with it, tho. I will rise like the phoenix and write this damn novel. Please write soon. Have a tequila for me.

Love,
Margaret

ps. I really like Gary, and find him good to talk with. Also, as often happens, when one talks with Phyllis alone, you find how intelligent and great she is. […]

---

1. Margaret Atwood was at this time married to the writer James Polk (b. 1939).

Elm Cottage
1 March 1971

Dear Al–

Isolation! This goddamn postal strike! Friends going to Canada will give this letter to D. Billington, who will try to ascertain your whereabouts (Mexico? Hiroshima? Ameliasburgh?) and post it. I feel so bloody cut off from the world – no post for nearly 2 months and no sign of strike ending. Brief message now, because I have no faith this will ever reach you.

Situation with me is as follows:

    1. Deprivation on account of no letters from or to friends.

2. Domestic chaos … David fed up with his school, wanting to take remaining 2 yrs somewhere else; me trying to find out about Technical colleges etc etc. Jocelyn about to quit university, on account of not interested in courses and not convinced now that she wants university under any conditions. She has also fallen in love with the young Canadian, Peter, who I encouraged to come here as a boarder thinking how nice it would be for David to have the company of a friend (Peter is 22). This is okay, and I like Peter, but it sure makes the household a complicated and dramatic business, much of which I could at this point do without, because of:

3. Deep depression over news that J.G.McC is going broke (Mordecai, Peggy Atwood and self having long phone converse, but detailed news scarce). Sent J.G.McC a cable with words of Geo Stephens to Donald Smith in 1884 re: fund-raising for CPR … (motto of Grant clan) … "Stand fast, Craigellachie".[1] But probably not possible for him at this point. Also – and worst of all – (I save the gloomiest bit till last) …

4. Have realized within last week that the novel I've been working on is the wrong novel. That is, it stemmed from an idea I had many yrs ago, and I have outgrown the necessity to do it. BUT – (ray of light?) – I was trying to combine it with other more current and pressing fictional matters, and now begin to see that the real (I *pray*) novel may possibly have been growing under the surface while I was sweating and straining at the other one. This has happened before, but I only just realized recently what was going on. So I'm back in my own territory, in a sense, both geographically and spiritually, and who knows? However, to throw out 6 months work and the ideas of some 8 yrs is difficult, not to say painful, and last wkend I felt well-nigh suicidal tho not quite. Mistake has been in trying to salvage ideas from the past and in fighting against what the novel itself may want to do, instead of accepting that & not attempting what I might want it to do or what I think might be interesting to readers. Hell with

readers. Nobody may want to read this one which may possibly begin sometime around now, but I do not care. It has taken me months to come back to myself, after last yr.

Hope you are okay. Will see you and Eurithe in June unless I am broke, dead or in mental hospital.

Woke up this morning and began to sing Onward Christian Soldiers, To Be A Pilgrim, Battle Hymn Of The Republic, Little Joe The Wrangler, and others. Must be a good omen.

Love,
Margaret

---

1. George Stephen (1829-1921) was the first president of the Canadian Pacific Railway (1880-88). His cousin, Donald Smith (1820-1914), a wealthy Montreal financier and a director of the Hudson's Bay Company, was a principal shareholder in the CPR and drove the last spike upon completion of the railway. In 1884, the railway company, vastly over-budget and pressed by its creditors, was in danger of financial collapse. Stephen, who was in Britain to raise money, sent his famous transatlantic cable to encourage Smith.

Ameliasburgh
15 March 1971

Dear Margaret,

Greetings and all that – after the silent interlude of mail strike. I wrote you a long letter just before it started from Mexico which came back to me – Won't send it now, since it was mostly about Geddes, who seems a bit irrelevant after two mos.

I returned, with Eurithe of course – *we* returned – to find snow up to the hubcaps of a brobdingnagian chariot (always knew I'd use that word sooner or later), and Jack McClelland issuing statements that he must sell the company, perhaps to an

American firm, imminently. Guess it's not sold yet tho. But it would be very odd to say the least if he sold out to a U.S. outfit, he being co-chairman of the League for Canadian Independence. How could he justify that? I'm sure he would, but how?

My much bashed-about purdy-edited book, Storm Warning, about to be published (unveiling in Toronto Mar. 22), myself going to Japan in early weeks of April. Will send a copy along to you before leaving.

We are staying in a friend's house near Belleville, on accounta the snow is too deep at the lake, and besides there's inadequate heating. He (the friend) is in Florida. My own mood is ghost-like, for unknown reasons – All the landmarks – my own and physical ones – seem to shift so constantly, that in some ways I scarcely know I'm back in Canada or that this is a familiar world. The strangeness of Mexico might even be more appropriate to existence.

How is your novel, which in fiction-reality must cling to compass points? I say no more than ask the question, because if you're not writing and working at it, even the query is dangerous.

I wrote 33,000 words of bio-crit prose in Mexico, got up every morning for three weeks and coffee and typewriter, banging out two-three thousand words a day, then revision and re-typing. Ron Everson went over the manuscript in Florida – where we stopped at his place on the return journey – and now the damn thing has to be done again. Also a few poems, only one seeming much good to me. Which is a fairly shoddy poem-result of the trip. But then, it never really was an enthusiasm of mine when we left, but Eurithe's. She'd like to be there still. I was sick to death of the place when we left. The prose mentioned is a personal autobiography of 1950 to '60, living in Mtl., etc., verging into criticism by discussing Lowry,[1] Layton and Acorn as I was involved with or knew them. Dennis Lee at Anansi talked about such a book from me before I left, and I thought it a good enough idea to go ahead. But Anansi had a bad fire at their warehouse a coupla weeks ago, and I guess it makes their situation pretty shaky. Seems also they are backed by new Canadian money, in the form of the Walls, two U.S. emigres.[2] Seems Dave Godfrey made a point of saying this to the press, causing Dennis Lee to issue a statement explaining the Walls – and I would guess there is now an acerbity between Lee and Godfrey.

Have just read a new book of poems by Ramon Guthrie, *Maximum Security Ward,* a 73-year-old U.S. poet, which is very fine. Good review in N.Y. Times caused me to buy it. Pick it up if you see it. $7.50 in U.S. (Jesus!). Re books, I paid $1.50 for Lady Chatterly, at used book store in U.S. This no cause for comment, except, "Privately Printed, Florence, 1928." Know what that means? Not sure I do myself, except that I think it's one of the most valuable of modern first eds, and guess anywhere from $50 to $200. Got on the ordinary fiction shelves by mistake – in Philadelphia – and I paid for it while being careful the cashier or owner didn't examine it at the time. Regard it as something like picking up Hemingway's Ten Stories, for $1.50. Quite a number of good buys, cheap, like Klein's Poems, 1944,[3] for 25¢. Callaghan's first book, Strange Fugitive, which is worth around forty bucks at Canadiana prices. And four or five Groves. The Groves seem to me crap, but their price has gone up fairly high. And this is the side of my character aborted by the 20th century, when I might have been a gold-seeker in the Yukon in '98.

Love,

Al

---

1. The novelist Malcolm Lowry (1909-57) had lived in Vancouver from 1937-54. Purdy met him twice in 1954 and described these meetings in "Lowry: A Memoir," *Books in Canada,* January/February 1974, 3-4.

2. Ann and Byron Wall. Ann Wall became a major shareholder and president of Anansi Press.

3. Abraham Moses Klein (1909-72), poet and novelist.

§

Elm Cottage
[30 April 1971]
tomorrow is May 1st ...
that must mean something.
good omen, I take it.

Dear Al–

I think a couple of our letters must've crossed, as we seem to have two lots of letters going simultaneously, if you see what I mean. Never mind. Hope this catches you in your pre-Hiroshima days.

Got yr letter of Apr 20 a few days ago. Farley sounds in good form. I think you know that when I first met him, I thought he was a slob, but now, over the years, have changed my mind and find I really like him, altho still somewhat on guard with him (except that well-remembered occasion at your place when Farley and I sobbed on each other's shoulders, revealing drunkenly to one another how inadequate we both felt in various areas of our lives – ah well.) I agree about Claire[1] – I think she's a really *good* person, without being "good" at all in the conventional sticky sense of the word, and she is charming and I think it's genuine. Farley is lucky, and I think he knows it very well.

Glad you are finished the Levesque piece.[2] Load off the mind, and money in the bank – no trifle, that. I will light several thousand mental candles to the success of your Hiroshima visit ... "success" in whatever way you mean it; poems. Even if it is somewhat ghostlike for you – and I think I know a bit how you mean about that word; I've felt it even when travelling in Egypt with my kids – guess that is why I wanted them along, to lessen the sense of my own unreality in those circumstances. But it'll be okay, whatever it turns out to be.

I'll phone Eurithe when I get to the shack, and maybe she will come and see me – I hope so. When you do not drive, you get to

219

be an expert at conning yr friends into coming to yr place. I am v.good at this gambit.

Well, Al, it has begun. I think. I pray. Not anything like I thought it was going to be. I don't even know where the hell it's going, except in a general sort of way, but even then it could all change. For the first damn time since I finished The Fire-Dwellers, and that was in 1968, I don't mind getting up in the mornings. I tell myself with cautionary gloom that it won't last. It will, though. I dunno if anyone else will want to read it – it's a bit unlikely, I feel, but I do not care one iota. This I'm writing for only one person – myself. The hell with everything and everyone else. I'm not even sure I will want it to be published. Marvellous to go broke over something you aren't even sure you ever want to have published. But I don't feel worried. I think my problem for one whole goddamn year has been that I was thinking of something that I thought would make "a good novel". Something that grabbed them with the first sentence. But that is shit. I am not sure this will grab anyone at all, ever. But this is what I've been trying to get to – I know that. It'll be terrible to write, but my God, it's fascinating, too, because I really don't know what's going to happen next, and can hardly wait to find out. If it turns out to be an unpublished or unpublishable novel, I'll let you see the typescript one day. I'm treading so damn warily that I do not intend to mention it to anyone except you and Adele, and would be glad if you did not, either. I'm still so bloody scared it may quit or go sour like the other one. And yet, I know what went wrong before – the attempt to write a theory as a novel, which will *never* work for me. As a theory it was great; as a novel it was dead before it even began, which was why, basically, I found myself re-writing the first page ten million times and never got much beyond that point. Some unknown quantity or quality usually saves me from outright disasters, in work. But my connection with this new thing (it's not so new, really, as it has been trying to bring me around to it for some time) is still so uncertain that I feel both joyful and petrified. Wow, does that sound melodramatic. I should re-write that sentence, but won't bother. Anyway, should you feel inclined, please offer up your own brand of prayer for what I hope may be happening. I don't feel any sense of strain, oddly enough. Well, we will see. Maybe. Or maybe not.

Let me know your address in the Land Of The Rising Sun, eh? And luck. And God bless. Etc.

Love,
Margaret

---

1. Claire Mowat and Farley Mowat married in 1963.

2. "Lévesque: The Executioner of Confederation?" appeared in *Maclean's*, October 1971, 28-29, 83.

Hotel Takanawa
Tokyo
10 May 1971

Dear Margaret,

I guess I write this more for myself than you, since I'm feeling baffled by logistics, defeated by language and discouraged by my own shortcomings – Hey? I'm in Tokyo, in case you hadn't guessed and feeling very sorry for myself. The logistics bit is transportation, which ties in with language. Boy, just try and get around in this country without someone telling you exactly how and who knows Japanese. Tomorrow I take a train to Hiroshima, on accounta if I take a plane I hafta wait another day. It's around 500 or so miles south, so might be a bit warmer. But I hafta change trains, and just try and read the signs here. But I know the time, and a kindly gal travel agent made the hen tracks to say please look after this pore guy, he's a little simple. Also managed to reserve a room thru aforesaid gal, whom I would reward suitably if I could think of a way other than money. Discouraged by my own shortcoming – I feel goddam old, not being able to overcome all these lousy circumstances on my own. I'm almost sure the language will fuck me up in Hiroshima too, but hell, I gotta try. I will too. But now drinking the end of my tax free VO, I feel like cryin on your far away shoulder. Had intended to stay two mos, now doubt more than one, since I'm sure the language will get me down completely by that time.

So my more cheery news. Finished the piece on Levesque (it's lousy) and get the eight hundred bucks, also travel expenses in both Mtl. and Tor. (the last for re-writes) which amount to another three hundred. Let me amend that lousy bit, and just say it's not great. I guess it's passable or Peter Newman wouldn't use it. But I felt I just couldn't turn down that much money, and besides, liked the idea of meeting Levesque (got him to autosign his book) (of course). (Incidentally, brought some canned goods and books, now throwing away and eating everything to save carrying weight. Jesus I'm lazy!) Then I suddenly get on a poem-writing binge, and write about five I like as well as one or two throwaways. At the same time as I write the poems I do a review of a book on beer-making – get that, eh? Only way to do that is non-serious, for Jack Jenson. Then he has a book I do want to do (just did the other because I like him, really): Paul Kane's Frontier, 48 colour plates and 2/3 hundred black and whites, big picture book, $27.50[1] – You know about Kane? Frontier artist and all that. Contemporary of George Catlin,[2] but in Canada. Then, for Chrissake, while I'm writing poems and things, Globe and Mail send me a book, not knowing I'm off to Japan in two days. 550 some pages, Alexander Mackenzie's Journals etc. I don't turn that down either. But hafta take it to Vancouver where I hole up in a hotel for three days reading and writing it.[3] Jesus! Of course it's sixty bucks, but really ain't worth it when you consider the blood on my typing fingers. Also drinkin like hell all the time … But the

Kane book was great, and I enjoyed doin it – the other two, well, you know ...

[. . .]

Hey, I forgot to tell you. Wh[ile] I was at MacLean's, decided not to miss the chance and took a poem into Chatelaine, having met the ed. previously on the Elwood Glover show. So they took the poem.[4] I bet neither Birney nor Layton can say that: a poem in Chatelaine. For twenty-five jesus deflated bucks. (VO is getting low, may not last much longer.) As an English citizen, I send you the enclosed clipping.[5] Also quote a passage from one poem, which you'd better like – or else!

> "Now the mind's diamond drill points
> straight at you but untouches you
> reconstitutes your face and what you said
> sings you with the same silly madness
> prehistoric men were embarrassed about
> over the sound-proof centuries ..."[6]

Okay, it's the prehistoric man bit I like. So I just come up with another line writing this. Right after "what you said" insert: "counterfeits your pale body like a forgery" – So what the hell, it might work ... It's romantic tho, eh? I shall buy a gee-tar. Before I left Van. found Mel Hurtig was in town, and he phoned me after I left my hotel number. Wanted me to see Charles Tuttle (big U.S. publisher and printer of Hurtig's books in Tokyo). So I stay here to do that, today, and it's like we never met. Neither makes any impression at all. Time wasted as well as cab fare. Did pick up a coupla books in the big used book area of Tokyo. Tokyo itself? Well, my impression right now is very similar to any big western city, only bigger. It's a goddam rabbit warren of a place. Eaten no meals at restaurants, tryin to cut weight I hafta carry, the two books having added to it. Been here two days and seen little, but doesn't look worth seeing, since exactly the same as the west. Concrete block buildings, cars, roads, busses etc. Well, I'm pleased with recent poems, tho I guess with not much else. You may chastise me for not loving life, as a result. You, Dr. Laurence, are suitably qualified to do that. I like the thought in the above passage of prehistoric men, in a brutal hunting society, where women were probably chattels or worse, still being plagued with the tenderness of love, and probably not knowing what was wrong with them. Or like I said, if they did know, too embarrassed to admit it. That tickles me. I will try and send you an address later, as exigencies of place and time permit. Since you will be at your cottage this summer, will likely see you, since I think a month here is all I can take. Must now pack etc. for tomorrow's early rising. Still feeling disappointed with myself for not having written great Great GREAT poems instantly. So how's that lousy novel of yours?

> love
> Al
> (no VO) (alas, alas)

---

1. Purdy's review appeared in *Books in Canada*, May 1971, 16-17.

2. George Catlin (1796-1872), American painter, writer and student of the American Indian, was older than Paul Kane (1810-71), the Canadian artist-explorer, who had been inspired by an exhibition in London, England, of Catlin's Indian paintings.

3. "Who Will Pay the Price?" Review of *The Journals and Letters of Alexander Mackenzie*, ed. W. Kaye Lamb. *The Globe and Mail,* 17 July 1971, 14.

4. Probably "Observing Persons," *Chatelaine,* January 1972, 48. The poem was later included in revised form in *Sex & Death.*

5. Missing from the correspondence.

6. A draft fragment of "8.50 a.m." included in *Sex & Death.*

§

RR 11
Peterborough, Ontario
3 September 1971

Dear Al–

In case you do not remember what you wrote in yr letter from Fort Frances,[1] I mean those deathless lines of something-or-other, I will refresh yr memory, as it is pertinent to the valuable document enclosed herewith.

> "All my loves are lost loves
> And all my deaths are journeys
> to love and die are all my life
> and fuck St. Paul forever ..."

Well, it just seemed to me that the Die bit was only too relevant to my own stance, but could also be phrased another way, namely Live. So, as is my unselfish wont, I consulted my Friendly Armorial Bearings Specialist ("*Your* family's coat-of-arms for Only $2.95, no cheques accepted"), and received by return carrier pigeon the enclosed Purdy coat-of-arms, like it says in The Clans & Tartans Of Scotland, complete with motto, war cry, plant badge and pipe music.[2] This is a gift ... you do not need to send the $2.95 ... I have promised to advertise my Friendly Armorial etc in my next novel.

On to serious (?) matters. Yeh, I read Irving's article in Maclean's.[3] I really like Irving, but what he said about immortalizing his people was a whole load of crap and I am glad it struck you the same way. Good heavens, we all have to have a Sturdy Ego to survive, but that is going too far. I thought Bill Howell's article on truckers was disappointing.[4] I have never known a trucker that well, but when Jack was working in Northern B.C. I talked to a lot of them, and also gleaned a lot from Jack's conversations with them, which is what I used in the Buckle Fennick scenes in both A Jest of God and The Fire-Dwellers, plus knowing one trucker in England very well (*ex*-trucker ... he ended up a ham-fisted bank robber, then a driving instructor ... after his sojourn in Wormwood Scrubs,[5] then finally I lost touch with him after his common-law wife had a nervous breakdown in my house ... but that is another story). I thought Howell's article was more superficial than it needed to be, and the long letter from him to his woman was sort of tacked on ... could have been reworked and interwoven, but he did it the easy (ie sloppy) way.

Will be low on supplies this week, and serve me right. J.G.McC was here day before yesterday ... did a TV show in Peterborough then came out here for dinner and spent the night. Naturally, the inevitable happened ... we drank a lot of scotch, which, surprisingly, affected him more than me ... at least I was able to haul him into his bedroom around 3 a.m. and deposit his limp semi-corpse on the bed. I even turned out the lights in the house, locked the door, and folded my own clothes neatly on my bedroom chair, how? First time in my life I ever actually *put* anybody to bed, not took them. Come the morn, and J.G. seems fine ... how? I, on the other hand, was in poor shape, so unable to go shopping. Instead, when the taxi came at 10:30 a.m. to pick me up, J.G. tottered into it and said "Take me to Toronto". The driver now obviously thinks I am even more eccentric than he thought before. I spent yesterday in a state of great fragility, reading improving things like Rudy Wiebe's v. Christian novel First and Vital Candle,[6] and thinking what a much nicer person Rudy is than I am. Not as good a writer, tho. No – I shouldn't say that – I may be stricken blind. You know the kind of thoughts. Come this morning, reborn like the phoenix, I did laundry, cleaned house, all those virtuous Presbyterian things, plus 14 letters written. Now I feel that God may not strike me dead with a thunderbolt after all.

Have hardly written a word for about 2 weeks, well, ever since the day you and Eurithe were here (nothing to do with yr being here, just masses of visitors ever since). On one hand, it does not really make much difference, as 2 weeks away from the novel will not determine its final nature nor hold up its final production that much. On the other hand, I get nervous and begin thinking how the whole thing so far is shit and why don't I throw it in the fire? Won't, of course. Main problem at this point is not just its present length, which is ludicrous … 200 pp and only a quarter through! … but the fact that I am still inwardly fighting the long haul it will be, and the awfulness of having to get deeper and deeper inside it. Have sections One and Two done in first draft, but section Three is demanding a price I really am unwilling to pay. Will have to, of course, but it will be more difficult than what I have so far written. Read an article by Richard Hughes (High Wind In Jamaica, Fox In The Attic, etc) which said he takes to travel like some writers take to the bottle … in order Not to write. I understand that perfectly, both travel and drink. Have done both in my time, as have you. What I must learn is:

(1) Patience.

(2) To be able to work with all hell breaking loose around me, as is normal when I am home in Elmcot with my loved ones.

(3) Not to be too scared by what I am trying to write.

(4) To be calm.

Well, (2) and (3) may prove possible; the others won't. But why do I feel time growing shorter, when someone like Richard Hughes, who is 71 (repeat … Seventy One) is cheerily working on a long novel? When you say in yr letter you need some Laurence vitality, oh heavens, friend, I ain't got it! And I am NOT young compared to you, either. Maybe if I could be quite calm, and not ever drink or smoke, and lead a totally controlled life …? hell, I'd be dead! My trouble is that all my own natural inclinations go against everything I was brought up to believe. Also, I now begin to perceive not just in myself but in others who are my contemporaries, the sense of time drawing in like an inexorable curtain … and we fight it, why not? Yeh, but have to accept it, as well. No room for pretense. As my incredibly wise step-mother used to say, "No one should try to be mutton dressed as lamb". But the other side of the thing is that I believe we have to live, in some ways, as though we had forever. The two concepts are not mutually exclusive. Man (or so we imagine, but cannot know) is the only creature who knows he must die. And some of us don't know that, even; those of us who *do* know it, feel we must inform the rest of our fellow creatures about this interesting fact. And we are right. There is a sense in which Live and Die mean the same thing. A process. As you have said often, in poems.

Outside my window, two flickers are getting at the bugs on the elm tree. When they fly up, the dark feathers of their wings light suddenly with the gold feathers underneath. Which is why they are called Yellow-Shafted Flickers. Maybe this means something, maybe not.

And I think of my kids, whom I love, and don't want to go back into the loony bin that Elmcot will be in the autumn when I arrive, the kids with enormous deep problems (Who Am I? Where Am I Going? etc) and me feeling Heavens, it is I who have handed on all those hangups to them, so what should I do? Not knowing. Hope to God I can get into work after about a month back there. When you write, guess you should write to Eng. Will be back there Sept 28th.

The prairie articles will be okay … don't worry about them. They will be hell to write, that's all. Certainly, awful to take time from yr real work. Learn patience … but how?

Love,
Margaret

P.S. Love & greetings to Earle.
P.S. Some Days Later … Sept 7 to be exact …

I can only post letters once a week unless Mr. Villerup[7] is going into town in between my shopping days, so am constantly adding postscripts which make my letters into mini-novels.

This is just to report that the gloom has lifted! (Obviously if I ever really flip my lid I will be a manic-depressive). This is not exactly a manic phase, but I began work again today and now feel what I really need is a hut near the Arctic circle, with no people around except a resident Gamekeeper of the Lady Chatterley's variety, altho with a difference ... he will make some of the meals *as well*. Seriously, I began Section III and found that I could get into it after all. Worked for five hours, went for a long walk to unwind my head, have now just come back from a swim, and I feel Great! All will be well, I now feel. Of course it won't last, but feels good while it does. Like some kind of phoenix, I keep rising (staggering up, rather) from my own ashes. I wonder how long I will be able to keep on doing so? Right now I don't care. I am into the third section and that is all that matters. Spent two damn-nearly-sleepless nights while portions of this opening part of S.III were composing themselves in full technicolour in my head. Too tired to get up and write it down; unable to shut the TV inside off for the night. Terrible. Got up and scrawled down key words, and in morning would look at them and think "what did I mean by *jerusalem*?" (Altho in fact only too sober during nights; tempera-ture nearly 100 and me quaffing iced tea and cursing weather). Today it began to come together. Probably it is crap but that is a gamble we must take. If only I had more time to be here alone. Lots of friends still to come before I depart, and want to see them. But. Split mind. In a sense, don't want to see anybody. However, if I were able to be alone for six months, say, with meals dropped by helicopter, I would go out of my mind, I know. It seems to me that writing a novel is some kind of struggle of opposites ... I get so goddamn lonely and hassled I really need to talk with friends; on the other hand, I can only work when I have an assured (at least) four hours a day with no one around and not too great a feeling of things and people pressuring me. The right balance I have never in my life found except some days this summer. But I guess that does not matter, except that it is so bloody difficult to get inside a novel and so difficult to get out once you're in.

Do you have this sense of living a double (if not triple or quadruple) life?

You mention the people talking inside my head. Yeh. I guess in some ways you know something about them, actually quite a lot altho not in their own individual personae, which is I guess the peculiar thing about fiction and maybe (yes) poetry as well – the people are both the writer and not the writer. You could make some shrewd guesses about the main character in this novel (even apart from what I have ever said about her) and you would be both right and not right. Well, we will see. The division between fiction and so-called reality in my life seems an awfully uncertain one.

Good luck with the prairie articles, and hope poems come also out of the whole deal.

love,

M

---

1. This letter has been lost. The Purdys were travelling by car to Vancouver.

2. See illustration on p. 231.

3. "Irving Layton's Canada." *Maclean's,* September 1971, 14-15, 80.

4. "Pushing the Big Rig." *Maclean's,* September 1971, 32-37, 71-72, 74. Bill Howell was one of the poets included in *Storm Warning: The New Canadian Poets.*

5. British prison located in London.

6. *First and Vital Candle* (1966) was the second novel by Wiebe (b. 1934).

7. Jack Villerup was Margaret Laurence's elderly neighbour.

PURDY

Clan: A sept of the Clan MacStalwart

Coat-of-Arms: (seebelow)

Armorial Description of Coat-Of-Arms:
  A nymph rampant on a background of heaven proper (azure) and
far-off pastures obscure (green).

Motto: Live Cum Love. (The second word derives both from the Latin and from
           what is known as the old tongue.)

War-Cry: Fuck St. Paul Forever. (origins obscure)

Plant Badge: Formerly, an ivy leaf, appropriate. Now usually a scarlet
    maple leaf, brazen.

Pipe Music: O'er Faroff Pastures to Sky.
      also: Goddamn The Naysayers; Rot They Will Soonest
      also: Moosehead's Lament (a pibroch)

ဪ

906 South Springer

Burnaby, B.C.

10 September 1971

Dear Margaret:

Enclosed a carbon of the eulogy to C.C.[1] The jargon about "philosophical and interpretive portrayal" is, of course, to impress any academics who may be reading it. I expect you too are concerned about your dimensions. Hope it suits.

We got here Friday, and I seem to have had a hangover ever since. I wrote six poems along the way and one section of the projected article. One of the poems I think hits nearly top level.

This is just a short note, because I wanta get it in the post. But the trip has seemed very worthwhile: Churchill, the 94-year-old survivor of the N.W. Rebellion, Batoche two days, riding a combine with a farmer near Moose Jaw, and tour thru Dinosaur Valley. Spent money like water, seemingly, but a note from Peter Newman mentions expense money later.[2] Jesus, I hope so, something like six hundred bucks in three weeks! The flight to Churchill was $67 plus train fare return. And I think there must be a gas tank leak, the way this monster gobbles fuel.

Love,

Al

---

1. Not traced. Laurence was applying for a Canada Council Writer's Grant.

2. Newman had left the *Toronto Star* to become Editor of *Maclean's*. Purdy had agreed to write an article for the magazine based on his cross-Canada travels, which appeared as "A Feast of Provinces," *Maclean's,* April 1972, 48-55.

§

R.R. 11
Peterborough, Ontario
16 September 1971

Dear Al–

Thanks a million for the letter to the C. Council – it is just great. Almost makes me feel impressed with myself! I'm really grateful to you, and also for doing it so rapidly.

Your trip sounds as tho it had been a great success. I am amazed you could get so many poems done, plus part of the article, while in the exhausting process of driving, etc. $67 for the flight to Churchill doesn't sound too bad to me – I think I really am going to try to get there next summer. Maybe if I set myself some goal, such as – I can go to N. Manitoba if I get the first draft of the novel done by then?

Have decided to leave here in a few days time, and stay with Adele in Toronto for awhile before flying back to Eng on Sept 27th. I got a bit more done on the novel, but then the visitors began again, so I have closed the writing shop for the time being. The last couple of weeks in a place are never good for me for writing, as in my mind I am already packing and leaving. Heavens, will I miss this place, though. It has been such a damn good summer in every way – writing; seeing friends.

Have reviewed a long long novel called *Bartleby* for Books in Canada.[1] Jack Jensen phoned me last week to ask if I would do it, and oddly enough, I had heard about the novel from Gary Geddes and also from Phyllis Bruce[2] (she was out here for a day, not long ago) as they know the author, Christopher Scott. I knew it was long, and oh God, was it ever! About 460 pp. And not easy reading, either. I spent one whole day reading it, and the next morning doing the review. It's a stunning novel in some places, its main flaw being that the writer gets too clever in places, too many literary references, and also indulges in some pretty cheap knocking of novelists such as Styron.[3] One wants to say … listen, kid, wait until you can write as well as Styron before you criticize him like that. If that time ever comes, tho, he wouldn't be so free and easy on the draw.

Suddenly it is cold as Greenland here, after a heat wave, and my inner thermostat is having trouble adjusting. After Labour Day weekend, all the local cottagers disappeared, and it is so peaceful here now that I really hate to leave.

How long will you be in Vancouver? Did you get the other letter I sent to Earle's? When you write, please write to Elmcot. Good luck with the article.

Love,
Margaret

ps. Eurithe's card from Batoche made me realize I really *have* to go there.

1. "Fiction About Fictions." *Books in Canada,* November 1971, 3-4.

2. Phyllis Bruce (b. 1939) was co-editor with Gary Geddes of 15 *Canadian Poets* (1970), an anthology that included Purdy.

3. William Styron (b. 1925), author of *The Confessions of Nat Turner* (1967).

Ameliasburgh
2 November 1971

Dear Margaret,

You really are a home for dis-homed authors. Janes, yet.[1] I can well imagine you're different. Also you and your goddam articles, and me in the same boat.[2] One more for Newman, and he wants me to go to maritimes, which I do in another week or so, and so busy I can't think, talk etc., but I'd better be able to write.[3] Eurithe and I ended up the trip hating each other's guts, she particularly mine.

234

The selling reviews bit is finding money, which I always like the feeling of[4] – No, never thought of that, since I sell all my crap in one place so long as they don't double-cross me (you recall the U. of Sask bit)[5] ... Besides, I could never keep any one thing or many things in good enough order to find them when needed. Anyway, articles weigh on me, but poems don't. Simple or not. I look at these enormous piles of books around me and think how nice to sell em all but a few and go live with a nutbrown maiden somewhere or something – impossible tho, they're all millstones.

Birney telling me he sends his books to the U.S. mag hoping for a review, finally gets the mag and thinks AHA, this is it. Then sees a review of Purdy and thinks Oh shit what do I hafta do?? The review ends: "These are the two most essential Purdy books to own & Purdy, whether he is Canadian or not, it doesn't matter, is a most essential poet to read." Now isn't that sweet? Makes me feel great, read me because the curse of Canadian might never have descended and I might even be American if no one says different.

Well, I wrote eight poems on the way west, a couple not much good, four-five a little better, and two-three *might* be good. One was a five page, single-space poem about dinosaurs yet![6] I should say *one* might be good. About the battlefield at Batoche, but even then I dunno.[7]

Selected comes in Jan. or Feb. and McStew (Jack, I suppose) having hassle with potential Br. publisher. To hell with it. Storm Warning sold 2234 copies in first report, which is pretty bad. But my own books sold much worse.

Well, if this seems unadulterated gloom I don't mean it that way. Fuck book sales! I wrote some poems, and there may be some merit in them. Which is important to me. I felt good when writing two of them, felt here's something. They will be a long time coming in books, since Selected has nothing but poems already in books.

Talked to Layton on phone last time in Toronto to see Peter

Newman. Told him his Nail Polish was terrific – which it is. Not all, but much. You see it? Also reading Atwood's Power Politics – migawd, it's good! Also monotonous if you read right thru. Same tone, same woman, same feelings mostly. But jesus, does she get it across! But I must admit that she strikes me as inhuman in some way, tho I like her personally much. The woman bit is carried too far in her, just as the man bit is in others. Male and female just cannot react against each other that hard, and still remain real people to themselves and others. We're all fallible whatever the gender. Maybe your bit about being forlorn and bereaved because a woman writer etc is true. Neither man nor woman ought to have to somehow compete on the same ego trip as writing. Or any other way, I expectoo. (Take your tweezers and separate those words.)

I really don't see why I'm dividing this into paragraphs, because there isn't a genuine paragraph in the letter, only a kind of pot pourri, a pot pourri being something like an omelette upside down in a pot.

I accepted a job for two weeks teaching (creatively, of course) at Banff next year, and they sent me some literature on the place, one bit which is a scream, pleasurable or tortured.

THE BLISS CARMAN AWARD FOR BALLAD OR LYRIC POETRY

This award was established in 1956 by Edith and Lorne Pierce[8] in memory of the Canadian Poet Bliss Carman (1861-1929). The award will be for the best example of ballad or lyric poetry submitted by a full-time student of the Banff School of Fine Arts.

"All entries must be submitted to the Director, Banff School of Fine Arts, Banff, Alberta, and must be received not later than July 23rd, 1971.

"Entries may be ballads or lyric poems of not less than 30 lines. Alternately a competitor may submit two sonnets. Entries must be typewritten on one side of the page only.

"The award will be made by a panel of judges appointed by the Director of the Banff School of Fine Arts.

"If no poem of sufficient merit is received, an award will not be made.

"The winner of the award will receive a ring once owned by Bliss Carman and now the property of the Banff School of Fine Arts. The ring will be presented on a suitable occasion and a replica of the ring will become the winner's personal possession." (No comment by me!)

REMEMBERING HIROSHIMA [9]
In the darkness is no certitude
that morning will ever come
In dawn spreading pink from the east
is no guarantee that day will follow
nor that human justice is more than a name
or the guilty will ever acknowledge guilt
All these opinions arrived at in years past
by men whose wisdom consisted of saying things
they knew might be admired but not practised
arrived at by others whose wisdom was silence
And yet I expect the morning
and yet I expect the day
and search for justice in my own mind
abstracted from mercy and kindness and truth
became a much more personal thing
I search for it in myself
with a kind of unbearable priggishness
I detest in other people
And yet the I/we of ourselves must judge
must say here is the road
if it turns out wrong take another
must say these are the murderers
identify them and name their names

must say these are the men of worth
and publish belief like fact
must say all this in the absence of any god
having taken a gleam inside the mind
having grown an opinion like rings on a tree
having praised quietly the non-god of justice
having known inside the non-god of love
as our peers did once in the long memory of man
Self righteous and priggish of course
not humor will save it from that
nor the laughter of clowns
but it is all a man can offer the world
a part of himself not even original
the strength he uses to say it
the time spent writing it down
the will and the force of solemnity
are his life tho his life ends tomorrow
and it will and he's wrong   Ameliasburgh, Ont.

Margaret: the line, "become a much more personal thing" is added in this typing.

Yours,
Al

---

1. Percy Janes (b. 1922) had published with McClelland and Stewart his second novel *House of Hate* (1970) for which Laurence later wrote a critical introduction when it appeared in the NCL series in 1976. He was staying at Elm Cottage and working on another novel.

2. Laurence had promised Newman an article for *Maclean's* "My Canada" series, and "Where the World Began" appeared in *Maclean's*, December 1978, 23, 80. In addition she had contracted for six articles with the *Vancouver Sun*.

3. Purdy's account of his trip to the Maritimes was included in "A Feast of Provinces."

4. Laurence had sold to York University for $800 all the reviews of her books from 1961-71.

5. Purdy's papers were purchased by Queen's University in 1969, 1981, and 1987. In the early 1970s, he sold some of his papers through an agent to the University of Saskatchewan, but his relationship with both parties subsequently went sour because of money and other disagreements.

6. Probably what was eventually published as *On the Bearpaw Sea* (1973).

7. Probably "The Battlefield at Batoche," included in *Sex & Death*.

8. Lorne Pierce (1890-1961) was editor of Ryerson Press (1922-60) and a Canadian nationalist who published, among others, F.P. Grove, Earle Birney, Dorothy Livesay and P.K. Page.

9. A revised version of this became the concluding poem in *Hiroshima Poems* (1972).

Elmcot

15 November 1971

Dear Al–

I was relieved to hear from you – when I don't hear from friends for awhile, I begin to be both paranoid and anxious – are they mad at me or are they ill? Glad to know you are only out of your mind with those bloody articles.

ARTICLES! Migawd, do you know that within the past week I have written five articles, 1500 words each? All I can do, Al, is climb into the typewriter, go into some quite different gear, and do the bloody things. They sometimes amuse me, but are far from deathless prose, and indeed, I have so many ambiguous feelings about them. For example, I hope the Van Sun never knows that I writ five articles in a week.[1] On the other hand, despite the fact that these articles will provide me with the necessary bread for the next year so I can relax (ho!) and get back to the novel, I still wish that I could really write them easily. I don't. I write first draft, in typescript, then do second draft also in typescript, then re-write by scribbling all over the piece with pen. I sweat blood. I suffer. Vocally. All those around me get bored to hell by my moaning. I was never one to suffer in silence. However, all I now hope is that Pat Nagle of the Sun will accept these 6 articles. I have 2 more to write[2] and will write them this week or expire dramatically in the attempt. Got word from my agent and from Macleans that Peter Newman likes my My Canada article and has already paid for it, good man that he is. I haven't yet got hold of your article in that series, but have read Irving's, Phyllis Webb's[3] (both v. good except for Irving's odd stance towards the people he thinks he has immortalized in pomes) and Mavor Moore's[4] (awful, I thought – concepts 20 yrs out of date; us poor Canadians, always on our knees, bunch of dullards ... well, nuts to him). Incidentally, M. Richler's comments on yr article (which he did in Sat Nite) seemed pretty nit-brained to me.[5] Same with the article he did (which I should have saved and sent to you but didn't) in the Sunday Times on Canada[6] ... out-dated concepts, again; dullards that we are; Can is so boring we yawn ourselves to death. Well, Mordecai's own novels give the lie to that, but as well, I would like to tell him about a lot of other things going on, which he does not seem to know about. Had dinner with my publisher, Alan Maclean, last week and he said, "Margaret, you're the most nationalistic Canadian I know." I gazed at him in astonishment, and then said, "Well, first, you ain't seen nothing, and second, you all have kind of driven me to it, in a way." If Can poets not published here, what is my response, ultimately? It can only be – the hell with Eng publishers. If Can novels either not published or (in my case) reviewed très condescendingly (how amazing that a Canadian should be able to write something that passes itself off as a novel), one's ultimate response must be – okay, chaps, we write for our own people; if anyone else is interested, fine; if not, also fine. I will NOT be looked down unto, any more, as a Can writer, nor will I seek acceptance among the halls of the élite, either in

London or New York. The hell with it, Al. They must come to us. And really *must,* when you see the paucity of striking poetry or novels in this country. This country more and more seems to me like the Emperor's New Clothes ... everyone is afraid to admit there ain't much there. Yes, of course, Sylvia Plath, Ted Hughes, Al Alvarez,[7] and one or two others. But so much else here seems dried blood to me. Same with novels. The old-line greats, like Graham Greene or Angus Wilson, and now William Golding.[8] But apart from that, the trendy novelists who make the Sunday supplements and you really wonder if many of them could speak to anyone except the trend-oriented few, and in this country alone? I am not hopeful here, Al. I get more and more to feel that I have to go back home and just work in my own area and the hell with everything else. Especially, the hell with being accepted as this week's mini-marvel. Oh no. Never. I am sorry Earle cares as much as he does, about being published in Eng. Maybe he should happily forget it. Maybe it doesn't matter one good goddamn, which is what I now think. I'm glad you are now getting such great reviews in the US & A, but also feel as you do that – well, you could *almost* be an American, if no one said.

The last Hiroshima poem[9] is so much better than any except maybe 2 of the others, or so I think. Thanks for sending it. The last lines, as always in yr best poems, hit like the spirit of god between the eyes, "Tho his life ends tomorrow/ and it will ..." Oh my friend, yes it will it will even without Hiroshima. [...] (See, if still interested, Airletter #2).

#2 Airletter

from M.L. to A.P.

Don't know if I've really got all that much more to say, but seemed to have more than One Airletter. I wrote to Peggy Atwood today, as had not told her what I thought about Power Politics. Wow, that is some book, eh? The beginning poem ...

"You fit into me like a hook into an eye …" I thought that was really something. I don't think her poems are bitter; they are sometimes vicious, as creatures who know about traps sometimes are. But also knowing that there is possible a kind of relationship between a man and a woman, even if it never happens yet, where neither hassles the other. I admire her poetry more than I can say. I also love her as a human, and somehow, once we really talked, did not find her frightening, as I thought I might. Instead, I felt I could level with her. And probably did. Okay, let's forget my bit about being forlorn & bereaved because a woman writer, Al – that is probably true but not really central to anything. Yeh, I guess it matters to me. It would, of course, matter much more had I never related to a man deeply, and to other men peripherally, and had I never had my kids. *Then,* I might have been really vicious about the whole subject. But ain't, now. I had to do what I had to do, and have to live alone in some way now forevermore but honestly that does not any longer bug the hell out of me. Like, it would bug me more if I'd *not* decided to go my own way, if I'd let the writing go. Once I thought you could have everything if you tried hard enough; now I know you have to make choices. Everyone's choices are different, but probably all writers' choices are connected with the survival of the writing. I had to go alone, possibly, in order for it to survive; you have had to remain within what is your vital battle area, for the same reason. Which is why the "hating each others' guts" bit is very true and also temporary, or maybe not temporary but fluctuating. You and Eurithe, over a lot of years, have learned to fight so well together. I got to know you separately; you first, a little, because of yr writing, and then her, a little, when you were here that time. Value you both, now, beyond any measuring. Having begun, a few years ago, to under-stand somewhat what it was with you both, can't think of anyone I know who fights so bitterly and to the death, and with such caring and love. No charge, Al – YE OLDE AMATEUR HEADSHRINKER

Yeh, neither man nor woman ought to have to compete re: writing, but hell, man, you *know* we *don't,* not really. It isn't a competitive business; it isn't man vs woman or person vs person; those who think it is are mistaken and will suffer much for that particular mistake. In writing, how could we knock each other down? If we do, we must be bloody uncertain of our own writing. The longer I live (and as you know I am older than God but without wisdom), I see that we are a tribe and we had bloody better look after one another.

Well, enough of this high emotion. Yr excerpts on the Bliss Carman Award were much appreciated. It happens everywhere; Canada ain't the only place where the nits gather.

Write when possible … I mean a letter. And let us hope these christly articles, yrs and mine, will get done and earn some bread and that will be that.

Love,

Margaret

---

1. In the next thirteen months, Laurence published five articles in the *Vancouver Sun*: "The River Flows Both Ways," 11 December 1971, 6; "Put Out One or Two More Flags," 25 February 1972, 6; "Voices from Future Places," 23 April 1972, 6; "Hello Aunt Nelly, I'm on the Telly," 17 June 1972, 6; "Living Dangerously … By Mail," 23 September 1972, 6. The sixth article was "The Wild Blue Yonder," 1 September 1973, 6.

2. Perhaps "commentary" for *Journal of Canadian Fiction*, 1, 3 (Summer 1972), 74-75, and "Time and the Narrative Voice" for *The Narrative Voice*, ed. John Metcalf (1972), 126-30.

3. "Phyllis Webb's Canada." *Maclean's*, 1971, 8-9, 47, 49.

4. "Mavor Moore's Canada: A Place to Kneel." *Maclean's*, November 1971, 20-21, 92.

5. "Al Purdy's Canada" (*Maclean's*, May 1971, 14-15) was the first in the magazine's "My Canada" series. Richler's comments were articulated in

"Perceptions and Portents: The New Canadian Style," *Saturday Night*, September 1971, 44-45.

6. "Canada." *London Sunday Times Magazine*, 7 November 1971, 99-102.

7. Alfred Alvarez (b. 1929), poet, novelist, critic, short-story writer.

8. Angus Wilson (b. 1911) and William Golding (b. 1911), whose latest novels were, respectively, *The Pyramid* (1967) and *No Laughing Matter* (1967).

9. "Remembering Hiroshima."

[Progresso]
[Yucatan, Mexico]
It might be Saturday,
and it might be
Feb. 14 or 15 [1972]
(one room)

Dear Margaret:

We are now camped in a sort of cottage by the sea, great waves roaring in etc. Hoping to rent a house for a month tomorrow. If we do will say so on outside of envelope, and you can write to us c/o American Express, Merida, Yucatan, Mexico. We are now at Progresso, which is 20 miles from Merida. Just came from Valladolid, where there was a Mardi Gras that kept us awake most of the night, and feel blah. Night before at the Isla Mujeres (Isle of Women).

Well the beer is great, ditto the people, but Mexico is not my bag. That is, I cannot write poems here. Wrote three or four last year, but things turn into crap in 1972. I should, of course, be satisfied with 1971, which was a very productive year (and I am), but still wanta write wherever I am. It isn't a dry spell so much as just writing badly here. Just not interested enough, I guess. I hope you are not the same. Knew this would happen before I came, which may have helped it to happen. Of course, some of the archaeological stuff is great – old cities spreading for dozens of acres. The big swimming pool at Chichen Itza is worth anybody's time. 140 feet wide, 65 feet below the surface of the ground, black and ominous, with a big stone platform where the priests hustled in virgins and children without soap. It really does look like an evil place, and one might think so even without knowing its history. The sort of spot where your backbone tingles on accounta that watered down Keltic blood.

But Palenque was the spot that impressed both Eurithe and I most. A city in the jungle foothills, where a huge tomb was discovered inside the pyramid in 1951. Middle aged man buried, or rather entombed there, fancy sarcophagus of stone, his bones smothered in jade and gold – shades of Tutankhamen. And the city of old grey stone spreading for acres and acres, abandoned by the builders long before the conquistadores came, which gives it a sense of mystery. The big pyramid has 120 steps leading to the top, a wee bit tiring at the end – Still, I don't feel like writing poems about these things, as I would in Canada, or as I would anywhere that I was certain of – For instance, I know I'll write a few poems in South Africa next winter – (I have an application in for another C.C., which I'll probably get –)

All the area around here, as well as farther north, is where Hernan Cortes and his men finagled the Indians out of the country – I'm reading a book by Bernal Diaz del Castillo,[1] who was a conquistadore under Cortes, and one can marvel at the two-facedness of Cortes. He told so many lies to the Indians (hard to think of the Maya as Indians) that if you took the opposite to what he said he would always have told the truth. Bernal Diaz wrote sometime around 1560, and died about age 90. One gathers that Cortes conquered the country mainly by using the Indians against each other; if there were any natural enmities he simply enhanced them, using one side against the other, and actually have some hundred thousand Indians along who were hostile to Montezuma when he took Mexico City.

When we first got to Merida we were trapped in a toilet factory in a hailstorm. Big bullets of hail enough to kill a bald man. Then a coupla inches of rain in an hour or so and a big wind. The sewer system couldn't handle it, and water roared down the street outside the toilet factory, running downhill, six and eight inches deep. Inch thick boards floated past the window. We priced the toilet fixtures and tile – very high, don't buy your toilet in Yucatan. The people seemed to think the storm was a great joke. Afterward, I went to a bar for a drink, stepped thru the door into eight inches of water – Incidentally, Eurithe tells me it's Sunday. I'm a day older'n I thought. In Merida we kinda marvelled at the Montejo house, circa 1549, built by one of Cortes' men's sons. Bearded Spaniards in grey stone carved on the front, and unless I'm mistaken some of the smaller carvings have their balls showing. Could I be mistaken? Not like Louis Riel in Regina, no cloak to cover these boys.

I'm down to a svelte 190 lbs, face like a hot dog with highlights of red, whereas Eurithe has gained a pound or two from eating the bread. All I do is drink beer and throw in a bun once in a while to soak up the moisture.

Eurithe has blown fuses with her electric frypan all the way to Cape Horn. Very embarrassing sometimes, to look at the motel lady with innocent face while she searches for a new bulb she thinks is burned out and apologizes to you. But here, in this cabin-motel, we hafta use sterno, since even the coffee pot makes the moon go dim when we turn it on – the coffee pot I mean, not the moon. Address: Me, c/o American Express, Hotel Panamericana, Calle 59, Merida, Yucatan, Mexico. IF IF we get the house. See outside of envelope.

Love, from both,

Al

1. Diaz (1492-1591) wrote *The True History of the Conquest of New Spain* (1632). There have been numerous English translations, among them *The Bernal Diaz Chronicles: The True Story of the Conquest of Mexico,* translated and edited by Albert Idell (Doubleday, 1956), and *The Conquest of New Spain,* translated and introduced by J.M. Cohen (Penguin, 1963).

§

Elmcot

19 February 1972

Dear Al–

Got yr last letter (Feb 15) today, which was pretty quick. Hasten to reply, now that I have an address for you. I may say I have been insanely envious of you and Eurithe, as I got yr communications saying "85 in the shade", etc. It has been cold as charity here, and the coal strike has gone on for 6 weeks and still not settled. Vast power cuts, of course. We have now had 7 power cuts, each about 6 hours. As our house is heated largely by electricity, this is sad. However, we're luckier than some – at least we have (a) a gas stove for cooking and can turn on oven and open it, for heat; (b) a coal boiler in kitchen (as long as our coal hangs on, which will only be another 3 weeks ... then no more hot water; and (c) 2 fireplaces and a fair supply of firewood. We are hoarding candles and using only a few at a time, as no candles to be bought anywhere in the country. Not surprisingly, I have developed a filthy cold, which doesn't add to my joy. It does have its slightly humorous side, however. The other day I was sitting in my study, writing – it was morning, but pouring with rain and the day was dark as pitch; the power was off; I was wrapped in 2 sweaters, an Irish wool shawl and an eiderdown. And I was writing a scene which takes place in Ontario on a boiling July day! I thought, well, if I can make *that* imaginative leap, I can do anything. Bloody winter. Actually, I feel more and more and more how much I want to

247

move back to Can. I know things [are] awful there in some ways, too, but if I'm gonna suffer I'd rather suffer in my own country, with at least some good friends about. What I'd like to do, really, is sell this house in a year (or maybe two, if it works that way) and buy a small house in Peterborough. I hate to sell Elmcot, but it is not realistic to think of keeping it forever. Anyway, couldn't buy a house in Can if didn't sell this one. The kids still yell with horror, when I mention it, but they will just have to adjust. I am *not* going to live here alone with cats and roses. No way. Also, can't afford to run this place for too many more years – costs a bloody fortune.

I ordered that book for you, but haven't received it yet. Do you want me to send it to you in Mexico? Airmail? When do you get back to Ameliasburgh? And THANKS A MILLION re: sending me The Horse's Mouth – I really love that book, and that edition is beautiful.[1] I haven't sent you Wm Golding's latest yet.[2] Want me to send to Mex or not?

Mexico sounds pretty fascinating to me. Odd about the guy from Calgary.[3] Meeting him on the ruins, I mean. I also like your being stranded in a toilet factory during a storm. You have a flair for the bizarre, I guess.

Sorry about poems. But migawd, Al, we do just sometimes go through periods of not writing anything that really comes across, or not writing anything at all. All last year here, remember how frustrated I was? Couldn't do anything. Began when I went to Can last summer, and got a lot done there. Since things have simmered down here, after Christmas, I'm back at it, and it is growing, at least in size if not in quality. I'm scared to read over what I've written, lest it appear a load of fatuous rubbish. And it is far far too long. But I just have to let it come the way it wants to be written, and struggle with it afterwards. It isn't that it hasn't got a form – the form is there, and basically sound, I think, altho kind of complicated. But it's the flesh and blood which is growing to huge proportions. I know why, and I know all that is faulty about it, but cannot think of any other way to handle it, so am just going on. When actually writing, I feel happy. When not writing, I worry about it and think it's crap. Each chapter is hell to get into. But at least it's getting down on paper. I keep putting in too much detail – well, never mind. At this point I don't give a damn if no one else likes it. I like writing it, and that matters. I was getting pretty hassled around Christmas – I like all the Can kids here, but it all went on too long, too many people. Now it's okay. Of course, the personal anxieties still continue – the other day Dave had a minor accident on his motorbike. Was brought home by the couple whose car he had grazed, and I damn near passed out when they came to the door. However, no bones broken, and only surface cuts and bruises. But it shook me for some days, needless to say.

I like the sad tales of Eurithe's electric fryingpan. She missed her calling – ought to have been an actress; all that innocence act! Don't the motel ladies smell the frying food? Or do you burn incense?

I'm going to Toronto May 15th. Out to P'borough on May 20th. Trent U giving me an Hon.D.Litt. Convocation May 26th. Back to Tor, then, and to Montreal May 30th for meeting of Univ Teachers of Eng, which I've said I'll be on a panel or something.[4] Then Toronto June 1st, as U of T giving me Hon.D.Litt … getting embarrassing, and also, wish there were some $$$ attached. They have asked me to give convocation address, and as I cannot think of a plausible reason for refusing, other than that I shake uncontrollably with nerves on such occasions, I've said I will. Gloom. Horror. Have writ speech, and I think it is probably a load of shit but have re-writ it 4 times and am not going to work any more on it. Some staff will think it too radical, while kids will think it (likely) too conservative.[5] Nobody wins 'em all. Then, June 2nd – out to blessed shack, and WORK, for whole summer, pray God. Odd, you know, Al – I love Elmcot, but I think my fated period of life here is nearly over, and I really long to be back in Can. Can't wait to get back to shack and writing there and seeing friends on weekends and all that. Hope you manage to rent house. Please write soon.

Love,
Margaret

---

1. Purdy sent Laurence as a gift his copy of the novel, a special edition with Cary's illustrations. It had been edited by Andrew Wright and published in 1957 by George Rainbird in association with Michael Joseph.

2. *The Scorpion God* (1971).

3. In a letter to Laurence of 7 February, Purdy had described his surprise at being recognized at Palenque by a visitor from Calgary who had attended a poetry reading given there by Purdy the previous autumn.

4. Laurence participated on a panel, which included the novelist Hugh MacLennan, at the annual meeting of the Association of Canadian University Teachers of English held at McGill University.

5. In her address, Laurence compared the contemporary university to the contemporary novel and said that both were "undergoing profound inner changes."

§

Elm Cottage
24 February [1972]

Dear Al –

Brief note, as I feel it may not reach you. As the Irish saying goes, if you don't get this letter, let me know.

Several things to say. First, the Joyce Carey arrived yesterday. Many many many thanks! It is so great an edition. Really wonderful. I thought I must read it again, but scared to do so yet, as if I do, I'll go out and hang myself instead of finishing this novel I'm working on. Guess I wouldn't, really. But you know what I mean. Someone's done something so bloody well – why try your own mini-approach? Because it is damn well one's *own* approach, and therefore unique, is why. And anyway, who knows how it will turn out? Might not be so mini after all, just possibly. Also, not really the same areas – just similar. Many differences – e.g. Carey isn't concerned about Louis Riel! Incidentally, did I ever mention – my character turns out to be not a painter after all but a writer? Hell, Al, what do I know about painting? Sweet nothing. That was one evasion I worked through. Different with Carey, who *was* an artist as well, at least to some extent, and who knew. Anyway, I really like to have the book, and am grateful. I think it was really good of you to send it … don't think I could've been so generous. (That's you, kid, generous to a fault!)

Second, when Rosemary Eakins last was here, she gave me the address of a bookshop in Eng which handles all kinds of old books, and apparently is the best in the business here, and you could write for catalogue: Richard Booth (Bookseller) Ltd., Hay Castle, Hay-on Wye, Hereford, England.

Third, got a letter today from Sheppard Press – the book you want will be out end March,[1] and will be £2-10 including postage. I'll send cheque and they'll send book to me when it is out. The new edition, that is. So will either take it to Can when I go, mid–May, or post to you.

Am having hassles re: the Companion of Canada. Seems they don't post the pretty little brooches, if you can't attend Investiture. They want me to attend the next one, end Oct, as I can't be there for April 12th. No way I can, Al. I have to return to Eng mid-Sept, as Joc and Peter can only stay that long and I can't leave Dave on his own. He would be miserably lonely in this huge dump by himself, and also, what if he had an accident on his motorbike? He did have a minor accident, week before last, and it damn near turned my hair white. No real harm done … only minor cuts etc. But it was traumatic. Have decided that if anyone is going to be PUT OUT TO SOME CONSIDERABLE DEGREE, I would rather it was the Gov Gen of Canada than any member of my family. The Sec of the Order wrote saying in some very few cases a private Investiture is arranged, so I have writ to say I'd be glad if this could be arranged in my case. Kind of funny, when you think of it. I'll probably propagandize Michener about Women's Lib — how a woman who is bread-earner and also fortress-keeper can't just gaily whip off on jaunts to Ottawa whenever she likes! Wow.

Won't write more now, as have no faith you'll get this. If you *do* get it, let me know, eh? And please write.

Love,
Margaret

---

1. *Booksellers of North America.*

§

[Progresso]
[Yucatan, Mexico]
26 February 1972

Dear Margaret,

well, eight days from Feb. 15 to here ain't so good, and that's about what it takes to and from Canada too. You musta hit a favourable air current with the last one.

I write quickly, on accounta, dunno how long we'll be here. Eurithe's dad had an accident, and she is haunting the telegraph and telephone offices. Badly injured, in hospital etc. Now slightly better. And since I am here as more or less a helpless puppet of hers anyway, this is an opportunity for rebellion. No, Mexico is fine re lack of snow, but I am as prone to boredom here as ever. It is a "fascinating" place if you're interested in ruins and ancient peoples etc. I am — in a way. I like the rum too, three bucks a litre. $2.50 if you buy two litres. And have now written two poems;

but your book sounds as if you're more enthused than I am about the poems. And one thing about Canada in February, there's something to be snarly and miserable about. The weather, I mean, which you can't possibly give up in your own case. I'm sure you'd miss that nasty English weather that is responsible for the Anglo Saxon race reaching its 1,000 year nadir. Huh? I have re-written Callimachus' translation of "Herakleitos" – or at least re-told it.[1] There, you transplanted Manitobaite chew on that. Learning, that's what it is. Mention just one more Hon. D. Litt. (whatever that is), and I will bite the typewriter. Does, by the way, or do I should say, three Hon. D. Litt's equal one book about a living author(ess)? The point about my not writing tho, is I'm losing enthusiasm for things, I don't feel enthusiastic about a damn thing right now, even rum. Or am I being self-conscious? Was I ever really enthusiastic, youthfully eager and totally involved in poems? Of course I was. Can you recommend me a bad head-shrinker so I can fuck him up too. Well, I take it you are still using your guts (etc.) (meaning, what you've gone thru recently, the things that hurt and feel good at the same time – hey, that ain't a bad line either) in writing. Don't think I am. I am here and don't really wanta be here, but couldn't think of very good excuses not to come. Which is part of it. Pain is deprivation of the unknown, which is a queer way to phrase it. I am feeling miserable, which oughta produce poems. Ergo (I like that word "ergo") why not? Answer, I oughta be where I wanta be, and it ain't here.

But enough of this amateur psychoanalysis. The one pome I write might begood a little possibly. But it (i.e. pome) doesn't really hit me anywhere. So what the hell.

No sympathy from me for your woebegone besweatered and be-Hon-D.-Litt-ed state, as I expect none from you re my psychic morass (I'll snap out of it when I get to South Africa – or, I hope, before that) – Let us say what the coal strike is good for your soul wielding a ghostly quill pen some time around Richard 3, as probably my extreme discontent is good for me now.[2] Hard to figure why when you go thru it tho. I have lost my lost feeling in one sense, but the paucity of commas and semi-colons means I'll get it back.

Re the Book Sellers of N.A., please send it to me at Ameliasburgh. Yeah, the Golding too. Will send money as soon as hit the home area. Funny, I'll be in England some time next fall, so I want U.S. book sellers. Did I say I got three or four good things? One, "John Carroll of Carrollton's visit to Canada in 1776", this being as one of the three U.S. commissioners during the revolution to try to induce Canada to join the revolution (and, of course, the U.S.). Pubbed in 1845 by Maryland Historical Soc. $25. Lousy book tho, but it's worth a hundred at least in Canada.

I do hope you actually remove home yourself. Expect it's a matter of counting your friends over there, as against same in Canada. Other less important considerations too, I suppose. Or: are you comfortable and at home over there? Much of your Hon.D.Litts and recognition comes from here, Canada. Does that make a difference? But I would think, as you say, the most important thing is friends. And those goddam cats and roses, you can have em anywhere. I applaud (as a non-mother and with little sympathy for maws of any kind except for labor pains and not enduring parental love) your apparent decision that the kids just gotta get used to maw bein human too. Jesus, no more paper.

love
Al

---

1. Callimachus (310-240 BC), Greek poet, wrote a famous epigram on the death of his friend and fellow poet, Herakleitos of Halikarnassos.

2. Purdy is recalling the opening lines of *Richard III*: "Now is the winter of our discontent/Made glorious summer by this sun of York."

§

Elmcot

9 March 1972

Dear Al–

Christ knows when you will get this letter. I am sending to A'burgh, on account of your last letter (Feb 26) sounds as tho you will be going back there shortly. At least, this is what my Celtic Second Sight tells me. I am very sorry re: Eurithe's dad, and hope he is okay now and out of danger. I sense, however, that even if all is well there, you'll be back home soon. Hence I write to you there, and probably you'll be in Mex for another 4 months and won't get this until July. However, you seem to be fed up with the tropical climes, so no doubt you'll find your way back to better (ie worse) climate soon. Well, if Mex isn't for you, it just isn't for you, that's all. Personally I feel I'd hate it, but maybe that is because I've *had* the tropics and all that. Fascinating ruins or no, I think I now prefer northerly climes, altho not so far northerly that I totally freeze the blood during 9 months of year.

Have written to Sheppard Press and sent £££. They'll send me book when it is out and I'll forward. Will send the Golding when I get around to packaging it up; soon.

Did you get my letter in which I said I received the Cary book you sent? If not, MANY MANY HEARTFELT THANKS ETC ETC. It's beautiful.

No. Cannot recommend a good headshrinker. ARE there any? Never been to one, personally, as feel I would argue so much it wouldn't be worth my money. Also, no money. I can see you at a shrink's – *he* might learn something!

Don't consider sending £££ for book – will let you know how much it amounts to in $$ and you can bring scotch some-time this summer, if, as I hope and trust, you'll be in Can same time I am.

I have about 3 friends in this country. I have about three dozen in Can (not all v. close, of course, but quite a lot whom I do love).

Of course it's a matter of friends, where you live, among other things. But I do feel I've been right and okay to live here, these years. Now, tho, it is time to go back. Will do when can arrange it. Soon, I hope. That is, within next 2 yrs.

Thanks for yr lack of sympathy re: my having to sashay to universities this spring. Okay, I don't expect much for that. I give you my sympathy for yr psychic hangups because that's what I've got too in some ways and who wants or needs sympathy for anything less? All the minor details are just a load of nothing, but all the same, I get nervous when I consider my schedule for this summer – I go to Can May 10, and from then until June 2 it is all go-go-go to universities and panel discussions and lots of nonsense. However, come June 2, I am off to shack and NOTHING is going to stand in my way. My words to my shack are (thanks, whoever wrote THE HIGHWAYMAN, Alfred Noyes?) ... And I'll come to thee by June 2nd, tho the Gov Gen should bar the way! [1]

Have finished Part III (out of V parts). Part V will be quite short. All others terribly long. What to do, except keep on and see what transpires? I hate to leave it, even for a day; it really slays me to have to break off, but I do have to. I have let everything else go for one solid month now. How to live Several Lives Simultaneously, by trying awfully hard and swearing all the way. How I want to be in the shack, alone for 5 days per week! If anyone interrupts me weekdays then, I will quite honestly stab them to the heart. I am getting positively nasty about all this. I know so bloody well what I want to do with novel, but of course am not actually getting it done, as it should be – between the idea and the reality falls the shadow. Still. Am getting something down, and the re-writing may bring in something more.

Got a card from Earle, from Ghana, thanking me for sending him addresses of a few people who might put him in touch with various Afr writers. He is having a fine time, it seems. Must say I admire his energy and so on. I don't think I could undertake a tour of Africa, doing readings. I guess what I admire really is not his energy (which I've got too) but his nerve!

Guess I'll pen 2 words to you to Mex, in case. By the by, your *learning,* re: Herakleitos etc, staggers me. I am a country illiterate from way back, sorry. Who is Hera. etc? I have some dim notion of Gr phil, but not much. I know what a Yellow-Shafted Flicker looks like, though. I can also recognize Poison Ivy once again (after a gap of years), but that's thanks to you, if you recall, at my shack. Anyone want to know about the basis of the Afr tribal systems, or the W. Afr concepts of the deity? I'm good on that.

For god's sake don't worry re: poems. They'll come. In their own time. I know how it feels to be convinced nothing will ever happen again. But it somehow does. I can say that now, but you know how I feel in between novels. The passionate convictions of despair. But the hell with that. It'll come. Of course, the real point, I know, is that *someday* it won't come. The spook behind every writer's shoulder. And a real one, of course. But that's only to say – someday I'll quit breathing. And we will. But need not do it until it actually happens.

Love,
Margaret

---

1. The lines from Noyes's (1880-1958) poem are: "I'll come to thee by moonlight,/though hell should bar the way."

Skyway Hotel
London Airport
12 December 1972[1]

Dear Margaret,

Tried to phone you on arrival this morning but operator couldn't find your listing despite my detailed & intricate etc.

– So what the hell – ! Eurithe and I will be over in late March I expect –

Got your letters yesterday – didn't write after arranging passage (your reservation helped) in the end I had *two* reservations. BOAC at Tor. told me.[2]

Any way, tumbled into bed here around 9:30 after abortive phone call. Dead weary, etc. Now 3:40, my flight at 7 pm.

Yeah, read Atwood's *Survival,* think it's admirable. Creating a lot of arguments too, which is good. Of course the victim bit is true, but you can't make as much of it as A does, because it's one of the major themes of world lit – The part about the five obscene sexual positions is also relevant, altho she's making political awareness perhaps a larger part of Canlit than it is. Best part of book is impression here's a sharp mind that read & thought & decided – One doesn't have to agree with her all the time – Anyway, what such a book does is tend to create a critical climate for one's own work, viz Eliot[3] – Any poems or fiction Atwood writes now is liable to be measured with her own yardstick. She is, in some ways, saying: this is how poems & fiction should be written –

I would find it difficult to think of Hagar as victim despite her being trapped & dead at the end. Or Duddy Kravitz. David what's his name in Buckler, yes[4] – Nor do I think of my own poems as a whole demonstrating the victim thesis. So much one could say – but too long & tiresome. I'm in a fair state of malaise right now myself. The point of grimness where you say, what do I really want to do next & how important is it? This is where the Zorba-thermostat ought to cut in. But it ain't up to now. Will write you from Jo-burg.

love
Al

1. Purdy was on his way to South Africa.

2. Laurence had, on Purdy's request, also made an airplane reservation for him.

3. T.S. Eliot (1888-1965), the Anglo-American poet, was the author of several works of criticism, among them *The Sacred Wood* (1920) and *After Strange Gods* (1934).

4. Hagar is the protagonist of Laurence's *The Stone Angel* (1964), Duddy Kravitz of Richler's *The Apprenticeship of Duddy Kravitz* (1959), and David Canaan of Ernest Buckler's *The Mountain and the Valley* (1952).

c/o Clients' Mail
American Express
1st Floor Merbrook House
Cor. Commissioner & Vonbrandis Sts
Johannesburg, S.A.
16 December [1972]
will be held there. It better be!

Dear Margaret –

At this point I am wondering what the hell I am doing here! You know the sort of feeling –

Three days here now (at hotel on reverse) & leave Monday for Cape Town on the Blue Train. It's almost 700 miles. Met a S.A. novelist, Nadine Gordimer[1] & husband Thursday, went to dinner there & attended a play written by blacks at university. Not bad – and I wrote a poem after return, but no typewriter, so I can't look at it.

Well, the papers are not just propaganda – S.A. sure is a racist country. Makes a good pair with Uganda. I hope to get an address or two from N. Gordimer (forgot my own address book), but so far nothing to hold onto with the mind for writing purposes – i.e. I don't feel like writing – I hope your novel is going well. I might leave here earlier & see you before going back to Canada – Eurithe will be in Fla. by now, of course – a place that doesn't stir me with anticipation either. Hope this doesn't sound too depressed. Incidentally, send me your telephone #, eh? Operators don't know nothin – Reading something called "Brill Among the Ruins": Vance Bourjailly[2] – Not bad – the hero [has] so much vitality I'd be bound to dislike him. Ain't natural. Burned out core that won't give up, whereas I feel like it. Also reading John Berger's essays in Penguin which seem intellectual shit.[3] Odd thing: I am well aware that, with an act of will, I can write poems. Here or anywhere I've exercised this will sometimes. And yet, much of what I wrote was written as I breathe, as I talk or consider something pleasurable i.e. involuntary. I see novelists as always exercising this act of will – until they get lost in what they're doing – you can't to my mind sit down every morning at a typewriter without exercising the will. Most of the time I don't remember exercising the will in order to write, at least initially – now I must if I am to write at all. Or is this sort of self-argument sophistry? Anyway, I might see you sooner than expected. And tell me if this is a poem:

> Write me in April
> and tell me if June is coming.[4]

love

Al

---

1. Nadine Gordimer (b. 1923) had recently published a volume of short stories, *Livingstone's Companions* (1971).

2. Vance Bourjailly (b. 1922), American novelist. *Brill Among the Ruins* (1970) was his sixth novel.

3. Probably *The Look of Things* (1972) by Berger (b. 1926), British novelist, playwright, and short-story writer.

4. These lines became the epigraph to *Sex & Death*.

§

Dear Al–

Thanks much for your letter, which certainly took a long time to get here – it's dated Dec 16 and I got it yesterday. Christmas mail, maybe.

I hope you're feeling less depressed now. Oh, *well* do I know the feeling. It *will* pass, but at the time it is difficult to believe that. I dunno about novelists having to write by an act of will – I think it is both an act of will and an act of faith. I always feel that the Will part comes in mainly by taking the pen in hand every day (or sitting down at the typewriter, as the case may be). But once I get into the thing, it isn't Will but something else which is operating, same as with poems, I guess. Of course, re-reading yr letter, I see that this is in fact what you have said – yeh, it *is* an act of will until one gets lost (or found) inside the thing itself.

Phone number (please write it down in a safe place) … Penn 2103. The reason you couldn't get my number was that the operator undoubtedly did not realize that Penn is in the Oxford Area phonebook, not in a Bucks County directory, so she looked in the wrong place. This has happened before, and always happens with people with whom I really would like to talk, *never* with the young Canadian who phones up and says she or he is a friend of one of my nieces or someone and can they come out and spend a few days – those kids always somehow get through!! Anyhow, thanks for trying. If you decide to leave S.A. sooner than expected, you know there's always a room for you here, any time.

Glad you got to meet Nadine Gordimer, a really fine novelist whose work I have long admired. Have also admired her staying there, rather than leaving as so many S.A. writers have done or have had to do. It must have been awfully difficult for her at times, maybe all the time. I'd be glad to hear your impressions of her. Do you know her work?

Odd things are happening here. I'm bashing on with the type-script and think I can get it done in another 2 months if I work hard. But the astonishing thing is that I have penned 3 songs for the novel! Yeh, I know you said "Margaret, don't do it", but these three seemed to come of their own accord. They're songs by Jules ("Skinner") Tonnerre, one about his grandfather, old Jules, who fought with Riel at Batoche when a boy, one for his father Lazarus, and one for his sister Piquette who burned to death with her 2 kids when the Tonnerre shack in the valley caught fire one winter – this has to be the most repetitive death in fiction, as it is told about in The Fire-Dwellers, in A Bird in the House, and now again in this novel. I wonder why it haunts my imagination so much. Anyway, Ian Cameron has composed music for the songs, and when he sings them with his guitar they really sound like real songs. Two other friends put down the musical score, so I hope it can be printed with the novel if the damn book is ever done and published. I'm also going to get a tape of Ian singing them. I may become like Leonard Cohen yet! (Awful thought, eh?) (Not that I'd mind being able to write poems like his).

Weather here is gawdawful … mist, fog, etc. But don't let that prevent you from visiting … the house is warm. We had a fine Christmas and I'm just beginning to get back to work now. One whole week with no work, and I begin to get impatient and anx-ious. The Camerons, and also Joc, have gone away for a few days leaving me with their cats, so I now have 2 black kittens, known as The Zany Black Panther Sisters, in addition to Topaz. Calico got run over, which was a great loss to all. The kittens are demons and the kitchen looks as though a hurricane had hit it. But I am calm, or mostly.

Dave will be away tomorrow, and altho he and Ian and Sandy and Joc and her man etc will be here New Year's Day, I shall for the first time ever be alone on N. Year's Eve. I am kind of looking forward to it. N. Year's Eve appeals to me much less than Christ-mas, and I hate the pretense of jollity that I have to put on. Shall quietly empty a bottle of wine by myself and think inspiring thoughts. Will drink to your defeat of depression and to lots of good poems for you in 1973.

Love,
Margaret

ps. I think I'm not going to sell Elmcot for a few years – Ian & Sandy will rent it. Think I can still whomp up enough for a house in Can, if I sell shack, which I think I'd do anyway, as who needs 2 houses? Am planning Project Canada, re: moving back in spring.

§

Elmcot
21 January 1973

Dear Al:

Forwarded Eurithe's letter to you to A'burgh, with a short note from me, but expect you won't get same until you return from Florida.[1]

My cold is as bad as ever, and I feel lousy and septic and not long for this vale of tears. However, I am bravely pressing on with novel, and think I can get second draft typed by end of next week. With what can only be described as a stroke of pure brilliance, I have now employed Jane and David as housecleaners – the agreement being that I pay them £1-50 per week each, and they do all cleaning. They did their first stint today, and I typed 20 pp., so it seems a good notion. Joc and Pete moved out today, so the old dump is somewhat quieter. However, we did have 10 people for dinner last night. Sandy Cameron cooked, however, so once again I was free to work all day.

Since you left, the weather has been unremittingly foul (nothing to do with yr leaving, unless you are a closer friend of the Almighty than you are even of Trudeau). Fog, rain, misery, woe, etc. I think I would prefer snow and sunshine. Eng winters are getting me down.

It was great to see you and to have a chance to talk, even tho I was not at peak form owing to cold, sinus, etc. Still, we seemed to get quite a bit of talking done. I wonder how you are feeling now about the South Afr poems? Less depressed, I hope. I can see how you must have felt, re: responding like a white liberal, etc, but I honestly do not believe there *are* more than 2 responses to South Africa – it is, literally, a black and white situation. Within those 2 responses, of course, there must be a lot of subtle variation. I haven't read much of the writing of black South Africans, but I would guess that some of the work of Ezekiel Mphalele, Alex LaGuma and Lewis Nkosi[2] would give a pretty accurate picture.

I dunno how much rewriting I'm going to have to do on this thing. I still hope to cut out some more from the 2nd draft. I'm finding it kind of a strain, just about now, to keep on going and not to rush the whole thing too much, as my natural inclination after nearly 2 years is to want to get the damn thing done and be rid of it. Must try not to succumb, however, as it is still in relatively sloppy condition.

How long are you going to be in Florida? By the way, I still haven't heard from Western U – maybe they have changed their minds about wanting me for 1 term as w-in-r. I wish they'd let me know. I've written to them, but no response.[3]

All for now from the bleaknesses of wintry Bucks.

Love,
Margaret

ps. nearly forgot main purpose of this letter – would it be okay with you if I quote 2 lines from one of yr poems at the beginning of this novel, ie just after title page? They are from Roblin Mills Circa 1832:

> but they had their being once
> and left a place to stand on

The whole ancestral thing, summed up. Over the past few months, I've thought of all kinds of different quotes to use at the novel's beginning, including those lines of yours (which I forgot to mention to you when you were here), and re-looking at all of them (Dylan Thomas, etc etc etc, including some lines of Psalm 39, and so on), I thought – oh for heaven's sake, why put in all that bezaz. Actually, not every theme in the novel is summed up in those lines of yrs, but the most important themes are, so I'd like to use them if you have no objection, as I'm sure you won't.

---

1. On his way home from South Africa in early January, Purdy had stayed with Margaret Laurence. After a brief return to Ameliasburg, he joined his wife in Florida in late January or early February.

2. Ezekiel Mphahlele (b. 1919), Alex LaGuma (1925-85), and Lewis Nkosi (b. 1936) were all South African writers.

3. Laurence was writer-in-residence at the University of Western Ontario from September to December 1973 and then at Trent University from January to April 1974.

Elmcot
21 January [1973]

Airletter 2
Dear Al–

Oh hell and goddamn. The scribbled-out bit on back of air-letter 1 [1] is because I realized I'd misquoted and said re: yr poem Roblin Mills Circa 1832, and it is actually Circa 1842. Then I started checking, and find that in Wild Grape Wine, it is: Roblin Mills (circa 1842) and in yr Selected it is Roblin's Mills (2). If you agree to let me use the 2 lines at the beginning of my novel, which title do I give the poem? For my purposes, quite frankly and selfishly, I'd like to get the 1842 in there, but far be it from me (she says hypocritically) to mess about with a poet's title for a poem, except that this poem obviously has been published with diff titles. How about Roblin's Mills (circa 1842) … hm hm?? Anyway, could you let me know what to put down, always supposing you aren't gonna say hell no don't use the lines at all.

Love,

M

ps. I am thinking of getting a small project underway to cheer you up – about 300 Can writers all write to you on April 1st, saying June Is Coming. Or better still, send telegrams, which would totally confuse yr local telegraph office and no doubt embarrass both you and Eurithe, but it sounds a kind of cheery idea to me.

---

1. The scribbled-out part is indecipherable.

811 – 8th Street
New Smyrna Beach
Florida
[2]6 January 1973

Dear Margaret:

Did get your letter afore leaving, and replied. Mail service to U.S. lousy tho, took ten days for a spec. del. letter from there to Eurithe to reach here. Jesus! Typewriter also lousy.

Course you can use the verse. Reason for difference in title is there were two poems of that "Roblin Mills" title, and had to differentiate. In one book, I mean. Of course, use the circa 1842 tag. At the lake I had ten days of 35 to 50 degree weather, then suddenly it was 15 below zero. I killed a rabbit to use for a jock strap.

Three of the poems I wrote are good, the rest very ordinary. But it's a comfort to get three.

Glad to hear you are bravely pressing on with unremitting vigor in order to give the world another masterpiece. My sentiments precisely. Us artists must take courage, fuck the philistines and sacrifice our lives for our art. Hey?

Talking about cuts, Don Obe, that bastard at Maclean's, wanta to cut my piece some more.[1] I said no with extreme vigor. It was cut to ribbons the first time in Dec. when he said that was enough. No no a thousand etc.

Sun is shining here, temp anywhere from 70 to 80, neons flash bravely at night amid the roar of drinkers' conversations ... drowning the ocean surf. Here till Feb. 15. No use you writing, on accounta mail del. really is awful. Eating sea food with Ron Everson yesterday, he wanta us to go to a poetry reading Wednesday. I told him I have to go to my own readings, but nobody else's. I wouldn't go to my own if they'd use a record and send me a cheque.

Maybe I said, don't think the quote from Friday very suitable for me after all. Tournier has another novel out called "The Erl King" (modern), pub. Collins, won the Goncourt prize or something in France, best book of year or some damn thing.[2] Thot you might be interested ...

I do not actually think June is coming. June is a time of the spirit rather than chronology. It is a novel or poem. I have, by the way, applied to Ont. Arts for more money, despite your own moral and puritan inhibitions. Milk em as long as I can. Beer with Acorn goin thru Toronto. His sole conversation is still himself and politics, mostly himself.

This typewriter is work. Hafta hit it like a sledgehammer.

love,

Al

1. Don Obe was Associate Editor at *Maclean's*. Purdy published nothing in the magazine in 1973, but two articles appeared in 1974: "The Agony of South Africa," April 1974, 34-35, 83-84, 86; "Caught in the Net," May 1974, 26-27, 85, 87. In the May issue, *Maclean's* also published "Face to Face," Margaret Atwood's article on Margaret Laurence, 38-39, 43, 44, 46.

2. Michel Tournier (b. 1924), French novelist and author of *Vendredi ou les limbes du Pacifique* (1967), translated as *Friday* (1969), and of *Le roi des aulnes* (1970), which won the Prix Goncourt and was published in English as *The Erl King* (1972).

§

Elmcot

3 February 1973

Dear Al–

Am writing to you to Florida, as I imagine you'll have left A'burgh by now. Thanks for yr letter of Jan 22, which certainly took long enough in getting here, as I got it yesterday – the mails are going to pieces; things ain't what they used to be.

Glad yr poems seem better than they did. I had a feeling they might, when you got away from the depressing atmosphere of S. Africa and also yr own sense of depression and of having reacted like a white liberal – which, in my view, is pretty well inevitable. How else can one react? There are, alas, only a narrow range of responses available in such a situation.

Thanks for sending Maximum Security Ward – I look forward to reading it. I have heard of it somewhere, but can't recall where.

Lucky you, going to Mexico. Actually, a cousin of mine in Rome (her husband works for the Can Diplomatic Corps, and sounds *awful,* but she is quite nice) has written to invite me to go there for a visit, and I am seriously considering it.

Migod, the clipping from Maclean's! [1] Why why do people do it, and what have I done to deserve such an embarrassingly fulsome outburst? In this vein, I was furious yesterday when I received the NCL edition of THE FIRE-DWELLERS. Some oaf at M& S has used on the jacket the quote from that lady on the Cleveland Plain Dealer, "there is no better novelist writing in English today." Like Edmund Wilson's remark about Callaghan (comparing him to Turgenev)[2] that damn remark follows me around, and I wish to heaven M& S had had more sense than to use it. It makes me look ridiculous – I don't mind looking ridiculous if *I'm* the one who has done it, but this is too much.

Well, now for the Big News:

MY NOVEL IS FINISHED. NOT JUST THE SECOND DRAFT. I HAVE NOW GONE OVER IT AND DONE AS MUCH FURTHER REWRITE AS I CAN AT THE MOMENT. IT IS *DONE*!!

Actually, of course, supposing the publishers accept it, I know there will be some further work to do on it, but by that time I should be outside it, so it won't be as difficult and nerve-wracking (I hope). Right now, I just cannot do any more to it – I keep getting it out and flicking through it, in a state which fluctuates madly between thinking "Hm, not bad" and "Migod, what garbage", so really my judgement is just lost for the moment. Jocelyn is going to type it out for me, as the typescript is readable. Thank heaven I won't have to type it myself. Another friend (one of Joc's ex's) who also works at ICL (you met him; John Valentine) is going to do 2 xerox copies from the one fair copy Joc will do. Also, Sandy has come up with some portraits of some of the characters, and they really are astonishingly good, so she is going to get duplicates of those, plus the musical scores for songs, at ICL. Little does International Computers Ltd know how they are assisting the arts! Joc is typing it on ICLmachine, altho I have gone so far as to buy the paper!

I am really exhausted, but damn glad to have it done, at least for now. But now I enter the worst stage – waiting until I hear what the publishers think of it. In my head I write terrible reviews of it

– and oh my God, one could, one *could*! Then, to cheer myself, I mentally write favourable reviews of it, and one could do that, too. I know FOR CERTAIN that both Auberon Waugh[3] and Barry Callaghan would hate it, so that cheers me somewhat. Actually, for me this is a bit worse than the usual withdrawal symptoms at the end of a book, because in fact this is the end of a 12-year involvement with Manawaka and its inhabitants, and as the wheel comes full circle in this novel, it will be the last of those. There will, if this one is published, be 5 books concerning the town and its people. Little did I think, when writing THE STONE ANGEL, that it would all work out like this. So I feel a bit odd, and empty, as though part of my inner dwellingplace has now been removed from me. I don't know where to go now – this is why I've always said this would likely be my last novel. I have been preparing myself mentally for this day, but now that it is here, I guess I'm not really prepared for it after all. I don't mean I'm in the depths or anything – I'm really not. Just feeling sort of aimless. I have one or two things in mind, but not involving in the same way as this fiction has been to me. However, one really does not know what is going to come along.

I feel slightly apologetic about your cold, as I feel sure you must've picked it up in this germ-laden house and taken it back with you. I have only just got over mine, and thought it was becoming chronic.

Good luck with Ont Arts Council.[4]

Love,
Margaret

---

1. A letter from Sandy Watson in praise of Laurence's "Where the World Began" was published in *Maclean's,* February 1973, 12. Purdy had cut it out and mailed it to Margaret Laurence.

2. Edmund Wilson (1895-1972) had made this comparison in *O Canada: An American's Notes on Canadian Culture* (1963).

3. Auberon Waugh (b. 1939), journalist, critic, and at this time chief fiction reviewer for *The Spectator.*

4. Purdy had applied for a writer's grant.

[Florida]

11 February 1973

Dear Margaret:

Great news the novel done. I hope it comes fairly close at least to your own difficult original vision, so like turning yourself inside out and then finding what you were after has reversed itself. You know what I … Secondary wish, I hope it's a novel others also think is fine, deleting the word "great" and Barry Callaghan chokes when he reads it as he must to verify his own mistakes. I am personally pleased to see you get into something that, while it includes the personal vision, also moves to a greater degree into objective narrative. Obviously you were not with the Selkirk settlers, except in the sense that a novelist is always with his or her people, therefore it gives you a different kind of creative scope. As you may have guessed, I have misgivings about the accompanying song bit and all that, but regard it as unimportant window dressing. I guess you don't. Well, the spinal cord is the writing, just as it must be in this picture book McStew projects for me next year with photos etc. a la Farley.

Reverting to that project, it's been decided that "In Search of Owen Roblin" shall be the poem, and not "country" or "rural" poems for the photographer. You remember the garbage dump bit that's part of the longer poem. It's probably the best part, incidentally. I wanta do more on that poem (In Search of …), but can't now. Fuck being objective too. Perhaps like a novelist in this instance, I wanta get everything about me into this, obviously ego eh? If I inhabit those goddam early settlers then they are me and I am them. I'd like to get a farmer in there who's a failure, can't keep up with more successful ones, dies trying and knows his own failure. How in hell do I do that? One poem would do it if I can write it. You'll have to see this one of mine. It both fails and succeeds in different places ...

We went to Cape Kennedy the other day, on accounta I wanted to see the rocket graveyard, now called a museum. Read a book in Africa that made me think a poem possible re the graveyard. Outmoded rockets and all that, now mouldering into rust. But they're not mouldering, painted and trim as new corsets or working model of a ballista. Had to take a two hour tour by bus of the whole shebang, bored the hell outa both Eurithe and me. Some 120 people in two buses. Two tours of places, rest of time in bus. Eurithe got out first time, viewed computers and lunar modules like a cynical martian housewife and got out first of all the 120. I was second. Second out-of-bus was for the biggest building in the world, the rocket assembly building, which has weather of its own, huge big large monster great heaviest farthest most wonderful – she stayed in the bus, wouldn't budge, all alone. I too all alone among the 120 and bored. The poem reflects my boredom, just lousy. Maybe I oughta turn it around that way, to boredom of the big and wonderful wow explosions. Makes me think of north poem I wrote in the arctic with me in a boat and all the world south, so that for the first time in my life I could piss on the world.[1] Metaphorically of course. Before going there I had visions of whole city blocks of black rafted into the sky and burning to ashes, meaning the money spent on rockets that would not be spent on slums. And two terrified little monkeys (Able & Baker) in 1959, clinging to each other in outer space, and wondering where are they now? Buried among the poisonous snakes and alligators of Cape Kennedy. Human graveyards at Cape C. too, those of the earliest settlers, not much attention paid to them of course when astronauts are there for autographs. (Hey,

Dr. Lawrence what about your auty-auty-graph?)??) (??) (go ahead and say it, I dare you).

The hero-worship letter, not important really, as you know. I *don't* think it makes you look ridiculous, no, what the hell, part of this age like others, and it influences one other person to read your books great eh? Look at me being Walt Whitman to Canada according to Dennis Lee[2] ... Walt Whitman Purdy aha aha ... As you know I don't agree that when the Manawaka circle complete that you're complete. You can always collaborate with Simone de Beauvoir on how awful it is to be a woman.[3] But the old sausage-grinder doesn't stop that easy. You're thinkin of the vital things like sex and children and all that. "An aged man is but a paltry thing/Unless could clap its hands and sing/And louder sing/For every tatter in its mortal dress ..."[4] Why the hell not? Up to you to find out how. And I don't mean Ayn Rand.[5]

Do read MAXIMUM SECURITY WARD.

Probably good to get away so you can be miserable in comfort.

love

Al

P.S. address in Yucatan:

    c/o American Express,

    Hotel Panamericana,

    Calle 59, No 455,

    Merida, Yucatan, Mexico

Leave here in three days.

---

1. "South" in *North of Summer* (1967).

2. "Running and Dwelling: Homage to Al Purdy." *Saturday Night*, July 1972, 14–16.

3. Simone de Beauvoir (1908–86), French novelist, philosopher, feminist, and political activist.

4. From "Sailing to Byzantium" by William Butler Yeats:

> An aged man is but a paltry thing,
> A tattered coat upon a stick, unless
> Soul clap its hands and sing, and louder sing
> For every tatter in its mortal dress.

5. Ayn Rand (1905-82), American novelist and champion of individualism, known for her two best-selling novels, *The Fountainhead* (1943) and *Atlas Shrugged* (1957).

Elm Cottage
17 February 1973

Dear Al–

Thanks for your letter. Lucky you, to be in sunny clime. Hope all goes well, and that this time you and Eurithe aren't endangering all the electric wiring in every motel you stay in! I've almost decided to go and visit a cousin of mine who lives in Rome – her husband is in the Can Diplomatic Service, or whatever it is called, and she has invited me to go. Think I'll sashay over about end March. I am beginning to feel a great desire to get out and do things, as I have virtually been inside this damn novel for 3 years and feel I've hardly surfaced in that time, and now feel an exhilarating sense of being free for awhile. I'll have to do more work on the novel, probably this summer, but nothing will be possible for a few months.

I think maybe you misunderstand the nature of this novel ... my fault, for giving wrong impression. I don't re-create fictionally the Selkirk settlers bit, really – it comes in first as really quite wildly inaccurate legends, told to Morag when a kid, and later it comes in as History, related briefly as such, but with an admitted and obvious bias. Later still, as a resumé of a novel which she writes, so the history is mixed up with her characters, who are in some ways influenced by people in her own life. I'm not sure this latter device works well, as yet, and I think the resumés of her various novels will need more work. To do a resumé of a novel (even if that novel is, in external reality, not really written, if you see what I mean) is difficult, because one has to simplify a lot, and the danger is in making it sound too simple or else pretentious. However, I don't think I can re-write those bits yet – will have to distance myself, and would like the views of a couple of editors, altho' I feel pretty certain these will only serve to confirm my own views. Anyway, it's good to have it out of my hands for a few months. Yeh, I agree about the songs, actually – it's just that I've enjoyed doing them, as it is very different from anything I've ever done. The novel does not hinge on them at all, and in fact they take up a very small part of the book. They simply express a part of Jules which he could not express in ordinary speech, or would not.

Yes, I recall the garbage dump bit in the poem – it *was* very good. Hope the book works out okay – how many poems will be in it, and how many pics? I wasn't quite certain, from what you said, whether there will be more than 1 poem, or what.

Cape Kennedy sounds gruesome. I suppose it is a good thing to see it, just to know how gruesome it is.

I just received Maximum Security Ward, and have begun reading it. It really hits me. More comment on it when I've read it all. Thanks v.much for sending it.

Have been reading Mervyn Peake's Gormenghast trilogy[1] ... a strange and totally gripping fantasy world, beautifully realized. At least in the first two, Titus Groan and Gormenghast. The third not so good. At last am getting caught up on reading – feel a bit strange, sitting around all day reading. But why not?

Have written to Manitoba Tourist Bureau, asking re: trip to Churchill. Hope they send me all the info.

Re: being finished writing – no, I don't intend to quit writing. I sometimes feel I will, but I guess I probably won't. It's just that I feel a bit peculiar having finished the Manawaka books, that's all. I'd really like to do another kids' book,[2] for light relief, if I can. After that, who knows? Can't force things, as you know. But maybe something will come along.

Have recently discovered (from an old newspaper clipping … article on my grandfather, John Wemyss … sent to me by my aunt) that my family believed themselves to be descended from the Picts – the aborigines of Scotland! How about that? I always knew that Wemyss meant "cave-dweller", and it is true that Fife is ancient Pictish country. I am delighted – I really love to think that in my veins (much diluted with other strains) there flows some blood which belongs to the Picts, a dark and magic people! I always wondered why I felt like a witch – and ho ho, now I know! Also learned from clipping the exact year my great-grandfather settled in Manitoba – 1880. My grandfather went to Canada, to Winnipeg, the year Riel was hanged, and two years later settled in Neepawa, 1887.

I wish I could teleport myself and assets back to Can, without having to go through the terrible business of clearing and selling this house, in summer 74. But I now see I will have to sell it, sentiment notwithstanding. Can't afford to hang onto it, and if I do, I would have to pay Capital Gains Tax on sale, if I left it for a couple of years. That would be more than a quarter of the money I got for house, so that is out of the question. Selling a house here is more complicated than buying one, if that is possible.

Hope the ancient Aztec ghosts are friendly to you.

Love,

Margaret

---

1. Mervyn Peake's (1911-68) trilogy comprised *Titus Groan* (1945), *Gormenghast* (1950), and *Titus Alone* (1959).

2. Her children's books after *Jason's Quest* were *Six Darn Cows* (1979), *The Olden Days Coat* (1979), and *The Christmas Birthday Story* (1980).

§

Dear Al—

Thanks for letter, just received. I wonder if you got mine (probably crossed with yrs) saying Elmcot now sold? Very relevant to what you said in yr letter! Actually, I could have (probably) made about £5 thou more if I had sold to a developer. But I would have felt like hell about it. As it is, it has worked out (unless any snag develops) very well for me in ways other than financial, as well. Mr. Wilson, the buyer – the "squire" across the road at The Beacon – will not tear down Elmcot nor cut down the trees; he will rent it to a couple or a family for a pretty low rent until such time (if ever) that one of his sons wants the place. Anyway, as long as he or his sons have it, the house will remain. He's giving me the price I wanted for it – that is, the price I reckoned I could reasonably expect from a private buyer, not a developer, namely £25,000. Well, that is 3 times what I paid for the house; even reckoning the money I've put into it, it is twice the total amount of my investment in the place. Who needs more? More than that, and one is really getting greedy. I'll have had 10 good years here, very productive re: writing and a very good place for the kids to have grown up, and the house will now provide me with considerably more £££ than I put into it. The great side-effect of all this is that Ian and Sandy Cameron will be renting the place for the next year, from Wilson, which is good in itself, and which also means that David can stay on for awhile, until he decides where he wants to go. So – I'm not complaining. I *was* determined not to sell to a developer, and as luck or chance would have it, it's turned out well for me, which is gratifying, as doing what one considers the right thing to do very seldom brings any kind of bonus! This house has always been lucky for me.

I've sent novel to publishers now. I'm not exactly pacing floor, but nearly. During this past week, I've re-read my manuscript

copy twice, trying to see if the damn thing is any good or not –
how crazy can you get? I've got twenty million things to do, re:
clearing out house, but can do nothing until I hear about novel. I
know that the editors are going to ask for a lot of cutting on the
manuscript, *if* they accept it at all. I just don't feel like going back
into it, Al. What to do? I don't even think it can be cut all that
much. Well, we'll see.

Have bought myself a cassette tapecorder and am fascinated by
it. Am going to go in for cassettes and not bother about a record
player when I get to Canada. Will just get some of my favourite
records put onto tapes. It's really marvellous. And so simple that
even I can work it without difficulty.

I'll bet anything that Eurithe wouldn't sell the farm to an
American, when the chips were really down.[1] And I know damn
well you wouldn't. This "highest bidder" bit is such a specious
argument, isn't it? It's why we now don't own large amounts of
our own country. No point blaming the Yanks for that. It was all
sold by Canadians.

I should be back in Canada by July 23 or around there. Oh
heavens, how will I ever get everything done here by that time? I
will, of course, but I do panic a bit sometimes.

Love,
Margaret

ps. it may be quite true that everybody has their price – in fact it
probably is true. But it isn't necessarily in monetary terms. It
depends on what one wants the most, which isn't always money,
given a certain basic coverage in that area – I mean, if one was
starving, naturally one would do almost anything in order to eat. I
guess we all have areas of vulnerability – I'm not sure what mine
are; it must be something to do with either writing or my kids, or
both. If I *knew*, absolutely for certain, that THE DIVINERS
would *never* be published, by anyone, unless I cut out several

scenes which I consider essential – would I do it? I think now I wouldn't, but I guess I can't be sure.

_____

1. In an earlier letter, Purdy had described how his wife had said that she would sell her land to the highest bidder, whether or not that person was American.

Ameliasburgh

30 April 1973

Dear Margaret:

Okay, congratulations, and apologies. I probably said you'd sell to highest bidder. Maybe Eurithe wouldn't sell to an American when chips prone, but she says she would. But she won't get the chance.

Of course it's our own damn fault for selling out, whatever — (*interruption*) it is: but what happens afterwards, how the people act who do the buying, is only indirectly the fault of the sellers. i.e., the buyers have a vested interest, a power lobby in both U.S. and Canada if there are enough buyers (and there are), an effect on their employees (Canadian, that is) – "We won't sell to such-and-such, our worse mousetraps or our better detergent etc." All sorts of ramifications, as you know. Anyway, I wronged you, and I hate to wrong a woman let alone a man, altho if it comes to that I'd prefer to wrong a woman, and wouldn't you prefer to wrong a man?

What the interruption was: Mel Hurtig in Edmonton asking me to write a history of Ontario, 150,000 words, taking two years, with an advance of living expenses for that time.[1] Jesus, did he take me aback and forrard. Phone call that is. I'm too shell-shocked at this moment to pursue any line of thought. It would call for intensive research of all kinds, interviews – I should say "popular history" – since his History of Alta.[2] sold 140,000 copies, which is the reason he thinks Ont. might do much better. Again, i.e., money. I am happy to sell out for money, unless ... On the other hand I'd wanta do a good job by my standards – which is liable to take a goddam lifetime.

I'm sorry, when I began begun started incepted took off with this letter, meant to say hell it's gotta be a good book. I mean, didn't the great Laurence write it? Else what's that ink-stained gremlin wound up with typewriter ribbon doin in the corner looking cowed and four ounces underweight? What it amounts to is: you can't do fuckall until you know do they like it – The writing itself has gotta be good (since that's you), but what you wrote about: does that hold together? (I feel the same way when I write an article, and hearing your outraged snorts, say humbly that this is a matter of personal insecurity about creativity: it may have left us and we don't even know it or feel the departure of what we didn't know we had when we did have it except for smug pride that's all in the past and memory being what it is may never have existed except as smug pride now that we once might have been writers. (Commas, where you want em.) I mean, this is the visceral disease of writers; is what I write any good? I don't think you could now write anything really bad, not as to the prose style etc ... Subject matter and a sort of overall thing – that's what you're worrying about I expect. How well do the style and the inner feeling of this-is-right meld in with the structure, so-called plot etc. God, I hope it does.

I am still thunderstruck by the Hurtig proposal. It's too big a thing to glibly say yes I will or no I won't. I doubt my own capacity, by which I mean vitality and energy to do all the research etc required. More specifically, I get tired – my eyes do – after a certain amount of reading (which calls for an eye doctor of course) ...

What do you want most, since you say either writing or kids – no, that's wrong, those are your areas of *vulnerability* you think ...

And yet, they're gone eh? The kids I mean. They're not really yours, except in a kinda loving memory sense. They don't need you as they did. What remains? Something apparently. Maybe, for a woman, and perhaps some men, a clinging to a different kind of life, when one "was needed" when the juices all flowed at a different rate etc. That's kinda simple, I guess. Writing: the writer normally says he/she hates it, but loves moments of it (or is that normal?) … But I look back, think, did I ever really love it that much? Dunno. Might well have hypnotized myself about it somehow. I mean about the good moments. Were there any. Sure, I know when I write a good piece, you do too. But doesn't one idealize and romanticise that, in the past, into something more than it is? Is it all that great, really? Or is it the capacity itself rather than the moment of doing it? Dunno, again. I love the ability and capacity that I sometimes think I have to write well, but the subjects I'm interested in grow less and less, i.e., I write about the blacks in S.A. from my own cynical no-purdy-won't-be-a-guerilla stance, instead of stirring saddle songs of revolution and the bro-hood-of-man.

Hurtig has really fucked me up, the bastard. After being lost about writing, my thoughts inevitably go back to his offer. A "popular history" (his Alta history sold 140,000,* or did I say that?) is one thing, the way I'd wanta do it is another. He knows my prejudices and would expect em, but I'd also wanta do a factually accurate book, but an arty one as well – by that last I mean not just a personal recital of fact and interpretation. I'd be liable to shave dialogue between Tiger Dunlop and John A.[3] into the section on the settlement of Upper Canada. Well?

love,
Al

* yes, I did –

1. The sentence following the italics was typed in red.

2. James Grierson MacGregor (b. 1905) was the author of *A History of Alberta* (1972), published by Hurtig.

3. William "Tiger" Dunlop (1792-1848) was a journalist, politician, and an official of the Canada Company, whose *Statistical Sketches of Upper Canada* (1832) was designed to bring settlers to the province. John A. Macdonald (1815-91) was the first prime minister of Canada.

Elmcot

4 July 1973

Dear Al–

I think you owe me a letter but at this point I am sure of nothing. Where are you? At the w-in-r job?[1] Surely not yet. Here all is very very organized chaos. Am dealing with: (a) clearing house of 10 yrs rubbish; (b) doing all the financial dealings re: income tax and transferring assets to Can etc etc etc etc etc etc etc; (c) doing the revisions on novel, which now turn out to be a massive amount of work. Had a long six-hr session with my Amer editor,[2] about a month ago, and she is just great. She (and also Mac's[3] and M&S – J.G., actually, no one else there has commented and they bloody better *not*) and I are pretty much in agreement about areas of weakness, and her remarks mostly confirmed my own feelings. I disagree with all 3 eds in some ways, but in major ways it is all pretty plain – I knew things needed to be done and I knew which things needed to be done, but at the time of the 2nd draft I did not want to know. Now I think in a month I've gone in again and done most of what is necessary – about 100 pp have melted away, to the great good of the novel, because now at last I could finally see what had to be cut. Have also done a hell of a lot of detail changes, and a 40 pp sequence totally rewritten from scratch. I do not feel at all tired, but I know it is going to hit me when I reach Trona. I've only got 2 speeds ... Fully On or Fully Off, and as I am Fully On at the moment, it seems better to try to get revisions done now, as I suspect that when I hit my home-and-native, having burned all bridges, on July 22, I may just switch to Fully Off for a bit. I'll be staying with Clara Thomas[4] for a week or so – phone 489-5421. Then to shack, to collapse and also to write intro for Ludwig's ABOVEGROUND for NCL and to get a lecture (performance; reading) together for Regina in Oct. Etc. So won't be able to collapse entirely. Main thing now is to get corrections made on 1 other copy of novel, so I can have 1 right copy and my ed in NY can have the other ... all 3 publishers have agreed this time that Judith Jones shall be my only editor, not because she is Amer but because she is the best goddamn editor I've had, and we can relate – she is a very hard and scrupulous lady, but then, so am I, when it comes right down to it. Anyway, I can work with her. The rewrite has been incredibly difficult and long, but I think I can see the light somewhere hm hm. The damn thing is better than it was in the 2nd draft, I do know. At least all 3 publishers think it is interesting, and all 3 criticize the same things that I myself felt unhappy about. We will see. I will get to Can and become for awhile a vegetable.

Love,
Margaret

---

1. Purdy was to be writer-in-residence at the Banff School of Fine Arts in August 1973 and at Loyola College (now Concordia University) for the 1973/74 academic year.

2. Judith Jones of Knopf in New York.

3. Caroline Hobhouse.

4. Clara Thomas (b. 1919), Professor of English, York University, had written the monograph *Margaret Laurence* (1969) for the McClelland and Stewart "Canadian Writers" series. She would later publish *The Manawaka World of Margaret Laurence* (1975).

§

Dear Margaret:

Sure, I owe you a letter, and I guess some other people too. Didn't feel like writing, main reason I guess being that I am building a work rook 12' x 13' on the far side of the present shed, moving some 300 wheelbarrowloads of earth to build a foundation that will endure the millenniums.

You seem comfortable about the novel now. I mean with 100 pages less. Odd how our feelings change about such things. Not long ago you were swearing red white and blue oaths that not a word should be cut. The main thing is, obviously, that the completed book should be the best that's in you. Not whether you have a good or bad editor, but whether you believe in the book now before you. Because it won't be the editors who will get shit if the book isn't good. And I think it's difficult sometimes not to be carried away by another person's personality and opinions on your work, simply because they have read it and are presumed to be interested. I still claim, no matter how good your editor is, you hafta make the decisions. But you do say that all three eds agree on the weak spots. If that's the case how can one editor be better than another?

I've turned down the writer-in-rez job at Loyola.[1] After much cogitation of course. They were gonna have me teaching a writers' workshop once a week. I coulda gone for office hours twice a week and meeting interested students, but not a regular teaching job however seemingly easy – not again gawd no. But I wish you joy in yours, or at least some kinda content somehow. I leave for Banff at the end of this month, and even that is too much. I resigned that too a while back, but they talked me back into it.

Lots of small bits of news here. Newlove[2] was here along

with Jack and Mary Lu and Ron Everson. At 2.30 a.m. he and I in the kitchen when – suddenly suddenly – he is on his ass on the floor, a five foot wave of water is sweeping me toward the door. I grab a door knob and save myself, Newlove struggles feebly in the tidal rush. We get him to his feet, but neither he nor I remembers what happened. He knocked over a five or ten gallon plastic thing fulla water when he fell, which accounts for my narrow escape from drowning. Thought he's sprained his ankle, and his upper lip was so stuff it cracked. Then next even we decided to go to hospital which he had resisted. Turns out it's broken in two places. Everson says take him to his hotel and he'll pay the bill. Eurithe on the phone says take him to a more reasonable place, which I nix on accounta it's no time to disagree about money when Newlove is like this. Anyway, Belleville Hosp. puts on a cast and says when he gets to Toronto they'll have to take it off there and put a pin in his ankle and another cast. Which they do, but bawl out the Belleville people for not having done all this in the first place. [...]

I have corrected galleys for next book,[3] and taken advance for one after that.[4] Also doing a coupla prose pieces for magazines. Have accepted Mel Hurtig's proposition. Remembering a while back when you felt Hurtig was unreliable or some such, I hafta disagree. Do think he's a good man, doing valuable work in many ways. Can't remember what you said, but it seemed uncomplimentary at the time. Anyway, I get paid $500. a month for two years until the book is finished.

But I have one really good feeling. A poem writ about three-four days ago. Shipped it off pronto to Bob Fulford at Sat. Night and he replied quick taking it.[5]

I look forward to your book. So much talk about something of which I am entirely ignorant. It will be pleasant to just sit down and read it – I read few novels these days, whereas I guess you read many –

I'm down to 196 pounds incidentally, from working on my

work room and sweating buckets. Ring me when you get to Toronto.

love,
Al

---

1. Purdy later reconsidered and accepted.

2. The poet John Newlove (b. 1938).

3. *Sex & Death*.

4. Probably *In Search of Owen Roblin* (1974).

5. Purdy published two poems in *Saturday Night* in the latter part of 1973: "The listening child (& Jacques & Suzanne Lanctot in Cuba)," August 1973, 5; and "Dead march for Sergeant Macleod," September 1973, 43.

478 Regent Street
London 24, Ontario
N5Y 4H4
27 September 1973[1]

Dear Al–

I'm writing this at the office, on the antique typewriter which turns out to be second-cousin to a tractor – it sure as hell sounds like one, anyway, and when I push the carriage back there is a horrible groaning rasping sound. However, wanted to get a line off to you in yr misery.[2] I don't intend to offer you any words of real comfort – I would if I knew any, but I guess I don't. Yeh, the job. I don't know why we do it – I'm not all that broke right at the moment, but I think my Depression sense of insecurity is still very operative. Odd – on the one hand, I feel I have to stash $$$ away for my old age, and on the other hand I am convinced I won't live to see 60. I do think this kind of job is worse for you than for me – I think you're right about that. I don't think I handle the job any better; I just think it probably isn't quite so hard on me. And I think the reason is that I'm a novelist and I have just finished a book and don't want even to think about my own work for at least another year. Whereas a poet's writing doesn't move in the same kind of cycle. With you, or anyway this is my impression, the possibilities of a new poem coming along are always there, and you really want to keep open to them, and this kind of job makes it very difficult and even impossible. I don't wonder that you are depressed. Also, migawd, 18 kids in one week!! Do they just all arrive at once? They must, obviously. I guess that gets it over all in one fell blow, though. I see kids 9 hours a week – 3 hours each afternoon on Tues, Wed and Thurs. One at a time for an hour each. They send in their writing first … at least most of them do. The ones who don't do this seem to arrive with a sheaf of writing as thick as your arm, and this is kind of daunting, as there's no way I can read it all through right on the spot. However, altho the first week was pretty tiring, I'm actually beginning to enjoy it now, but expect I'll continue to arrive home about 5 p.m. feeling like a limp dishrag. I must say that I've been getting some interesting writing from the kids – mostly prose, thank God. I specified in the poster that I would rather get prose, altho I wasn't going to turn poets away. I don't do too badly on the poetry – don't know a damn thing about technique, but neither do they, and at least I can spot a cliche when I see one!

In many ways I'd rather be in my house in Lakefield,[3] but in some ways I think it probably is better for me right now, having just finished the novel, to be getting outside myself and my own house for awhile, especially with things so screwed up for Dave[4] … if I was alone in the Lakefield house all the time now, I would probably be drinking myself into an early grave. Here, at least I'm seeing people every day and have to stick to a reasonably healthy life or I'd be dead at once. Also, I'm much less isolated here than I was in that office in Massey College … hardly ever saw any of my contemporaries there. I see now how cut off it was, and that was partly why I was so uptight that year. Here I can pass the (damn this typewriter)[5] time of day with Eng Dept people in nearby offices. Lawrence Garber is teaching here, and he is really a nice guy. Have only just met Reaney,[6] so can't say about him yet. There are also a couple of good people in next door offices.

I certainly hope things improve a bit for you. How is the commuting working out? The milk train sounds like a drag. I understand you share an office with John Metcalf[7] ... he is a very good guy, and I like him a great deal. Also a good writer.

... first client due now. More later.

Belleville High School wants me to go out there sometime in the winter – I wrote and said maybe I would, but spring would be better. What I was really wondering was when you and Eurithe would be at A'burgh? Are you going to move to Montreal for winter? If so, when will you return? I don't want to go to Belleville unless I can combine it with a visit to you. Could you let me know? It would mean free transportation and enough of a fee to buy a crock of wine.

Your Quebec wine sounds wonderful. I really laughed when I read that you plan to import a gallon a week until you have a decent stock – I just can't see you stock-piling wine!

I've met Peter Buitenhaus and Elspeth[8] – liked them very much.

What is On The Bear Paw Sea?[9] I don't recall your having told me about it. Any more news of Sex & Death? It's par for the course for it to be overdue, naturally, but maddening all the same. I haven't been able to get hold of a copy of Sept's Sat Nite. But am going to univ bookshop next week so will try them.

Didn't know you had been in touch with Billington in Montreal. He is a very good guy, and a dear friend, as you know. I wish he did not have reverence for writers ... he would deny that he has, probably. No, there's nothing to be revered – but on the other hand, it is pretty damned annoying to find kids who have not heard of yr writing! Some kids here come in and say apologetically "I'm afraid I haven't read any of your books". What am I supposed to say to that? Yes, I knew Dave and his wife had split up – Helen stayed with me in Elmcot for a month just before I left England. She is working in London now and I haven't written to her but have got some news via Ian and Sandy.

Re: wasting yr life – yeh, I know we cannot either help or hinder young writers, really, and that makes this job seem a bit futile. On the other hand, you've had the feeling before (as I have, too) that you would probably never write again, but something else has always come along, eventually. I know – you've said the same to me when I've said this is my last novel. How do we know? Impossible to tell. Maybe we should just look at it in this way – even if you never write another word, you won't have wasted yr life. You have written a hell of a lot of good poems. I can hear you saying in rage that you don't want to rest on yr laurels. Well, who does? But at least it's a thought – that you *have* done something. It's better at this point than having to think you've done nothing. I wish you weren't sad, though. Don't worry, however … you'll survive until you die.

Have to go to Trona this eve – CBC interview tomorrow morn, and a weekend of executive meetings for Union. Why did I take that job?[10] Shall I get out of it in Nov? Dear Mr. Landers, please advise! I keep getting flak from the CAA about the Union, and have not even replied – dunno what to say.[11] Polite flak, but flak all the same. CBC is putting me up at the Four Seasons tonite … how about that? I could have stayed with friends but decided that as they had offered to book me in at the FS, I didn't mind taking advantage of the offer. Think I'll order iced champagne and put it on bill.

This bloody typewriter doesn't have a workable margin yet … hence the odd margins on the left. It also frequently sticks … hope you can read this.

There are moments when I'd give up my whole year's salary just to be in my shack. Did I tell you Mr. Villerup died? I'll miss him a lot. But have decided not to sell shack. Lot in Lakefield only 55 feet by 160, and not on river. Good place for winter.

Typewriter getting tired and rebelling. Better quit. Take heart, eh?

Love,

Margaret

---

1. Margaret Laurence had recently begun her term as writer-in-residence at the University of Western Ontario.

2. Purdy had written that he was not enjoying his duties at Loyola and was exhausted from weekly commuting by train between Ameliasburg and Montreal.

3. In late August, Laurence had bought a house.

4. She was experiencing concern for her son who was living in England.

5. The typewriter's spacing was defective.

6. Lawrence Garber (b. 1937), an experimental novelist, and James Reaney (b. 1926), poet and playwright.

7. John Metcalf (b. 1938), novelist and short-story writer, was also teaching at Loyola.

8. Peter Buitenhuis (b. 1925), Department of English, McGill University, and Elspeth Cameron (b. 1943), his wife and a member of Loyola's English Department.

9. *On the Bearpaw Sea* (1973), a long poem inspired by Purdy's visit to Alberta's badlands in the late summer of 1971. It first appeared in *Waves*, 1, 2 (Autumn 1972), 27-33, and was then published by the Blackfish Press of Burnaby, B.C.

10. In the Spring of 1973, Laurence had agreed to be Interim Chair of the fledgling Writers' Union of Canada which was officially established in early November 1973.

11. The Canadian Authors' Association had been established in 1921 and was suspicious of its new rival.

§

4 October 1973

Dear Margaret:

Thanks for sympathy. Now I'm liable to rebel from the sterile straitjacket in which I assign myself – so writ a poem.

Yah, mine all arrive at once, at least they're split between morning and afternoon on Tues. I drink seriously Mon. rum.

You have it exactly right re the poet, or so I think. One wants to "keep open to them" etc. So you must have the novelist right too. Trouble is also one gets sick of too much writing, whether pomes or novels (prose), which puts one off writing oneself. Also, as apart from writing, one (you and I) I think tends to take the first chunk of cash that comes along that isn't obviously Cia[1] tainted or something … If something tremendously interesting arrived unheralded tho, one can't throw up the damn job and just fuck off to do the interesting thing. Blighted romance, thwarted adventure, etc. Guy layin concrete blocks here, outside the door, while I type. I'm thinkin the mortar he uses is the same as the junctures of our lives, when we make decisions. Mortar ensures each block be in its exact place; it then hardens into decision. I guess that's crap, but just the same …

Plans here right now, are, I guess, commuting till very early January; then believe Eurithe wants to get a place in Mtl. to end of Mar. Then back here. How would this work in with your possible trip to Belleville? Could you take a night just before Christmas, say, or sometime in Apr.? My days at Mtl. are Mon. & Tues. I have, insicendentally, been buyin Bordeaux wine by the gallon, $8.50, which works out to about $1.30 a bottle of 25 oz. and it's damn good wine. (Little tendrils of red curl out from the stool)

I'm stayin with Dave every Monday, buy a case of 24 which we drink with much loud talk. He is feeling a bit noble lookin after Dai, bakin his own bread gettin meals and the like. Mourns for Helen tho. We get along well, Watch football games, yak about love and life so that the whole neighbourhood is one low roar of thunder.

It's a lousy thing to say one has written something worthwhile, and therefore one's life is not wasted – We both know it's lousy. Yes, I am sad. But last two Mondays been drinkin rum with a blonde prof, which makes me feel better. Amazing the simple things that solace. And I did write one erotic obscene pome addressed to her Not by name which also makes me feel better. I've always had (or for a long time) the idea that how I live my life will make all the difference in the way and quality of what I write. If I read this book or that, if I take a chance here and not there, if I am large and magnanimous instead of small and mean, etc etc. It turns out tho, that I hafta be what I am, without much choice. For if I don't like a book I can't read it; if I don't like a person it's all I can do to be polite. Which I suppose the writing has to reflect too. I turn out to be not very close in some ways, to what I think I ought to be, but fairly close in other ways. Which the writing also reflects. But the writing also tends to have me reflecting itself, I mean I reflect the writing too, so there must be a continual back-lash – what's the other word? – reciprocating current? What the hell, there's a better word. Feedback between two things. What about you? Is it the same, or have you thought or not thought of this? I am a product of my own writing, or vice-versa, or both? Alphabet soup. I'm turning into a goddamn machine for writing, liable to leap at any blonde prof soon.

The Bearpaw Sea pome was writ two years ago when we druv the trailer to west coast. Pub in one mag and brcast on cbc, the Blackfish kids wanted poems, and when they saw that a book was decided. It's six manuscript pages single-spaced, so when they used the Jap. or Chin. method of folded double pages, it comes out a fairly bulky little book with five pencil drawing and tissue guards, in three diff. eds. About a duck-bill dinosaur named Albert (by me) whose love life and disposition were ruined by havin his tail buggared by tyrannosaurus.

I am not sure that I'm sad or discontented because that's the situation, or because I'm mostly sad and discontented. If you were here we would laugh and drink and talk. So what the hell? "I'm laughin with tears in my eyes"? But jesus, I do think my life is frantic with sadness and drinkin, boredom and excitement, stupor and tingling nerve-endings alternating, black depression and euphoria etc. So what's different, except I'm dwelling on it more? I'm still mean, generous, all the opposites, sometimes simultaneously. Goddammit, I'd still review that guy Bromige and say "it is with great pleasure that I note this writer is fully as bad as I had hoped and expected" – (Boy, did that get repercussions!) [2]

[. . .]

No, you didn't mention Mr. Villerup. Come on – will you really miss him? Don't all the gaps and interstices of people get filled in by other people? Sure they do. Momentary somberness yes, momentary twinge of rage at me for saying this, but it's true. Only the closer communicating people does one miss very much. The others are examples of transience only that happened to impinge. Go ahead and tell me I'm fulla shit besides treadin on your sacred feelings and delicate sincere emotive emotions.

Yr right about stock piling wine – first three gallons got drunk by people and me, mostly me. Fourth gallon produced stern resolve, will drink beer until I have ten gallons, then drink all ten in a one-week drunk that will light up the sky red around A-burgh. I will die of course, and be buried in the foundation of new room bein built here.

[. . .]

Clients you have? For chrissake! All I got is lousy versifiers.

love,
Al

1. Central Intelligence Agency, the espionage arm of the United States government.

2. "After a Hundred Years Canadian Poetry Certainly Is ...," *Queen's Quarterly*, 76, 4 (Winter 1969), 710-18. This omnibus review included David Bromige's *The Gathering* (1965) and *The Ends of the Earth* (1968), which Purdy panned in noting, "That some of Bromige's poems have a degree of merit is a fact that I find personally regrettable, but take comfort that most of them are fully as boring as I had hoped and expected" (715). Several years earlier, Bromige had himself written a dismissive appraisal of Purdy in "Craftsmen and Others," *Canadian Literature,* No. 4 (Spring 1960), 85-86.

478 Regent Street
London 24, Ontario
17 October 1973

Dear Al–

Had meant to reply sooner to yr letter but oh heavens my life is becoming circus-like once again. This week: Monday – frantic efforts to overcome Sun-nite hangover, get business letters done, and in eve a reading and discussion at one of the colleges here. Tuesday – saw kids of 2 huge Can Lit classes in vast auditorium, they shooting queries at me; Wednesday (today) saw kids individually afternoon and have actually agreed to be supervisor for a guy in Library School who wants to get the Dean to allow him one course to write a novel instead of regular course – I've seen this guy three or four times now and read his half-finished first draft of novel and it is very promising. Thurs – seeing kids individually. Friday – giving readings as part of Western's Open House, whatever the hell that is. Saturday – collapse, probably. Sunday at dawn – I go west to Regina, Moose Jaw & Edmonton for the long Reading performance. I will be dead when I return on Oct 28th. Then the weekend after that is the Writers' Union conference in

Ottawa. Dear lord, how much can I stand? Actually, it's not at all bad, altho I feel beat at the end of the day.

You are right about us taking the first chunk of cash to come along. With this in mind, I had the courage to turn down 2 offers of w-in-r for next year – I thought, hell, what is the use of the $$$ if I am dead? Two years in a row at this job and I *would* be dead. I have got to settle into the Lakefield house (now mine, all mine) and unwind for about a year before I do anything. I see myself filling the time by writing something very frivolous – any suggestions?

I'll suggest to the Belleville High School that I go sometime in the Spring, April probably.

[. . .]

Yeh, being a product of one's own writing. I *know* I am, partly. Reciprocating current is exactly right. I create the novels and the novels also create me. Spooky? Yes. Sometimes seem prophetic, too, the novels – in various ways as tho I partly drew from my own experience in order to write them, and on the other hand, partly acted out in my own life what I'd already written about, altho in some different form – but related. Don't leap at blonde prof too soon. Or maybe I should advise the reverse. So leap, leap!

I saw about The Bearpaw Sea somewhere, after I'd asked you. Where did I see about it? An issue of Can Lit? Dunno.

What can you do, if anything, about the fishing article? I am not totally surprised. I had some doubts, as you recall, because what you were saying, or some of it, struck me as kind of radical for present Macleans. I think it is VERY DISHONOURABLE (how about that for a phrase?) of them not to print it. Of course it's not the point that they paid for it. [1]

You're not treading on my sacred feelings re: Mr. Villerup – what you say is undoubtedly true. I'll miss him next summer, briefly, when I first go to the cottage, and then I'll no doubt think of him less and less, as one does with people who die. Don Bailey,[2] incidentally, is trying to buy Jack Villerup's cottage – some uncertainty as the estate split 3 ways and all 3 have to agree and so on, but it would be nice if Don got it.

I have decided not to run as Pres of Writers Union. I began having Freudian accidents – first, wrenching my back; I'm damn sure that was tension-caused. Next, about 2 weeks ago, hurrying one morn, I slammed the fridge door against one bare foot and I think broke a bone. I did not go to the doc because with busted toe bone nothing but time can heal, as with broken heart. But I was furious. I knew then I had to cut down somewhere on the stress and strain. The W. Union is just too too much for me to handle whilst doing this job. Or anytime. It just ain't me, Al. I cannot do it. I'll go on a committee, but I will not be front person. I have the opportunity of getting out in Nov, at conference, and will take it. Feel a bit guilty, but must think of own survival. Also – and please, this is in confidence – I have serious doubts now about the organization. I hope it can accomplish something, but some of the younger writers think the revolution is at hand, and it isn't. Also, there are bound to be a lot of disagreements and flak, and I don't really have much of a masochistic desire to make a lot of enemies; life is difficult enough without that. Someone who is younger and less single-minded and also probably more radical than I am at this point should take the job. I'd like to talk about this with you sometime but some of the issues are ones I kind of hesitate to put on paper – suppose it fell into THE WRONG HANDS? Wish I could spend a Mon eve with you and Dave. Drinking wine.

[. . .]

I am still trying (vainly, I think) to persuade M& S to put out a 45-record with each copy of THE DIVINERS. McClelland thinks it is a lousy notion, but might be okay to do some for publicity purposes. That would satisfy my craving to break into the Pop Song business!!

[. . .]

Got to go to a Reception in Faculty Club. For me. Oh joy. Hope it isn't just sherry. Need a double scotch right now. It's been a long day.

Love,
Margaret

ps. tried to think of some embarrassing comment I could make on the envelope, to get back at you for yr comment about the postal code, but couldn't think of anything – I will, though, in time! [3]

---

1. Purdy was frustrated at *Maclean's* delay in publishing an article he had written on the west coast fishing industry. It appeared in the spring as "Caught in the Net," *Maclean's*, May 1974, 26-27, 85, 87.

2. Don Bailey (b. 1942), poet, novelist, short-story writer.

3. At the top left-hand corner of the envelope containing his letter of 4 October, Purdy had typed his name, address, postal code – KOK 1A0 – and had added "(you made me selfconscious about that postal code)."

§

[Ameliasburg] [1]
31 October 1973

Dear Margaret:
This is likely a note, since I ain't got no energy. Suggestions for something frivolous: Jason in the Underground Tunnel to Peterboro?

297

I had Monday off on accounta Quelection.[2] So down to Mtl. and back in one day. Jesus.

I forgot what I said about postal code.

Yah, that nice cash! Shit on it tho. I am drinking too much, smoking too much much, sleeping too much, and still tired as hell – Kids are okay at Mtl. I guess, but but still … I can't see myself writing at all …

Traumatic event: went to see Angus[3] after long lapse, turned into his driveway, see a brown flash fifty feet in and it's Oliver, Angus' dog, killed him. In his death throes, he bit Angus, bit Eurithe. We drive to Napanee to the vet with him, he's dead (Oliver) when we get there, to hospital for shots for Angus and Eurithe. Jesus, I liked that dog, but above that shoving grief into someone else's life … Even over a dog, you ask? Well Mr. What'shisname next to you stirred something so I guess a dog can too, tho not principally directly … Shit, I felt like a murderer.

Been asked to talk half an hour on CanPo for Prov. Library Services. $150. I took it. First chunk of cash? See current Books in Canada,[4] get my come-uppance for first time in ten years or so, re record. First ever bad review of that record. Book review so-so I guess – but the signs are all there. For this book I get the shit I've missed a long time. Obviously can't complain, on accounta everybody said nice things so long, with unimportant exceptions like Callaghan. Did you get the book incidentally, sent from McStew?[5] Odd/funny thing is I still object to remarks like "discursive" which, while true in some instances, is a mark of a style changed somewhat in last five years. i.e. I'm indignant, no, I wanta argue with the bastards about their opinions. They are right about the fact of, say, discursiveness; but I claim, not about its effect. i.e., if they were to argue straight that the poems are not good, didn't hit any more, okay, I hafta say that's so if you think so. In this case I disagree with reasons given. I think it's possible to be discursive and very interesting. Think readers will find it that way, I say, in a burst of ego. We shall see of course. (Selected now being reprinted.) Maybe I'm getting aggressive as Layton, tho with his example before me I shall apply curbs. Or shall I?

Peter Newman sent me my book to sign, saying also keep us in mind for articles. In a burst of frankness (unprecedented?) I say, well you cannot really think that or you'd use the ones you have.

I have forty days off at mid-term, Dec 4 to Jan. 14 ... Wow! Whyn't I hear about the academic soft life afore?

Yah, Dave and his roaring ... okay, I like him anyway, but sometimes wonder if his awe at writers, particularly you and me, allows any very close relationship ... But who do I have close relationships with anyway? Maybe yourself, in some odd sort of way I guess, but most of the others are people wanting to know me, then putting up with me when they do ... That sounds egotistic but isn't ... I'm too turbulent and aggressive in some ways to keep the old old friends, or call it that for want of – Even Eurithe seems like an old friend to me more than a wife. Is that shocking? I have hordes of people I can yak with freely; but that's another thing isn't it? Life seems to arrive at point where time, or whatever, only allows the infatuation of brief friendship then passing by again. Essentially I feel always a loner, the lighted rooms in my head have doors ajar perhaps but never open to anyone or very many ... Do you know, I feel and think far more freely with you than with anyone else, which includes Birney and whoever ...? No distinction I disclaim hastily, just is so. There are times when I feel so much of a goddam institution that it isn't possible for anyone else to approach me in any other way. Which is alarming and may seem a bit fatuous or again egotistic. But people do approach you, I'm sure you too, from that angle most of the time. And Dammit, I'm not my work not only anyway. Am too of course.

Anyway, we're goin to Spain for the mid-term break I guess. I'm working so much here it really will be a holiday. Or Mexico? Dunno really.

1. This letter exists only in carbon copy.

2. The Quebec provincial election of 29 October.

3. Angus Mowat.

4. Fraser Sutherland, "Purdy's Wordy," his review of *Sex & Death* in *Books in Canada*, October 1973, 4-5. In his review, Sutherland noted Purdy's "windy rhetoric." In the same issue, in a review entitled "Al Locutions" (12-13), Kelly Wilde dismissed the recording *Al Purdy's Ontario* (CBC Learning Systems) as having "not a spark of genuine communication" (13).

5. *Sex & Death*.

478 Regent Street
London 24, Ontario
14 November 1973

Dear Al–

At long length, an epistle from yr exhausted friend the Canlit apostle. Man, are they working me hard in this place. But I have to admit because of my innate or inane honesty (no, I'm not drunk – yet) that it is largely my own doing. I said I'd see students 9 hrs a week, plus some seminar classes etc, and that is what I'm doing, plus going out to some high schools on account of I hate to say no and also because my motto is Grab 'Em For The Cause Of Canwriting, Young! I suffer pangs of indigestion, quaking knees, sweating palms etc before I face one of these classes – they shoot questions at me and I field same, in my warmhearted, yet intellectual, yet slightly humorous fashion. When I get going, I can handle it all in my warmhearted, intellectual yet slightly etc fashion. I guess what I worry about, Al, is that I'm becoming a performer. The kids are pretty level, tho, and don't go in for a lot of worshipful bullshit … it's the teachers (High School) who give me that bezaz, and much as I don't want to knock them, I don't like that "Geewhiz a real writer" kind of thing. It does nothing for my ego. It bores and embarrasses me. I don't know how to handle it politely, so smile and say little. The kids are better – as I say, they don't go in for a whole lot of bullshit, and altho they start out being very hesitant about talking or asking questions, they always end up by speaking their minds and are sometimes more frank than university students … one kid said "I've read The Stone Angel twice, and I still don't see what the hell the stone angel is supposed to mean" … I liked that. However, the PER-FORMER bit does kind of worry me – I sense in myself that once the performance gets going, I begin to enjoy it, and I suspect that that is not devoutly to be desired. One *could* get to depend on that kind of thing, what must basically be a kind of ego-trip, enchantment with the sound of one's own voice and all that. I got myself into this, and I am not about to quit now, and I imagine at Trent it will be much the same, but I am determined at least (a) that at Trent I won't do the High School circuit quite so much, and (b) I gotta deploy my financial forces if possible so that I don't have to take on this kind of job again, for several years, if ever. It is not the same for you … you aren't doing the High-School, Univ Women's Club, etc things that I numbly have agreed to do, and much much better that you shouldn't. But I'm ambiguous as well – I mean, like on my Western Trip – end of Oct – I haven't writ-ten to you since then, have I? No, I haven't. Anyway, I did read-ings from THE DIVINERS and played tape of songs. Well, I have to state that if one is gonna put a show on the road, it had better be as good a show as possible. I do have a kind of feeling of profes-sionalism about that. I think that sort of thing is probably like a poetry reading – had never done such a thing before, so really had not known how it would feel. How it felt, in Moose Jaw, Regina and Edmonton, was – I was desperately nervous beforehand, but in one corner of my head quite cool and absolutely determined that the thing would go well. Got together with the sound tech-nician in each place, to get right what I wanted done re: the songs. And faced audience with a kind of heart-sinking but nonetheless feeling that the goddamn show, feeble tho it might be, must go on. I don't think that kind of being a performer is bad at all. They've come to hear you do a reading; you do a christly reading to the best of yr ability. That is sure as hell no ego trip; it is just being professional in another area, one that had not before been mine. Mind you, I don't think I could do it too often. I finish the eve as tho I'd been through a battle. Working alone at writing seems kind of simple and infinitely preferable by comparison. I guess you'd agree there.

More news – before I get to answering some things in yr letter and also to the main thing, which is I've just read SEX AND DEATH. But first ... the Writers Union of Can was formed officially in Ottawa a week ago, and I did have the strength of mind not to stand for President. I just couldn't. However, I can at least feel I was the first Pres, even if Interim, and that all of us on that interim Executive worked like slaves to get the thing going, and it got going. It was a hell of a good conference ... maybe you saw Bill French's report in the Globe. Much much more happened than he said, but it wasn't a bad report. I'm on the membership committee, and also heading something called the Emergency committee, aid and help to them in need of various things such as help with grant letters or just a place to stay in another city where one of us finds oneself. Haven't yet got this off the ground, because pile-up of correspondence and manuscripts to read here at Western was just unbelievable, after a week in west and almost another week spent either at conference or preparing for same. But there was a very good tribal feeling. We worked out a constitution (the interim exec had drafted one), and did a lot of practical business, and in the evenings, talked talked talked. Great. Great to see people I hadn't seen for some time, and to meet writers whose work I knew but hadn't met them before. We elected new officers on the Sun morn, and Marion Engel[1] is Chairwoman, a very good person and will do a good job, in my opinion. Other 2 on Exec are Harold Horwood[2] from Newfoundland and Rudy

Wiebe from Alta … what could be better? National Council represents all regions, and the question of regionalism was a tough one, but I hope we overcame it. There is: Exec, National Council, Committees. Sounds a drag, but I hope it will be kind of radical, the way we started.

My personal best moment was so dramatic and unforeseen – on Sat nite we had hired a bus to take us to a country club (us impoverished writers!) for dinner. I was talking to Kent Thompson[3] and his wife, as they had to leave then and wouldn't be at the dinner. I looked out the lobby door of the hotel and saw the bus and realized I was the last person and the damn bus was about to leave without me. I had on my long greenblue silk robe and a long black cape lined with scarlet silk – I flew out looking like a combination of an Indian witch and Batwoman, and dashed onto the bus, and good christ, they gave me a hand! From the members of my tribe, yet, and done with love and mockery, it was somehow pretty nice. As the bus came home that nite, with all of us kind of drunk and singing "The Maple Leaf Forever" and "Farewell to Nova Scotia" and "The Red River Valley", Leo Simpson[4] was heard to remark enigmatically, "If this bus crashes, two of Canada's finest writers will be killed."! Farley was there, and was great, and Berton[5] also was there, and to my surprise and pleasure, was really concerned and gave out at meetings with some very practical thoughts about money (of course, but still … he is one hell of a pro, let's face it, and we needed that kind of practical thing). God, if the bus *had* crashed, damn near every serious practising prose writer in the land would have been killed! There are, of course, many whom we need and who aren't yet members. Do I sound like a member of the Old Left? Oh Al, I am, I *am*.

[. . .]

Thanks a whole lot for sending SEX & DEATH. I'd read some of the poems, but not all. How have the reviews been? I've only seen a couple, good ones, because I just don't see any Can publications on account of my subscriptions have all run out and I haven't renewed yet. What amazes me about the book is yr range – both emotional and (if I may say so) spiritual, and also geographical ... this latter may sound odd, but what I mean is that in the geog way, something does happen and you can actually go to Greece, or Mexico, or whatever, and poems result. I couldn't do that, with prose, and it impresses me. Why is it we are always impressed by the things we can't ourselves do? The collection seems to me to reach a kind of new and perhaps more sombre tone. It's very very good. I like a lot of the poems, but the ones which really and truly knock me out are: Dead March For Sgt. MacLeod; The Horseman of Agawa; Old Man Mad About Painting; Freydis Eriksdottir In Greenland; RCMP Post; Wilf McKenzie; The Double Shadow; Hands; Iguana; 8:50 a.m.; Excess Of Having; I Am Definitely On The Side Of Life; In The Foothills; The Beavers of Renfrew; The Time Of Your Life; Remembering Hiroshima. I don't mean I don't like the others – I do. But these particular ones are my favourites, and, I think, brilliant. Them's my sentiments. I've commented previously, at various times, on some of them which you sent from time to time in letters. Seems to me this collection contains some of yr best poems. You've got an awful lot of best poems, at this point, when one comes to think of it. Anyway, thanks – I don't just mean for sending the book; I mean for the fact that the poems are.

What a terrible thing to happen re: the dog. Do you mean Angus *Mowat*? Shoving grief into someone else's life – sure. Even over a dog.

Hope yr state of mind is less bleak now. I feel pretty cheery at the moment, but then I sometimes think maybe my permanent state of mind is pretty bleak and I hardly notice it any longer. Dunno. Yeh, old friends ... not too many of those. I have also hordes of people with whom I can talk, especially writers, as was shown at the conference, but there aren't too many with whom I can really talk about things that matter the most, not even many writers with whom I can talk about some of the real things I feel about writing. Mostly it's on the kind of gossipy level, which I enjoy, but it doesn't go very deep. You and Adele, I guess, and maybe óne or two others sometimes – can't really go very deep with anyone else. I guess with friends, you have to know a fair amount about one another's life as well as work. Migawd, do I ever know what you mean by feeling sometimes like an institution – I never thought it would happen, but it has. That is one thing I don't like about the kind of year I'm having now – so many people *do* approach you as tho you were a stone in the National Gallery's edifice. I hate that. It makes me feel I must be dead already. But I'm not, damn it!

Think the novel will be out in April. They're doing large-size pages so it won't appear so long! So far, my battle re: the record goes on, but McC isn't giving in yet.

I'll be in Trona about Dec 15. Will you be gone to Spain or Mex by then? I'll be at Clara's for a week, then Christmas with my aunt and uncle in Newmarket, then to Adele's for a week before Trent. Am not going back to Eng for Christmas … I sense that it would be a mistake.

Wish I were in the Lakefield house and all this w-in-r stuff were over. I like the kids, and some are promising writers. But I'm so damn tired. Never mind. Only another 3 wks here.

Love,
Margaret

---

1. Marian Engel (1933-85), novelist and short-story writer.

2. Harold Horwood (b. 1923), novelist, essayist, anthologist.

3. Kent Thompson (b. 1936) had recently published his first novel, *The Tenants Were Corrie and Tennie* (1973).

4. Leo Simpson (b. 1934), novelist and short-story writer.

5. Pierre Berton (b. 1920), popular historian, best-selling author, and

Canadian nationalist, at this time best known for his two-volume history of the Canadian Pacific Railway: *The National Dream* (1970) and *The Last Spike* (1971).

§

8 Regent Street
Box 609
Lakefield, Ontario
KOL 2HO
22 May 1974[1]

Dear Al–

This is An Historic Letter. At last, praise God, I have got my old Remington back again, out of storage and fixed up, after more than a year without it. This is the first letter I am writing on it. Migawd, it feels as tho it were an old friend ... all these terrible typewriters I have been coping with for the past year, that don't understand me!

Was going to phone, but not sure where you are. Too tired to talk on phone, anyway. I have born up nobly, or at least somehow, and book is now out, and publicity stint in Trona is over, thank God, and I am home at last. Reviews so far appear puzzling, at least some do. P. Grosskurth in Globe[2] said nothing about novel – talked about my other books, then said what a hell of a fine thing it was that I used so many 4-letter words in the novel, and how great I described sex. Well, well. She is fence-sitting, of course. (My typewriter obviously not properly fixed ... if you hit the "f" with more than a light touch, it sticks. That must have been the key that flipped and that they replaced ... will have to learn how to write without "f" ... severely limiting to those 4-letter words). Bob Fulford in Star[3] gave a reasonable outline of some of the themes, then went on to say he couldn't hardly notice anything, first time through, except the flaws ... why did he bother to read it again, I wonder. He also said he thought no good editor had looked at it – that hurt, because I thought of all the revision I had done and how Judith Jones had read it damn near as carefully as I wrote it. He also said the England section was unnecessary – how wrong he is. The thing that burns me up is that I had a long CBC interview with him (for Anthology) the day before the review came out. He was friendly to a degree, even bland … his questions were so innocuous that I felt I was having to try to put some guts into the reply, to make it even mildly interesting. He did not once level any criticism – why didn't he say he thought the England section was unnecessary, and let me have a word about it? But no. Next day, as I was on the bus coming home, I read the review and wondered somewhat. He does not seem to understand or grasp the form of the damn thing at all. Well, the hell with it. Screw him. I like (liked?) the guy, tho. I don't blame a person for giving a rotten review, but I do think it is dishonest to interview the writer on radio and not bring up one single criticism which will then appear next day in the written review. Anyway, I have to admit he has got Sat Night on its feet. We must not be bothered by reviews. And actually, I am not, for very long. Just a bit mad about unfair statements when they appear. Later, it will be unimportant. Oh – he also quotes a bit re: Morag and sex, which is plainly romantic, and which in his context is awfully corny, but what he misses is that that interpretation of sex was for her when she was very young, with her newly married husband, and *of course* it was romantic … didn't the twit think I saw that? The view of *everything* in the Past bits is how Morag would have viewed it, at that particular age, or so I hope. That whole age bit, as reflected in the narrative tone, seems to have escaped Fulford. Well, as I may have mentioned before, the hell with it.

Trust you got the copy from M&S which I signed. Marge was going to send you a copy before, but I thought I'd do another one for you, signed now, with thanks for lines from Roblin Mills, instead of waiting until you are able to come up and see my house

(not that you are interested in seeing my house, but Eurithe will be, I hope, and anytime will be fine, if you can fit in a visit in between your many engagements in the field of Canlit.)

The week in Trona was awful, but it all worked okay, more or less. The launching party was, for a change, fun. It was a Divining Contest, and we had yer real actual old diviner there, name of Lawrence Maltby. What no one guessed was that 7 real other diviners from various small towns in S. Ontario would turn up. They did. It was kind of nice. Maltby had divined 2 water courses outside the Ont Science Centre, and the point where they intersected. The winner was the one who got closest to the intersection. Three prizes ... a case of French burgundy; a huge bottle of champagne; a bottle of brandy. I need hardly say that all the prizes were won by the real diviners.

Autographing party at Longhouse[4] was a near-disaster ... I was quite cool beforehand, but arrived and saw all those people, and panicked. Started to shake. I can always get through an interview, or reading, even if shaking, because voice does not shake and I know I can rely on it. But had never done an autographing thing before, and had never thought of problem ... how to sign books if hands shaking? No way. First 20 or so books, my signature was totally illegible. After about 10 minutes, with Clara Thomas on one side (desperately summoned by me) and Beth Appledorn on the other, speaking calm words of reassurance, I simmered down and then it was okay. A moment of panic, tho. And I was at a table in a tiny corner, with people converging on me – my main thought was – RUN! Couldn't, of course. Earle Birney came, which was damn nice of him. Didn't know he was in Trona. Had me sign a whole pile of paperbacks for a young (Chinese?) friend of his. Life is certainly never dull for him.

Joc and her husband[5] arrive day after tomorrow. Dave and girlfriend about a week later. They are all in Trona now. Seem okay. Dave still in a cast with busted leg, from motorbike accident.

Migawd, am I glad to be home. And this place does feel like home now. Especially now that the Remington is back.

Try to come for a day or so, or wkend. I dunno about you, but I am turning down all invites for every kind of performance … if I can't be here quietly for the next year, I'll collapse. And *refuse* to do that. Of course, now that everything is more or less over, I mean the excitement, I have sprouted a terrible cold. But all is more or less well. Hope same is true for you. Wrote to Sheena Paterson of Wkend,[6] saying I'd like to do more articles. We'll see.

Love,

Margaret

---

1. Laurence had moved into her Lakefield house on 1 May.

2. "A Looser, More Complex, More Sexually Uninhibited Laurence: And Never an Atwood Victim." *The Globe and Mail,* 4 May 1974, 35. Phyllis Grosskurth (b. 1924) was a member of the English Department at the University of Toronto and had won a Governor-General's Award for her biography *John Addinton Symonds* (1964).

3. "It's Fascinating Despite the Flaws." *Toronto Daily Star,* 18 May 1974, H5.

4. The Longhouse Book Shop handled Canadian books exclusively and was co-owned by Beth Appeldoorn and Susan Sandler.

5. Jocelyn Laurence had married Peter Banks in May 1973.

6. Sheena Paterson (b. 1942) was at this time acting editor of *Weekend Magazine* where Laurence had just published an article: "Loneliness Is Something That Doesn't Exist Here," 11 May 1974, 7.

❦

3 June 1974
Aboard S.S. Golden Hind
in the Gulf of St. Lawrence,
or damn close thereto –

Dear Margaret:

Well may you ask what the hell I am doing here? (Margaret: "Al, what the hell are you doing there?" Me: "Uh, well, I think I'm gonna write a piece about life on the ocean wave in the River and Gulf of St. Law.")[1] It's now Monday, and I've been here six days, Going by bus and train to Toronto and St. Catherines, catching the ship at Thorold, then riding the thing to a spot a few miles from the Gulf, where we have been anchored for two days. There's only been three days of travelling time outa that six on the non-briny. Seems there is labour trouble at Baie Comeau, also ships ahead of us to get unloaded, so we're stuck out here in a thirty mile-wide river or gulf, just waiting. Another ship has been waiting about three miles away (parked there) for eleven days.

I hope you're slightly interested in all this, because it's about all I have to talk about. I probably mentioned this trip to you before, but it finally was arranged quite suddenly. Sheena Paterson (who may have gotten in touch by now, I think she said she wrote you or was gonna visit you at Lakefield) was supposed to send a photographer aboard at the Beauharnois Locks, but it was night when we got there. I phone her from below Montreal, on a gadget where you say "Over to you" and things like that. I felt like a grounded or watered-down Spitfire pilot. Anyway, the ship is 620' long and some 68' wide, with cabins and things like that at either end, so you have to walk seeming miles to get meals in the Officer's Mess (where I eat, naturally). I kept going to the crew's mess at first, because I thought it would be more interesting, and would show my democratic nature in the story I wrote. (see next page for continuing this interesting story) Then the captain kept calling at my cabin for meals, and I think: is my aristocratic

310

lineage and upbringing apparent in my face? Does blood call to blood? Anyway, when it's rain you damn well get drowned going from the forward cabins to aft dining rooms. I've talked to many of the crew, decided they lead a fairly dull life, and they think so too. I'm well aware you can go into their lives intensively, and find out more about them personally and then they ain't dull. However, I can only treat them fleetingly in a piece like this – for instance the 2nd cook from Barbados was torpedoed off Cape Hatteras in WW2 on a CN ship, and his brother died in the same life boat. The man who hauled him into the lifeboat, Luther Beckles, also survived, but died on a lake boat a few weeks ago near Rimouski. His body was sent back to the West Indies by Air Canada, but the authorities sent it back because the Canadians hadn't made out a proper death certificate giving the cause of death. Beckles wife accompanied the bodies [sic] on its flights back and forth. That seems a bit horrible to me. Two of the 18-year-olds on this ship went to a whorehouse in Baie Comeau a few weeks back and the Fr. girls thought they were English cops and wouldn't serve them. Of course the kids were drunk. Does this strike you as interesting?

You are a last resort. I must talk to someone (having drunk the two bottles of Scotch I brought along and made as many notes as seems worthwhile). Like I say, we've been parked, uh – I mean anchored – in this goddam gulf or river for two days, and I may be here for weeks. If we finally do get to Baie Comeau, I shall quickly jump ship, and take a train back west if there is one. Incidentally, a guy named Parker in April went to the mate to get paid off at 4 a.m. in the morning (you can get paid off in any port in Canada), but mate rightly refused to wake the captain. So he left the ship, stole a milk truck and drove it to Forestville 70 miles asked for directions there. But people got suspicious, called provincial police and they nabbed him. He got 15 days, which ain't bad for car theft. Once he would've been strung up to the nearest tamarack for stealing a hoss, or drawn and quartered or something. Anyway, meals are great, three choices of meat noon and evening; room is about 12' by 14' with big bathroom and shower. Television in rec room which you can only get the Rimouski channel (near which town Beckles died. I think it was his heart.) And there is something frantic about sitting in a ship doing nothing. I've finished my wine-making article, at least the draft before the last, drunk 65 ounces of Scotch in six days, exercised at night by doing a hundred toe-touchings (and gotten a blister on my ass as a result, and now bandaided, can't do any more) ... Incidentally, I wrote near 4,000 words of the wine piece, and it will have to be cut. There are some damn interesting things in wine history. I feel like quoting you one paragraph, in which, tongue firmly in cheek, I am talking about women related to wine. It's expressed in such a way that no doubt the piece will get a reaction from every women's lib devotee in the country. But I hope it's amusing. You might like to see 2-3 paras.

"In 1955 my first play was accepted and produced by the CBC,[2] so we moved to Montreal so that I could reap the rewards for my genius. And my wife went to work to support me, as any well-behaved wife should and must. I wrote. And made beer with a couple of friends, one of whom was the same Doug Kaye mentioned previously. His marriage had foundered on alcoholic shoals. Henry Ballon, a third member of the trio, was a pharmacist. His job enabled him to buy health malt wholesale, also a supply of returnable mineral water bottles. We then scrounged a fifteen-gallon oak whiskey barrel and were in business.

"Over the winter of 1956-57 the three of us had fifteen gallons of beer brewing in the barrel, the same amount maturing in bottles, and fifteen gallons that was ready and had to be drunk every five or six days. We had to drink it because the batch in the barrel had to be bottled, and there weren't enough extra bottles in which to store the stuff. We brewed ourselves into a tight alcoholic circle from which escape seemed impossible. We drank beer for breakfast, beer for lunch and beer for dinner. It was coming out of our ears. We gave the stuff away, with strong injunctions to return the bottles by, say, Friday, when the next batch was ready to bottle. I began to smell of malt; dogs sniffed me suspiciously on the street; I crossed the road to avoid policemen. Friends began to drop away ...

"There were other handicaps as well. The bathtub was filled almost continually with mineral water bottles being washed in advance of our deadline for the next batch of maturing beer. My wife couldn't take a bath for weeks, months even. She complained bitterly and I think unreasonably about this. After all, we had to wash those bottles somewhere. It would have been unsanitary otherwise.

"Women are sometimes very intolerant creatures, while at the same time possessing many good qualities. My wife kept on complaining. If I had been aware at the time of some of Pliny's writing in ancient Rome, I would have mentioned them to her. Pliny says that Roman women were forbidden to drink wine (I've never forbidden my wife anything), and that Egnatius Maetennus' wife was clubbed to death by her husband for drinking wine from the vat. But I didn't know history was on my side in 1956. Nor was I aware that in 2000 BC the Code of Hammurababi says no priestess shall open a wineshop nor enter one for a drink: if so she shall be burned. In a matter related to alcoholic consumption an interesting Syrian law states that if a woman perpetrates certain sexual transgressions on a man, then both her nipples shall be torn out. Of course those dark days are long past, as witnessed by my own enlightened attitudes. Anyway, women's lib obviously didn't exist in ancient Rome and Babylon. But it's well to remember that the state of women is always reversable."
So there. Do you pulse with righteous indignation, or just feel it's trivial? I was somewhat amused at first, but then wondered about it, begins to seem worse and worse the more you look at something like that ...
Like I said, we've been here two days, and may be here much

313

more. When we finally get to Baie Comeau, I shall jump ship, fly or bus back if there's no train. I've written about six poems here, one of which might be okay, another can't be published because of personalities, finished article, read some Rilke poems from a Penguin (I'm sure the translation by a guy named Leishman is awful, because they're metric, stilted and words shoved in to fill a metric space like mortar)[3] and getting depressed about life … Times like that one should be with friends and weep together and drink to make up for dehydration. You talk about The Diviners being your last novel, and I think lately I haven't been able to break thru to another stage another thought I might flatter myself is original, either in saying or meaning. I wonder if that's what you mean — the feeling you've absolutely said all you can, and there's nothing left in you. The feeling your brain has discovered as much as it can discover. I can't figure that out entirely. Can only speculate: if I had more vitality would content matter less and form more, could I then deceive myself that I was having brilliant ideas, or else would the less-brilliant ideas be expressed so well thru the aforementioned vitality that their less-brilliance wouldn't matter? I seem to grow less and less sure of my own philosophic (to make it sound more dignified and impressive than it is) base sometimes: i.e., is all worthwhile, or nothing worthwhile, or just some things worthwhile. There is a feeling in Rilke that all, any situation, is worthwhile if you can manage to extract or appreciate. I'm much too fallible and human to feel that myself. And yet, I write six poems in a boring situation, writing a boring letter to you as if I were talking (tho I'm not sure I'd talk like this, some things can only be written) … Writing has always seemed worthwhile to me, and yet does mediocre writing, is mediocre writing still worthwhile? Goddam Rilke! There is one passage tho, in which he and a companion are looking at some Egyptian ruins, I think near Akhnaton's hangout (wasn't he the boy-king who started a new religion in Egypt?) which is meditateable on:

> Man and beast appear
> to keep at times some gains from the god's eyes.
> Profit, though difficult, can be secured;
> one tries and tries, the earth can be procured,
> who, though, but gives the price gives up the prize. [4]

These clever paradoxes! Very rational, but Rilke conveys emotion or feeling badly, does it through exclamations, oh and ah. Yet I'm sure some would say the opposite. Emotion, rationality both must be fused in a natural language. Here something jars, perhaps because of Leishman.

Two stone castles in the Thousand Islands, one of them Pickford's, "America's Sweetheart" [5]

> Time that with this strange excuse
> Pardoned Kipling and his views.
> And will pardon Paul Claudel,
> pardon him for writing well.
> And indifferent in a week
> To a beautiful physique ...
> Worships language and forgives [6]
> Everyone by whom it lives ... [7]

And yet, in some ways the world has not quite forgotten Pickford, has it? The absolutes and exaggerations of poems and prose do not always hold. Must stop. This letter is getting out of hand and envelope.

love,

Al

---

1. The piece was published as "The Rime of the Fledgling Mariner: Retracing the Route of Canada's Early Immigrants Along the St. Lawrence." *Weekend Magazine,* 10 August 1974, 3-9.

2. Probably "A Gathering of Days," produced by John Reeves.

3. Probably *Selected Poems by Rainer Maria Rilke* (Penguin, 1964), translated and introduced by J.B. Leishman.

4. From "From the Poems of Count C.W." by Rainer Maria Rilke.

5. Mary Pickford (1892-1979), stage name of Gladys Mary Smith, famous Canadian-born star of silent films, who became known as "America's Sweetheart" because of her innocent film *persona*.

6. In the space to the right Purdy had typed "(Worships language and forgives. W.H. Auden ...)."

7. Purdy had re-arranged lines from "In memory of W.B. Yeats" by W.H. Auden (1907-73). The pertinent stanzas are:

> Time that is intolerant
> Of the brave and innocent,
> And indifferent in a week
> To a beautiful physique,
>
> Worships language and forgives
> Everyone by whom it lives;
> Pardons cowardice, conceit,
> Lays its honours at their feet.
>
> Time that with this strange excuse
> Pardoned Kipling and his views,
> And will pardon Paul Claudel,
> Pardons him for writing well.

Lakefield

12 June 1974

Dear Al–

Thanks much for letter and also for Scott Hutcheson's Boat,[1] which arrived this morning. I found the poem tremendously moving – I dunno, it made me feel sad and yet hopeful at the same time. I guess it expresses an attitude that I feel myself quite a lot of the time, the same kind of thing I tried to express (yep, it took me 382 pp to do it – as I've mentioned frequently before, the conciseness is one thing I envy you) in The Diviners. The sense that the past is always the present is always the future, and that the future, altho in one way totally unknown, in another way *is* kind of known to us. There *will* be someone, "far from this Quinte shoreline" … someday, somewhere, who knows what men like Angus (and you) were all about, altho they may know it and express it in very different ways. And you're right – it damn well *better* be right. Not for nothing are these articles of faith passed on. Or am I being too optimistic (or are you?) to feel that anything really will be passed on? I think not. They *are*. And many of the kids who, a few years ago, affected to believe that life and history had begun with their own tiny births, are now (I've heard them) beginning to wonder how they link in with a past that is so distant as to be only available in legend and myth, and also a past so recent that it still resides in the skulls of their living parents or grand-parents. One thing I have always loved in your poetry is the recurring themes of the connectedness of life – which is why, in yr poems, deeply out of Canada, you can make reference to the Greeks (ancient, i.e.) and the old Egyptians, etc etc etc, with perfect ease and naturalness, because it fits and we are not isolated nor ever have been, if only we can see it that way. I guess in The Diviners a lot of the same ancestral feeling comes across (I hope), and the sense that in some ways, after a certain time, *the ancestors* are everyone's ancestors – mine, in some ways, are not only the Scots but also the Métis; I was born in a land which they had inhabited, shaped and invested with their ghosts. You take it further in the poem – by implication, the ancestors are also the ancient Egyptians and the Minoans and all sea-going peoples who knew about the nature of boats. And oh Al, we *are* haunted by more than our deaths. Not necessarily haunted in a way which is ultimately frightening, either – haunted in some ways in a reassuring sense, or so it appears to me at this point in my life. As you may now have gathered, I think it is a very excellent poem, and what comes across more than anything, I mean the emotion or whatever, under the words and under what you are saying, is a kind of sombre and yet enormously strong affirmation of life and continuity – the kind of thing that you could not possibly have written 20 years ago because you didn't know it yet, not in that way. Perhaps at this point in life, if we do anything at all, we begin to address ourselves not to our own wounded psyches or our un-understanding lovers or anything like that, but to our inheritors. Like Tiresias or Cassandra, maybe – "Listen!" But then again, maybe not quite that prophetic. Anyway, Al, it's a fine poem, and they certainly produced it beautifully. Who did the photo of Angus? It is great. John de Visser's photo of the boat was the one they used in the article, I think. Also – thanks for sending me copy number 1 – I feel honoured! (Actually, I really do.) I take it that the poem can be included in a future collection? I hope so. Incidentally, what an incredibly fine-looking man Angus is.

The letter from the S.S. Golden Hind (did you get to choose the boat for its name?)[2] I found fascinating, partly because of the sense of awful boredom – how do seamen stand it, I wondered. Also because of the stories you picked up from the crew. An entirely different world. And yet not so, of course. How much of all those stories can you use without getting libellous? Or is that a problem with that kind of article? I ask for my own information, actually. Am never sure what one can use, or not, when it is non-fiction.

I note, re-reading yr letter, that you say you feel you haven't been able to break through to another stage, etc etc. Maybe you have done it somehow without realizing it. See my remarks on the poem, above.

To convey the knowledge of mortality, but with the sense of some kind of continuity, of something going on after oneself – that's real, and it's not anything that a young writer can possibly do, not even a young writer who is convinced they'll die young

... Keats ... "When I have fears that I may cease to be/Before my pen has gleaned my teeming brain ..."[3] Okay, fine. But it's "I", "I", "my", "my" all the way. You can say – "dead but pre-knowing we're there/till someone like Angus or me ...",[4] which quite frankly, moves me a lot more than Keats does.

Yeh, this may be my last novel, and this no longer breaks my heart or even worries me. The only thing that worries me is money, and maybe articles for such publications as Weekend will look after that for awhile.[5] Not that I'm broke – I'm not, and I'm deploying my financial resources as best I can in this uncertain world. Will certainly keep shack as long as I can, as I love it. But house is paid for, and also shack, and whatever was left over has been put into Royal Bank investment certificates which draw quite a lot of interest, not enough to live on, of course, but a help. But re: the writing – guess I'll always write something, but it may not be another novel. It isn't that I think I've quit growing or being able to understand more; it is just that (without my knowing or realizing it, initially) I seem to have had to deal with a particular area and time, and I now seem to have completed what it was I had to do, there. And that is okay. Migawd, I might have died of a heart attack or alcohol before I'd finished those 5 books. Not that the world would have crumpled in sorrow, but it mattered to me, anyway. Don't see a time when I won't have a thing to do or be interested in. But that damn novel took a lot more out of me than the goddamn reviewers can possibly realize, and I am not sure I really could ever again be prepared to enter the field in that way. Reviews have been mostly favourable, but some pretty stupid. I won't go into all that again. The hell with them.

My unfortunate medical condition: I have decided that I can stick to the diet when I'm alone, or when my family is here, because juggling with the cooking is quite easy, and the diet isn't too limiting, really. But I have also decided that there is NO WAY I'm going to stick to it utterly when out for dinner ("Sorry, I can't eat that casserole; please do me one meatball with 4 lettuce leaves"). Also, altho I accept that my heavy-drinking days are over, there is also NO WAY I'm going to quit having 1 or 2 drinks before dinner, and when I'm out or have people in, a glass of wine or two with a meal. I aim to tell my doc this. If he is willing to give me some kind of medication to cope with the realities of the situation, fine. If not, well, then maybe I live a few years less – hell, I don't want to see 80 anyway. Also, altho I will be more circumspect than of yore, when meeting with dear friends from time to time, I do not intend to sit the whole eve and sip at soda water. I would no doubt feel differently if I were 21, but at 48 (in July) I am prepared to ease up on the booze but not to change my life style entirely. The hell with it. I'll take my chances. My aunt and uncle visited me last wkend … Mord (my uncle by marriage)[6] is 72; has been mildly diabetic for years; his mother died of diabetes. He eats 3 butter tarts (made by my aunt, and about 97% pure sugar), drinks about 5 ryes in the course of the evening, and consumes baked potatoes with butter, plus about a ton of roast beef, etc. He says he takes a pill every day. Hell, I wouldn't mind taking a pill every day, and I'm not about to eat all those butter tarts, etc, anyway. The doc will probably hate me, and the Clinic (where I have to go for a 3-hour lecture of brainwashing me about health) will wash its hands, no doubt. But I am prepared to do certain things – e.g. lose 20 lbs; stick to diet when alone; strictly limit the booze, etc … but other things I am not prepared to do, and bloody well won't.

Going out to shack this Friday, with carpenter, to see about various repairs, and Dave & Jane will go out and stay there for awhile. Dave may be getting cast off leg soon, I hope, in which case the swimming in the river would probably be a good thing. Don Bailey, I think, has bought Jack Villerup's cottage, so he maybe will be there soon – I hope so. I love my kids (as I may not need to mention), but really, Al, what I'm looking forward to is September in the shack, BY MYSELF. Friends on weekends. Weekdays spent in contemplation, bird-watching, and other innocuous and restful pursuits. Actually, I'm far far less tired than I was a month ago, or after the awful publicity week in Trona.

A few weeks here, with not too many pressures, seem to have restored me. Reckon I can't be in that bad physical shape if I feel pretty okay. Anyway, I refuse to spend the rest of my life obsessed with diet and health – what a bore.

I thought Sheena Paterson sounded quite nice over the phone, and really want to talk about articles with her. This area abounds in local history and personalities, but they are very jealous of their history and I don't think they would take kindly to an outsider from the prairies writing articles about it. Best not to write any-thing about any place in which one is actually *living,* I've found, until you've lived there a few years, at least. I am still feeling out this community and of course it is mutual. So I think the articles will have to be in another area. Next year, Churchill, maybe, but not right now. Sheena says she has some ideas, but as I told you on the phone, this rarely works for me. Haven't really applied my mind to thinking about article-ideas as yet, but that is partly why I need to be ALONE in the shack for awhile. I may get this phone unlisted – I get some awfully odd calls. About 2 minutes ago, a gal from the Tor Star phoned – they're doing a list of summer reading and want various writers to recommend 2 Can paperbacks for folks to take on vacation. I said, off the top of my head, Ernest Buckler's THE MOUNTAIN AND THE VALLEY and Mor-decai Richler's ST. URBAIN'S HORSEMAN. Why, the girl asked, would I say those two. "Because they are two of the best novels ever written in this country," I replied coldly, "and they're both long but haven't got a boring word in them, and if you're only gonna read two novels during your vacation, you may as well get value for yr money, in both length and quality." I thought she was going to ask for a list of 12, but no, it seems that 2 books is about all the holiday reading the average Star reader is capable of. Well, well.

Yr remark that you write a letter to me as tho talking, but not really as tho. Yeh. Some things *can* only be written, or at least they're easier to write than to say. Which is why you and I fence humorously a lot of the time when actually meeting, but don't do too much of that in letters, and also why I don't get on too well with the telephone when talking to real friends. Letters are better. Possibly we are word-oriented and in relation to the printed page. James Thurber[7] once said he felt it would be better if he never saw any of his friends ... just wrote to them. I've sometimes felt something the same. Altho I guess seeing people is important in ... hm hm ... nonverbal ways. Just to see that the other people are still there, I suppose, in some way that letters doesn't prove.

Yes, I do quite often feel I've discovered as much as I can discover. That isn't nothing, but it isn't everything, either. What I don't want to do, ever, is to write a mockup of a novel, an invented rather than created thing. I could do it. Frankly, I know I could, and a lot of people would not know the difference. Some of the reviewers would probably even prefer it to the real thing. But that isn't allowed – it's the one thing I am afraid of doing, of finding myself doing it just in order to write something. That would be the real death. It just isn't on *at all*.

Thanks for the inscription in Scott Hutcheson's Boat.[8] I always want to write something I mean in books for friends, but am no damn good at it at all.

Try and come up and see my new abode, The Old Anderson Place, ex- Funeral Home, now looking as tho me and mine had lived here some time.

Love,

Margaret

---

1. The poem was published in 1973 in a limited edition of 223 copies in the Caledonia Writing Series, Prince George, B.C.

2. Francis Drake (1541-96) circumnavigated the globe (1577-80) in his ship "The Golden Hind."

3. The opening lines of "When I Have Fears" by John Keats (1795-1821).

4. From "Scott Hutcheson's Boat."

5. Laurence published two articles in *Weekend Magazine* in 1974: "Loneliness Is Something That Doesn't Exist Here," 11 May 1974, 7; "The Greatest Gift of All," 21 December 1974, 2-4.

6. Morden Carter had married Norma Wemyss, the sister of Margaret Laurence's father.

7. James Thurber (1894-1961), celebrated American humorist.

8. "For Margaret – for being Margaret – and much more than much, or little multiplied by marvellous. love Al —"

Lakefield

18 September 1974

Dear Al–

Received IN SEARCH OF OWEN ROBLIN a few days ago – very many thanks. I'd ordered one from Longhouse, actually, but will give that copy to someone for Christmas ... Jocelyn, I think. I hadn't known whether you'd send me a copy or not, it being a kind of costly book. Anyway, I'm really glad you did ... and thanks for the inscription,[1] as well; yours are always kind of original; I can never think of anything to put down except either Love or Best Wishes, pretty corny.

I read the book last night and had a lot of fun trying to sort out which parts had been in previous poems, with alterations. Don't know how accurate my guesswork was. It's a very good long poem, Al, and gets across a lot of the feelings you have about the ancestors, the land, and all. Both Owen Roblin and your grandfather began to take shape in my mind as real individuals ... you can do that. I've always thought that some of the poems about your grandfather are among the best you've ever written. He must have been some man. And yes, I know you fictionalize or mythologize him ... that comes out, too. I'd like to have heard the whole thing read on the CBC ... except that in many places, reading it, it was *your* voice I could hear, and I assume you didn't actually do the reading yourself ... or did you?

I think the production job is very good, and the photos could in some places be better ... or clearer, I'm not sure. Some are v. good, tho, and the old photos are great.

I also received the bookclub copy of The Fire-Dwellers which you sent, and now cannot recall whether you sent it for me to keep or if you wanted my priceless signature in it for your own collection. Please let me know.

Things more or less okay here. Joc and Pete having their problems ... I am a listening ear from time to time, but they have to sort it out, and either will or won't. David still in Eng, and of course hasn't written, but at least if I don't hear all the problems I don't worry about them. Am starting back 1 day a week at Trent, as of next week. Spent a week in Vancouver and Victoria, seeing one or two old friends, but mainly went to see my aunt age 86 ... god forbid I live that long, altho it isn't likely. She's got all her marbles and is pretty cheery but can hardly walk and is nearly blind.

My ancient Remington finally packed in – flipped a key for about the 10th time throughout the years, so I decided it was time I put it out to pasture and so went to town and bought this one, a Monica Olympia, which I hope will work out better than the last time I bought a new typewriter – I got my old one fixed and decided I liked it better so gave away the new one.

I got the old Remington fixed (a flipped key) just about 3 months ago, so this time I'm not going to bother, as it's about $15 each time. I am a bit superstitious about that typewriter, I guess, as I've typed all 10 of my books on it. Sounds like My Grandfather's Clock, doesn't it? Do you suppose it *knows*? Well, I don't aim to start another novel but I'd kind of like to do a kid's book this winter. Or some articles. Still can't decide what to do about the many articles ... we discussed this when you were here. I feel very ambiguously about the whole thing. I change my mind daily, not that I think about it that much.

Adele's novel should be out soon. I'm reviewing it in the Globe.² Also did a review of Dennis Lee's 2 books of kids' poetry, which will be out soon.³ I really liked them, altho you might not. But there is a great verse from his poem called 1838: (the last verse)

> Mackenzie was a crazy man,
> He wore his wig askew.
> He donned three bulky overcoats
> In case the bullets flew.
> Mackenzie talked of fighting
> While the fight went down the drain.
> But who will speak for Canada?
> Mackenzie, come again!

I really think that should be taught in every public school in the country. We were brought up on Drake's Drum,⁴ which is fine, but nothing about *here*. There's another verse you might enjoy ... the whole poem is good, but this is the last verse ... the poem is called Homage to Moose Factory, Ont:

> Jack declared the Giant wasn't
> Worth a hill of beans.
> Samson flexed his armpits
> And destroyed the Philistines.
> Sir John A. built the CPR
> With words and Scotch whiskey;
> Pygmies all, beside the men
> Of old Moose Factory!

Got a whole stack of new books from Longhouse ... $52 worth; well, if I can't buy books when I want to now, when will I? Have about 3 doz. books not yet read, here and at shack ... will keep me going the winter. Got Earle Birney's What's So Big About Green? Haven't read it, just leafed through. It seems kind of odd. I don't care for his visual poems much. I guess they were fun to do, tho, and that must count for something, I suppose. Read Tony Kilgallen's book on Lowry while in Toronto recently[5] ... migawd, what a fancy production job! Too fancy, in my opinion. The book is interesting but not, I would have said, definitive in any way. A lot of gossip, which one always reads assiduously and afterwards wonders just how significant it is, probably damn little meaning. I've bought Day's book on Lowry, too, but not read it.[6] Am going out to shack tomorrow after I see the dentist (woe). Will have to commute, more or less, coming in here on Mondays & Tues.

What does the winter promise re: you? Are you going anywhere? Are you writing? What about the state of your soul, etc? I hope you aren't depressed, as you were awhile back. Corragio – Avanti.

And again thanks for book.

Love,

Margaret

---

1. Not traced.

2. Laurence reviewed *Crackpot* in *The Globe and Mail,* 28 September 1974, 33.

3. Laurence's review of Lee's *Alligator Pie* and *Nicholas Knock and Other People* appeared in *The Globe and Mail,* 5 October 1974, 35.

4. "Drake's Drum" by English poet Henry Newbolt (1862-1938) was widely anthologized in Canadian school texts.

5. *Lowry* (1973).

6. *Malcolm Lowry: A Biography* (1973) by Douglas Day.

§

Ameliasburgh
26 September 1974

Dear Margaret:

Your own book was in an edition you didn't have, so it's for you, not signing.

No, I didn't do the reading – and some of those were really fruity CBC voices. I'd have preferred more natural harshness.

I'm going nuts here. Had two more pieces to do for Weekend, then Sheena Paterson phoned to ask me to do a profile of Earle Birney,[1] who was just taking off round-the-world. So I've just done a first draft of that. So I'm a journalist now. It pays.

I had that Dennis Lee poem in Storm Warning. As I remember, the title was a typo: should've been 1837. Altho maybe I'm wrong if the same title was in his own book. Sure, I think that poem should be in the schools too. It's fine.

I reviewed both the books on Lowry, the Day one being a pretty complete job, complete with doomed alcoholic theories. Dunno if you saw the full-page piece I did for Dave Billington's Gazette [2] – Jesus, ordinary newspaper pay is bad – I got a hundred bucks for a full-page article.

I haven't read Lee's children's poems, apart from that one. Makes you want to try them out on children when you as an adult enjoy them.

This is really just a note – I hafta get back to work on stuff … Seems like I'm gonna be at Univ. of Man. next year, and the horror of a Wpg. winter is gonna drive me to Peru this year.

My soul is lousy, corrupt and black – on accounta I'm in the usual rut and it has street lights and hand holds. Writing a few poems now and then, but not in the outpouring I seem to have lost forever. Maybe that's good tho, because much of what you "outpour" is crap. But much of what I'd write now, if I wrote poems, would be repetition, or about things in which I'm not very interested. Reversely, I wrote before whether I was interested before writing, but got interested when writing. No answer to these puzzles.

Must stop.

Love,
Al

---

1. "The Man Who Killed David." *Weekend Magazine,* 14 December 1974, 16–17.

2. Purdy's review of the two books, "Malcolm Lowry – private hell in the public eye," appeared in *The Saturday Gazette,* 9 March 1974, 43.

Lakefield
14 February 1976

Dear Al–

Happy Valentine's Day and thanks for your letter. I haven't replied sooner because (a) I've been thinking, and (b) I've been caught up in an idiotic situation which I'll explain in a moment.

Re: the U of M[1] – could you convey to them, please, that I just don't think I can go in the coming year, although perhaps another year I could, and I really would love to spend a year in Manitoba. The winter does not daunt me – in fact, I think it might be preferable to the icy streets which we have here at the moment; it thaws then freezes, and walking is all but impossible. If I did go at some point, there would be some problems which I can't yet see my way around … one would be transportation from apartment or whatever to U of M, as I don't drive. Guess I could learn how to go by bus, like students. The other would be that I would have to rent my house here. However, at some point all these things no doubt could be dealt with. But for the next year, and possibly two,

I really feel I have to stay home and do my own work. I can't seem to combine writing with being writer-in-res. It is an either/or thing for me. When I am w-in-r, I don't seem to have any psychic energy left for writing, not to mention time. But perhaps when I've got this kids' book done, and hopefully some stories ...

I've got the manuscript done with the collection of essays, articles and so on ... 14 articles in all, out of about 30 over the years, so we will see what J.G.McC says about them.[2] I got a xerox copy for myself yesterday at Millage's Plumbing in the village (yep, and one can buy rubber boots at the Bowling Alley). Posted it to M&S today, thinking Feb 14 was a propitious day. Now I have to do an Intro for the NCL,[3] 2 book reviews, an article, and my income tax, before beginning on the kids' book. My correspondence alone is damn near a fulltime job. I feel a bit swamped.

The idiotic situation is this: THE DIVINERS was banned in the Lakefield High School, by a superintendent in the Board of Ed's office, who received complaints from 2 parents. The Peterborough Examiner reported it at great length, although not with total accuracy. The Star and the Globe picked it up; it went out on CP; I received phone calls from everyone ranging from friends to the Vancouver Sun. The local high school teachers of English rallied, and the book now is still on the course lists and will presumably go to the Textbook Review Committee, a committee set up to deal with books on which complaints have been received – this is the proper procedure, which was not done in the original banning. The same thing has happened in another area school with LIVES OF GIRLS AND WOMEN, this time banned by the principal, but it, too, will now go to the committee. The Eng Dept heads in area high schools throughout P'borough County have met and are united and will defend the 2 novels. So we shall see.[4] But what a storm! Several nasty letters in the Examiner and Globe, saying, yep, it's a dirty book all right. Others in Examiner, Globe and Lakefield Leader, in support of novel. I made one statement to the Examiner and one to the Leader, but am now maintaining a dignified silence … what else can I do? I don't think I need to defend my own novel. Probably it will be good for sales … I hope the local bookshops are getting in fresh stocks! It's a bit ironic to have this happen where I live. I wonder who in Lakefield hates me?

Otherwise, life is uneventful. The local ruckus is enough eventfulness to be getting on with.

Thanks for the poem.[5] Have you been writing much recently?

I'm thinking of writing a pornographic kids' book so it can be banned in the local primary school as well.

Love,

Margaret

ps. Joc said she had an interesting evening with you and Hans Jewinski.[6]

------

1. As writer-in-residence at the University of Manitoba, Purdy had written Laurence on behalf of the Department of English to offer her the post of writer-in-residence for the 1976-77 academic year.

2. The manuscript was published as *Heart of a Stranger* the following September.

3. *House of Hate* by Percy Janes.

4. The novels remained on the curriculum.

5. In his letter of 28 January 1976, Purdy had sent a typescript copy of the poem "Lament," published later that year in *Sundance at Dusk*.

6. Hans Jewinski (b. 1946) was a Toronto poet and policeman, author of *Poet Cop* (1975).

[Department of English]
[University of Manitoba]
[Winnipeg]
21 February 1976

Dear Margaret,

Yeah, I read about that book banning thing. Seems so silly in this day and age. Wonder when they'll look at my stuff and do the same.

Congrats on the articles book. Mine is ready too, and with McStew.[1] They'll likely do yours and turn mine down. Alice Munro was out here, nice gal!

I just came back from six readings in five days, for money of course. But wow, it takes it outa you.

Odd that in your new home town, that was the place they fixed their prurient eyes on your book.

Sorry you can't take the job here, it seems a lotta money.

love
Al

---

1. *No Other Country* (1977).

§

Ameliasburgh
13 February 1977

Dear Margaret,

Recent poems. Altho Starlings dates from around 1968, give or take a year. I managed to overlook it directly after it was written, and now spent a little time touching it here and there. It will be in Q.Q.[1] A Handful of Earth in CanFor, also as title of a small book.[2] Prince Edward County I don't know as yet.[3]

331

I phoned you after your own call, but expect you went to bed early.

Hope you enjoy the television. The one here (aerial) cost $300., and an extra booster for it another $125., so cost damn near as much as the tv set. But you'll be much closer to Toronto where you are.

Expect to see you at Hamilton – and I wonder if the papers will pick up the incongruity of Mowat finishing ahead of Laurence in the novels sweepstakes.[4] Incidentally, I just (a month back or so) read The Diviners, and have all sorts of thoughts, but don't dare mention them to you. Shall we ask Dave Godfrey what he thinks? I shall be very sorry if you don't write one more – and always the cry is just one more, whether poem or novel. I think: just one more poem that I can regard as among my best. And I'm not sure but what Prince Edward County, or possibly Starlings, is not among my best. But can't count Starlings, given that 1968 date. For you, I don't see how you can't not try to write another, despite this double negative. If you don't write one, you'll feel so goddam useless. At least that's the way I feel when not writing what I think is well. I mean, what are we here for if we don't make the effort, fall flat on our faces maybe, but damn well try. Which is the reason for all the comebacks of athletes and everyone else in the world, they keep trying. I don't want to end with a whimper, nor necessarily a bang, but something something I'm not ashamed of.

Colombo in the same category as Woodcock and Creighton,[5] and Berton with them too, ahead of both Creighton and Wood-cock – this is like putting Richard Rohmer[6] beside Dostoyevsky.

Yours
Al

PRINCE EDWARD COUNTY[7]
Words do have smell and taste
these have the taste of apples

332

brown earth and red tomatoes
as if a juggler had juggled
too many balls of fire
and dropped some of them
a smell and taste and bell sound
in the ear of waves
— not princes

Conservative since the Romans
— altho it's only animals
that are true conservatives
using the same land and water
and air for countless generations
themselves their own ancestors
each their own child
rabbits and groundhog tenants
porcupine leaseholders
and the wide estates of foxes

This is an island and you know
it's like being dressed in lace
as only a woman may be
and not be laughed at
around her neck and throat
the silver dance of coastlines
and bells rung deep in limestone

Animals having no human speech
have not provided names
but named it with their bodies
and the long-ago pine forests
named it with their bodies
and the masts of sailing ships
named it to the sea
and a bird one springtime

named it bobolink bobolink
even a small unremarkable flower
I saw last april blossoming
that died shortly after
named it for herself
trillium

And we – the late-comers
white skins and brown men
no voice told us to stay
but we did for a lifetime
of now and then forever
the fox and flower and rabbit
and bells rung deep in limestone
for any who come after
you have heard our names
and the word we made of silence
bobolink and –

Al Purdy, R.R. 1, Ameliasburgh, Ont. KOK 1A0

STARLINGS
The starlings strut jaunty and raucous
with just that little swagger which says to hell with you
        bud
orioles glow like orange napkins at the world's dinner
        table
by two always by twos being lovers
things shine internally and it's spring
everything is all that it is and complete as it is and the sun
just coming up

By contrast:
before I returned to the house this spring
three starlings were trapped

334

in the shed between wire mesh and door glass
and died there shitting and squawking
with heads projecting inward thru the wire their bodies
    rotting
and I left them there for I'd be sick
if I tore them out with pliers
This morning the shed floor was covered with cream-
    coloured maggots
wriggling worms helpless as human babies
having abandoned host bodies of the three starlings
dessicated and part mummified in the shed window
while other sub-microscopic organisms held high revel
in the corpses and fester onward in the condition which is
    life

At times it is brought home to one
as personal viewpoints change according to age and
    exuberance
this continuing process
– as human bodies are shovelled quickly into the ground
decaying soldiers on battlefields glimpsed only briefly
by burial details and cameras   a single maggot crawling
    from nostrils
evoking casual grunts of horror on television
rioting students die outside chemistry classrooms
guns bark muted and witnesses give brief testimony
then move on elsewhere into a morning more or less like
    this one

No reason to write a poem
except to say that the morning is bright
your breasts my dear are lovely
and suspended somewhere between birth and decay in a
    single moment
melancholy fuses with wonder   the body alertly stiffens

as if something had been hinted at
– vouchsafed perhaps the word is? – or the realization is
   achievement?
– pinned down by particular words – arrived at like a
   streetcorner?
while the grass grows an eighth of an inch as the maggots
   converge
like arrows   labels on medicine bottles read backward
            the colour
of thoughts turns grey   bacteria glimmer in the stars'
   experimental
stations   your breasts are lovely
while three dead starlings strut onto the lawn stage jaunty
   and raucous
and impossible to do without
it is a bright day

Al Purdy, R.R. 1, Ameliasburgh, Ont. KOK 1AO

A HANDFUL OF EARTH
      – to René Lévesque

Proposal:
let us join Quebec
if Quebec won't join us
I don't mind in the least
being governed from Quebec City
by Canadiens instead of Canadians
in fact the fleur-de-lis and maple leaf
in my bilingual guts
bloom incestuous

Listen:
you can hear soft wind blowing
among tall fir trees on Vancouver Island

it is the same wind we knew
whispering alon[g] Cote des Neiges
on the island of Montreal
when we were lovers and had no money
Once flying in a little Cessna 180
above that great spine of mountains
where a continent attempts the sky
I wondered who owns this land
and knew that no one does
for we are tenants only

Go back a little:
to hip-roofed houses on the Isle d'Orleans
and scattered along the road to Chicoutimi
the remaining few log houses in Ontario
sod huts of sunlit prairie places
dissolved in rain long since
the stones we laid atop of one another
a few of which still stand
those origins
in which children were born
in which we loved and hated
in which we built a place to stand on
and now must tear it down?
– and here I ask all the oldest questions
of myself
the reasons for being alive
the way to spend this gift and thank the giver
but there is no way

I think of the small dapper man
chain-smoking at PQ headquarters
Lévesque
on Avenue Christophe Colomb in Montreal
where we drank coffee together six years past

337

I say to him now: my place is here
whether Cote des Neiges Avenue Christophe Colomb
Yonge Street Toronto Halifax or Vancouver
this place is where I stand
where all my mistakes were made
when I grew awkwardly and knew what I was
and that is Canadian or Canadien
it doesn't matter which to me

Sod huts break the prairie skyline
then melt in rain
the hip-roofed houses of New France as well
but French no longer
nor are we any longer English
– limestone houses
lean-tos and sheds our fathers built
in which our mothers died
before the forests tumbled down
ghost habitations
only this handful of earth
for a time at least
I have no other place to go

Al Purdy, R.R. 1, Ameliasburgh, Ont. KOK 1AO

---

1. "Starlings" was published in *Queen's Quarterly,* 84, 2 (Summer 1977), 227-28, and in a slightly revised version in *A Handful of Earth.*

2. "A Handful of Earth" appeared in *The Canadian Forum,* April 1977, 27, and in *A Handful of Earth.*

3. "Prince Edward County" first appeared in *A Handful of Earth* in a slightly revised version.

4. Purdy had participated for several years in the annual Canada Day seminar at Mohawk College in Hamilton. Initiated in 1970 by Jim Foley, nationalist and teacher of Canadian literature in high schools and then community

colleges, the seminar featured well-known Canadian writers. In preparation for the Canada Day seminar to be held on 23 April 1977, it appears that an informal survey had been taken to indicate the popularity of Canadian writers: Purdy's essay on Foley – "Norma, Eunice, and Judy" – was included in *No Other Country.*

5. Donald Creighton (1902-79), pre-eminent Canadian historian.

6. Richard Rohmer (b. 1924), lawyer and author of best-selling popular fiction dealing with national and international affairs.

7. Purdy had written in the margin, "For Margaret – recent stuff from Al Purdy".

§

Lakefield
15 February 1977

Dear Al–

Thanks much for your letter. I think that A HANDFUL OF EARTH is one of the best poems you have written. Draws upon a lot of your past poems, the place to stand on, and in the end expresses what I feel, too, and I suspect so many of us do ... "I have no other place to go." But it's an expression of faith and also heartbreak, not the awful reproach that so many WASPS seem to be laying on Levesque[1] these days, or worse ... the indifference ... "let 'em go; who needs 'em?" Well, we need them and they need us, for the reasons you say, which are deeper than the reasons of currency, passports, etc, industries, and so on. I thought the other 2 poems were fine, as well, and if I focus more on A HANDFUL OF EARTH, I guess it is just because of the point we are at in our history plus the feelings I have had myself about this land for a long time. I think STARLINGS must date a bit later than 1968?? I remember going out to A'burgh ... and I think, altho I'm not sure, that it may have been 1970, when I was at the U of T, and I recall your telling me then about the trapped

339

birds in your study/library, which was then still in an almost shed-like state. You had come home after a winter away and found them ... or such is my memory of it.

After I talked with you on the phone, I looked for a bit at Hockey Night in Can and then went to bed. The phone rang and I didn't answer it. Of course, I didn't know it was you. I have so many nut phone calls that when I don't feel like talking and coping with odd people who always seem to want something from me, I just don't answer any more. I guess I should get an unlisted number. Have you?

Well, not to worry about the popularity poll. It shows who is being read, and that's okay. At least some of our books *are* being read, and that's a nice change from about 15 years ago.

Why didn't you tell me before that you had not previously read THE DIVINERS? If I'd known you hadn't read it before, I would not have taken on so, in bygone times. It's okay not to read a book, but to read it and not *say* anything ... well, let's not go into that again. That is over. But if you have all sorts of thoughts, whether positive or negative, I would like to hear an assortment of them ... and I am not saying this in any wish that you'll approve or disapprove of the book, you understand. I think one values the assessment, either way, of one's peers, that's all.

[. . .]

Re: my writing. I wish people wouldn't think that I am in a state of despair, or am bowing out of life. Gee. It's not that way at all, Al. I hope I'll write another novel, and if I can get all these damn people who keep writing me letters of requests for interviews, etc etc, off my back, I may even have some time to think. If another novel is given, I'll be grateful. If not, I won't be too upset. I don't think I'm useless in this life unless I'm writing – I would have thought that if I hadn't done the writing I was compelled to do, against great odds, I may say, then I would not have lived my life the way I was meant to live it. But I did my work and I raised my kids and I kept a roof over the heads of us. If another true real novel comes along, and it may, then that will be a gift, a bonus. If not, then so be it, and I won't feel goddamn useless at all. To me, life depends on doing what you are given to do, and no excuses. And if one door may close, then another opens. We will see, but I am not alarmed, nor do I feel it is a matter of constantly "proving" ... proving what? That is not where it's at, in my view of myself. What a lot of people, maybe including you, old friend, don't seem to realize about me is that I'm not trying to force anything, and I'm really happy here ... try to believe it. I am.

Love,

Margaret

P.S. of recent times, you have been very thoughtful and nice to me, after a kind of friendship-absence on the part of both of us, and I do recognize it and reciprocate. Old friends matter more as time declines, and that is not a gloomy statement

---

1. René Lévesque (1922–87), leader of the separatist Parti Québécois (1968-85), had been elected premier of Québec in November 1976. Under his administration (1976-85), a referendum on Québec sovereignty took place in May 1980 and the pro-independence cause was defeated.

§

Ameliasburgh
18 February 1977

Dear Margaret,

Thanks for the good word on poems. And yes, the point about a country is it means a lot more than economics. Many people don't seem to realize that. I've written other poems besides those three, but they seem to me much the best. And maybe you're right about the date of Starlings, but sometimes the past seems to become the future indefinite, not lost but floating in a place without time, and all three tenses are applicable. And this is a peculiarity about time for me, that apart from definite dates which rarely seem very important, I seem to become a compendium of both past and future. All things have such varied aspects and facets that I see them from many viewpoints. For instance, I'm going to the Yukon shortly. And just looking at a photograph of the thronging main street of Dawson, when the town and area had a pop. of 25,000, later down to a little over 700, and thinking I will write a poem about that, contrasting it to now.[1] Which doesn't sound very good, but the point is I hold both that past and present in my mind, also the possible poem, plus unrealized things that may happen. Probably unfigureoutable.

[. . .]

The Diviners? I have all sorts of feelings about the book, one of them being one you perhaps don't prize as much as I do: the fact that you seldom or never write a line that isn't, of itself, interesting. I mean in a surface way, apart from whatever the total book adds up to. And I think that is damn rare. There are things I did think about the book, as I remember: that the earlier years in it overmatched the other sections in some degree. But the best part of it was what I talked about in the first para. of this letter, the homogeneity of time and what happens, how incidents float in time. Or am I being obscure? I do think it's one of the three top novels written in/of/about this country. And when one develops the ability to do this, I think one should go farther. Always farther, exploring, developing etc.

I doubt that people think you're "in a state of despair" and "bowing out of life." That's a wild exaggeration. And people who keep pestering you to do this and that, well, one learns to dispose of those things in order to do the important things. I am saying: a talent is to be used, even if you let it lie fallow for a time. If you never write another novel, you won't think you're useless in this life, as you say. Of course not, and that's not the goddam point. Because neither novels nor poems are entirely gifts, only in one sense. The qualities that enabled you to write your novels are still there, and one owes both one's self and other people. Don't tell me that's shit either. And life is only partly what you are given to do, which is carrying fatalism to its absurdio. To have written what you did changed you, gave you tools and equipment in your mind to do other and different things. I don't say one should drive and push one's self into those other things, I do say one should not seem to bar them out with fatalism. i.e. they were gifts, I'll wait and see if there's another gift. That's passive and inert. Of course it's not what other people want of you either, but what you need from yourself. But we are liable to miss each other's point if I continue like this. What happens in the mind is so damn mysterious anyway ...

Incidentally, I don't think A Handful Of Earth is as good as the other two, but since it's about the subject it is, perhaps for that reason ...

I'll see you at this coronation or whatever it is, the Mohawk College thing.[2] Which will be a lousy place to talk, one can't. I may go to Mexico after the Yukon trip, dunno. But maybe we can drink some wine in Hamilton. And hey, I think you're a pretty nice person, if I haven't said so lately – much larger than you know about.

love

Al

---

1. Possibly "Hail Mary in Dawson City" in *The Stone Bird*.

2. The annual Canada Day seminar.

343

§

Lakefield
30 July 1977

Dear Al–

My brother[1] and his wife and their 2 young teenage daughters have been with me all July – hence the delay in replying to your letter. They left yesterday to return to High Prairie, Alta. It was great to have them here, although I have to admit to a few silent moments of feeling hysteria mounting as I realized I wouldn't get ANYTHING done this month, not even a few letters. It was all I could do to get the cheques written out to pay the bills. However, what is one month more or less in the eternal scheme of things, or even in my own life? Well, I guess it's one month without work, neither more nor less. But it was good to see them – don't manage it too often, they living so far from here.

Thanks much for A HANDFUL OF EARTH. I don't see why you might suspect it's "bottom of the barrel". It isn't, as you really know. I haven't read them all yet, but I like the S. Amer ones. Also, as I think I told you before, I think that "A Handful Of Earth" is one of your best. That whole subject – well, more of that later.

Good good news that you'll be w-in-r at Western!! [2] They will probably work you quite hard – at least, that was my experience. If you only see students 3 days a week, tho, as I did, and not go into office on other days, it won't be too bad. They also like the wir to attend some Canlit classes, but not as teacher. Or so it was when I was there. Horwood was there last year, and enjoyed it. I thought I worked hard, but Harold surpassed anyone – he is an energetic fellow. However, I must say that I found (no, I didn't *find,* I *met*) more really promising young writers there than I have almost anywhere else. A few of them have since been published. It's nice when that happens.

Incidentally, Western phoned me (and now, having mentioned it, I hesitate to mention it … just as you said in yr letter about the job … however, this is in confidence, and I mean

344

strict), I suppose because I was an ex-wir there, and asked if I knew anything about your ability with young writers. I said, truthfully, that I knew plenty and that you related with young writers extremely well and had indeed helped a lot of young writers with getting published for the first time, etc ... I mentioned STORM WARNING I and II, and people like Suknaski and Marty.[3] I think I have had something to make up to you for, and hope I have in honour now done that. Would have said the same thing even if this had not been the case, of course, not because you are a friend but because it is obviously true.

I agree with you about Clarke and Thomas.[4] I didn't know they hadn't taken out citizenship. Now I know.

I was invited to the Halifax thing but declined.[5] Gee, I get sick of all those conferences and banquets and so on. No more. Not EVER. I swear it!!

Re: the Can thing – I got a letter from a friend in Ottawa who had just seen the Can Forum issue (the last one)[6] in which the Committee for a New Constitution or whatever it is, including people like you and me, were presented as signatories of that statement which said, in effect – we hope and pray that Canada will remain one; we need a new constitution which will take into account the rights of all parts of the country, the special needs of Quebec, the grievances of the West and the Atlantic provinces and native peoples; if, however, all fails, we must give thought to keeping the rest of the country together. This really is my point of view. I think we have to think the "unthinkable" ... it isn't going to go away, and I sure as hell am not prepared to see my country go by default to the USA *if* Quebec separates. Anyway, said friend, who is NDP, (as I am!), wiped the floor with me ... practically accused me of being either a knave or a fool, and said that this group was the last gasp of Upper Canadians who would benefit from the separation of Que! Who, me? Purdy? Atwood? Mel Watkins?[7] I nearly had a fit, from surprise and anger. She is, I think, falling prey to the same error as Trudeau & Co ... if you even *breathe* the possibility that the country may separate, you are advocating separation. Ye Gods! The separatistes aren't just going to conveniently disappear. Of course we *must* do all possible to keep confederation, but not as it now is. And if it fails, I believe we must *not* simply panic and start learning the words of The Star-Spangled Banner. My God, she cares about this land as much as I do, but what is the sense in absolutely refusing to think the unthinkable? I honestly think your poem is about the best statement I've read so far – it puts the thing in both historical and personal terms. I agree with everything you say in it. But I think that many people, including both you and myself, feel that if the worst does, tragically, come to the worst, we *must* be prepared to say … what now?

Don't worry. More poems will come. I don't say this in a facile sense. I, too, mourn the fact that things don't come with the speed and ease they once did … ideas, I mean; the writing never did come with ease, although sometimes with speed. I have some vague ideas, and am reading in a rather eclectic way, sort of freewheeling out of some instinct. Some characters are there, too, or the embryonic beginnings of same. But – so many unsolved problems of how to approach what I think I want to do. I can't hurry the solutions, although I *can* think about them, and I desperately need silence and privacy, which as usual for me aren't apparently all that easy to obtain. The unlisted phone, the form letter and the determination to turn down all invites have helped a bit. I need to know a lot more, about various things and about how I really feel myself. Also, when I think of another long haul like a novel, I get scared. But – I hope it may come.

The book of essays should be good. NO OTHER COUNTRY is much much better than A.P.'s Can.[8] It is good to have things coming out, too. I have a feeling that with myself it will be years and years and … ho hum. I take no interest in reprints such as Seal book editions, except for the money. However, I'm not really depressed … just sort of subdued for the moment. So little time, so much to do. The *doing* would be okay, if I were ready, but I'm not. Anyway, we bash on somehow, I guess.

Love,

Margaret

---

1. Robert Wemyss (1933–86).

2. Purdy was writer-in-residence at the University of Western Ontario for the 1977/78 academic year.

3. Andrew Suknaski and Sid Marty (b. 1944) had been included in *Storm Warning: The New Canadian Poets.*

4. Austin Clarke, a native of Barbados, had come to Canada in 1955. Audrey Thomas (b. 1935) was born in Binghamton, New York, and came to Canada in 1959. Purdy had argued for Canadian citizenship as a condition of funding by the Canada Council.

5. Laurence had been invited to attend the meetings of the Halifax Federation of Writers in June.

6. "Canada and Quebec: A Proposal for a New Constitution." *The Canadian Forum,* June/July 1977, 4–5. Laurence and Purdy were among the signatories to the proposal.

7. Melville Watkins (b. 1932), Canadian nationalist and Professor of Economics and Political Science at the University of Toronto.

8. At one point, the collection of Purdy's essays was to be called *Al Purdy's Canada.*

Ameliasburgh

3 August 1977

Dear Margaret –

Many thanks for your good offices with Western. That $16,000 is nice. But you scare the shit outa me with your mention of a heavy workload. I intend to have office hours two days a week, morning and afternoon, as at Wpg. And of course I'll be in

347

class sometimes, was told that by Collins,[1] the chairman. However, I figure the main duty is talkin to young writers, and that is what I'll do.

Three months drought ended with a coupla poems, one quite long. Enclose em as part payment for your help at Western. No Second Spring is a line I swiped from the folk song Loch Lomond, and also got a bit of Wordsworth into the poem.[2] It is, of course, science fiction, and I hope it's a few other things too. It will be a small book later in the year. (I have five books coming this year)[3] The Bible quote was fortunate, since Mount Moriah is mentioned several times in Bible (It's where ol Solomon was gonna build a temple too), and wouldn't it be great to have names like Hezekiah, Obadiah, etc. in the poem. I had an ancestor named McDagg Purdy. How ya doin, McDagg?

You shoulda been at Halifax. John Moss[4] and I got together and worked out a plot to write a book on the sexual lives and scandalous affairs of Can. writers, and we had a publisher's rep named Lewis slavering to get the book. We dangled it in front of him, trying to work a large advance. We were drinking at the time of course, and finally Lewis got disgusted and departed. I made myself unpopular with a black girl who wore a very low-cut dress, by looking at the mammary glands significantly several times. She would have blushed if she could. I was flattered so outrageously by nearly everybody that it delayed my suicide for a few months. Anyway, you can get the picture.

My latest peeve is Don Obe at the Canadian. I go west to Vic next Monday, and they just return my Dryland Country story with requests for all sorts of changes which must be in by Aug. 15.[5] And I hafta phone Ottawa, an MP there, and find out the latest on the Grasslands Park. Re-write the piece in three days. Jesus! From what they'd said before, I thought the piece was set to go. It would've been too, but delay to coincide with pub of No Other Country has made them want to bring the park info up to date.

I hate the photo on that book. Makes me look ten years older. I think Eurithe did it on purpose. I'm trying to get a pro photog's picture for the hardcover that is yet to come.

I'm sick to death of the Quebec thing. But it won't go away. And yes, we must think the unthinkable. "the last gasp of Upper Canadians who would benefit by the separation of Quebec ..." How's that again? How the hell would the Wasps benefit? It's not like you to have the floor wiped with you in an argument. In my own experience with you, you just raise your voice six decibels and proceed merrily with your fallacious argument.

I can say the same to you – the stuff will come. You write all your life, and you can't stop even if you do feel drained until later. I suppose if I knew the formula for writing I'd use it, but in a way I'd hate it if there was a formula. But I see you are doin all sorts of bureaucratic judging, of writers for Retreat (why not advance?) and bein helpful. Personally, I hate young writers! The bastards are all around me if I go to a reading, giving me their crummy poems and wanting to be told they're geniuses. I mean, a puritan like me, who works like hell, and these kids want it easy. Of course so did I, exactly the way they are now. But I resent seein my own image in them. Of course if they're any good, that's different.

Of course you need privacy. The old song and dance about the writer bein solitary etc is exactly true. I am discontented as hell right now, and more or less solitary, since Eurithe is off much of the time on her business doings. But that's okay. Like they say, if you can't take the heat get outa the kitchen.

I'm pleased you like some of the poems. I do think title poem, Starlings and Prince Edward County are best. Incidentally, some guy named McBurnie writ Jack McC. tellin him how lucky he is to have Purdy on his list, genius etc. Which tickles me, on accounta Jack thinks the sun shines outa Layton's ass.

And yes, the prospect of the essays pleases me. I thought at first, before reading, that yours wouldn't be too good. But I was pleased to be wrong (except for your heart-warming Christmas piece),[6] and realized they are very good. I predict that now you will do a collective biography, entitled Famous Women in Canadian Subsoil. Trouble is, one is too close to one's own writing, I mean with prose. I finally lose sight of whether there's merit or no. In my low moments, I think, not another jesus book on Canada, and I'm doin and writing like everyone thinks I will, if they know me, write a heart-warming book on Canada, or pome as the case may be. I'd love to write a poem on all the pollyana sentiment that's gushing from the Canadian woodwork, like Scott's The Canadian Authors Meet.[7] However, I settle for No Second Spring, I guess.

Must stop.

love
Al

No Palgrave! You cheated![8]

NO SECOND SPRING[9]
(Proposed atomic waste site at Mount Moriah in Hastings County)

I

Five thousand feet straight down
a shaft driven thru billion-year-old granite
equipped with electric elevators:
and there we shall hollow out great rooms
and place in those rooms the spent uranium fuel
contained in glass boxes
which shall again spend itself for 250,000 years
laying waste its powers of death
under the mile-high granite mountain
uranium "bundles" so hot the stone itself
would melt if not protected

350

shielded and guarded
under Mount Moriah

The noonday shadow of man
that lengthens and dies at evening
night-crawler on the face of time
– having given birth to a monster
turn in your sleep to see its face
this face outliving good and evil
magistrate above and below judgment
destroying all our categories
a black thing shaped like the human brain

The difficulty to be sure
is to be quite sure
whether that quarter million years
of monster time travels forward
or that it possibly travels backward?
– or perhaps both ways at once
with a monster flip-flop
permeating time it becomes time itself?

2

We entered a turquoise continent
we hunters
following the mammoth with spears
falling rain painted the turquoise columns
and blue grottoes ran gleaming with rain
we were blue men we were turquoise men
we hunters
in light that filtered over our bodies
Our pursuer was a monster
a black man from the old time
with beast jaws and red gleaming eyes
then turning I saw that what followed us

had changed into a man
a man exactly like myself
then saw my own face reflected in rain
it grew black hair with great beast jaws
and had changed into something else
I turned then to pursue my pursuer
We stalked each other all that day
on the ice above Mount Moriah

3
"And it came to pass after these things
that God did tempt Abraham
and he said unto him Abraham
and he said Behold here I am
And he said Take now thy son
thine only son Isaac
whom thou lovest
and get thee into the land of Moriah
and offer him there for a burnt offering
upon one of the mountains
which I will tell thee of —"

And it came to pass
while a black face peered from granite
and soundless heat gushed in the stone

4
In the caves of wood
we squatted and waited the knowing
— the caves once built by men
for so it was told to me
by a different one
whose voice spoke in my head
and who still had something called sight

instead of this knowing we have
whether a thing is round or square
whether it is good to eat or not
friendly or unfriendly
or concerns a thing or a thought
and which we know for only a short time
then lose the knowing
and cower in the rags of our caves
and hide till we know again
It is of small importance perhaps
but remains in my mind somewhat longer
for once it was told to me
that we are the children of men

                    5
Long distance to the Ontario Hydro
Candu Reactor at Pickering

(Introductions, explanations, etc.)

Me – What does it look like? I mean
when you throw the stuff away?

Distant Voice – Black is the colour
of my true love's hair.

Me – Whaddaya mean by that?
Don't play games with me!

Voice – We don't throw the stuff away;
we store it carefully and safely
in underground caverns. It is very
hot stuff. Have you heard
about hot stuff?

Me – (patient and resigned)
I'm sure you'll tell me.

Voice – Black and liquid,
sometimes solid, containing
plutonium. So hot we call it
the China Syndrome.

Me – What's the China Syndrome?

Voice – (dreamily) The stuff is
so intensely hot it can melt
rock and sink all the way down
to the other side of earth and
reach China.

Me – I'm supposed to be the poet
here, not you.

Voice – I read your stuff.
You're a lousy poet, dad.

Me – Have you known how the blackness
covers your soul, and there is no light
anywhere; you cannot even imagine
light? When birds turn to cinders
in the sky, and beasts are carriers
of darkness? Have you known –

Voice – Shit!

Me – What?

Voice – Like I said: sometimes solid,
sometimes liquid, and hot as hell.
Loathesome and crawling like.

Me – That's all you have to say?

Voice – What would you suggest?

Me – Nothing more …

6

No second spring again
for you and me my love
our half life is thirty years
there is no second coming

We stood on Mount Moriah
counting from one to ten
light flooded our understanding
we didn't know what it meant

Sleep – would that have been better?
– it is so – it becomes the same
when stars soar out at evening
my dust forgets your name

We invented ourselves into human
we explored the moon and sun
now the gates of the world spring open
but the time has come to go

Reach out your hand my love

Al Purdy

AFTER RAIN [10]
The world pulses and throbs
bathed in a thick gold glow
the world is a heavy
gold bangle on the universe
burnt brown grass turns live yellow
the shithouse is a green dollhouse
even grey muffin-shaped stones
are throbbing small hearts
across the dark south

lightning semaphores north
Suddenly – say ten seconds
– everything thickens
as if someone had stirred
and mixed in another colour
I am almost what I was
a bored child again
experiencing magic
now that's a lie
I never did experience magic

Now I'm old as Houdini
without any sleight of hand
and know there is nothing
nothing I could possibly need
or want more than is here
only this thick brown-gold glow
turning the tall cedars
into one-dimensional cutouts
the shithouse a gingham highrise
Oh yes one thing more
come to think of it I saw
a blue heron this morning
on the lawn like a fake ornament
but he was blood real
I held my breath and didn't move
and the world stopped shoving
then he stopped being
a work of art and changed
his shape becoming
a bird flying in my mind
Of course there's death
cruelty and corruption
likewise shit in the world

to hell with that
one day at least stands
indomitable as a potato
its light curving
over the roof of the world
a samovar of the sun
enclosing my guest
the great blue heron
including a hunched figure
myself
on some porch steps
between lightning flashes
writing

Al Purdy, R.R. 1, Ameliasburgh, Ont. KOK 1AO

---

1. Thomas Collins (b. 1936).

2. The penultimate line of the third stanza of "Loch Lomond" reads "But the broken heart it kens nae second spring again."

3. *A Handful of Earth, At Marsport Drugstore, Moths in the Iron Curtain, No Second Spring, No Other Country.*

4. John Moss (b. 1940), critic and author of *Patterns of Isolation in English-Canadian Fiction* (1974).

5. "The Grassland Question: Who Shall Inherit the Earth – People or Prairie Dogs?" *The Canadian,* 19 November 1977, 12-16. In revised form as "Dryland Country," it was included in *No Other Country.*

6. "Upon a Midnight Clear."

7. The poem by F.R. Scott (1899-1985) is a satirical description of the Canadian Authors' Association.

8. In his introduction to *A Handful of Earth,* Purdy had mentioned his editor's curiosity about the identity of the lady in one of the poems in the collection, "Postscript to E.B.B." He asked, "Does anybody out there know?" and stated, "Send me your answer and two cornflakes boxtops (in triplicate) and I'll reward you with a copy of Palgrave's Golden Treasury (in softcover)." On the

back of the envelope containing her letter to Purdy of 30 July 1977, Laurence had written, "P.S. – Elizabeth Barrett Browning. Please send Palgrave. Corn-flake box tops will follow."

9. A revised version of the poem was published separately in 1977.

10. "After Rain" was published in *Being Alive: Poems 1958-78* (1978).

Ameliasburgh
23 August 1977

Dear Margaret,

Take a look at this Graham Greene.[1] I think it's possible you haven't read it. He saw a much different Mexico than I did, and hated it, detested it. All possible generosity was gone from him when he went there. The book starts a bit slowly, and he's defi-nitely padding it here and there, since I gather it's a commissioned book, or was years ago. I've had the book a long time, but never read it until I went west and took it along for casual reading.

It was strange for me to read the book, and see how he disliked everything he saw and some things he didn't see. I think it the book of a recently converted person to Catholicism, who has to some degree let religion take over his good sense. And yet his acute observation remains; some of his descriptions are marvel-lous. Hope you enjoy it.

Al

See Page 157 for his description of Palenque –

P.S. I wrote William Golding, asking him if he'd sign his books etc. He wrote back, sending me twin signatures like a crossword puzzle, that I could clip and, as he said, "deface his books" – It broke me up to see those signatures; I chortled for half an hour. Like Gabrielle Roy,[2] who wrote "to be continued" in each book.

358

1. *Another Mexico* (1939) in the Viking Press edition.

2. Gabrielle Roy (1909-83), French-Canadian novelist and short-story writer.

Lakefield
28 September 1977

Dear Al:

It was good to see you last week, even if only briefly. I've owed you a letter since August … I don't know where the summer has gone; I feel as though it's disappeared without my quite hav[ing] been aware it was here. Although in other ways it's been a good summer for me – no writing, but much eclectic reading and some thinking.

Thanks for the poems. No Second Summer is *very* good, I think, albeit chilling. But that was what was intended. Thanks also for pic by Harrington … I note it's the one used on jacket of No Other Country. Wow! You look handsome and *stern*!

I had read some of the pieces in NO OTHER COUNTRY; others, not. I think it's an excellent collection. I have always thought the piece on Angus is one of your best. I hope he saw the book before he died. I saw about his death in the paper the other day.[1] I also think the Labrador piece is one of your best. I like the dedication of the book.[2] Don't worry about not getting cloth binding … it's cardboard all the way these days, unless you're Charles Templeton[3] or Berton. The old firm doesn't make that kind of money out of you and me, pal. Every time I attend a board meeting I come away feeling so depressed I think I can't stand to remain on the Bd. I don't think I will, either, after the year I promised is up, in the spring. What good do I do? None. The Board is only a figurehead … Jack and Anna[4] have already decided exactly what to do. Every time I raise my voice, or write long letters to Jack, he listens attentively or replies in an equally long letter, and pays not a scrap of heed. All the news seems bad, financially, which means they will take fewer and fewer risks with first novels, or with any thing remotely experimental or different. At times I just want only to stop thinking about it all. I get disrupted for days afterwards – emotional retrogression; it takes a week to get back to something resembling peace of mind. It's a high price to pay for receiving all the books on their list free.

I'm still at the shack, but it's getting cold. I'm going to move back home in a week's time. I have to go into the V.M. (Vile Metropolis) next week for a union meeting. I hate Toronto.

I hope Western is okay. Don't let them work you *too* hard. On the other hand, when I was there I met really a lot of promising young writers. I had just moved over from England, and I had a small portable typewriter which I naturally wanted to have at the house I rented. The university could not find a spare typewriter for me, for the office, so I had to rent my own! Apart from that, I enjoyed the stint. Quite a few good people in the Eng. Dept, some of them old members of what we are pleased to call the Manitoba Mafia, so I enjoyed reminiscing with them.

Love,
Margaret

ps. have you rented a house, or what? Is Eurithe with you?

---

1. "Angus" was a celebration of Angus Mowat who had died six days before on 22 September.

2. "Argus in Labrador" described the unsuccessful air search for two Eskimo hunters, Jacko Onalik and Martin Senigak. Purdy dedicated *No Other Country* to them.

3. Charles Templeton (b. 1915), journalist, broadcaster, and McClelland and Stewart author of two best-sellers, *The Kidnapping of the President* (1974) and *Act of God* (1977).

4. Anna Porter, vice-president and editor-in-chief of McClelland and Stewart.

❦

Dear Al–

Haven't heard anything about you for ages. How are you? Where are you? Is all well? How was the year at Western? Exhausting, probably. I only had one term there and I thought I would pass out with fatigue. Plans for future? (No, this is not an interview and no, I'm not writing an essay on you. Do you get that sort of letter? I do, and damn it all, I refuse to write kids' essays for them).

All more or less okay here. I'm out at the shack now, thank God. An exhausting and hectic winter and spring, as usual. Where does the time go? Just had 6 guys from the NFB for 8 hours a day for three days at my house in Lakefield last week. They're doing a half hour documentary on me.[1] I only agreed because they are paying me pretty well. A nice bunch of guys, but a very strange and slightly gruelling experience to be in front of those damn cameras for hour after hour. They really only did a total of about 3 hours filming, including some at the cottage. Most of the time spent in waiting around nervously while they fixed up lights and got camera angles right. They'd been to Neepawa and talked to a whole lot of people – I wonder what people said about me? ("What a brat she was as a kid"; "Snobby – the lawyer's daughter"; "Kind of – well – odd, even then"; I dare not think). The researcher seemed to have turned up nearly everyone I've ever known, coast to coast. A friend phoned from Vancouver to say "Who are these guys? And shall I tell them to get lost?" (I said Yes, do that)

Still not into another novel. Depressing. I don't know whether I'm not allowing myself enough space in which to think, or whether the novel just isn't there, or whether I'm just scared. I suspect the latter. We will see.

Drop a line when possible and let me know how you are. Give my regards to Eurithe.

Best,
Margaret

1. *Margaret Laurence, First Lady of Manawaka,* directed by Robert Duncan, National Film Board of Canada, 1978. The documentary was lengthened to 52 minutes.

Ameliasburgh
6 July 1978

Dear Margaret,

I'll try and answer your questions first: I don't know where I am; I don't know what I've been doing. I'm not being ambiguous, because I doubt that I've been doing anything, except the usual readings and writing a few poems. Not many of the latter. Guy wanted me to write the libretto for an opera, which idea I toyed with for a coupla weeks then decided against it. Referred the composer to Newlove, which no doubt he will thank me for. It boiled down to: why the hell would I wanta write an opera? Of course Norm Symonds[1] had a great basic story, a factual thing, which a small part of my mind regretted abandoning.

About the film people asking questions about you: do you really care what people say? You've undoubtedly changed to a degree that any possible answer about you old acquaintances or friends might give could come as no surprise and only a large degree of indifference. If they read your books, it will be out of curiosity as to what makes you tick. The real audience is somewhere else. I can't imagine Eurithe's family reading anything I write for any reason but curiosity about me, certainly not for what I might say.

Western? More or less usual, I guess. Did meet a guy, one of the univ. governors, whose name I seem to have forgotten already, whom I went to school with, and who had kept those school mags you get. Therefore I was able to gaze with horrified eyes at the first poems I wrote at age 13. They're just as lousy now as then. Odd that this old schoolmate should become an army colonel then a univ gov.[2] We went to dinner there one evening, and he had assembled any literary people he and wife knew. The intention was good, but the only way to endure such gatherings is imbibe as much as is enough as quickly as possible.

I think there's a fine line between writing a poem and not, and suspect it might apply to prose too. If I have some sort of thought or idea, it's a question of whether I do or do not write some of it down. If I don't I might have lost a fine poem; if I do I'm pretty sure to have lost it anyway, because it's almost always bad. But I have to write a little to find out if it's gonna be bad, or if I get no more words arriving from nowhere. I suppose the comparison with prose falls down, because a novel needs so much more planning? You don't just write a novel from the top of your head, the way I can sometimes write a poem, when conscious and subconscious merge and flow together. But I do think there's a *right* time to write a novel, when all the omens are propitious and the entrails read go, the lares and penates grin at you approvingly, etc. As I think I've said, a novel is such a huge job, so much bloody work, I'd only try it thru ambition which is the same case with the aforementioned opera. Still, there's gotta be a parallel with poems in all this. I suppose the real question is (which leads to the novel): what is the most interesting thing in your life right now, what preoccupies you the most, etc etc.? Even if this subject doesn't connect directly with a possible novel, there are certainly ways of making it connect. Being a surface dilettante of life, I flit from subject to subject mostly superficially. But I think ageing and the changes I see in myself and my own attitudes are probably foremost. And it's tough to make poems from that. Of course there are other things that interest me, but it's an interest strongly tinged with indifference. As long as other people's opinions (unfavourable ones) aren't overt, I couldn't care less. And "caring" is one of the necessary ingredients of poems in most cases, as of anything. In some sense, I think a poet writes one long novel all his life, just as the novelist ... Now what the hell was a gonna say there, something philosophic and profound no doubt.

Incidentally, I've a 200-page selected called Being Alive to differentiate coming this fall. Dennis Lee edited for this one book with McStew, and several poems were changed and revised at his prompting. He really does have a keen eye and perceptions. This will be the longest and best book I've published. Other books no doubt have themes that predominate more, but if there's any mood or area in which I wrote best, that must predominate in a book like this. I mean, other books undoubtedly had more poems written in other countries or love poems or whatever, but if those poems weren't what I do best, they won't be in this book. Therefore, in some ways a Selected is liable to be misleading. Must stop.

Yours

Al

---

1. Norman Symonds (b. 1920), jazz musician and composer.

2. Colonel Charles F. Way, at this time Secretary of Western's Board of Governors, was born in Wooler, Ontario, and had attended Trenton High School.

§

Lakefield

24 July 1980

Dear Al–

Like everyone else in the world, probably, I hate to admit that I have been wrong. However, there is an important matter in which I *have* been wrong, I think, so I had better admit it. (Interesting beginning to a letter, no?)

I always said that I would burn all my personal papers before I depart this vale of tears, and I always disapproved of writers selling their papers to a university. However, I have now changed my mind. In an attempt to simplify my life, and also feeling that it was not fair to leave a ton of papers for my kids to sort out eventually, I began sorting through old papers. Found I had indeed kept letters from other writers, from about 1962 onwards, and that there was very little of a terribly personal nature, nothing of a scandalous nature, but a whole lot of very interesting material about what people were working on at the time, the relationships with publishers, their comments on my work, etc etc etc. I began to see that this stuff was of historical value and should be preserved. I found, after the vile job of sorting out the letters and assigning a folder to each writer, that I had letters from 109 Canadian writers, and some from a few British writers. Some files only a few letters, others (such as yours) very large. I sorted through most of them, and removed a few letters that seemed of a too personal nature ... there were surprisingly few of these, however.

I have put all these, together with a ton of business letters, etc, on deposit at York U in Toronto until such time as I decide to sell them. This means they are kept there but are not accessible. I did not previously understand the legal position, but now I understand it. I own the actual pieces of paper, but the writers of the letters hold the copyright, so nothing can be published or quoted without their permission. However, *unless* conditions are made to the contrary, anyone may read the letters and virtually paraphrase parts of them. I am concerned to protect the privacy of the writers of the letters, and therefore plan to make appropriate conditions. I have drawn up a tentative list of same, and I would like your opinion of it. The final clause (9) was added in the event of someone wanting copies of their own letters but not being personally able to get to Toronto to get same.

Naturally, I have absolutely no idea where my own letters to other writers are, but I'm not too concerned about this at this point. I wonder if you have sold any of your papers, and if so, what conditions you have made? I would be glad of any info, simply to see what a few other writers have done.

All well here, but too busy. I have sold the cottage, as it was getting a bit too much to have 2 places to look after. I don't really feel the need of a cottage any more – I think it served its purpose for ten years. Hope all is okay with you.

All the best,
Margaret

Margaret Laurence's Papers … Deposited At
   York University, Toronto.
Tentative List of Conditions … To Be Finalized
   Upon Sale of Papers

1. These papers are not to be accessible until such time as they are sold.
2. Should they remain unsold at the time of my death, my heirs and executors, Jocelyn Laurence and David Laurence, will sell them with such of the conditions as still pertain.
3. Upon decision to sell, York University shall at its expense have these papers evaluated and shall have the first opportunity to buy.
4. Future papers, comprising business correspondence, personal letters from other writers, letters from readers, desk calendars, shall be included in the York University

collection, with no further payment, and shall be deposited there from time to time. Any such papers left in my effects at the time of my death shall also be added to the York collection, with no further payment.

5. When the papers are sold, the business correspondence, the memorabilia, the original manuscripts, and everything else, *unless specified herein,* will be immediately accessible, with the usual copyright conditions that nothing can be quoted or published without the permission of the writer of the letter or the firm involved, or, in the case of material originating with me, my permission.

6. When the papers are sold, personal letters to me from other writers or critics, etc (in the separate files) will be accessible after my death. Copyright conditions will of course pertain, and no one may quote from these letters without the permission of the writers, or, in the event of their deaths, their heirs. In the case of persons who are medically judged to be mentally incapable at that time, permission will be sought from their nearest relative or legal guardian.

7. Both before and after the sale of these papers, I will have access to them. I agree not to remove such papers from York University, but may make notes or copy portions for purposes of memoirs, etc, it being understood that I may publish or broadcast such portions only with the permission of the writers of same, or their heirs.

8. Both before and after the sale of these papers, in the case of personal letters from other writers to me, each writer shall have access to her or his own file of letters, provided that each writer agrees not to remove these letters from York University. After their death, their heirs shall have access.

Margaret Laurence
Lakefield, Ont.
18 July 80

367

9. Under special circumstances that may from time to time arise, the personal correspondence may be accessible to John Lennox of York University, with the written permission of myself and the writers of the letters.

§

Dear Margaret:

You wrong? Perish the thought etc.

Interesting conditions for York. When I sold (over eleven years ago), I was too stupid to include all those conditions. Or ignorant, which I prefer.

Your own letters, an enormous pile, are stored in a box, among the some twenty boxes of my papers for the last eleven years. Taking up a large amount of room. I ought to do the same thing you did, have the univ. (Queen's) store them under the same conditions. They may not be sold until my death, but it'd sure be helpful to get em out of the way. Of course I also have some ten thousand books here, which are also crowding us out.

Anyway, as Eurithe has pointed out, the only weak spot in those conditions: York University has your stuff evaluated and has first chance at buying. They have the evaluation done, therefore can arrange to have any price put on the papers they think suitable for their budget. I don't say they would, but the opportunity is there. (Eurithe thinks of these things.)

Yeah, I can see how the cottage would be too much bother after a while, but you'll miss the water. Any books coming? I'm just working on the final version of a new book with the McStew ed. Ellen Seligman, for pub in January.[1] Amazing how many things come up. Readings all over the place, including the Yukon in Oct. I get a little sick of them, but can use the money. Am doing some reviews for Heritage Canada which I enjoy. Enclose one of them.²

love

Al

---

1. *The Stone Bird*. Ellen Seligman had joined McClelland and Stewart as senior editor in 1977.

2. The review follows. It appears never to have been published.

Collecting Canada's Past, by Jean and Elizabeth Smith, photographs by Ken Bell, Prentice-Hall of Canada, 220 pages, $29.95

This is a lavish coffee-table tome, with many coloured and black-and-white photographs picturing antiques of all shapes and sizes. The authors tell you what to collect and how to collect, plus the history of furniture design, woodenware, native artifacts, ceramics, and just about everything it's possible to collect except early sailing ships, dromonds and triremes. It's even mentioned that some people collect a few or all of the eighty varieties of barbed wire used to surround and protect farmers' fields.

From the Preface: "Collecting is a highly individual way of expressing oneself. A discriminating collector will produce a unique expression of personal taste." Here I think the writers are being slightly ridiculous. Does collecting barbed wire amount to a unique expression of personality? And Doulton ceramic figurines – do they confer their undoubted grace on the possessor?

No, I think collecting things is the pack rat desire for acquisition. In many cases junk is piled up that the owner can't possibly use, with a sheer greedy joy in possessions. And does a pack rat have personal taste?

But collecting also has its admirable aspects: if people hadn't collected things we would never know what our ancestors were like, how they lived and what their tastes were. That last is entirely legitimate, but is only part of the pack rat mentality.

I don't get off this self-created hook so easily myself, since I collect books. I dote on fine bindings, exquisite tooled leather, octavo, quarto and folio. (There's a pseudo-learned jargon attached to everything.) I write books as well, having achieved octavo and quarto, but am still yearning hopelessly for folio. And here a question: does the virtue or beauty of old and fine things, whether furniture or books, rub off on the possessor? I doubt it. There's a literary tag that seems applicable: them as can does, them as can't teaches. To which I would add, them as can't create collect creations and write books about it.

Of course I'm being a little unfair, since C.C.P. has undoubted merit – for pack rats and collectors. Ceramics and furniture pictured in the good photographs are functional: food in the china, a hat and jacket tastefully draped over a bureau, if "bureau" isn't too mundane a word for these *rare antiques.* (italics) Some furniture items have been carted outside by the photographer, where they confer unique personal taste to the shrubbery. A Regency style dish dresser blushes becomingly among lush ferns. But I am slightly disappointed, hoping to encounter a genuine 19th century pioneer with genuine dirty sweat on his honest but discontented face, just come from clearing timber or making potash – hoping to meet this man or his tired wife nursing her baby among the photographs. But since not much remains of pioneers, how about a genuine 19th century skeleton?

But leave us not be quite so facetious about the noble pastime of collecting things. I like the book. I like the furniture (and wish I could afford some). I like the ceramics and other stuff too. And no doubt there's emotional feeling attached to some of the pictured articles. It's a good bet that some pioneer wife loved a particular ceramic piece because it once belonged to her mother in the old country. And she probably hated the new country because of the rough life, the cheap and plentiful drunkenness. And without doubt some bush farmer fondled at least one of these antiques, some bowl or mug say, which someone loved habitually drank from until they died. But that intangible feeling hovers no longer among these old things, is supplanted by the collector's feeling for rareness as a "unique expression of personal taste."

Still, the book does help to preserve "Canada's past." The people who once owned this stuff were our ancestors, our fathers and mothers. So were the Greeks and Romans. So was the single-celled amoeba. He wore no pants and owned no furniture, and has left little trace in the rocks of our planet. But he – or it – too was Canada's past.

Al Purdy

Lakefield

3 November 1980

Dear Al:

I was going to get back to you about sale of papers (mine) to York U, but nothing has happened. Ho hum. They said they'd get back to me when they had them assessed; I went to a lot of trouble – nay, expense – to consult my accountant about the complexities of how this kind of sale can be declared under Capital Gains Tax rather than as income – maybe I told you about that. I understand perfectly what my accountant told me, at the time, but in the intervening months I've lost my grip on exactly what it means, but never mind, I've got it all down in an appropriate file and can look it up when and if the time ever comes. Hart Bowsfield,[1] (who I've known forever … an old Winnipeger), Archivist at York U, did phone me some considerable time ago to tell me that the letters from other writers were not worth nearly as much as they would have been if I'd kept copies of *my* letters to them.

Exactly what you told me many years ago. I said "tough apples … I didn't, so what I want to know is not what they *might* have been worth but what they are." However, I want to tell you this because it might make your own collection worth quite a bit. This about-face on my part may strike you as odd, but I am getting so damn concerned about writing and publishing (serious stuff, I mean … like you and me … wow, how pretentious can one sound, but you know what I mean) in this land, and I just am getting around to feeling downright angry about the whole situation. Do not mis-understand me. I am not against academics in any way – without their interest, our books would not be on university courses, so god bless 'em and all that, and I mean it. But still, when I consider that the work of writers such as you and myself and quite a pile of others, have become a kind of growth industry in the academic world, and here we are, damn it, wondering every January if we're going to make enough to live on this year. So I think – okay; pro-tect one's privacy and the privacy of one's friends, as much as pos-sible, re: sale of papers, but if one can get some security, go ahead and sell. I think that your collection right now should be worth a lot, and my spies tell me that now is a good time to sell, because with cutbacks, etc etc, in 5 or 6 years the universities may not have the money. I pass this on for your edification, and will pass on any further little bits of knowledge I may acquire about this sordid subject.

I know you said in your last letter that you didn't too much mind some of the readings, but I dunno, Al … I just feel that at this point, if you really feel like doing some, that's fine, but you should not *have* to. We all know that life is not exactly filled with Ye Olde Perfect Justice, but nonetheless, I get pretty angry when I think of writers like you, who have never hedged their bets, who have never (except for brief stints as w-in-r) been associated with universities or had pensions or tenure or any of them thar perks. Well, obviously I feel very strongly on account of I've been one of them, too. We damn well have to do what we can to earn a living, but I don't think that at this point it should have to include barn-storming unless desired by *us*.

How are you and Eurithe? Are you going anywhere this winter? How is the general picture? You mentioned some trouble with your back, I think. This is, believe me, not idle curiosity on my part – just the concern of an old friend.

I'm okay – should stop smoking, as I daily tell myself as I cough and wheeze my way into the morn, but I don't and no doubt will pay for it in due course, probably sooner than later. I still have not got into this new novel, if indeed it is there to get into, but do not entirely despair – in fact, feel okay much of the time, but it is very frustrating not to be writing. A little kids' book came out recently ... a re-telling of the Nativity; panned *very meanly* in last Sat's Globe.[2] I first wrote it 21 yrs ago, when my kids were 4 and 7, and *like hell* I didn't know how to tell stories to little kids!! However, this babe, Jacquie Hunt, reviewed THE OLDEN DAYS COAT last year and said exactly the same as she said about THE CHRISTMAS BIRTHDAY STORY this year ... text *awful,* pictures swell. The critics (reviewers) have a power that they love to use, not even recognizing how unfair it is that we don't have any redress against their diatribes. Well, the hell with them. I used to be hurt by that kind of thing. Nowadays I only get angry ... a more healthy reaction, I think. Kids seem to like the books, so that is what matters.

Best, and please let me know how things are –

Margaret

---

1. Hartwell Bowsfield (b. 1922), Canadian historian, was York University's Archivist (1970-88).

2. In her review of *The Christmas Birthday Story* in *The Globe and Mail* of 1 November 1980, Jacquie Hunt described Laurence's retelling as "a simpering domestic drama" whose tone was that of "didactic condescension" (Entertainment, 15).

§

Ameliasburgh

7 November 1980

Dear Margaret:

Thank you for that good letter. It seems you haven't yet sold your own papers. Well, I may have changed my own mind about readings. I've done some forty this year, with five more to go, and I'm sick of the sound of my voice and it's ruining my own poems for me. I just got back from eight in the Maritimes, and a week before this last safari, I did ten more in the west. And yeah, the money is necessary. Eurithe and I are paying part of her sister's rent in Victoria (the sister has agoraphobia), but she's a very fine lady, and I don't mind that. Eurithe will be going out again to Vic. (she just came back) to see if she can help. Isn't it odd that the name for a Greek marketplace is used for this mental illness?

Yeah, the usual back trouble, and arthritic knees. But I live with it. A bone doctor in Toronto told me it wasn't bad enough for surgery – yet. I like that yet. Sure you should stop smoking and drinking, and so should I. But what the hell …

And yes, it's easy to be smart and show-off reviewing, not so easy to write the kind of book they're panning. My articles book got the same kind of panning: "Purdy should stick to poetry." Well fuckem.

I may or may not have told you: finished this last McStew book, The Stone Bird, about two months or three back, and haven't written a thing since. Don't mind and I do mind. But the book is as good as anything I've done, or so I feel, and makes me realize that the time between 1970 and 1979 produced only inferior books. Well. What else is new, as you say. Still, I'm enthusiastic enough about this new book to forgive myself for not writing a thing lately – or almost.

It isn't surprising that you're writing a new novel. How could you not? Just as I'm sure I'll be writing more poems, in whatever time it takes.

Now I have to get ready to go to Toronto for this CanFor[1] anniversary thing. Maybe you'll be there. Still, it's hard to say things in person sometimes that are easier to say in letters.

Okay, take care of yourself, and I do mean that.

Al

---

1. *The Canadian Forum* was celebrating its 60th year of publication.

1572 Vining Street

Victoria, B. C.

V8R 1R1

31 December 1986[1]

Dear Margaret,

I've heard you are ill, were ill, or whatever it is. So I want to wish you the best.

Eurithe and I are out here to escape the snow. So far we have. And the place is lousy with writers, whom I have very little to do with. Went to hear Ted Hughes when he was here, lunch with Pat Page,[2] and that's very nearly all.

Had a "Collected" out last Oct., and now taking pleasure that it's on both the TorStar's and TorGlobe's best ten list. What does that mean? I've no idea, except one does want some kinda recognition or acknowledgement. I'm sure you know what I mean. And I think it's probably my last book …[3]

The climate here is good, but must admit it's a kinda dull town – We expect to take a two-week break in Mexico shortly …

love

Al

P.S. Heard you have a new book –

1. Laurence died six days later on 5 January 1987.
2. P.K. (Patricia) Page (b. 1916), Canadian poet.
3. It wasn't. *The Woman on the Shore* was published in 1990.

Index

Books by Margaret Laurence

A Tree for Poverty: Somali Poetry and Prose (1954)
This Side Jordan (1960)
The Prophet's Camel Bell (1963)
The Tomorrow-Tamer (1963)
The Stone Angel (1964)
A Jest of God (1966)
Long Drums and Cannons:
Nigerian Dramatists and Novelists 1952-1966 (1968)
The Fire-Dwellers (1969)
A Bird in the House (1970)
Jason's Quest (1970)
The Diviners (1974)
Heart of a Stranger (1976)
Six Darn Cows (1979)
The Olden Days Coat (1979)
The Christmas Birthday Story (1980)
Dance on the Earth (1989)

Books by Al Purdy

The Enchanted Echo (1944)
Pressed on Sand (1955)
Emu, Remember! (1956)
The Crafte So Longe to Lerne (1959)
The Blur in Between: Poems 1960-61 (1962)
Poems for all the Annettes (1962); rev. ed., (1968); 3rd ed. (1973)
The Cariboo Horses (1965)
North of Summer (1967)
Wild Grape Wine (1968)
Spring Song (1968)
Love in a Burning Building (1970)
The Quest for Ouzo (1970)
Hiroshima Poems (1972)
Selected Poems (1972)
On the Bearpaw Sea (1973)
Sex & Death (1973)
Scott Hutcheson's Boat (1973)
In Search of Owen Roblin (1974)
The Poems of Al Purdy (1976)
Sundance at Dusk (1976)
A Handful of Earth (1977)
At Marsport Drugstore (1977)
No Other Country (1977)
Moths in the Iron Curtain (1977)
No Second Spring (1977)
Being Alive: Poems 1958-78 (1978)
The Stone Bird (1981)

Bursting Into Song: An Al Purdy Omnibus (1982)
Birdwatching at the Equator (1983)
Morning and It's Summer (1983)
The Bukowski/Purdy Letters 1964-1974 (1983)
Piling Blood (1984)
The Collected Poems of Al Purdy (1986)
A Splinter in the Heart (1990)
The Woman on the Shore (1990)

BOOKS EDITED

The New Romans: Candid Canadian Opinions of the U.S. (1968)
I've Tasted My Blood: Poems of Milton Acorn (1969)
Storm Warning: The New Canadian Poets (1971)
Storm Warning 2: The New Canadian Poets (1976)
Wood Mountain Poems. By Andrew Suknaski (1976)